HRC

H R C

STATE SECRETS AND
THE REBIRTH OF

HILLARY
CLINTON

JONATHAN ALLEN
AND AMIE PARNES

CROWN PUBLISHERS ▲ NEW YORK

All rights reserved.
Published in the United States by Crown Publishers,
an imprint of the Crown Publishing Group,
a division of Random House LLC,
a Penguin Random House Company, New York.
www.crownpublishing.com

CROWN and the Crown colophon are registered trademarks of
Random House LLC.

Library of Congress Cataloging-in-Publication Data
Allen, Jonathan (Jonathan J. M.)
    HRC: state secrets and the rebirth of Hillary Clinton / Jonathan
Allen, Amie Parnes.—First edition.
    pages   cm
    1. Clinton, Hillary Rodham. 2. Women presidential candidates—
United States—Biography. 3. Presidential candidates—United
States—Biography. 4. Women cabinet officers—United States—
Biography. 5. Cabinet officers—United States—Biography. 6. United
States—Politics and government—2009– 7. United States—Foreign
relations—2009– I. Parnes, Amie. II. Title.
    E887.C55A49   2013
    327.730092—dc23
    [B]   2013037029

ISBN 978-0-8041-3675-4
Ebook ISBN 978-0-8041-3676-1

Printed in the United States of America

Jacket design: Christopher Brand
Jacket photograph: Marco Grob/Trunk Archive

10 9 8 7 6 5 4 3 2 1

First Edition

CONTENTS

Part IV

Introduction

H illary stared at the screen, eyes wide open.

The American consulate before her stood at the edge of civilization, in one of the most lawless places on the planet, amid an epic struggle between moderates and extremists. The diplomats inside believed they were there to help; the anti-American terrorists at the gate most certainly did not.

Frame by frame, in a video-equipped conference room on the seventh floor of the State Department's Washington headquarters, Hillary watched terrorists attacking the outpost. The stultifying images had been captured from a security camera at the American compound. Hillary wanted her top aides—about two dozen of them had gathered in the conference room with her—to "get a sense of what people were facing inside these posts," as one of them later put it.

The screening was held shortly after the April 5, 2010, assault, two and a half years before Ambassador Chris Stevens would be killed at the U.S. special mission compound in Benghazi.

Attackers had nearly made it inside the American compound in Peshawar, the gateway to the tribal region of Pakistan that had become the world's most notorious haven for terrorists. They detonated a truck bomb when it hit a barrier fifty feet from the consulate's entrance, and they launched a second-phase assault with guns and grenades. Pakistani employees of the consulate were killed in the attack, but the terrorists were repelled before they could breach the compound. Though in a similarly dangerous region, the Peshawar compound was more fortified than the one at Benghazi because of its status as a consulate, a step below an embassy but still a more permanent installation than the special mission in Benghazi, which is often referred to as a "consulate."

The slide show was intended as a wake-up call for the State Department brass. In Peshawar, the attack had been thwarted in large part by a pop-up vehicle barrier and the quick reaction of Pakistani soldiers, who provided host-nation support to the consulate.

Increasingly, the drumbeat of threats against American diplomatic facilities could be heard not just in Iraq and Afghanistan, where the United States had military forces on the ground, but in other places that weren't live combat zones. Diplomats were having a harder time doing the basic function of their jobs—interacting with the locals—without the menacing accompaniment of heavily armed convoys and rigorous security precautions.

When Hillary had taken over as secretary, she had spoken at length to Ryan Crocker, the veteran ambassador to Pakistan, Afghanistan, and Iraq, who told her that, despite the dangers, diplomats weren't effective if they were constantly hunkered down in heavily barricaded embassies and consulates. She knew that Peshawar was one of the most precariously situated American posts in the world, amid Al Qaeda, Taliban, and other jihadist forces. There were constant threats to the diplomats who ventured into the surrounding community, but this was an attack on their home base.

When Hillary heard about the incident, and the success in holding off the terrorists, she asked Pat Kennedy, the undersecretary who oversaw diplomatic security operations, to brief her team. I want to see it, she had told Kennedy.

Thank God we had the pop-up barriers, she thought, when she watched the images. Whenever there was an attack on an American diplomat or facility, a chorus of voices would argue for pulling back from the site. But Hillary believed that the United States couldn't afford to leave vacuums in troublesome regions. American embassies and consulates, and the diplomats who worked in them, were important tools through which the United States could influence the rest of the world. They were also platforms for intelligence, military, and commercial activity.

Yet the perils of modern diplomacy were clear. American diplomats in war zones were at just as much risk of coming under fire as the military. The difference was that diplomats didn't carry machine guns. Hillary understood that engaging in diplomacy in hostile parts of the world was a calculated risk. She had made the case, within the administration and on Capitol Hill, that funding for the security of diplomatic posts in war zones should be as sacrosanct as the money spent on arming and equipping troops. She had included Pakistan on a list, with Afghanistan and Iraq, of countries where embassy security budgets should be protected by law.

The decision to take time out from one of her tightly run meetings for an embassy security briefing sent a message to the people in the room that Hillary believed at that moment that "this is the most important thing for us to be talking about," said another source who was present.

It wouldn't be the last time.

Near the end of her tenure at State in September 2012, the Benghazi attack—essentially the three a.m. call she had campaigned on in 2008—interrupted the smooth narrative arc of Hillary's political comeback. For four years, from the day she accepted Barack Obama's invitation to join his cabinet, Hillary had been engaged in a peripatetic rebuilding and rebranding campaign. All at once, and with disciplined follow-through, she had enhanced the State Department, America's relationships with some foreign countries, and her own brand at home. The mission required a survivor's strength, a gatherer's cultivation of political capital, a hawk's vigilance, and the ambition of a woman who believes she should be president. Taking the job had been a risk, just as continuing to engage in diplomacy in dangerous parts of the world was a risk.

Hillary explained, both before the Benghazi attack and after it, her view that the United States couldn't simply pull back from the most precarious parts of the world because of the danger to diplomats. Instead of avoiding risk, she argued, it was the job of the State

Department to mitigate and manage it, a point of view that reflects her own personal calculations about risk and reward.

Hillary also harbors a related trait that one source calls "a bias for action," which influences her decision-making process. It can be seen in her approach to going after Osama bin Laden, in her building of a coalition to intervene militarily in Libya, and even in the way she encourages her aides to innovate and improvise, whether in building partnerships, aiding rebels, or, in the case of Richard Holbrooke, searching unsuccessfully for the right recipe for peace in Afghanistan.

From the outset she demonstrated a deep understanding of the levers of power within the American government and in international politics. As a result, she became an increasingly influential voice within the Obama administration, moving from the realm of campaign-trail rival to valued counselor and executor of the president's will. Some of her initiatives are still taking root, and it may be that she is forced to watch as others take credit when they blossom. Her advocacy for a "smart power" approach to dealing with other countries was most evidently successful in Burma, but it could also be seen in the management of more difficult relationships in the Middle East and Asia.

To the disappointment of even some of her most ardent supporters, Hillary's legacy is not one of negotiating marquee peace deals or a new doctrine defining American foreign policy. Instead, it is in the workmanlike enhancement of diplomacy and development, alongside defense, in the exertion of American power, and it is in competent leadership of a massive government bureaucracy.

Through inside-the-room stories, this book tracks the arc of Hillary Clinton's last rise, a tale of political resurrection for which the final chapters remain unwritten. Part of that story is the temporary return of the reins of the family's political operation to Bill Clinton, whose work on behalf of Barack Obama's reelection— and on punishing Hillary's enemies on the campaign trail—helped lay the groundwork for Hillary to run again in 2016. But even as she insisted that she was out of the political game while serving as secretary, Hillary continued to build the Clinton political network, acquiring new allies within government, Democratic political circles, and the business world who would help form an expanded base for 2016.

Of course, at the time of the writing of this book, Hillary still had not announced a decision about her plans. However, most politicians looking at higher office do everything in their power to preserve their option to run until they make a final call. Hillary is no different in that regard. But she has shown a willingness to take risks—from signing on as Obama's secretary of state to staking out positions in his Situation Room that might not play well either with the Democratic primary base or with the full electorate—because it was her duty to give the president her loyalty and her unvarnished counsel.

Loyalty, for better and worse, has been the defining trait of Hillary and her tightly woven inner circle, from her days as first lady through the Senate and State. She values it in herself, demands it in her aides, and often gives it too much weight in judging the people around her. The failure of her 2008 presidential campaign could be attributed in part to the way she rewarded longtime allies with jobs that they were ill-equipped to execute, and even her fiercest advocates often wonder whether she truly learned enough from that experience to elevate competence over loyalty in building a second bid for the Oval Office.

As she weighs a run, the bias will be for action, the risk will be calculated, and the candidate almost certainly will be reborn.

PART

I

ONE

Hillary's Hit List

Inside a cramped third-floor office of Hillary Clinton's once-bustling presidential campaign headquarters in the Ballston neighborhood of Arlington, Virginia, Kris Balderston and Adrienne Elrod put the finishing touches on a political hit list. It was late June 2008, and Hillary had dropped her bid for the presidency. The war room, where her brain trust had devolved into profanity-laced shouting matches, was empty. The data crunchers were gone. The political director had drifted out. A handful of Hillary's aides had already hooked up with Barack Obama's campaign in Chicago.

Balderston's salt-and-pepper beard gave him the look of a college English professor who didn't need to shave for his job. Then in his early fifties, he had been with the Clintons since their White House days, serving as a deputy assistant to the president and later as Hillary's legislative director and deputy chief of staff in the Senate. The official government titles obscured Balderston's true value: he was an elite political operator and one of Hillary's favorite suppliers of gossip. After more than a dozen years spent working for the Clintons, he knew how to keep score in a political race.

Elrod, a toned thirty-one-year-old blonde with a raspy Ozark drawl, had an even longer history with the Clintons that went back to her childhood in Siloam Springs, a town of fifteen thousand people in northwestern Arkansas, on the Oklahoma border. She had known Bill Clinton since at least the age of five. Her father, John Elrod, a prominent lawyer in Fayetteville, first befriended the future president at Arkansas Boys State when they were teenagers. Like Bill Clinton, Adrienne Elrod had a twinkle in her blue eyes and a broad smile that conveyed warmth instantaneously. She had first found work in the Clinton White House after a 1996 internship there, then became a Democratic Party political operative, and later held senior posts on Capitol Hill. She joined the Hillary Clinton for President outfit as a communications aide and then shifted into Balderston's delegate-courting congressional-relations office in March. Trusted because of her deep ties to the Clinton network, Elrod helped Balderston finalize the list.

For months they had meticulously updated a wall-size dry-erase board with color-coded symbols, letters, and arrows to track which lawmakers were leaning toward endorsing Hillary and which were headed in Obama's direction. For example, the letters "LO" indicated that a lawmaker was "leaning Obama," while "BD" in blue denoted that he or she was a member of the centrist Blue Dog Coalition on Capitol Hill.

As one of the last orders of business for a losing campaign, they recorded in a Microsoft Excel spreadsheet the names and deeds of members of Congress. They carefully noted who had endorsed Hillary, who backed Barack Obama, and who stayed on the sidelines—standard operating procedure for any high-end political organization. But the data went into much more nuanced detail. "We wanted to have a record of who endorsed us and who didn't," said a member of Hillary's campaign team, "and of those who endorsed us, who went the extra mile and who was just kind of there. And of those who didn't endorse us, those who understandably didn't endorse us because they are [Congressional Black Caucus] members or Illinois members. And then, of course, those who endorsed him but really should have been with her . . . that burned her."

For Hillary, whose loss was not the end of her political career, the spreadsheet was a necessity of modern political warfare, an improvement on what old-school politicians called a favor file. It meant that when asks rolled in, she and Bill would have at their fingertips all the information needed to make a quick decision—including extenuating, mitigating, and amplifying fac-tors—so that friends could be rewarded and enemies punished.

Their spreadsheet formalized the deep knowledge of those involved in building it. Like so many of the Clinton help, Balder-ston and Elrod were walking favor files. They remembered nearly every bit of assistance the Clintons had given and every slight made against them. Almost six years later most Clinton aides can still rattle off the names of traitors and the favors that had been done for them, then provide detailed accounts of just how each of the guilty had gone on to betray the Clintons—as if it all had happened just a few hours before. The data project ensured that the acts of the sin-ners and saints would never be forgotten.

There was a special circle of Clinton hell reserved for people who had endorsed Obama or stayed on the fence after Bill and Hillary had raised money for them, appointed them to a political post, or written a recommendation to ice their kid's application to an elite school. On one early draft of the hit list, each Democratic member of Congress was assigned a numerical grade from one to seven, with the most helpful to Hillary earning ones and the most treacherous drawing sevens. The set of sevens included sen-ators John Kerry, Jay Rockefeller, Bob Casey, and Patrick Leahy, as well as representatives Chris Van Hollen, Baron Hill, and Rob Andrews.

Yet even seven didn't seem strong enough to quantify the be-trayal of some onetime allies.

When the Clintons sat in judgment, Claire McCaskill got the seat closest to the fire. Bill and Hillary had gone all out for her when she ran for Senate in Missouri in 2006, as had Obama. But Mc-Caskill seemed to forget that favor when NBC's Tim Russert asked her whether Bill had been a great president, during a *Meet the Press* debate against then-senator Jim Talent in October 2006. "He's been a great leader," McCaskill said of Bill, "but I don't want my daughter near him."

Instantly, McCaskill regretted her remark; the anguish brought her "to the point of epic tears," according to a friend. She knew the comment had sounded much more deliberate than a forgivable slip of the tongue. So did Hillary, who immediately canceled a planned fund-raiser for McCaskill. A few days later McCaskill called Bill Clinton to offer a tearful apology. Bill was gracious, which just made McCaskill feel worse. After winning the seat, she was terrified of running into Hillary Clinton in the Capitol. "I really don't want to be in an elevator alone with her," McCaskill confided to the friend.

But Hillary, who was just then embarking on her presidential campaign, still wanted something from McCaskill—the Missourian's endorsement. Women's groups, including EMILY's List, pressured McCaskill to jump aboard the Clinton bandwagon, and Hillary courted her new colleague personally, setting up a one-on-one lunch in the Senate Dining Room in early 2007. Rather than ask for her support directly, Hillary took a softer approach, seeking common ground on the struggles of campaigning, including the physical toll. "There's a much more human side to Hillary," McCaskill thought.

Obama, meanwhile, was pursuing her, too, in a string of conversations on the Senate floor. Clearly, Hillary thought she had a shot at McCaskill. But for McCaskill, the choice was always whether to endorse Obama or to stay on the sidelines. In January 2008 she not only became the first female senator to endorse Obama but also made the case to his team that her support would be amplified if Governors Kathleen Sebelius and Janet Napolitano came out for him at roughly the same time. McCaskill offered up a small courtesy, calling Hillary's personal aide, Huma Abedin, ahead of the endorsement to make sure it didn't blindside Hillary.

But the trifecta of women leaders giving Obama their public nod was a devastating blow. *Hate* is too weak a word to describe the feelings that Hillary's core loyalists still have for McCaskill, who seemed to deliver a fresh endorsement of Obama—and a caustic jab at Hillary—every day during the primary.

Many of the other names on the traitor side of the ledger were easy to remember, from Ted Kennedy to John Lewis, the civil rights icon whose defection had been so painful that Bill Clinton seemed to be in a state of denial about it. In private conversations, he tried to explain away Lewis's motivations for switching camps midstream, after Obama began ratcheting up pressure for black lawmakers to get on "the right side of history." Lewis, because of his own place in American history and the unique loyalty test he faced with the first viable black candidate running for president, is a perfect example of why Clinton aides had to keep track of more detailed information than the simple binary of *for* and *against*. Perhaps someday Lewis's betrayal could be forgiven.

Ted Kennedy (another seven on the hit list) was a different story. He had slashed Hillary worst of all, delivering a pivotal endorsement speech for Obama just before the Super Tuesday primaries that cast her as yesterday's news and Obama as the rightful heir to Camelot. He did it in conjunction with a *New York Times* op-ed by Caroline Kennedy that said much the same thing in less thundering tones. Bill Clinton had pleaded with Kennedy to hold off, but to no avail. Still, Clinton aides exulted in schadenfreude when their enemies faltered. Years later they would joke about the fates of the folks who they felt had betrayed them. "Bill Richardson: investigated; John Edwards: disgraced by scandal; Chris Dodd: stepped down," one said to another. "Ted Kennedy," the aide continued, lowering his voice to a whisper for the punch line, "dead."

For several months, as the campaign intensified, Balderston and Elrod kept close tabs on an even smaller subset of targeted members of Congress, who were still undecided after Super Tuesday. Because Hillary and her team made such an intense effort to swing these particular lawmakers in the final months of the campaign, they are the first names that spring to mind when Hillary's aides talk about who stuck a knife in her back and twisted it.

For Balderston, the betrayal of Jim Moran, the congressman from Alexandria, Virginia, was perhaps the most personal. The two men were social friends in the Del Ray neighborhood of Alexandria, about six miles from campaign headquarters. They were even in the same book club. For months Balderston had casually pressed Moran about his endorsement. Moran played coy. He praised Hillary but came up short of promising an endorsement. Then in January 2008,

Moran left a voice message for Balderston: I'm all in for Hillary, he said. Naturally, Balderston was excited. The courtship of delegates hadn't been going well, and adding a new name to Hillary's column was welcome news. But Balderston's joy was short-lived. "What the fuck?" he exclaimed a couple of weeks later as he read the news that Moran was set to endorse Obama. He called the congressman, his old chum from the neighborhood. "Do not ever call me again!" Balderston said. He stopped going to the book club.

Bill was particularly incensed at California representative Lois Capps. He had campaigned for Capps's husband, Walter, who knocked out an incumbent congresswoman in 1996, delivered the eulogy the following year at Walter's congressional memorial service—calling him "entirely too nice to be in Congress"—and then helped Lois Capps win her husband's seat in a special election. The Cappses' daughter, Laura, had even worked in the Clinton White House.

"How could this happen?" Bill asked, after Lois Capps came out for Obama at the end of April.

"Do you know her daughter is married to Bill Burton?" one of Hillary's aides replied.

Burton worked for Obama as a high-profile campaign spokesman and would go on to join the White House staff, but this did little to assuage the former president's frustration. Bill and Hillary were shocked at how many Democrats had abandoned them to hook up with the fresh brand of Barack Obama. The injuries and insults were endless, and each blow hurt more than the last, the cumulative effect of months and months of defections. During the spring and summer, the Clinton campaign went days on end without adding a single endorsement.

It reached the point where Hillary—in a stale, sterile conference room at the DNC headquarters—asked uncommitted "superdelegates" to give her their word, privately, that they would back her if it came to a vote at the convention, even if they weren't willing to take the political risk of coming out for her publicly ahead of time. Unlike the regular delegates who were elected in state party primaries and caucuses, the superdelegates, a group of lawmakers, governors, and other Democratic officials, could support whichever candidate they wanted to at the convention. As a last resort, Hillary pleaded with them to simply refrain from adding their names to Obama's column. Bill would make that pitch, too, in phone calls and when he crossed paths with lawmakers. Please, just don't endorse Obama, he cajoled.

Balderston and Elrod recorded them all, good and bad, one by one, for history—and for Doug Band, Bill Clinton's tall, balding, postpresidency aide-de-camp. A former University of Florida frat boy, he had a fierce loyalty to the former president that competed with his instinct for accumulating wealth and status. One longtime associate, reflecting the view of some others in the Clinton world, described him as "always looking out for number one." But if that was true, Bill Clinton came a very close second. As a young man, Band served in the Clinton White House and then went on to help create and oversee the vast Clinton web of charities.

Most important for politicians, donors, and journalists alike, he became the gatekeeper to Bill Clinton. Few question Band's strategic vision in setting up Bill's postpresidency philanthropic empire, and he counts Huma Abedin, Hillary's top personal aide, among his close friends. But some in Hillaryland take a dim view of Band's influence on the former president. He can be so abrasive that Maggie Williams, the person closest to Hillary, told friends at one point that she quit working at the Clinton Foundation in large part because of Band. But Band was in charge of the Clinton database, a role that made him the arbiter of when other politicians received help from the Clintons and when they didn't.

"It wasn't so much punishing as rewarding, and I really think that's an important point," said one source familiar with Bill's thinking. "It wasn't so much 'We're going to get you.' It was 'We're going to help our friends.' I honestly think that's an important subtlety in Bill Clinton, in his head. She's not as calculated, but he is."

▲

Dining with a few friends at Cafe Milano in Georgetown in 2012, Bill Clinton recalled what he considered to be a major rebuke from a junior congressman, Jason Altmire, who had been helped by the Clintons early on in his career. "If you don't have loyalty in politics," the former president said, "what do you have?"

If there was a poster boy for the betrayal-and-revenge narrative, it was Altmire, a tall, broad-shouldered former Florida State University football player who had won his western Pennsylvania House seat in the midterm Democratic landslide of 2006. Altmire had worked for six years as a congressional aide, a stint highlighted by his selection to work on Hillary's health care reform task force in 1993. It was the only big job he'd had in Washington before winning an election, and he knew it had been an important springboard in his career. He was a prime target for Hillary as she courted superdelegates in the spring of 2008.

Humbling herself, Hillary met with many of these superdelegates in one-on-one sessions in the second-floor conference room of the Capitol Hill building that houses the DNC and the Democratic Congressional Campaign Committee (DCCC). When Hillary wanted to elude what she called the "paparazzi," she held the meetings at the nearby Phoenix Park Hotel. But it wasn't just the press that Clinton wanted to avoid at the DCCC. The House Democrats' campaign arm was controlled by House Speaker Nancy Pelosi, a technically neutral power whose private leanings had been made clear when her entire inner circle of House members jumped on the Obama bandwagon in late January and early February. Brian Wolff, an Arkansas native and the executive director of the DCCC, worked with Balderston and Elrod to redirect lawmakers who were in the building into meetings with Hillary and also to keep tempers cool. At least once, at a time when the tension was running high, aides to Clinton and Pelosi had to scramble to keep the two women from encountering each other. "It would have been a problem," said one source. Some of Pelosi's friends chalked up her hostility toward Clinton's groundbreaking run as motivated partly by jealousy and partly by a desire to tap into Obama's base. "I think it was very calculated, that support," said one friend of both women. "It was obvious that was going to bring in a whole new constituency of voters that were important to the Speaker, and that's politics."

The DCCC and the Phoenix Park Hotel, both within walking distance of the Capitol, were chosen in part so that it would be harder for the almighty superdelegates to say they didn't have time to meet with Hillary. It was telling that a former first lady, New York senator, and onetime presidential front-runner had to worry about members of Congress avoiding her. It was also telling that Hillary's heavy push for superdelegates, particularly those like Jason Altmire who hardly registered on the Washington power meter, didn't begin in earnest until after Super Tuesday in February. She had thought the nomination would be hers by then, and in any case, she detested asking lawmakers and donors for votes and money. She preferred to be the magnanimous one, dispensing favors rather than collecting them.

Hillary had begun to lose Altmire long before she realized she needed to compete for him. While it took her until the spring of 2008 to get her delegate outreach into gear, Obama had first approached Altmire in the summer of 2007. By October of that year, the junior Pennsylvania congressman was invited, along with Representative Patrick Murphy, to attend a speech that Michelle Obama gave to a group in Philadelphia. After the speech the two congressmen spent the better part of an hour backstage with the future first lady, who sat on a couch and sipped a bottle of water as she explained her husband's strategy for beating the Clinton juggernaut. Even though he had slipped far behind Hillary in the national polls, Obama would win Iowa and New Hampshire, turning the race into a three-way fight with Clinton and John Edwards. Edwards would drop out of the race soon thereafter. "When it's a one-on-one battle, that's when Barack's going to shine," Michelle told the two junior Democrats. "She's not going to know what hit her."

Four years later Altmire was still impressed with Michelle Obama's presentation. "She called exactly what happened," he said. "She was wrong about New Hampshire, but she called exactly what was going to happen." Murphy, a close friend of Altmire, already had endorsed Barack Obama, joining the future president at a time when the outlook for his election was bleak. Altmire, rumored to be ready to join up, too, held off—he would keep his powder dry. Obama made another appeal on the floor of the House of Representatives during President George W. Bush's 2008 State of the Union address, asking Altmire if he was "ready to come over," then made contact every six weeks or so to check in and see if an endorsement was forthcoming.

Hillary finally reached out to Altmire on February 29, 2008. She called his house and left a voice message. "The momentum's on our side," she said, alluding to the Texas and Ohio primaries set for the following Tuesday. From a public relations standpoint, they were must-win contests. If she failed to at least win the popular vote in either state, her campaign was over. The delegate count was a different matter because the general public, and even many experienced political journalists, didn't really get how important it was. Win or lose in those states, Hillary couldn't catch Obama in the national delegate math without an implausible wave of superdelegates rushing to her side. But she wasn't ready to give up on flipping them into her column, and neither was Bill.

Altmire got a phone call from one of Bill's aides on the morning of March 4, the day of the Ohio and Texas primaries. He was told to hold for the former president, but Bill never came on the line. The races were still too close to call. Once it was clear that Hillary was going to capture the popular vote in both states, Altmire got a second call. This time Bill was ready to make the pitch.

"He comes on the phone. He is flying, you can hear it in his voice," Altmire recalled.

"We really need you," Bill told him.

But Altmire worried that Hillary would fail to connect with the conservative voters in his Pennsylvania district. Bill pushed back, citing the margins of his own victories in the district in 1992 and 1996. He knew the voters there as well as Altmire did. Hillary, Bill argued, had been a popular state-level first lady in rural, conservative Arkansas and had won her Senate seat twice in part because she had done better than expected in conservative upstate New York. Calling an old favor to mind, the former president also thanked Altmire for his work on the 1993 health reform task force. As he had with Obama, Altmire told Clinton he didn't like the superdelegate system or the idea that his vote would carry more weight than those of each of his constituents. He didn't plan to endorse anyone, he told the former president.

But the Clintons didn't give up easily. Altmire was one of about a dozen Democratic superdelegates invited to a cocktail party on March 12 at the Clintons' multimillion-dollar Washington house, nestled among foreign embassies and a stone's throw from the sprawling vice president's residence. At the party, Altmire asked Hillary a pretty simple question: You're way behind. What's your path to victory? "You all are superdelegates," she told the group, "and the purpose of superdelegates is to make up your mind and make a decision that might be contrary to what the voters have decided." That didn't make much sense to Altmire; nor did it appear to sway many of his colleagues.

On St. Patrick's Day, Obama visited a community college in Altmire's district and invited the congressman to join him. Like a football recruit at a major Division I university, Altmire was given a window into what it was like to hang out with the cool crowd. Accompanied by David Axelrod, he watched Obama deliver the speech, give a press conference, and sit for an interview with Gwen Ifill of PBS.

Then he clambered into the senator's SUV for a ride to Pittsburgh International Airport. Avoiding the primary elephant in their midst, Obama and Altmire talked about their daughters, who are about the same age. When they got to the airport, Obama signaled to his security detail to get out of the car and leave the two pols alone in the back of the SUV.

"I'm going to win this election," Obama said bluntly. "I'm going to be your president, and I want you to be on our team. . . . You don't have to commit right now, but I want your support."

Altmire said he was in a tough spot, with Clinton on the verge of winning his district by a big number. Obama reiterated his confidence and his desire to get Altmire on board, and then he signaled for a Secret Service officer to open the door so he could go to his plane.

But Altmire still had something to say. He wanted Obama to know that they had made a connection, and he blurted out his good wishes for Obama's upcoming speech on race in Philadelphia. "Hey, Senator, I know tomorrow is a very important day for you. Good luck," Altmire said.

Obama turned to the officer to signal that the door should be closed again. He leaned over toward Altmire with a look of determination on his face, brow furrowed, eyes squinted. "We're going to be fine," he said. "They told me I wasn't going to be able to beat Hillary Clinton, and I'm going to beat both Clintons. . . . This is just one more hurdle. Don't worry about me. I'll be fine."

The difference between the two campaigns struck Altmire as remarkable: while Hillary was begging for help, Obama didn't need it. As Obama delivered his speech on race the next day, Altmire thought, for the first time, "This guy is special. There's something about this guy that's just different than anyone else." It was Obama, not Clinton, whom he would endorse if he were pushed into that corner. Though he didn't tell anyone yet, Altmire had made up his mind—he wanted Obama to win. He felt as if he were actually doing Hillary a favor by keeping his thoughts to himself. In Hillaryland, he would soon be regarded as an opportunist because he had extracted so much face time from the Clintons—and then as an outright traitor.

In April, Altmire got word that Bill wanted to talk to him again. The congressman told Hillary's team that the two men could travel together between events at venues about an hour apart, a ride that Hillary's aides would later recall as another delicious plum they had given an ungrateful backbencher. Altmire got the full backstage and onstage treatment from the former president. Bill praised him in his speech at the first event, then put his hand on the congressman's shoulder and whispered in his ear, classic Clinton moves for conveying intimacy to an audience. When the event wrapped up, Altmire got in the car. Bill followed, cell phone to his ear, making it clear that he was talking to Hillary. In the SUV, Altmire gave the former president his now-practiced spiel about disliking the superdelegate process.

"I think you know as well as I know that Hillary is going to win in your district, and you should support the people of your district by supporting Hillary," Clinton said.

If there was anybody who knew what it took to be president, it was Bill Clinton, and the Clintons had been suggesting Obama wasn't ready to be president. That had caught Altmire's attention. What did he mean by that? What were his concerns?

"Why do you think that Senator Obama is so not qualified to be president?" Altmire asked.

Clinton looked up. "I didn't say he was not qualified," he explained. "I don't want to say that, but when I became president, when I look back, I made some mistakes early because of inexperience. I was not as prepared to be president as I thought I would be. This guy is not nearly as ready to be president as I was in 1993." Then Clinton turned bitter, saying Obama's "buddies in the media" would just "cover it up anyway" if he did make mistakes.

When the votes were tallied on April 22, Hillary won Pennsylvania by 10 points and Altmire's district by 31 points. The result increased the pressure on Altmire, who had been saying all along that he didn't like the idea of reversing the will of his own constituents. Now, having spoken, they had shouted, "Hillary!" Where they had once been a convenient shield, protecting Altmire from having to make a decision, they now became the point of Hillary's spear.

A miscommunication made the inevitable showdown even more painful than necessary. Through the union grapevine, Hillary's aides got the erroneous message that Altmire was ready to endorse her. They invited him to meet with her one morning later that week at the DNC's Washington headquarters. Clinton, weary from a six-week marathon of campaigning in Pennsylvania, rose early to meet with Altmire at eight a.m. Coffee and bagels were the standard fare in the small conference room that Hillary used to court superdelegates. There was a table in the room, but two chairs had been pulled away from it so that Hillary could talk to him face-to-face, at close range, with nothing separating them. She had previously told staff that pleading for superdelegate votes felt beneath her, beneath what the Clintons had accomplished, and beneath what they had become accustomed to in terms of treatment from fellow politicians. But now she had no other options. Clinton, expecting to get Altmire's endorsement, and Altmire, knowing she wouldn't get it, locked eyes.

Hillary started. President Clinton had enjoyed meeting Altmire, and she had enjoyed running up the score in his district. Now there was nothing standing in the way of Altmire endorsing her, just as the Democrats in his district had. Altmire said he was impressed by just how well she had done with them. Dispensing quickly with the small talk, Clinton pressed him on his decision as a superdelegate. Altmire retreated to familiar territory, explaining for the umpteenth time why he didn't like the system.

For the first time, Hillary realized that he wasn't going to endorse her under any circumstances. She had hit her limit. She didn't let him finish. She stood up, put her hand out to shake his, and said she appreciated his time. Pleasantries included, the exchange had lasted about seven minutes. For Hillary, that was seven minutes too long.

When Altmire was gone, she lashed out at her aides. "Such a fucking waste of time," she fumed, her voice full of disgust and frustration. "I thought you said he was going to endorse me."

She later apologized for the outburst, but the anger ran true and deep. The Altmire episode would remain a sore spot for Hillary and her aides for years. They felt he had milked his superdelegate status for all it was worth, exchanging the favor of his time for access to the former president and first lady. The Clinton team expected that at some point he might stop acting the coquette and just give it up.

"The hottest places in hell are for those who declare neutrality in times of trouble. He was one of them," one adviser recalled. "I'd rather have one of these guys come up to me and say, 'I'm not for her. Fuck you.'"

On the day before Thanksgiving 2008, after Bill and Hillary

had campaigned for Obama successfully, Altmire approached the former president at the VIP reception before a fund-raiser for Pittsburgh mayor Luke Ravenstahl. Bill was cordial but cold and minutes later turned downright icy. Taking the stage at the Steel City's Omni William Penn, packed with more than four hundred people, Bill launched into a hearty endorsement of Ravenstahl and another local pol, Dan Onorato, both of whom had backed Hillary in the primary.

Then, catching sight of Altmire at a table up front, he looked the congressman dead in the eye as he delivered the clincher: "And I am never going to forget the people who supported Hillary."

More than a year later, at the western Pennsylvania funeral of the legendary congressman John P. Murtha, Bill again gave Altmire a perfunctory greeting. Clinton would eventually get the chance to do more than turn a cold shoulder to Altmire or stare him down at a fund-raiser. The bill for Altmire's neutrality would come due nearly four years later, to the day, in the 2012 Pennsylvania Democratic primary.

While Hillary worked at the State Department, Bill used his influence, his fund-raising ability, and his campaign skills to tend to the family's political network. He helped nearly every friend of his or Hillary's when they needed assistance defeating an Obama acolyte—and even punished some who had remained neutral when the Clintons felt they were owed allegiance. Longtime party builders, the Clintons generally weren't into helping Republicans beat Democrats—though Bill's efforts resulted in a GOP win on at least one occasion. But no holds were barred in a primary. The message from the Clintons to the rest of the Democratic political world was clear: It's better to be with us than against us. Over four years, Bill racked up some high-profile victories in races matching one Democrat against another. These were practical as well as punitive: every victory by a Clinton loyalist ensured that Hillary would have a more powerful team in place if she ran again. And the Mossad-style, get-you-when-you-least-expect-it payback politics would have a chilling effect on politicians who thought about crossing her in the future. "They're into loyalty," one Clinton aide explained. "They're used to loyalty."

It would be political malpractice for the Clintons not to keep track of their friends and enemies. Politicians do that everywhere. The difference is that the Clintons, because of their popularity and the positions they have held, retain more power to reward and punish than anyone else in modern politics. And while their aides have long and detailed memories, the sheer volume of the political figures they interact with makes a cheat sheet indispensable. "I wouldn't, of course, call it an enemies list," said one Clintonworld source. "I don't want to make her sound like Nixon in a pantsuit."

Another one of Hillary's longtime advisers also sought to soften the long-term relevance of the list. "I'm sure Doug does have some sort of fucking memo on his BlackBerry like the rest of us," the adviser said, "but the notion that it is updated, circulated, disseminated, and relied upon is absurd."

In the summer of 2008, Hillary Clinton couldn't have known whether or when she would run for president again. But she knew who was on her side and, name for name, who wasn't.

TWO

"Be Gracious in Defeat"

On June 6, three days after the last presidential primary, Hillary invited about two hundred campaign aides, advisers, and friends to the family's $4 million–plus redbrick home on White-haven Street for a backyard get-together. The event was a final expression of gratitude for the brainpower, tears, and sweat they had poured into her cause for more than a year.

On this day, the sweat kept coming. It was a sweltering Friday in the nation's capital, with violent summer storms brewing in the suburbs, and Clinton's air-conditioned house was off-limits to guests, except for one bathroom that was accessible from the outside. Some of her aides kicked off their shoes and dipped their feet in the pool for relief. Hillary ignored the heat and stifling humidity to work one last crowd, taking pictures with midlevel staffers in sweat-soaked shirts.

Like a weekend griller, Bill Clinton held court in his own backyard, complaining about *Meet the Press* moderator Tim Russert to just about anyone who would listen. Russert had called the time of death on Hillary's campaign a month earlier on the night of the North Carolina and Indiana primaries. "Sometimes in campaigns the candidate is the last to recognize the best timing," Russert had said. "It's very much like being on life support. Once they start removing the systems, you really have no choice."

Much as Bill blamed big-media types for jumping on the Obama bandwagon, Russert was just reporting a truth that was evident even to Hillary. The narrowness of Hillary's victory in Indiana, where she had run the field operation for Jimmy Carter's 1976 presidential campaign, was just as telling as the pounding she took in North Carolina that night. The day after those primaries, on a conference call with the campaign's top executives, she issued the edict to cease and desist on attacks that could hurt Obama in the general election. The final month of the campaign was a slow march to her inevitable fate.

At the end of that slog, the backyard party had the feel of a wake, a bittersweet goodbye. Though the Washington air was thick with speculation about whether Obama might pick Hillary to be his running mate, the two former rivals had met the night before at Senator Dianne Feinstein's D.C. home and, unbeknownst to the partygoers at Hillary's house, Obama made clear that he did not intend to ask her. For the most part, the extended Clinton family of friends and aides tried to keep the mood in the backyard upbeat. But surface conviviality couldn't hide the fact that this journey was ending on the north lawn of the Whitehaven house rather than on the South Lawn of the White House.

While Hillary listened to battlefield stories, shared laughs, and posed for pictures, she gave no hint of the emotional and politically delicate task that lay ahead of her that night. As the last of the political operatives and press aides shuffled off the property, Hillary headed to her dining room to write the final draft of the highly anticipated concession speech that she would deliver the next morning to a nation of Democrats waiting to see whether she could endorse Obama with conviction. The dining room, separated from the foyer by sliding French doors, is the business center at the Clintons' Washington home, a 5,500-square-foot Georgian temple to the 1950s that they bought in 2000 so Hillary would have a place to live while she served in the Senate.

By the time Hillary sat down late that afternoon with aides Doug Hattaway and Sarah Hurwitz, the latest draft of the speech reflected the scars of a staff still riven. Nearly all agreed that Hillary had to endorse Obama and acknowledge her own supporters, but they couldn't come to terms on the best approach. For several days, her various communications advisers had been e-mailing drafts back and forth, fighting one another through edits to the text. The bigger camp, made up mostly of high-priced advisers like chief strategist Geoff Garin, demanded a full-throated endorsement of Obama that would convince his team, the Democratic Party, and the rest of the country that she was completely on board.

The smaller set, which included several of the women closest to Hillary, as well as Hattaway and Hurwitz, insisted that she couldn't credibly make the case for Obama if she didn't deliver a powerful acknowledgment of the historic nature of her own candidacy and particularly of the women who had supported it. At the heart of the matter was an existential question that had plagued the campaign from its earliest days: how should Hillary handle being the first viable female candidate for president?

For most of the campaign, she had sided with old-school professionals who believed she needed to project strength and thus keep the talk about being a woman to a minimum. She hadn't given a speech that called attention to her gender the way Obama had made a race speech. But her campaign had been resurrected by vulnerability, in a moment of emotional exhaustion, when a tear rolled down her face at a stop in New Hampshire. Those who felt she performed better when she showed her underdog side believed the concession speech gave Hillary an opportunity to talk about the very aspect of her persona that she had held back for so long and that appealed to so many voters.

When Hillary sat down with Hurwitz and Hattaway, the draft they reviewed included both an endorsement of Obama and an oratorical run about her place in history. For months, she had resisted the close circle of advisers who had wanted her to frame her candidacy in terms of history, the way Obama had. Now the text in front of her did just that. Jim Kennedy, a longtime Clinton hand, had come up with the phrase that melded Hillary with her voters in the continuum of the women's movement. Text-messaging his thoughts from his home in Venice Beach, California, earlier in the week, Kennedy said Hillary should speak of the "eighteen million cracks" that her campaign had put in the most fortified glass ceiling of them all.

Hillary had always favored making a robust endorsement, her aides said. But as she reviewed the latest draft at her dining room table, she still wasn't sold on the riff about her place in history. She was more inclined to show first and foremost that she was a team player—an attribute she prized in herself and that was important to preserving her political future. She had to be brought around to putting so much emphasis on honoring her achievement as the woman who had come closest to winning a major party's presidential nomination.

She scrawled a question mark in the margin beside the paragraphs about her.

"It wasn't about being a woman," Hillary said.

"Think about talking not about you as a woman but to the women who supported you," Hattaway countered, framing his argument in terms that might appeal to the midwestern Methodist who reflexively worried about the potential unseemliness of calling attention to herself. "This is a big accomplishment for them."

Hillary wasn't convinced. "Her head wasn't there," said one source. Then Hurwitz, a Harvard-educated lawyer and speechwriter who had been taking notes quietly, leaned forward and made the case. For one young woman with proximity to power, this was the moment to speak for the millions of women her own age, as well as for the mothers and grandmothers, who had stuck by Hillary. They burned to see the first woman in the Oval Office, choosing that cause over another cherished hope for many of them—to elect the first black president. This, above all else, mattered. It wasn't that Hurwitz was consumed with hatred for Obama. Within weeks, she would join his campaign, and she ended up landing a coveted job on the White House speechwriting team. But this moment mattered for so many women who had pinned their hopes on Hillary. In the end, Hurwitz's passion, and her reason, won out.

Okay, Hillary said, it stays.

The denouement was pivotal, as much for what it said about the evolution of Hillary's persona in the coming years as it did for the tenor of the speech she would give the next day. Hillary's toughness and her femininity weren't mutually exclusive; they were bound together. Voters, particularly women, identified with her precisely because she was a woman with an iron spine. Over that summer, from her dining room table in June to the Democratic National Convention in Denver in August, she started to develop a new narrative in which she embraced being a trailblazing political force in her own right.

Though the point in her speech was resolved, Hillary's night was far from over. There was a lot riding on this address, and she needed to strike the perfect chord with the endorsement. She couldn't afford to alienate her remaining loyalists. Her advisers even feared that supporters might walk out if she was too strong in her endorsement. She knew that 10 percent of them would never go over to Obama, but she had to make sure she could move the other 90 percent. Yet neither could she come up short in praising Obama. It wasn't really an either-or proposition. If she failed to give a hearty enough endorsement, she might severely and permanently damage her own standing in the Democratic Party. No one wanted to relive the awful moment when Ted Kennedy refused to join hands with Jimmy Carter after their 1980 primary fight.

Hillary stayed up with the speech past four a.m., and then it was circulated to top advisers. Garin, the chief strategist, was dumbstruck at the final version, which he thought had too much about Hillary and not enough about Obama. He e-mailed an F-word-punctuated missive that the revisions had to go.

To this day, there are still disagreements among Hillary's advisers about the degree to which edits were made that morning. "There was no resistance or reluctance to change it back," said one source who sided with Garin's view. "It's not like there was a real fight over this."

But a friend who favored Hillary's version disputed that conclusion. "There were a lot of attempts by some people in that other camp to [put in] more refrains about Obama," the friend said. "She kind of ended up where she was overnight."

The morning of Hillary's concession speech played out in inadvertently comic fashion—half royal wedding and half afternoon car chase. The news media staked out the Whitehaven house, so viewers knew the minute her motorcade left for the National Building Museum. The museum, defined by the seventy-five-foot-high Corinthian columns in its Great Hall, is a nineteenth-century Bureau of Pensions building that Congress converted into a memorial to "the built environment." Its Roman-themed interior was meant to house both the federal pension service and Washington's great social galas. That Great Hall, and the thousands of Clintonites who filtered into it, had to wait for Hillary, who was running late. Even the delay was turned into the kind of minidrama of speculation that the cable networks live for.

The final tweaks to the speech were made at the last minute. Hillary arrived nearly an hour late, well past even Clinton Standard Time, the term Washingtonians have long used to describe Bill's indifference to other people's schedules.

She had to bury her own campaign before she could praise Obama, and she delivered a long eulogy. It took more than six minutes, and almost seven hundred words, for Hillary to get to the two that mattered most: "The way to continue our fight now, to accomplish the goals for which we stand is to take our energy, our passion, our strength, and do all we can to help elect *Barack Obama,* the next president of the United States," she said.

In its final iteration, Hillary's Building Museum speech wove together the threads of her base, Obama's base, and the common Democratic values they shared. As is often the case with politicians and their concessions, it rated as the best speech of her campaign. But it will be most remembered for the stanzas that had made Hillary uncertain the night before.

"Now, on a personal note, when I was asked what it means to be a woman running for president, I always gave the same answer, that I was proud to be running as a woman, but I was running because I thought I'd be the best president," she said, building to an echo of the famous line—"Ain't I a woman"—that Sojourner Truth uttered at a Women's Convention in 1851. "But I am a woman, and like millions of women, I know there are still barriers and biases out there, often unconscious, and I want to build an America that respects and embraces the potential of every last one of us."

Hillary, having integrated the struggles of women and African Americans by subtly paying homage to Truth, retreated briefly from the building momentum, allowing the crowd to recover—for just a moment—before etching an indelible line in the nation's political memory.

"Although we weren't able to shatter that highest, hardest glass ceiling this time, thanks to you, it's got about eighteen million cracks in it," she said, as her supporters, some of them in tears, burst into applause. "And the light is shining through like never before, filling us all with the hope and the sure knowledge that the path will be a little easier next time."

With everyone in the building now rapt, Hillary bound her cause to Obama's through a more explicit marriage of the women's rights movement and the black civil rights movement. "Think of the suffragists who gathered at Seneca Falls in 1848 and those who kept fighting until women could cast their votes," she said. "Think of the abolitionists who struggled and died to see the end of slavery. Think of the civil rights heroes and foot soldiers who marched, protested, and risked their lives to bring about the end to segregation and Jim Crow."

It was a powerful pivot, from the emotional pull of the women's movement and the hope of electing the first woman president to the parallel arc of the civil rights movement and the possibility that her own followers could still make history by electing Obama. Women and African Americans, and no small number of activists who were both, shared the same struggle for equality and opportunity. Moreover, it was a personal struggle.

"Because of them, I grew up taking for granted that women could vote, and because of them, my daughter grew up taking for granted that children of all colors could go to school together," Hillary said. "Because of them, Barack Obama and I could wage a hard-fought campaign for the Democratic nomination. Because of them and because of you, children today will grow up taking for granted that an African American or a woman can, yes, become the president of the United States."

No doubt the same logic could be applied to rally African Americans, Hispanics, gays, and other minorities to her cause if she ran for president again.

The argument sounded so genuine because she, too, had to give up her dream, or at least defer it. It had once seemed so inevitable, her course to the White House and certainly to the Democratic nomination, and now she was being asked to support the guy nearly fifteen years her junior who had skipped the line to get in front of her. To ask her millions of followers to do the same thing, she needed to give a compelling explanation for her own conversion.

The two factions in Hillary's campaign had battled over the balance of eulogizing her own candidacy and endorsing Obama's for so long that talking points for the media were drafted in an anteroom *after* the speech was delivered. The speech was really hard to write, she thought, and just as hard to deliver. But it was credible because she didn't ask her supporters to do anything she wasn't willing to do. Like her candidacy, it was both aspirational and inspirational, and her decision to link herself so directly with the cause of women's rights was an early sign that Hillary was ready to take charge of a new political narrative that cast her more as a pioneer and an Obama loyalist than either her husband or his old political advisers would have liked.

Hillary disappeared from public view for two weeks after the concession speech, spent some time at the Clintons' primary residence in Chappaqua, New York, and in the Dominican Republic, then returned to the Senate with the pomp of a president on June 24, a humid Tuesday. When her mini-motorcade pulled up to the Capitol that morning, Clinton's staff met her on the East Front plaza outside.

They knew it would be a hard homecoming for their boss; staying in the Senate had never been the plan. So they set out to make her landing a little softer. In lieu of encountering "Welcome back!" banners and tear-jerking speeches, she entered her office to find a Ping-Pong tournament in midswing. Staffers clad in gym clothes—headbands, shorts, striped knee-high socks—paddled a ball back and forth. Dan Schwerin, a press aide who returned to the Senate after working with Balderston and Elrod on the campaign, had driven all over town to find the table in time for Hillary's arrival.

Clinton delighted in the boisterous, unlikely scene inside the Senate office that she hadn't seen much of in recent months. She let out a hearty laugh. To network anchors, the sound of her full-body laugh was a "cackle," a word that made her aides cringe; but to her adoring and anxious staff, it was a sign of normalization. "I love this!" she exclaimed.

She watched the match closely, as the ball was smacked in one direction and batted back in the other—a dynamic with which she was very familiar. She couldn't resist offering a self-aware admonition to the legislative assistant who ultimately lost.

"Be gracious in defeat," she advised.

In those weeks, Hillary was heeding her own advice, but she was having difficulty getting her die-hard supporters to follow suit. The campaigns booked a ballroom at the Mayflower Hotel in Washington two nights later, June 26, so that Hillary could gather her top donors and political supporters in a show of unity for Obama. It was a struggle to fill out the guest list, as many of Hillary's most loyal backers were still in no mood to shift allegiance. But the room was full by the time Obama and Hillary appeared together with Terry McAuliffe, the longtime Clinton family fund-raiser who introduced them to the crowd. Hillary spoke glowingly of Obama, and he returned the favor, recounting how his daughter Malia had told him it was "about time" for a woman to be president.

"I'm going to need Hillary by my side campaigning during this election, and I'm going to need all of you," said Obama, who announced that he had written a check for $2,300 to help retire

Hillary's campaign debt and had asked his leading donors to do the same. But his olive branch was quickly snapped in half. During a question-and-answer session, Hillary's supporters peppered Obama with questions that were thinly veiled jabs.

"Q and A really turned more into commentary, and some of her most significant supporters were very pointed and forceful," one participant recalled. "Obama was getting annoyed. It was not good. . . . Neither one of them were happy. It wasn't supposed to be that way. It was supposed to be a unity event."

Finally Lanny Davis, a Washington lawyer and Hillary loyalist, put a stop to the kvetching with a call for civility. While Davis was an ardent Hillary advocate, his own son was an Obama guy—a sign of a generational divide that had to be closed for the good of the party. "It's time for the family to come back together and act as one and take this because we need to win," Davis said.

Unity, it turned out, was more than just a sentiment for Hillary to express. It was also the name of a remote town she had to visit to prove her loyalty. Obama campaign manager David Plouffe was obsessed with the symbolism that Unity, New Hampshire, held for the forced union of Barack Obama and Hillary Clinton. Not only did the small town's name provide the ideal message for the absorption of the Hillary camp into Obama's fold, but Unity had given each candidate 107 votes in the February primary. Unity was a metaphor for Plouffe himself: the perfect marriage of data and messaging. Perhaps that's why he was so taken—much more so than anyone else—with the idea of staging the first public joint postprimary event in a tiny burg an hour west of Concord.

It would have been far easier logistically for Obama and Clinton to rally the Democratic faithful in northern Virginia, just outside Washington, D.C., in a major swing state. After all, they had been at the Mayflower in Washington the night before. To get to Unity, about five hundred miles away, the rivals, and their embittered aides, had to gather in close quarters on an airplane and fly about ninety minutes from Washington to New Hampshire. As if that weren't enough punishment, they then boarded a bus for an hour-long ride to Unity Elementary School.

Every presidential campaign event is carefully staged, but Unity was as precisely choreographed as a ballet. Staffers even e-mailed to make sure Obama's periwinkle tie would go with Clinton's pantsuit. The Obama campaign staff had never been assigned seats for a flight until they boarded the jet. An Obama aide dutifully made name tags for the handful of people on the plane, who were as recognizable to one another as a nose tackle is to a center. Obama settled into a window seat in the second row. Clinton sat beside him. She traveled light: Huma Abedin and traveling press director Jamie Smith were the only aides with her.

On the flight, Obama and Hillary discussed what she and her husband could do to help him in the general election. Hillary told him that they would go all out, but warned him that the rest of her base might be more difficult to sway. She felt obligated to push them, but it wasn't easy for her. She wanted Obama to understand that it wouldn't happen overnight; just like his backers wouldn't have jumped into her camp immediately if she had won the primary.

"Look," she told him as they flew north, "the harder part is going to be convincing my supporters at the grassroots, at the donor level, everything in between, to be enthusiastic about your campaign."

Enthusiasm on the plane could have used a boost as well. "A lot of people in Hillaryland were holding their noses while they were doing this," said one former top aide with knowledge of the trip. And the feeling was mutual. On Obama's side, Plouffe harbored an intense hatred for Hillary. The campaign had also worn on Hillary's relationship with David Axelrod, Obama's senior adviser. A decade earlier Hillary had spoken at the first annual fund-raising dinner for CURE, the epilepsy charity established by Axelrod and his wife, Susan, in honor of their daughter, who suffers from the condition, and Clinton thanked Axelrod in the acknowledgments of her memoir *Living History*. David Axelrod later said that Hillary was the "patron saint" of CURE and that she didn't "hold the sins of the father against the mother and daughter," but Susan Axelrod acknowledged that there was "a little discomfort" in the relationship during the campaign. Hillary compared a conversation with Axelrod on the bus from the airport to Unity to a "root canal."

"Hello, Unity!" she exclaimed, with a clenched smile, when she took the makeshift stage in an open field before a roaring crowd of about four thousand people. "Unity is not only a beautiful place, as we can see, it's a wonderful feeling, isn't it?" As she spoke, Obama appeared locked into her every word and was the first to applaud in the right places. When she wrapped up, he kissed her and thanked her. Hillary patted his back. "You're welcome," she said.

The crowd cheered with approval, but exhalation rather than elation characterized the Obama and Clinton camps when the event ended. "I remember it was a big relief when it was over because it had gone smoothly," one Obama aide recalled. "Her people made an effort to be magnanimous."

There may have been residual tension after Unity, but Obama and Clinton didn't have either the time or the mental energy to dwell in it. Nearly two weeks later they appeared side by side yet again for a couple of fund-raisers in New York, where they basked in each other's celebrity. For Obama, it was another introduction to Hillary's vast donor base. For Clinton, it was an opportunity to help pay off some of the backbreaking campaign debt—more than $22 million still remained—that she had racked up in her desperate attempt to catch Obama. (At one fund-raiser, Obama had to double back to the microphone after leaving the stage. He had forgotten to ask his donors to write checks for Clinton and had to remind them to fill out the forms at their tables.) For her part, Hillary still struggled with many of her top donors, cajoling them to bankroll a Democratic victory without her on the ticket.

Over that summer, as Obama marched toward the presidency, Hillary quietly held a series of postmortem meetings with aides and advisers in her Senate office and at the house on Whitehaven Street. Each had a slightly different tenor, tone, and purpose, but all were generally aimed at figuring out what went wrong, at learning from the mistakes, and at plotting the rest of her career.

It didn't take her long to figure out the basics of why the campaign had imploded. "I was struck by how good of a sense she had before I walked in there of the problems that were going on in [the headquarters]," said one adviser. "She had a mosaic pieced together that if you read a transcript of it, you would have thought it was someone who sat at headquarters every day, and it was remarkably accurate. . . . She just had it pegged."

In the meetings, almost everyone told her that she had hired the wrong people for some of the top jobs. Patti Solis Doyle, the campaign's first manager, and chief strategist Mark Penn bore the brunt of those complaints. But others, including communications chief Howard Wolfson and policy director Neera Tanden, also suffered from what one aide told her was an "arrogance of the people on top."

"Why didn't you tell me this?" she asked the aide.

"We did," he replied.

The reviews shouldn't have been much of a surprise, given that advisers had warned Hillary before the campaign not to make Doyle the campaign manager and that midway through the race Doyle had been demoted in favor of longtime Hillary confidante Maggie Williams. Of course, Penn, Doyle, and the rest of Hillary's high command were convenient scapegoats. Ultimately, Hillary was responsible for her own dysfunctional operation, and she would have a lot to learn about managing the next political campaign.

To the extent Hillary was dejected, she didn't let it show beyond a very small circle. "She wasn't doing cartwheels," said a friend, describing her mood as "more reflective than anything." But for many of her advisers, the midsummer sessions were more cathartic than forensic. They felt that they had personally failed her for not calling attention to problems earlier in the process.

Burns Strider, who had served as Hillary's link to faith-based groups during the campaign, had e-mailed her one day after the primary, while he was working on the House side of the Capitol. "I'm sad," he wrote.

"Come over," Hillary replied.

It was a hot day, and Strider—who later slimmed down with a diet and recipes sent by Bill Clinton—was very overweight at the time. He began to sweat as they walked together to the Senate floor and back to Hillary's office. When they finally sat down at her desk, Strider couldn't find words to express his emotions. Behind his glasses, he began to cry.

"You need to get your composure," Hillary admonished.

"Well," Strider replied in a thick Mississippi drawl, "I'm just sad."

"We're all mourning," Hillary said, acknowledging her own pain. Then she explained her coping mechanism.

"We all mourn in our own ways, and then we move on," she said. "We keep going forward."

Hillary felt like she had gone all out. She was exhausted but had found her peace with the result. She was proud that she had gone the full distance.

"I'm not somebody who dwells on the past or ruminates about 'what if, what if, what if?'" she said. "I have enough people around me who do that. So I don't need to do that. I delegate it."

She believed "a few breaks here and there might have made a different outcome," she said. "So, my view was, okay, I made history; I was the first woman to win primaries, I got all those votes, and I was very proud of the effort. But it fell short. So let's get to work making sure that what I cared about, which I had expressed in my campaign, was going to be continued through Barack Obama's candidacy. And so I had a very down-to-earth, practical approach to it."

For Hillary and her aides, forward was the only way through not just the devastating loss but the shock of returning to Congress. Visions of lofty White House jobs had turned back into the pedestrian reality of Senate life. The type-A personalities who drove her Capitol Hill operation were accustomed to being on the winning side; now they were all coming back with a big "L" in their column.

Hillary was hardly the first candidate who had to descend from the rarefied air of a presidential campaign jet to the slightly less elite Senate. Over the years, countless sitting senators had run for president and returned to its ranks. But the fall for her was longer and harder. She was at once more famous and less senior than those predecessors. There was no chairmanship of a top committee waiting for her on Capitol Hill. Beyond that, the Senate she returned to was a bit of a snake pit. Of the three top Democratic Party leaders, Richard Durbin (D-Ill.), the cochairman of the Obama campaign, might have treated her best over the course of the primary just by being up front about his stance. The other two, Harry Reid (D-Nev.) and Chuck Schumer (D-N.Y.), had advised Obama behind the scenes, even though Reid had technically been neutral and Schumer had publicly been in Hillary's camp.

"I do think she may have been hurt by the actions of some of her colleagues and friends in the Senate during the campaign," said an adviser who talked to her a few days after she conceded. "Those who endorsed Obama, those who just sat on the sidelines, and particularly those who were in the shadows."

Veteran Hillarylanders insist that Hillary was excited about diving back into her Senate work, eager to get back to business as soon as possible. The people of New York hadn't elected her to take a two- or three-month self-pity break. "From the moment she walked in, it was very much like she wanted to go back to business as usual," said an aide who stayed with her for years after the campaign. "She was going to go back to her committee life."

But her return was awkward for everyone on Capitol Hill, including one former aide who encountered her at a park near her Russell Building office.

"How are you?" Hillary asked from behind gigantic sunglasses.

"Senator, how are you?" the young woman replied, before adding, "Is it good to be back?"

Hillary's stone-faced response oozed contempt for a question with such an obvious answer, and she quickly excused herself from the conversation.

Outside the Capitol that June and July, a rising young executive assistant, Rob Russo, methodically completed a Herculean political task for Hillary. Russo, who had recently graduated from George Washington University and worked as an intern for campaign manager Maggie Williams, was put in charge of delivering 16,054 thank-you notes to an elite class of Hillary supporters, from top donors and volunteers to fellow politicians. The naughty-and-nice list that Balderston and Elrod assembled covered just a small corner of a political world full of people who had helped or harmed Hillary. Russo was responsible for making sure that folks categorized as particularly generous got a final "touch."

Presidential campaigns, often the last big run for a given politician, usually dissolved without top backers getting a last personal note from the candidate. Hillary determined that that wouldn't be the case with her operation. It was more than just a polite demonstration of gratitude from an old-fashioned midwestern girl, as her aides suggest. Just like the methodical autopsy she conducted on the campaign that summer, the massive get-out-the-notes operation hinted that Hillary still had electoral politics on her mind. It was a way for her to show extra love and attention to the very people she would call on for help if she sought the presidency again.

Most of the people on Russo's list received an e-mail message. But for almost two full months, the impeccably dressed young aide with black-framed hipster glasses delivered to Hillary batches of thank-you notes, state by state. During downtime in the Senate, she read the sixteen thousand typed notes, often making hand edits, and signed those that were ready to be sent. Russo went on to handle Hillary's correspondence at the State Department and in the Hillary Rodham Clinton Office that she set up after she stepped down from the Obama administration, ensuring continuity in her efforts to keep up with friends and supporters. The list of political and personal contacts, transferred from job to job, expanded her network every day.

With the Senate in recess and the thank-you project wrapped up, Hillary took most of August for herself before arriving in Denver at the end of the month for the Democratic National Convention, where she had once expected to be nominated for president. Instead, she'd be giving an endorsement speech on Tuesday night and for the second time that summer, the behind-the-scenes fight over the substance and style of a speech would help define Hillary's persona going forward.

For decades, as first lady of Arkansas and first lady of the United States, and even as a senator from New York, Hillary had been defined in large part by her relationship to Bill Clinton, perhaps the most charismatic man in the country. Even when she ran for president in her own right, the nature of Bill's role was a question that had to be dealt with not only by her rivals and the media but within her own campaign. But now, with Bill having embarrassed himself at times in his zeal to get her elected, Hillary's future political fortunes would depend less on him than they had at any time before. If she was to have a political future, she would have to take control of her own story—and not wrestle publicly with the role of her former-president husband in her career as she had during the campaign.

The Clinton team set up its war room that week at the Brown Palace, a posh hotel about a mile from the convention's security perimeter. The speech had been written over the course of a few weeks. Lissa Muscatine, now the co-owner of Washington's premier political bookstore, Politics and Prose, had taken over the lead from Hillary's younger speechwriters and set up shop with other staffers in a conference room with a long narrow table.

Late Monday night, less than twenty-four hours before her big moment onstage, Hillary met with several women in her inner circle, including Muscatine, Maggie Williams, Cheryl Mills, and Melanne Verveer, to discuss the text. It was good, Hillary thought, but it wasn't quite there. She left it to the group of women to spruce up the draft. Muscatine went back to work, sequestering herself in a corner of the hotel conference room to polish the speech while colleagues worked on other assignments at the table. By Tuesday morning, it was about 80 percent right—in good enough shape for Hillary to feel confident about the substance. At that point, the concern was mostly about style. How, for example, should she build the drama in a passage about Harriet Tubman, the Underground Railroad conductor? She was close to finished—or so she thought. She rode to the convention center to practice on a mock stage.

But that afternoon, when Hillary returned to the Brown Palace conference room for another run-through with a TelePrompTer, there was a new problem with the speech. As she started to read it aloud, she stopped short. The text had changed.

"What is this?" she asked, looking askance at her speechwriters and communications advisers in the room. She often expresses her displeasure with the scolding tone of a mother, and here it was unmistakable.

While she had been on the mock stage at the convention center, Bill had delivered edits. He had ripped up the structure and added some of his own poetic flourishes. Clinton aides, many of whom have worked for both Bill and Hillary, still referred to him as "The President." They had simply done what they had been ordered to do.

But Hillary was having none of it. Bill and the set of advisers she had hired from his 1996 campaign had proved disastrous at developing her message and strategy for the campaign. She was the one in the hot seat now. It was her make-or-break moment as a loyal Democrat and time for her to take control of the message.

"It's *my* speech," she declared as she left to find "The President."

When she was safely out of the room, Hattaway advised the other Clinton aides to put it back the way it was. Keep the president's one-of-a-kind turns of phrase—"the poetry"—he instructed, but reassemble the original structure of the speech. With just hours left to go until she took the stage, Clinton aides rushed to piece it back together like a jigsaw puzzle.

They moved paragraphs around and made last-minute tweaks to the words. Throughout the commotion, with the clock ticking toward the zero hour for the speech, Hillary was dressed casually. She still had to put on her evening wear, a bright orange suit that would stand out against the Democratic-blue backdrop of the convention floor. Hattaway's phone blew up: Obama team vetters kept calling to get a copy of the speech. It'll be there, he tried to reassure them. But everyone was anxious. Despite the photo-op in Unity, the Obamans didn't fully trust the Clintonites. The relationship had remained testy during the course of the summer as Hillary's team tried to extract promises that Obama would help retire Hillary's debt every time his high command asked the Clintons to appear as surrogates. And the drama of Clintonworld grated on the disciplined Obama campaign.

When Hillary and her speech were finally ready to go at about eight p.m. in Denver, a copy was e-mailed to the Obama team. Jon Lovett, a young Clinton speechwriter who would go on to work with Hurwitz in the Obama White House, clambered into a van with his laptop and a thumb drive with a copy of the speech in tow. He called ahead to advise that Hillary would soon be at the Pepsi Center, the site of the convention. Soon there was a mad dash through the warrens of the building to get the thumb drive to the folks running the TelePrompTer. "Never a dull moment with the Clintons," Jim Margolis, an Obama ad man, quipped when they arrived.

After final touch-ups to her hair and makeup, Hillary and her team walked through Obama's staff room in the arena, on the way to the stage. She stopped to say hi to a few top Obama aides, including Anita Dunn and Dan Pfeiffer. As she processed the speech in her mind, "she's feeling all this pressure," one confidante recalled.

A rump group of her delegates had shown up at the convention hell-bent on forcing the issue of Obama's nomination; they weren't listening to her appeals to just get on board. No matter how hard she tried to stop them, she couldn't. And she knew that she would take the blame if they disrupted the convention. That added to her tension as she prepared to take the stage. But for once, this would be a dramatic Clinton moment with plenty for Obama's team to love. It was the third time in less than three months that she would stand before a national audience to offer her testament. For its tenor and its timing, just before John McCain picked another woman, Sarah Palin, as his running mate, it would be the most pivotal of her endorsements.

When she finally emerged before a raucous crowd, with about twenty minutes to go before the end of prime time on the East

Coast, it was to chants of "Hill-a-ry, Hill-a-ry" and a thumping ovation. Clinton and Obama supporters alike waved white signs bearing her signature emblazoned in blue and underlined with a red
streak. A television camera captured Bill Clinton mouthing "I love
you" from his skybox.

After opening with a little riff on her pride—as a mother, a New
York senator, a Democrat, and an American—she hit the punch line,
calling herself "a proud supporter of Barack Obama." No one would
have been surprised if the Obama team backstage had been prepared to count the minutes before she said his name. But it was out
in a matter of seconds. There it was, for the world to hear. In the skybox they shared, Joe Biden and Michelle Obama leaped to their feet.

Then for the first time, Hillary dropped the gloves and threw
roundhouses at McCain, the Senate traveling buddy with whom
she had once done vodka shots in Estonia. "My friends," she said,
echoing—perhaps gently mocking—the Republican nominee's favorite rhetorical tic, "it is time to take back the country we love."

She continued, "I haven't spent the past thirty-five years in the
trenches advocating for children, campaigning for universal health
care, helping parents balance work and family, and fighting for wom-
en's rights at home and around the world . . . to see another Republican in the White House squander the promise of our country and
the hopes of our people. . . . No way. No how. No McCain."

But the heart and soul of the speech was a final section on finding the faith to persevere in the face of hardship. Extending the arc
she had first drawn in her concession speech of a shared struggle for
women and African Americans, Hillary used the heroism of a second black woman to drive home her point.

"On that path to freedom, Harriet Tubman had one piece of
advice: 'If you hear the dogs, keep going,'" Hillary said. "'If you
see the torches in the woods, keep going. If there's shouting after
you, keep going. Don't ever stop. Keep going. If you want a taste of
freedom, keep going.' . . . But remember, before we can keep going,
we've got to get going by electing Barack Obama president."

The crowd exploded in applause one more time as Hillary concluded. Bill and Chelsea beamed. Biden whispered his approval to Michelle Obama. He had been an ally of Bill's White House on Capitol Hill and later a good friend of Hillary's in the Senate and on the campaign trail. At times during the early presidential debates, when he was still a candidate for the nomination, Biden had seemed a lot closer to Hillary than to Obama, and Hillary was clearly much more fond of Biden than Obama. "Even when they were opponents in the primary, anytime someone would mention his name around her, she would get this little smile," one of her top aides said. "She really likes him. He really likes her."

Having heard her emphatic endorsement, Biden raced deep into the arena to Hillary's holding room. Finding her, he dropped to his knees and clasped his hands in a dramatic gesture of praise.

After the convention, Hillary turned most of her attention back to the upper chamber. Steeped in grandeur, tradition, and sloth, the Senate had never seemed like a perfect match for the former first lady, who had to learn to control her natural impatience.

"I don't know if I can take this," she had told an aide as they walked back to her office from a vote in the Capitol in her first year. "I don't know if I could stay in this job and just go back and forth and vote and go to committee hearings."

But over eight years, she had come to find rewarding aspects of her job. She'd fought hard to get this seat that was once held by Robert F. Kennedy, and she had used it as a power base far beyond the walls of the Senate. And while she had first won her seat in the shadow of the end of the Clinton presidency, she had soon begun to prove that she was a political force in her own right as a senator. She liked completing tasks, and the Senate afforded her a platform to make laws, have a voice in the national debate, and even attack issues from outside the legislative process. In a system designed, with checks and balances, to effect change slowly, Hillary constantly looked for ways to use both her official power as an officeholder and her celebrity to jump-start action on policy issues. Many of the projects she took pride in involved what she called the "power to convene"—her unique ability to bring together stakeholders from government, the private sector, and academia to solve problems. Few said no to a meeting request from Hillary Clinton.

Just as she would later creatively use her power to launch public-private initiatives at the State Department, Hillary established herself as a resourceful player in the Senate. All members of Congress introduce bills, vote, and help constituents navigate the federal bureaucracy when they have trouble getting veterans benefits and Social Security checks. But Hillary saw the job as a platform for connecting institutions in different parts of society to achieve goals. She persuaded Cornell University to link upstate New York farmers with markets in the city that were buying produce from New Jersey, and she played a helpful role in bringing about a settlement between the New York Power Authority and the Buffalo area to redevelop the city's waterfront.

Back in the Senate full-time after Labor Day, Hillary was excited about the prospect of working in a Democratic-led Congress with a Democratic president, which seemed to augur well for a new push to reform the nation's health care system. From the outside, she looked weakened by the primary loss. But inside the Senate, her allies were adamant that majority leader Harry Reid find a way to elevate her. That was particularly true among the women, and not just the group of them who endorsed her. A strong feeling had taken root that Hillary should be embraced, a sentiment of which Hillary was almost certainly aware.

The smallest senator in stature, Barbara Mikulski of Maryland, may have been the biggest Hillary booster behind the scenes. Mikulski, who had served twenty-two years in the Senate, and who had endorsed Hillary in the primary, prodded party leaders to find an enhanced role for her. Mary Landrieu of Louisiana was also among those who led the charge. The drawling daughter of former New Orleans mayor Moon Landrieu had regrets about the primary campaign. She counted herself among Bill Clinton's biggest supporters and among Hillary's greatest admirers. But when Obama came calling, armed with the fact that Landrieu was running for reelection and would need a big black turnout in New Orleans and across the state, she had privately committed to vote for him at the convention. Now Landrieu wanted to make things right. At one point, she pleaded with Reid to take care of Hillary. Reid responded by half-jokingly telling the oft-troublesome Landrieu that Clinton could have her spot as chairman of the Small Business Committee.

Reid ultimately blocked Hillary at every turn. He and Schumer weren't going to irritate other Democratic colleagues by giving Hillary a leg up. There was an inherent risk in giving her a more prominent role in the Senate, particularly on health care: she'd have a better spot from which to challenge Obama. If any Democrat was going to be the face of health care reform in the Senate, it was going to be the dying Ted Kennedy, whose endorsement of Obama was one of the most pivotal moments of the primary and one of the most stinging rebukes of Clinton. If it wasn't Kennedy, it would be his best friend in the Senate, Chris Dodd, the red-cheeked, white-haired son of a senator who had been Kennedy's carousing buddy in their salad days on Capitol Hill. Clinton asked Kennedy to give her control of a health care subcommittee, but he turned her down cold. Instead, he offered her a runner-up trophy as chair of a special task force on insurance industry issues—the very industry that had strangled her health reform effort in the White House.

Yet, while Reid ran the Senate, Hillary's advocates, including some surprising sources of goodwill, turned to Obama, the nation's new top Democrat, for help. Even Claire McCaskill privately made the case to Obama's aides that he should help find a position of prominence for Hillary, whether in the Senate or in his administration. "Her message was that Hillary and Hillary's camp needs to continue to be engaged by the Obama folks," said a source familiar with the discussion. "She had to be included. She needed some seat at the table."

THREE

Calculated Risk

The Clintons were out for a Sunday stroll in a wooded preserve in the scenic Hudson Valley, not far from their Dutch Colonial home on Old House Lane in Chappaqua, New York, when Bill's phone rang. It was November 9, five days after the election, and the president-elect was calling for the last Democratic president. But Bill wasn't getting good reception on his cell phone, and he asked if he could call back when he got home. When they finally had a sound connection, from the Clinton house, Obama explained that he was busy filling in the roster for his new administration, a project that former Clinton White House chief of staff John Podesta had been running behind the scenes for months, and he wanted Bill's thoughts on a couple of personnel moves. Before they hung up, Obama asked Bill to tell Hillary that he would soon want to speak to her as well.

A small set of Obama's top advisers knew the reason: she was his pick for secretary of state. Political insiders had started hearing whispers about Hillary at State almost immediately after the election. The day after Obama's victory, Andrea Mitchell of NBC News asked Philippe Reines, Hillary's senior adviser and spokesman, whether Hillary would land at State. He gave the same answer he would have delivered had he been asked whether Hillary would sign on as dog catcher: anything's possible.

Aggressive, with intense brown eyes, the Upper West Side native had earned his place in Clinton's inner circle with fierce loyalty and a sharp instinct for how to build and protect his boss's narrative, often in insult-laden e-mail exchanges with reporters. Reines relished petty put-downs like using the wrong first name for a junior congressman to indicate the lawmaker wasn't famous enough to merit being remembered, and he once described himself as a hockey goalie defending the Hillary net against the flying pucks of the press. Now he, too, wanted to know if the roller-coaster ride of the 2008 election was going to end at a new height—at the State Department.

On November 7, in an e-mail chain with several of Hillary's top advisers, including Maggie Williams, Cheryl Mills, and Capricia Marshall, Reines asked his boss whether she would end up at State.

He's going to offer you the job, Reines wrote.

"Ain't gonna happen for a million reasons," Hillary replied to the group. She thought it was ridiculous, even absurd. She told him she couldn't fathom where the rumor was coming from. But it couldn't be true, she wrote.

The call from Obama that Sunday night added to the intrigue for Hillary and her staff.

Longtime Obama scheduler Alyssa Mastromonaco then reached out to Huma Abedin, who handled Hillary's most sensitive personal and political tasks, and they plotted a trip for Hillary to Obama's transition headquarters in Chicago. Hillary was getting a lot of attention right after the election for someone who didn't think she was going to be asked to join the administration, but she still wasn't nearly as convinced as some of her aides that a job offer was forthcoming.

Inside Hillary's Senate office on the fourth floor of the august Russell Building, a century-old Beaux Arts mix of marble slabs and Doric columns where the squeaking shoes of generals and admirals can be heard as they come to testify before the Senate Armed Services Committee, aides were still wrestling with the question of how Hillary could continue to make her mark from Capitol Hill. After a summer of discontent, there was suddenly a buzz of excitement over the surprising possibility that Hillaryland might find a new home in the Obama administration.

On the other side, there had been deep misgivings among some of Obama's high-profile aides, including David Axelrod and Jim

Messina, who had discussed the choice with the president-elect in late October, shortly before the election. As early as the summer of 2008, Obama had been pondering what a Hillary-run State Department would mean for his presidency.

Axelrod had been dumbstruck when Obama first said he wanted Hillary for the job. "How can this work?" Axelrod asked. "We just had this very vigorous campaign."

"She was my friend before she was my opponent," Obama replied. "She's smart, she's tough, she has a status in the world. I'm sure she'll be a loyal member of the team. I have no concerns about it."

While she wouldn't be answering the infamous three a.m. calls she had discussed during her campaign, she would have a major role in dealing with them if she landed in the job. During their grueling primary fight, Obama had mocked her for overstating her foreign policy portfolio. Worldliness wasn't just about "what world leader I went and talked to in the ambassador's house, who I had tea with," he'd said. But as the primary battle wore on, Obama aides said, he became impressed with her persistence, her desire, as one put it, to "bust through a brick wall." And in the months after he defeated her, he admired her fierce loyalty to the cause in the general election.

Valerie Jarrett, the president-elect's closest adviser and friend, ultimately embraced the idea. The campaign had been painful for her because she had a relationship with the Clintons that went back many years and was developed through her cousin, Ann Jordan, the wife of Clinton confidant Vernon Jordan. Jarrett had always admired and respected both Clintons and was relieved by the prospect of mending fences.

Obama wanted Hillary on his team, and in making the case to his own aides, he knocked down the argument he had made on the trail that her experience was limited to tea parties. As important, having Hillary on the inside would let Obama keep control over perhaps the nation's most potent political force other than himself.

In a series of meetings in Chicago beginning two days after the election, Obama had gathered his brain trust, including Joe Biden, Podesta, Messina, and Rahm Emanuel, to pick the top officials in his

Cabinet. Because the economy was in free fall, the first decision was to ask Tim Geithner to take the reins at the Treasury Department. Secretary of state was second on the agenda. By that point, Obama had made clear to his campaign team why he wanted Hillary. Biden spoke up in favor of that decision, according to Ted Kaufman, his longtime Senate chief of staff, who was also in the room.

Biden had sought Bill Clinton's advice before entering the 2008 race, and, as a longtime friend of both Clintons, never endorsed Obama in the latter stages of the primary. Instead, he had offered his counsel to both Obama and Hillary as they battled it out across the country.

"The president was looking for what the vice president was going to say," Kaufman recalled. "The vice president was a strong supporter of Hillary."

When Obama went around the room to count the yeas and nays—his personal choice evident already—the decision was unanimous.

On November 13, four days after Obama's call to the Clintons, Mitchell reported that Hillary had been spotted on a flight bound for Chicago. Later that day reporters staking out the Obama transition office at a federal building downtown caught sight of a motorcade that didn't belong to the president-elect, raising the question of which other dignitary was visiting. Still, the two camps weren't talking about it publicly. The operation was so hush-hush that when Obama speechwriter Jon Favreau ran into Abedin at the office that day, he assumed Huma was being interviewed for a job in the administration; the thought that Hillary was in the office listening to Obama's sales pitch never crossed his mind.

Obama and Clinton huddled in a bland conference room, face-to-face without any aides.

Obama said he wanted her for the job.

"I'm really flattered, Mr. President-elect," Hillary replied, "but I'm going to go back to the Senate. That's what I really want to do. You've got great people to choose from to be secretary of state."

She offered up two names: veteran diplomat Richard Holbrooke and retired general Jim Jones, a former commandant of the Marine Corps.

"I can help you in the Senate, because it's going to be challenging to get your agenda through," she told Obama. "You've got the economic crisis to deal with."

But Obama had given it a lot of thought, he told her, and she was the woman for the job. While he was tied down in Washington with the financial collapse, he needed a star-power diplomat to represent him across the globe.

Hillary said no again.

Go home and give it some thought, Obama instructed her, as only a newly elected president could. He wasn't taking no for an answer. They could talk about it later, he said.

Hillary had plenty of reasons to reject Obama's first entreaty. She was coming to grips with returning to the Senate; she didn't want to run an agency full of Obama appointees; her husband's international dealings could become an unwanted distraction for Obama; and she wouldn't be able to pay off the $6.4 million debt that her campaign still owed to vendors if she held a post in the executive branch. Besides, why would she want to work for the upstart who beat her and look at his portrait every day in her office? And— never stated but obvious to anyone in politics—playing coy with Obama gave her leverage to extract a better deal if she ended up accepting. It all added up to a demurral.

Until their face-to-face meeting, all but a few insiders in each camp had been kept in the dark. But the *Huffington Post* reported the next day that Obama had offered her the job, citing two Democratic officials. Suddenly it felt more real. It was a lifeline for Hillarylanders who had once imagined themselves in the West Wing only to snap back toward Capitol Hill. The State Department represented a soft landing in between.

As Hillary began researching the job and soliciting opinions, she soon found out that her closest friends and advisers were divided on whether she should take it.

Madeleine Albright, the former secretary of state, was driving in heavy traffic on M Street in Washington when Hillary called to get her thoughts. A dozen years earlier Hillary had urged Bill to make Albright, then the U.S. ambassador to the United Nations, his second-term secretary of state. The two women had traveled abroad together during the Clinton administration, and their bond was enhanced by the common experience of a Wellesley education. Not only was Albright a friend of Hillary's, she was the only Democratic woman ever to serve as secretary of state and thus was uniquely positioned to offer counsel both about what the job entailed and about whether Hillary should take it. Albright pulled off onto a side street in Georgetown for what she correctly suspected would be a long conversation.

"She knew I'd liked the job," Albright said. "We talked about what the job was about, what you could do with it, how much travel there was, what the building was like."

What her friend was really driving at, Albright knew, was whether Hillary would enjoy being at State. "I told her obviously that I thought the job was terrific, that she'd be wonderful at it, and that it was something that she could take great pride in doing," Albright recalled. "Often people think foreign policy has nothing to do with domestic policy, and they're part of the same spectrum. So I just knew she would be good at it."

Mark Penn's knee-jerk reaction was that she shouldn't go to work for Obama. But ultimately he had a clear-eyed view of what was best for Hillary—especially when it involved plotting for a second presidential run. He came to see the political benefits that could accrue to Hillary if she took the job. Among them, it would bolster her credibility as a foreign policy expert; it would prove again that she was a good Democrat, not an out-for-herself freelancer; it would once and for all liberate her from Bill's shadow; and it would please the Democratic primary voters who wanted to see her and Obama join forces.

Penn had been so iced out of Hillaryland by that point, according to longtime Clinton hands, that his advice probably didn't matter much. But his personal ambivalence exemplified the divide within

Hillaryland. "Our office was kind of split because a lot of people didn't want her to do it," said one of Hillary's Senate aides. "A lot of people wanted to retain their jobs—they were kind of negative about Obama and bitter. Then there were others who thought this was a good opportunity for her."

Obama put on the full-court press. Working on his behalf, a long list of high-profile Democratic players urged her to take the post, and it became clear that Bill was willing to do anything to ease that path, including adjusting the nature of his charitable work and sharing his donor list with the new White House team. But he was sensitive to the criticism he had received during her campaign. While he made clear that he thought she should take it, he didn't pressure her.

Podesta became the key go-between for Obama and Hillary. He had suggested Hillary for the job during meetings in the summer of 2008 only to find that Obama had already given it thought. Podesta urged Hillary to take the gig and advised Obama on the strategy and tactics of getting her to yes.

For a week, news reports went back and forth on the question of whether she had actually been offered the job and whether she would take it. Behind the scenes, some Clinton and Obama aides worked hard to make a match. Reines and Andrew Shapiro, an adviser on national security matters, came up with a gambit for lobbying Hillary indirectly. Joe Biden's birthday was coming up in a few days, and they urged her to call the vice president–elect a couple of days early, knowing that once they were on the phone, Biden would apply friendly pressure. He did his part. Emanuel made his own appeal to Hillary.

But while the Clinton allies within Obama's high command worked back channels to persuade her, much of the rest of his team was unsettled by the prospect of trying to assimilate the Clinton universe into the Obama world.

"The majority of people, and I mean this not at the top echelons, but up and down the campaign, would not have suggested that she and her people become part of" the administration, one Obama insider said. "The majority of people who I knew were not for it."

As these subterranean fights played out between those who

wanted Hillary at State and those who didn't, the calculus flipped. At first it looked like Obama was on the verge of scoring a coup by getting Hillary to join a "team of rivals" cabinet. But with the public latched on to that story line, it became clear it would be an equally jarring embarrassment for Obama if she turned him down. That meant her own reputation was suddenly on the line, too—there could be a backlash if fellow Democrats read a rejection as a deliberate attempt to sabotage her former rival.

Hillary had been concerned about those optics from the moment she left Obama's transition headquarters. She instructed aides not to talk publicly about the offer, so that if she turned Obama down it wouldn't reflect badly on either one of them.

For several days, Hillary remained unsold. She was just getting used to the idea that her next act would be in the Senate, where a player with extraordinary contacts and political muscle could make a career as a serious legislator, even after a failed presidential campaign. Ironically, the model was Ted Kennedy. The cultural differences between Obama's camp and Hillary's raised serious doubts about whether they could all get along, and the candidates themselves had clashed some on foreign policy approaches during the campaign. While they had more in common than not, the contrast between them was real. During the primary, Obama had repeatedly knocked Clinton for voting to authorize the war in Iraq. Clinton had portrayed Obama as a naïf who would wilt in the face of troublemaker nations like Iran.

As the days crawled by, Hillary kept leaning no. Several of the women closest to her, including Williams and Mills, urged her to reject the offer, according to one adviser familiar with the discussion at the time.

But there was also a committed cadre who pushed her to get to yes throughout the weeklong flirtation. Reines pushed every button he could to get her to reconsider, and then asked others to do the same. "If you think she should be secretary of state, you better send an e-mail to her right now, because she is saying no," he told one colleague late one night.

Ellen Tauscher, a senior member of the House Armed Services Committee, was among those who reached out to Hillary in the final days before the decision. A Wall Street wunderkind who wandered into Democratic fund-raising after moving to California with her then husband, Tauscher had chaired Senator Dianne Feinstein's first two campaigns for the Senate. Running as a Clinton-style centrist, she then edged out a Republican incumbent to win a Bay Area House seat, as Bill Clinton won reelection in 1996.

She was tall and warm—and as tough as a Trident missile. Tauscher had befriended the first lady, and Hillary had helped talk her through a tough divorce from a husband who had admitted to extramarital activity at the same time Bill Clinton was on trial over the Monica Lewinsky scandal. After Hillary won the Senate seat, the two women grew closer when they worked together on military issues as members of the House and Senate Armed Services committees.

Tauscher believed that Obama, who had limited foreign policy experience, needed gravitas on his national security team. She had urged Defense Secretary Robert Gates to hold over from the Bush administration to help Obama sort out the wars in Iraq and Afghanistan, and she considered Jim Jones, the incoming national security adviser, a close personal friend. As chairwoman of the Strategic Forces Subcommittee, Tauscher not only liked the idea of having three allies in the Situation Room, she thought Hillary's skills, expertise, and relationships around the world could help restore America's battered reputation and focus attention on serious policy issues that the Bush administration had neglected. And Hillary wouldn't have to spend much time getting up to speed.

Tauscher got her on the phone. "You've got to do this," she said. Hillary laughed her familiar chortle and stammered a bit in protest. But then she started listening. Tauscher explained that Hillary would add value to Obama's national security team immediately, using a Rolodex matched only by her husband's to create a sense not just of push but of pull. The Bush administration had been almost hostile to the rest of the world, including longtime allies and potential strategic partners. In particular, Tauscher noted, the START treaty was expiring and America would need a superstar to repair its tattered relationship with Russia. "We've got to get this done," she said of the nuclear pact.

In all, it was a thirty-five-minute pitch, and it was one Tauscher would hear repeated back a few months later, nearly word for word, when Hillary asked her to leave Congress to become undersecretary for arms control and international security affairs.

Hillary also ran into her former White House chief of staff, Melanne Verveer, outside an event in New York. Verveer, who ran Vital Voices, an NGO supporting women in leadership around the world that Hillary had launched, urged her to take the job. Lissa Muscatine, the veteran speechwriter, made a similar pitch. Still, the many reasons to accept the offer didn't obviate or eliminate all the reasons to reject it.

Kris Balderston, sitting at Baltimore-Washington International Airport, waiting for his daughter to return home from college one night that week, tapped out a message to Hillary on his BlackBerry, laying out the arguments for why she should take the job. "You're an executive branch person, not a legislative branch person," he wrote, playing on Hillary's deeply held belief that Republicans are patient and Democrats are impatient. "You are impatient." It was a long note, one that would have taken up at least a page and a half on paper.

He wasn't alone. "Everybody sent their individual e-mails to her," one Clinton insider said. "There was a surge."

On Tuesday, November 18, five days after her trip to Chicago, Hillary' top advisers convened a conference call to discuss what a rejection of Obama's offer would look like. To ensure that Hillary's impending no wasn't revealed to everyone on the call, they also quickly chatted about what she would say publicly if she took the job. Of course, if she said yes, it would be up to Obama to make the announcement. The lion's share of the two-hour call was devoted to the "no" version.

Williams, Mills, Reines, Jim Kennedy, Abedin, longtime Clinton lawyer Bruce Lindsey, Doug Band, and others were on the call.

Reines divined a window of opportunity to stall Hillary's decision making. Obama's team was still in the process of reviewing potential conflicts between Bill's charitable work and the duties of the secretary of state. If she said no now, Reines argued, the press would read it as Bill failing the vet. She should wait until that process was finished, he advised, even suggesting that the Clinton camp deliver a full physical printout of all of Bill's donors—rather than just the coterie of $200,000-plus contributors Obama had requested—to the transition headquarters.

Band was initially resistant to the idea. Charities aren't generally in the practice of handing over donor lists, and Band was justifiably worried about potential headaches that could arise. He had to be brought around to the idea because "it was such a rash suggestion," said one source on the call. Bill's camp wasn't "prepared to be in this situation at all," the source said. But, in the end, Band agreed.

The list exceeded the capacity of a Microsoft Excel spreadsheet, and Maura Pally, a Mills confidante and Hillary loyalist, had to hop in a cab to hand-deliver the industrial-size printout to Obama's team. The stratagem bought the yes crowd a little bit more time.

By Wednesday, November 19, Hillary had heard all the arguments. "She knew who was where," said one aide. "Everyone who was for it was ineffective."

She tried to get in touch with Obama to turn him down. But he wouldn't take her call. At one point, to avoid the rejection, Emanuel told Hillary that Obama was in the bathroom. Finally, late that night, they connected.

Please say yes, Obama cajoled. I need you on my team.

"You're really making this hard for me," she said.

"I mean to make it hard for you," Obama told her. "I want you to take this position."

No thank you, Hillary told Obama, for at least the third time.

Once again, he refused to accept her rejection. But he made clear that he wasn't going to ask again. He needed an answer. If it was no—really no—he had to move on and give the job to someone else. He was ratcheting up the pressure. Sleep on it and give me your final answer tomorrow, he said.

The major roadblocks had been removed: Bill wouldn't be a problem, Obama already had shown some willingness to help her retire the campaign debt, and pivotally, he assured her that she would be able to fill the State Department with her own people, not his.

As the night wore on, Reines got no indication that Hillary would reverse herself. He prepared himself to send out a press release the next morning that would put an end to the drama.

By eight a.m., he was back at his desk in the Senate, staring at two computer windows, a Microsoft Word document with the statement up on the screen and an Outlook press list. He was ready to blast it out to reporters as soon as he got the final call. Though Hillary had made initial edits to the statement, she hadn't yet signed off on it. But the order wasn't coming. There was "radio silence," said one adviser who worked on the release. As the minutes turned to hours, Reines began to get a gut feeling that something had happened.

He was right. Around eleven a.m., Maggie Williams called. Reines moved into Hillary's personal office and sat at her desk to talk privately. Williams told Reines to take his finger off the button.

Hillary had called Obama back that morning.

"All right, let's start talking about the conditions that I would need if I were to do this," she said—a clear indication that she was taking the job.

Obama's persistence had paid off. He was thrilled with her decision, he told her. He was confident they'd make one hell of a team.

Ultimately, Hillary thought, she would want him to say yes if their roles were reversed. "What finally tipped it for me is I really started thinking about, suppose I had won, and suppose I was facing the same multiple crises that the president was facing—two wars going on, an economic meltdown—and I wanted him to be in my cabinet," she said. "And I had thought a lot about it, I believed he was the best person for the job, and I asked him, and he said no; how would I feel?"

The call of service was a strong motivator, too. "I'm old-fashioned enough to think that when your president asks you to do something, you better have a really good reason not to do it," she said. "And I loved being a senator. I thought I could be a really help-ful partner in the Senate. But this is what he wanted me to do, and he needed an answer."

FOUR

Us and Them

Hillary's deference had won out. The new president asked her to serve her country, and she couldn't turn him down. Left unspoken, secretary of state could be the perfect stepping-stone to the presidency, a four-year reprieve from domestic political battles and a hard-to-match foreign policy résumé all rolled into one.

Hillary had plenty of work to do to learn the nuances of foreign policy and win the confidence and trust of her new department, her colleagues in the cabinet, and Obama's fresh crop of empowered White House aides. Following the model she had used as a freshman senator, she began gathering political capital by keeping her head down and proving, through her work ethic and command of the subject matter, that she belonged in the job.

The trick of building a relationship with Obama's aides remained the toughest of all, and it got off to an inauspicious start. In early December 2008, two days after the president-elect introduced his national security team at a Chicago press conference, the *Washington Post* published a photo of Jon Favreau, Obama's twenty-seven-year-old speechwriter, mock-cupping the breast of a cardboard cutout of the incoming secretary of state. Another young man, standing on the other side of the Hillary cutout from a grinning Favreau, kissed the side of Hillary's head and held a beer near her mouth. Hillaryland had accused Obama of playing gender politics during the campaign, and the image, which had first been posted to Facebook, threatened to roil two camps still struggling to forge a new bond, both publicly and privately.

When the photo went online, Obama's campaign veterans and reporters assigned to cover the new administration were at the Capitol Hill bar The Hawk and Dove at a party honoring Robert Gibbs, who had just been named Obama's White House press secretary.

The reporters at the bar were blissfully unaware of the delicate diplomacy about to take place between the Obama and Clinton camps. Tommy Vietor, an Obama press aide, reached out to Reines to try to broker a détente before the image caused a major rupture in the fragile Obama-Hillary relationship. Reines stepped away from his dinner to jump on a conference call with Vietor, Favreau, and Jon Lovett, a former Hillary speechwriter who would go on to work for Favreau in the White House. The call was the first time Favreau and Lovett had ever spoken.

Together they tried to figure out the best way to defuse the situation—a sign both of goodwill toward the young speechwriter, who was liked in both worlds, and the recognition that it wasn't in anyone's interest to feed the story. Favreau and Lovett helped write a tongue-in-cheek statement that went out under Reines's name: "Senator Clinton is pleased to learn of Jon's obvious interest in the State Department, and is currently reviewing his application."

A distraught Favreau was eager to apologize directly. While he pondered the most elegant way to say "I'm sorry I cupped your cardboard breast," he noticed he had missed a call. Checking his messages, he heard Hillary's voice.

"I haven't seen the picture yet," she said lightheartedly, "but I hear my hair looks great."

Favreau was relieved. If Hillary wasn't going to make a federal case out of it, no one else could credibly do so. Together the Obama and Clinton teams had turned a potentially fraught situation into a moment of levity. It was the first test of the ability of the two rival camps to work as one, and these hard-charging young aides put aside their differences more easily than might have been expected.

"Little things like that matter," said one Obama aide, "because you have these conduits who would say 'these guys aren't total ass-holes over here' and vice versa."

The subtext of the statement that Favreau drafted for Reines even poked fun at the very real tension surrounding Hillary's power to fill the State Department with her own loyalists. That single promise from Obama to Hillary, while crucial to bringing her on board, created more friction up and down the ranks of the two camps than any other single factor through Hillary's first year at the State Department. In one stroke, the president-elect had excluded most of his own people from winning sought-after jobs at the State Department's headquarters in Washington's Foggy Bottom neigh-borhood, and he had guaranteed that Hillary would be able to reward some of the dead-enders from her own campaign who had never really warmed to Obama and weren't trusted by his team.

But he had left the pledge vague enough—it wasn't etched in stone or signed in blood—to set the table for a fight between his White House aides and Hillary's team over just what it meant. For example, Obama reserved for himself the right to pick a deputy secretary, the number two post at State, and the ambassadors to major countries. His aides also believed they would still be able to control the process for narrowing the list of hopefuls for particular jobs.

Most of the battles played out between Hillary consigliere Cheryl Mills and Obama adviser Denis McDonough. On occasion, they took disputes to Obama for a resolution. The White House hoped to exclude certain Hillarylanders by leaving them off lists of hiring options, according to a senior State Department official who watched the process closely. "The original fight was the White House thought they were going to send slates to [Hillary] and she would pick off the slate," the official said. "Cheryl said, 'No, we have total autonomy,' and that led to the first clash of the titans."

McDonough had been in the room when Obama promised Hillary she could pick her own staff, but that didn't mean the White House was going to give up easily on placing Obama people at State or blackballing hated Hillarylanders. There were examples of both, but they were the exceptions to the rule. McDonough found out quickly that Mills had no compunction about waving the president's promise in the faces of White House personnel officials. The tension was natural, Mills thought, and she had sympathy for the bind McDonough was in, having to explain to fellow White House aides why State was off limits. The two began scheduling weekly Saturday breakfasts, often at the low-budget Tastee Diner in the Washington suburb of Silver Spring, Maryland. If they missed a session, they'd make it up over coffee (McDonough) and hot chocolate (Mills). The need for a regular sit-down pointed to the volume and intensity of the personnel fights early on in the administration.

Staffing at State presented Hillary's first chance to correct bad personnel decisions that helped torpedo her primary run. Her friends had told her constantly throughout that summer and fall that she had been too loyal, and too forgiving, to aides who weren't equipped to do the jobs she had given them during the campaign, whose outside interests conflicted with her own as a candidate, or whose inability to play well with others sowed dysfunction. At State, she shut out the high-volume drama from her campaign, but she still relied on an intensely insular inner circle that prized loyalty to Hillary above all else. The campaign's hired guns, many of them veterans of the Bill years who had their own interests to tend to while moonlighting for Hillary, didn't fit into her plans at State. Instead, she surrounded herself with the small set of advisers who had most completely demonstrated that they would sacrifice themselves on the altar of her success.

Hillary would give Mills sweeping authority in the State Department, allowing her to merge two of the most significant roles in the agency, chief of staff and counselor, into a single power base. Widely respected for her competence, her loyalty to Hillary, and her sharp elbows, Mills would handle State's management and operations, as well as some sensitive political issues.

An Army brat and a Stanford law graduate, Mills had been a thirty-three-year-old aide in the White House counsel's office when she defended Bill Clinton during his Senate impeachment trial.

Through the various Clinton scandals of the 1990s, Mills's loyalty, discretion, and skills as a lawyer caught Hillary's attention, and Mills sealed their bond as a general counsel on the presidential campaign. Joe Lockhart, who was White House press secretary under Bill Clinton, described Mills as the "voice of reason" on Hillary's campaign. Her pugnacity as an attorney and aide reflects Hillary's own background as a lawyer and staffer working on the House impeachment proceedings against Richard Nixon, and she is perhaps even more direct than the blunt-spoken Hillary. "Secretary Clinton wants to know you're a team player, but she wants to hear it straight," Lockhart said. "And she gets exactly that from Cheryl."

Described by one of Hillary's campaign aides as a "ball-buster" and by one of her admirers in Obama's camp as a "pit bull," Mills could keep big egos in check. "Tell that man I'll call him back," she once said when Bill Clinton was trying to reach her. "We all worked for Cheryl," one of Hillary's senior State aides said. Indeed, she was the unquestioned leader among a set of three aides—known at State as "the troika"—whose final word on matters was taken as Hillary's gospel.

Before long into the transition, "The Huma Factor"—an echo of "The Hillary Factor" from White House days—became shorthand for the influence that Huma Abedin, Clinton's most trusted personal aide, wielded in Foggy Bottom. Born just a few years before Chelsea, Huma had worked in the White House at the tail end of the Clinton administration and became Washington's quintessential "body woman" as a high-ranking aide to Hillary in the Senate. In Washington parlance, a body man or woman is the person closest to an official, the one who makes sure that he or she gets from place to place on time, has all the materials he or she needs—a phone, lipstick, hand sanitizer—and keeps track of who he or she interacts with. Huma was all that and more. She demanded to be involved in everything the secretary did, according to one State Department source. "No one tells Huma no, even Clinton," that source said.

Abedin, by then deep into a relationship with Brooklyn-based

New York congressman Anthony Weiner, combined black-haired, brown-eyed South Asian beauty with political smarts and an uncommonly subtle grace. "She looks like what you can imagine Scheherazade might have looked like," one Clinton confidante at State said. "Absolutely gorgeous—exotic looking and gorgeous. And she is paradoxically one of the sweetest and nicest people you could ever meet. She does have this kind of iron-butterfly face that she can put on," the confidante said. "She's kind of the thinking person's body person."

Not everyone was so enamored of Huma. In particular, some members of State's career staff viewed Huma as aloof, more comfortable hobnobbing with celebrities than engaging with her new colleagues. They also felt that Huma wasn't willing to collaborate with them.

"She will not really be in touch with you for working on a project for the secretary or planning a trip, and then come in at the last minute and say that 'everyone has done a bad job, but I'm going to fix it,' and then do a few things and say that she fixed it for the secretary, and she'll take credit for it," said one midlevel official. "This was sort of her M.O. I know this because it happened to me, and I know it happened to several other folks."

Her presence created tension because she involved herself in substantive matters in which she had little apparent background or expertise, and she guarded her proximity to Clinton jealously. Hillary trusted her like a family member and empowered her to be a force within the department. Seldom farther than arm's length from Hillary at that time, Huma was chosen to serve as deputy chief of staff for planning, one rung below Mills. If there was one person who played best to Hillary's demand for loyalty, it was Huma.

The third member of the troika, thirty-two-year-old Jake Sullivan, had been planning to go home to Minnesota when Mills called him at the tail end of November to ask if he would run Hillary's Senate confirmation team, a job that also required him to become heavily involved in her transition planning. Sullivan had told friends that he wanted to reestablish his roots in Minnesota so that he could someday run for public office, but he chose to defer designs on launching his own political career.

Blue-eyed and pale-skinned, with thin, light brown hair swept across his forehead, Sullivan cut a figure as lean as Obama and stood out among Hillary's diverse set of advisers for looking much more like a traditional Ivy League–pedigreed State Department official. He didn't neatly fit into the cult of personality that defines Hillaryland, where many top aides are, like Madonna, known simply by one name: Huma, Philippe, Capricia. Or, at times, just by their initials. Reines is PIR, Mills is CDM, and Marshall is CPM. Hillary, of course, is in on the alphabet act, too, as talk-show host Ellen DeGeneres found out during an interview in 2005.

"What do I call you? Do I call you Senator?" DeGeneres asked.

"Just call me HRC," Hillary replied.

Sullivan was never initialized—just Jake—but Hillary trusted his judgment and discretion. He gained influence during the primary, and later at State, because his policy and political instincts mirrored Hillary's. Whether that was a function of natural affinity or of highly attuned mimicry is a matter of disagreement among Hillary's advisers, but no one doubts that she appreciated his ability to understand her thinking and follow through on it with little instruction necessary.

Indeed, Sullivan had done such a remarkable job preparing Hillary for the marathon of primary debates with Obama in 2007 and 2008 that the Obama campaign brought him in to help get the nominee ready for matchups with John McCain that fall. In those sessions, where bigger personalities dominated the training, Sullivan quietly typed up answers to possible debate questions, absorbing almost anonymously into Obama's operation. At State, he ultimately landed a job equivalent in rank to Abedin's as deputy chief of staff for policy, from which he later took over the department's in-house think tank, the Policy Planning Office, and often briefed reporters on policy matters too complex for her press team to handle.

"Jake did everything for her," explained one of Obama's senior aides. "You could go to Jake with a personnel issue, a policy issue, a communications issue. Jake is a utility player, and in Washington that's kind of an indispensable person to be able to go to." Not only did Sullivan handle a wide variety of tasks, he spoke for Hillary. "You knew if you were talking to Jake, he had her full confidence," the White House aide said. "Whatever was the front-burner issue of the day, you could go to Jake."

These posts, which didn't require a presidential appointment or Senate confirmation, were the top subset in a group of roughly two hundred political appointments at State, almost all of which were given to Hillary by virtue of Obama's promise. Veteran Hillary-landers tend to describe her operation—whether in government, a political campaign, or philanthropy—as consisting of concentric circles of trust. Only Hillary has a full view of every aspect of her formal and informal networks of friends, family, staff, and outside advisers, many of whom have a direct line to her over e-mail. Information is highly compartmentalized and tends to flow on a need-to-know basis, leaving most of her advisers with only a limited window of insight into her strategy and activities.

Informal power, gained through Hillary's favor, is far more important than the formal power of a particular title. Because Hillary had been in Washington for nearly two decades, it was nearly impossible for newcomers to earn the kind of trust that veteran Clinton warriors had built up over the years. Sullivan was an exception to that rule, having come on the scene for the 2008 campaign. But the people closest to Hillary at State were generally very familiar faces who could be trusted with the most sensitive information and political assignments. That's true for most secretaries, but Hillary's predecessors had much smaller universes of loyalists and less discretion to enlist them en masse. A new secretary can expect to bring in half a dozen to a dozen people. Because of Obama's personnel promise, Hillary tallied the power to appoint political aides by the score.

Reines, the Senate office spokesman who had been shunted to the side by Doyle during the campaign and ended up traveling with Chelsea Clinton, was named senior adviser and retained informal control over Hillary's interaction with the media. In addition, Hillary brought in Melanne Verveer, her chief of staff at the White House, as an ambassador for global women's issues, an office given the designation "S" to indicate it was under the secretary's direct purview and budget. Likewise, Hillary tapped hit list architect Kris Balderston to be the force behind a new global partnerships office—a State Department mirror of the Clinton Global Initiative that sought to bring together money and expertise from inside and outside government to address international problems.

Hillary would take criticism, both internally and externally, for her use of "S"-class offices to appoint special ambassadors, envoys, and representatives, as well as senior advisers, who exercised tremendous power to circumvent the department bureaucracy on various issues of concern to Hillary. But this same model, also used by some of her predecessors at State, has become standard operating procedure for the White House, which has built up economic and national security teams with hundreds of people who are loyal to the president and occupy jobs that do not require Senate confirmation.

The construction of Hillary's staff reflected lessons learned from the campaign trail, especially when it came to those who had caused difficulty or embarrassment. For a variety of reasons, the ambitious, highly combustible advisers who made her campaign war room so contentious—Mark Penn, Howard Wolfson, and Phil Singer among them—didn't accompany Hillary to State. During the course of her campaign postmortems in the summer and fall of 2008, Hillary had shaken out a number of aides like Penn even before she made the decision to go to Foggy Bottom. While a certain number of dependable, close-knit advisers—including Senate chief of staff Tamera Luzzatto and campaign manager Maggie Williams—chose not to follow Hillary to State, she brought with her those who had served her well in the Senate and during the campaign.

Loyal, but wiser, Hillary engaged some of her old friends off the books to draw on their intellect and information while keeping them out of her decision-making structure. "She has a group of people around her that have been incredibly strong, smart, and loyal," said one longtime Hillarylander who did not take a job at State. "Sometimes we have to figure out 'Does that person go into that slot or does that person go into this slot?' You have to make tough choices, and I think that prepared her to make tough choices in the State Department—and it certainly prepared her to make tough choices going forward if she decided to do anything."

Yet the difficulty of making personal staff decisions paled in comparison to that of the myriad challenges she found in transitioning into official State Department business. In short order, she needed to put together a leadership roster that mixed Democratic Party stalwarts with veterans of the nonpartisan foreign service, get up to speed on nuances of foreign policy, devise a plan to implement Obama's vision for the world, and start building relationships with key players on the president's national security team who would be valuable allies in bolstering State.

Hillary walked into the transition facing four major interdependent challenges. First, the president had picked her, he said, because he believed she was the best person to represent the United States abroad as it tried to regain its standing in the international community. President George W. Bush's pursuit of the Iraq War, his policies on the treatment of detainees, and his polarizing rhetoric had turned international sympathy for America in the wake of the September 11, 2001, terrorist assault on the United States into resentment. Bush's numbers were pathetic in parts of the Arab and Muslim worlds: in Pakistan, a crucial partner in pursuing Al Qaeda, confidence in Bush's foreign policy leadership stood at 7 percent during his last year in office and was just as bad throughout the Middle East, at 11 percent in Egypt, 7 percent in Jordan, and 2 percent in Turkey. The story wasn't much better among America's long-standing European allies: Bush stood at 16 percent in Great Britain and 13 percent in France.

Second, she had to rebuild the State Department's influence within the American government, a project that required buy-in not only from the president but from the military and the CIA, which had taken big bites out of State's portfolio during the Bush years, from diplomacy to development (which means distributing

American aid). Defense Secretary Donald Rumsfeld and Secretary of State Colin Powell had barely been on speaking terms, and Rumsfeld's relationship with Condoleezza Rice wasn't much better. With the leaders of the two agencies at odds, there had been no incentive for the rank-and-file workers at the State Department and the Pentagon to fight the natural tension between diplomats and soldiers.

Third, she had to win the confidence and rebuild the morale of the roughly seventy thousand people at the State Department and the U.S. Agency for International Development, many of whom felt beleaguered after years of playing second fiddle in the national security realm. Past secretaries had found it much easier to implement their agendas when the bureaucracy embraced them and much harder when the permanent class of foreign service and civil service officers rejected them. Hillary needed allegiance from the career folks to execute her plans.

Fourth, and most important should she choose to run for president in 2016, she had to fortify her own brand within the United States, a task that depended on her ability to execute the first three. Some of her aides vehemently dispute the idea that Hillary's brand needed any burnishing at the time—her numbers had been on the rise since the end of the Democratic primary—but public opinion polls are fickle, and the ground she gained by endorsing Obama and joining his team could easily be lost if Americans decided she wasn't up to the task of serving as America's top diplomat.

One of her first moves in the transition was to court General David Petraeus, the architect of the successful counterinsurgency strategy in Iraq who was moving into a new role as the head of Central Command, the Pentagon's unit overseeing both Iraq and the Afghanistan-Pakistan region. In that post, Petraeus would have significant say over American policy in Afghanistan and Pakistan, where Hillary's trusted lieutenant Richard Holbrooke would represent the State Department's interests. Though they had enjoyed a good relationship during most of her time in the Senate—and Petraeus was a protégé of Hillary's best uniformed pal, General Jack Keane—Hillary had rattled their friendship during an Armed

Services Committee hearing on Iraq in late 2007, just as the presidential campaign was heating up. She believed that Petraeus and Ambassador Ryan Crocker had delivered to the committee an overly rosy assessment of the success of the surge in Iraq. "I think the reports that you provide to us really require the willing suspension of disbelief," she said. Hillary and Petraeus had sporadic contact over the next year, but the relationship had grown cold.

Hillary made rekindling that connection a high priority. Petraeus was stationed in Florida, but while he was in Washington at the end of 2008, in late November or early December, she invited him to the house on Whitehaven Street. Petraeus understood what was going on, that Hillary wanted to make a gesture of reconciliation because she would need his help. But regardless of the calculation involved, he was grateful that she reached out to him. They sipped glasses of wine by her fireplace, and Hillary invited him to come back the next night, where he found Holbrooke, the veteran diplomat who had negotiated the Dayton Accords ending the war in the Balkans during Bill's presidency. The two men didn't know each other, but as Petraeus found out that night, they would soon be working closely. Petraeus, the highly educated soldier, and Holbrooke, the classic diplomat, were more alike than it might seem on first glance. They were both ideas men. And while they didn't see eye to eye on everything, they quickly developed a high regard for each other's intellectual firepower.

Hillary opened another bottle of wine, and the three of them sat down by the fireplace. It was mostly a social drink, a getting-to-know-you moment for Petraeus and Holbrooke, whom Hillary had picked to be the presidentially appointed special representative for Afghanistan and Pakistan. In that role, he would partner with Petraeus to develop civil-military plans for the region and meet with officials from the two countries, as well as American leaders, to implement those ideas.

Hillary's courtship of Petraeus would pay dividends, both on policy and personally. In mid-February 2010 she found herself stranded in Jedda, Saudi Arabia, because of mechanical problems with her jet. Petraeus, who had been in nearby Riyadh, redirected his own plane to pick Hillary up and bring her back to the United States. On the plane, Hillary picked Petraeus's brain on the region monitored by U.S. Central Command, an area encompassing twenty countries that spans from Egypt in the west to Pakistan in the east, and from Kazakhstan in the north to the waters off Somalia's coast in the south. During their conversation, it became clear that both Hillary and Petraeus were exhausted from their respective trips. So Petraeus, playing the part of an officer and a gentleman, offered Hillary his bed in the compartment at the back of the plane. As Hillary settled into Petraeus's bed, he stretched out on the floor outside the door to the compartment. She had won him back.

I nitially, Holbrooke had hoped to become the deputy secretary of state, but the Obama camp couldn't forgive him for threatening messages he had delivered to foreign policy experts during the campaign, vowing to deny them jobs in a Hillary administration if they signed on with Obama. Instead, Obama picked Jim Steinberg, a deputy national security adviser in the Clinton administration who had counseled Obama during the general election. Steinberg, then the dean of the University of Texas's public policy school, was with his daughter at a birthday party in November when Obama called to offer him the job. Disappointed that he wouldn't become Obama's national security adviser, Steinberg asked for one concession from the president: Give me a permanent seat at National Security Council meetings. That would ensure that he couldn't be shut out of the top level of the policy-making process. It's okay with me, if it's okay with Hillary, Obama said. Hillary liked that idea because Steinberg's presence would mean State had two seats at the national security table, and Steinberg was an acceptable number two because of his long-standing ties to trusted Clintonites.

Hillary sat down with Steinberg in early December in an apartment on Central Park South, overlooking the lush rectangle of gardens, fountains, and playgrounds that stretches from the northern reach of midtown Manhattan to the southern edge of Harlem. She used the apartment for a series of one-on-one sessions with advisers and potential hires that fall and winter. The location allowed her to meet with them discreetly, lowering the risk that reporters would find out who was up for a job at State, and in an environment cozy enough to promote comfort and informality. Once visitors stepped out of the elevator on the appropriate floor, Hillary's Secret Service detail—a perk of her status as a former first lady— guided them to the right door. Inside, Hillary played hostess, boiling pot after pot of green tea as she planned her execution of Obama's foreign policy vision. The apartment was dotted with pictures of the Clinton family, and Hillary seemed so at home in the dining alcove with the view of the snow-glazed park that, years later, Steinberg thought the apartment belonged to the Clintons. It didn't. It belonged to Doug Band.

For three hours, as afternoon turned to evening, they had what Steinberg recalled as a "lovely, long conversation where we talked about the excitement of getting these new jobs and the opportunities and what kinds of people we wanted to work with and bring into the department, and how we wanted to use our time, and how we would conceive our mutual roles." Hillary still didn't know exactly which jobs she could offer to which candidates, but she had a pretty firm idea of who she wanted at the top, what her agenda would look like, and what strengths she brought to the position.

Two main "meta" objectives informed everything she wanted to do at State: restore America's standing in the world, and infuse the theory of "smart power" into America's foreign policy. The term, coined by Clinton administration Pentagon official Joseph Nye, is shorthand for an approach to influencing other countries that combines traditional "hard power" such as military force and economic sanctions with the "soft power" of inducing foreign nations to change their behavior by offering carrots such as political or economic assistance. "Smart power is neither hard nor soft," Nye wrote in 2004. "It is both." A cultural shift toward smart power—and using both hard- and soft-power tools together to influence a single country—would take time. The more subtle and comprehensive approach to relationships with other countries often meant waiting for results. For the knee-jerk hard-power devotees, it looked weak in the short term. There was always someone in Congress screaming for the White House to take more aggressive action toward a rival, even if the hard-power route was likely to backfire.

More immediately, Hillary consumed herself with the question of how to reverse the damage Bush had done to America's reputation. "There was a lot of question globally about how was the United States using its power and how it was perceived in the world," Steinberg said, "and I think that strong sense of being able to project a different America and a different America abroad was her paramount objective. I think she recognized because of who she was and her own experience that she was particularly well suited to be the carrier of that message, of a different kind of America, an America that was going to protect its interests but could take into account the concerns and perspectives of others as well."

In that way, the objectives of using a smart-power approach and rebuilding America's standing meshed perfectly. America would increase its influence in the world by taking advantage of opportunities to engage other countries in trade, investment, philanthropic partnerships, and military coalitions. In particular, Hillary told aides in those early days, she believed it was vital to engage other countries at all levels, from top to bottom. Political leaders are responsive to their people, so engaging the public at the grassroots level could bolster America's ability to influence foreign nations.

"Her first priority, above all else, that she talked about in every single meeting, was how do we restore America's standing in the world? What's it going to take? And how do I reach not only to governments but to people to be able to convey the message about our vision for the future, about President Obama's and my commitment to the values that people appreciate about America?" said a source who was in the transition meetings. "That was, above and beyond, her biggest thing."

For Hillary to play effectively on the global plane and within the American government, she would need her house to be in order at

State. Even as she discussed a partnership with Steinberg, Hillary began circumscribing him. Steinberg was a gifted thinker in the public and foreign policy arenas but less talented as a day-to-day manager. Rather than handling all of the duties of the deputy secretary of state, Hillary told him, his job would be split into two. Congress had approved a second deputy slot at the end of the Clinton administration, but Bush hadn't made use of it. Now Hillary planned to bring in a Wall Street banker who had served as the cabinet-level director of Bill Clinton's White House budget office: Jack Lew. An Orthodox Jew with a zealot's devotion to public service, Lew would become Steinberg's equal if Hillary could lure him away from a lucrative job at Citigroup. Steinberg would be the deputy for foreign policy, and Lew would be the deputy for management and budget.

Lew wasn't Hillary's first choice for the new post. She had offered it to Wendy Sherman, who had been Albright's right hand at State. But Sherman declined. For his part, Lew had hoped to land a spot as chairman of Obama's National Economic Council. But when Tim Geithner was picked for treasury secretary, former Clinton treasury secretary Larry Summers slid into the NEC role. Geithner brought Lew in to discuss the deputy secretary slot at Treasury, and when Lew returned to his office, he had a message from Hillary, who wanted to hire him at State. Rahm Emanuel objected to Lew being hired at Treasury, not out of personal animus but because he worried that it wouldn't look good to put a Citigroup executive in that job in the midst of a Wall Street bailout. About a week after talking to Geithner and Hillary about their respective deputy secretary openings, Lew accepted Hillary's offer.

Between Sullivan's role in the formulation of foreign policy as a deputy chief of staff and Lew's control over the budget, the deputy secretary slot Steinberg got had been sliced into a much smaller fiefdom. Hillary told Steinberg that Holbrooke would be brought in as the special representative for Afghanistan and Pakistan, a post that technically reported directly to both Hillary and Obama. The main global hot spot, then, would be in Holbrooke's hands, at least as far as State's influence went in formulating so-called Af/Pak policy.

She also wanted George Mitchell, the former Senate majority leader, to become a special envoy to the Middle East to deal with the conflict between the Israelis and Palestinians, and Dennis Ross, a longtime Washington hand, would become a senior adviser to her on Iran. If Steinberg felt threatened by the A-team Hillary assembled before his eyes, he didn't mention it. Years later he insisted that he welcomed the news of Lew coming in to handle the budget, calling it the best personnel decision Hillary made at State. Her closest advisers maintain that Hillary welcomed Steinberg and had no intention of carving up his new job and parceling out choice pieces to favored lieutenants. But the proof was in the outcome—a much smaller domain for her new deputy—according to other aides who watched the process play out.

"It is fair to say that it had that effect. But I don't think that was the intent—to diminish Jim's authority. Jim and Jack got on well, as did Jim and Jake," said one high-ranking State official. "But Jake was clearly Hillary's guy, and Jim clearly was not. Hillary wanted her own people, and as they came in, Jim's turf was smaller."

Ultimately, whether they worked with him, went around him, or fought with him openly, senior State officials found that Steinberg could be marginalized, said another aide to Hillary.

"Even though Jack was principally focused on budget and management, he was also the lead deputy on Af-Pak and Iraq. He had the development agenda, which is typically a place where [Steinberg would have been] involved," said one senior State official. "Jake's role ensured that Jim was not the last policy official to talk to HRC, and it kept policy speeches mostly away from Jim."

Hillary made another major change to the deputy position that spoke more to the insularity of her inner circle than an effort to sideline Steinberg, but still had the same effect. In the Bush administration, the deputy secretary had authority over the S-class, a set of nearly a dozen offices under the secretary. But when Hillary came in, she removed her new deputies from the chain of command, meaning veteran loyalists who were appointed to run those offices, including Capricia Marshall and Melanne Verveer, did not report to anyone but her.

The use of special envoys, special representatives, and senior advisers was nothing new, but Hillary seemed to have a better understanding than her predecessors of how deploying them could circumvent the stodginess of the institution she was about to inherit. With direct access to the secretary and her explicit imprimatur, these aides were empowered to put policies on a fast track through a department in which change often became mired in bureaucratic inertia. These jobs, like those on Hillary's personal staff, didn't require Senate confirmation, but they carried a downside risk of Hillary failing to get credit if one of her lieutenants reached a break-through peace agreement. Still, the big-name diplomats offered Hillary a degree of insulation, too: if Holbrooke and Mitchell failed to solve a conflict, it would be more on them and less on her than if she had picked anonymous newcomers.

In group meetings with her top staff, including Steinberg, Mills, Sullivan, and incoming congressional liaison Rich Verma, Hillary pounded on the theme of finding ways to restore America's brand. It was clear that she knew, even in those early days, that her stature and confidence were chief assets in building a team at State, interacting with her peers in Obama's cabinet, and most important, reposition-ing America in the world.

"No other secretary of state could have convinced Richard Hol-brooke and probably George Mitchell to come work for them," said one senior State Department official. The same was true of Lew, who was moving down from the last post he held, as a cabinet-rank official, but felt intense loyalty to the Clintons and knew he could be a player from a senior post at State.

The construction of a top-notch staff mattered a lot in Hillary's case for several reasons. First, the mission of acting as the face of America abroad meant that she would be traveling almost continu-ously and had to delegate day-to-day management of most activities to trusted advisers. Each former secretary had fallen victim to pitfalls that Hillary was determined to avoid. Albright's failure to win over the career officials at State meant she had had to fight the bureaucracy rather than mobilizing it in support of her goals, and Condoleezza Rice had gotten bogged down in the details of a handful of crises at the expense of other issues that also needed attention. "We had necessarily spent the past eight years very focused on threats, and focusing on threats would always have to be a part of our foreign policy, but it couldn't be our foreign policy," said one top official who was involved in the transition planning.

Second, the heavy hitters—Lew in particular—gave State a leg up in its relations with the White House and other agencies, which strengthened Hillary's hand not only in the policy-making process but also in showing her new rank-and-file employees that her arrival signaled the return of influence to the State Department. Third, her operational model, in which information is highly compartmentalized and the lines of authority often run through informal channels rather than the official bureaucracy, requires competence among the true powers to function. She needed people close to her who could execute her will.

During the sessions in the Manhattan apartment, Hillary took notes on a long legal pad, which would become a trademark accessory during her four years at State. But even as she was starting to put together a staff in her mind, the details of Obama's agreement to let her do the hiring at State were already a sticking point with the president-elect's aides—and, at times, a convenient out for her. When she talked with Bob Hormats, a Goldman Sachs executive and longtime friend of the Clintons, Hillary told him that she couldn't yet offer him the undersecretary job she planned to give him. "I have to work out each of these jobs with the White House," she said, "because these are presidential appointees."

Hillary already had begun to scout the talent she was inheriting. Following the tradition for incoming secretaries, she and her team worked out of a transition space on the ground floor, where current State officials could visit her rather than risk the awkwardness of the outgoing secretary's successor wandering around executive offices. She brought Sullivan with her to a December 9 orientation visit there, where she met with Bill Burns and Pat Kennedy, among others.

Burns, the undersecretary for political affairs, was the highest-ranking foreign service officer, and he gave her the first briefing. An expert on the Middle East and Russia, where he had served as an ambassador during the Bush administration, Burns had white whiskers that stood out in the decidedly clean-shaven foreign service. Using notes scribbled on a three-by-five card, he gave Hillary a two-hour tour of world affairs and found himself impressed. She reminded him of former secretary of state James Baker in terms of her preparation and the grasp she already had of the material he covered. Mostly Burns hoped to help connect dots for her among various parts of the world and emphasize the importance of prioritizing in a job in which new crises hit every day.

In addition to foreign policy, Hillary pressed Burns about the institution and its people—a line of inquiry that demonstrated her political savvy. "It's a group of people both in the foreign service and the civil service who have a lot of energy and a lot of experience," he told her. "A little bit of attention goes a long way in terms of reaching out to people and doing an early town hall and going around to meet with more junior officers and things like that." He would come to be pleasantly surprised by the degree to which she not only followed the advice but sustained her effort to win hearts and minds in the building.

Hillary was impressed with Burns, too. "I gotta keep this guy," she told Sullivan.

The same went for Pat Kennedy, the undersecretary for management, whose penchant for micromanagement and bureaucratic maneuvering made him one of the most powerful figures in the foreign service. If a State Department employee wanted a BlackBerry or transfer papers for an assignment on the National Security Staff,

Kennedy had to sign off on it. Often his management style infuriated subordinates, but everyone needed something from Kennedy, and he had doled out a lot of favors over the years. Hillary remembered Kennedy from her husband's administration. By keeping Burns and Kennedy, respectively the most beloved and the most parochial institutions within the institution, Hillary sent a message to the career staff at the State Department that their views would be taken into account, even as she appointed a remarkably insular and loyal team of personal and political aides to exert power behind the scenes.

While Hillary was building her team and getting ready for her Senate confirmation hearing, Bill was reorganizing his life to accommodate hers. Doug Band helped negotiate a five-page memorandum of understanding between Bill and Obama's transition team that limited the former president's international activities. Dated December 12 and signed four days later by longtime Clinton lawyer Bruce Lindsey and Obama confidante Valerie Jarrett, the document dictated that Bill would publish the names of donors to the Clinton Foundation, separate the Clinton Global Initiative from the foundation, remove himself from an official fiduciary role in CGI, stop soliciting money for CGI, and prohibit CGI from accepting money from foreign governments during his wife's tenure at State. In addition, the White House and State Department would have to review his speaking schedule. Some Clinton aides chafed at the standards to which the former first couple were being held, feeling that they had been forced to go above and beyond the bar that would have been set for anyone else.

In the days before her confirmation hearing, Hillary met with vice president–elect Joe Biden, the former chairman of the Foreign Relations Committee, to get his advice, and she made sure she spoke to every living secretary of state, from Henry Kissinger to Condi Rice. When rumors had first surfaced that Obama might pick Clinton, some in Rice's inner circle wrote them off, but Rice herself intuitively knew it was true. She placed a congratulatory call to Hillary as soon as the official announcement of her selection was made. After eight years as national security adviser and secretary of state, Rice was eager to hand over the playbook to her successor and get back to academic life at Stanford. She reached Hillary in New York and issued an invitation to a private dinner in one of the most famous of all of Washington's political landmarks, the Watergate.

Hillary knew the confirmation process had much less to do with her public profile than with her ability to connect with her old colleagues on a personal level. She made sure to touch base with each member of the Senate Foreign Relations Committee, a banal ring-kissing exercise that was valuable in winning votes and softening any potential opposition. In a sign of respect—and because it had far greater concern about other nominees—the White House largely left Hillary alone to run her own confirmation effort, though Obama national security advisers Ben Rhodes and Denis McDonough attended her last prep session.

"The first thing you have to do are these courtesy meetings where you suck up and you call the senators and you say, 'Can I come to your office so you can lecture me on foreign policy and the pre-rogatives of the Senate for forty-five minutes?' And you have a lot of people who say, 'I'm above that. I know these senators individually,'" one White House official involved in confirmations said of a common pitfall. "She was absolutely charming on that front. She handled it like a complete pro. . . . I think that she did everything right so early on that we were like, 'It's going to be fine.' We were tracking it, but we weren't going to go office to office with her as we would with other cabinet secretary nominees."

In the end, Clinton, who aides said was entering a phase marked by the "reemergence of the nonpolitical Hillary," needed only to persuade her colleagues that she was qualified and competent in a Foreign Relations Committee hearing. While it wasn't expected to be as grueling as the firing line that awaited attorney general–designate Eric Holder, she spent the better part of several weeks huddled with close aides to prepare for the big moment in the Senate spotlight. She had two main objectives, one Clinton insider said. "One is how to frame the message of what kind of secretary of state you're going to be and how you're going to tackle the problems. And then there was how to deal with the Q and As. What sort of tough questions that would come up about money and the foundation."

No one can predict the future, and promises in Washington have a way of vanishing into the humid air, but to a remarkable degree, throughout her tenure at State, Hillary would stick to the philosophy and agenda she outlined in her confirmation hearing. Whether that's a sign of a sound strategy or stubbornness, the continuity is undeniable.

In her opening remarks, with Chelsea sitting dutifully behind her and Bill watching at home with Hillary's mother, Clinton laid out the framework for Obama's foreign policy approach. Rather than creating an Obama Doctrine, he would be nondoctrinaire in his dealings with foreign powers, she said. "The president-elect and I believe that foreign policy must be based on a marriage of principles and pragmatism, not rigid ideology," she said. "I believe that American leadership has been wanting but is still wanted. We must use what has been called 'smart power,' the full range of tools at our disposal—diplomatic, economic, military, political, legal, and cultural—picking the right tool, or combination of tools, for each situation. With smart power, diplomacy will be the vanguard of our foreign policy."

She also laid out the theory of the case for integrating diplomacy with military power and development, particularly in the most dangerous parts of the world. In particular, she said, it was imperative that the United States work to better the lives of Pakistanis and Afghans to help lay the groundwork for rooting out Al Qaeda and the Taliban. She toured the globe rhetorically, enunciating how the president would approach relations with Russia, China, Japan, African nations, and old European allies.

Hidden in her remarks was a hint of the emphasis that she would put on the State Department understanding and affecting actions by nonstate actors—terrorist organizations, political movements, and social groups—that presented new partnership opportunities and potential calamities. By the time "globalization" became a catchword, she said, "we were already living in a profoundly interdependent world in which old rules and boundaries no longer held fast—a world in which both the promise and the peril of the twenty-first century could not be contained by national borders or vast distances."

For the question-and-answer period, which might be hostile, her team had had to anticipate which senators would be antagonists and decide how she would respond to a variety of questions both about foreign policy and about Bill's international dealings. This last point was the X factor for Hillary's prep team, though there were other messy kinks to work out, too. They had to square her hawkish worldview with Obama's more nuanced policy prescriptions. "She can't show up the president. She can't appear like she's trying to formulate her own foreign policy," one aide told *Politico* at the time. The *New York Times* editorial page, never fond of Hillary in any of her roles, stoked the fires of doubt on the Sunday before her hearing. While expressing support for her confirmation, the *Times* begged the committee to examine "the awkward intersection between Mrs. Clinton's new post and the charitable and business activities of her husband."

She fielded six hours of mostly cordial questions on tough foreign policy matters, from Israel to Iran. "I don't get up every morning thinking only about the threats and dangers we face," Clinton told the committee. "In spite of all the adversity and complexity, there are so many opportunities for America out there." The line sounded like pure Rice, who famously noted that the Chinese word for *crisis* consists of the characters that mean "danger" and "opportunity." David Vitter, the Louisiana Republican best known as a client of the D.C. Madam, accused Bill of presenting a "multimillion-dollar minefield of conflicts of interest" and said he wouldn't vote for that. In the end, Vitter stood alone. The committee voted 16–1 to recommend Senate confirmation of her nomination, leaving just a perfunctory floor vote between Hillary and the Cabinet Room at the White House.

Though she prepared assiduously, there could have been little doubt in Clinton's mind that she would sail through the process. Less than a week before she was confirmed, an emotional private party was held for her one evening in the LBJ Room in the Capitol, where senators had their weekly policy lunches, just steps from the

Senate floor. A teary-eyed Clinton worked the room, hugging and kissing her colleagues, smiling for pictures, and thanking them for their camaraderie and support, reminding them that although she was leaving, she would be "just around the corner" in Foggy Bottom.

In a brief speech, once again with Chelsea at her side, Clinton told her colleagues that serving in the Senate "has been the greatest experience of my life" and that leaving them was "like leaving family."

Majority Leader Harry Reid, who had quietly thrown his support behind Obama and then deflected other senators' requests that Hillary be given an outsize role in the Senate, choked up as he addressed the crowd, his famously soft-spoken, hushed voice quavering. "Parting is such sweet sorrow, I have such sweet memories of you," said Reid, his insincerity evident to insiders. "I feel like crying."

Clinton's eyes welled, more because she was leaving her home of eight years than as a response to Reid, and she grew increasingly emotional. "This is not goodbye," she said. "This is just a wave, Harry. . . . We're going to be in each other's hearts and minds."

If Clinton was popular in her own caucus, she was also well regarded across the aisle. Republican senators Susan Collins, Lindsey Graham, Bob Corker, Olympia Snowe, Johnny Isakson, and John McCain showed up to honor her and her eight years in the upper chamber. And as her past collided with her future, she was joined at the reception by members of the Obama team—Rahm Emanuel, who had worked in her husband's administration and was Obama's new chief of staff; John Podesta; and her husband's final treasury secretary turned Obama economic adviser, Larry Summers. One after another, Hillary's colleagues shared stories and toasted her future. Chuck Schumer, the senior senator from New York, said he had "complete confidence" in the soon-to-be top diplomat, predicting that she would be "the best secretary of state this country has ever known." It was an easy time for Schumer to be gracious. He chased cameras with the same gusto that cameramen chased Hillary; now he would be the top dog in the New York delegation again.

Clinton smiled at her colleague but soon struck a more business-like tone, saying her goal was to create "a real partnership between the State Department and the Congress."

"Let's go out and make the future better than it is," she said. It was typical Hillary: forward-looking, positive, and a bit hokey.

The Friday before she took over at State, Hillary and Huma made a drape-measuring visit to Foggy Bottom. Rice and her aides had been working with Obama's State Department transition team for weeks, and they wanted to make sure it was a smooth transfer, not a repeat of the enmity that characterized the Clinton-Bush transition eight years earlier. The Bush folks were determined to make sure there wouldn't be any stories about political aides taking the keys off of computer keyboards or trashing offices. When Hillary and Huma made their way to the seventh floor to meet with Rice that Friday, Rice's aides took immediate notice of two physical attributes. Hillary was shorter than they had expected, and Huma was strikingly attractive. "That's Huma," one Rice aide whispered to another in awe.

Clinton met privately with Rice in the secretary's inner office, and then Rice walked her out to meet the staff—some of whom would be leaving in the transition and others who would stay on. In all, the visit lasted about ninety minutes and was described, like the ongoing relationship between Clinton and Rice, as cordial and pleasant. In their various interations during the transition, there was one dynamic that the Rice team took as foreboding in dealing with Clinton: Hillary still referred to her loyalists as "us" and to Obama's people as "them," according to a source familiar with the situation.

On January 21, 2009, the full Senate confirmed Clinton by a vote of 94–2. About an hour later she took the oath of office, putting her fourth in line to the presidency. When she was finally confirmed, Clinton, as promised, hired her own staff. And dozens of loyal aides from Clinton's past jobs—the White House, the Senate, her presidential campaign, and her HillPac political action committee—lined up to play a part in her new world. Obama's offer was a sign of the high regard in which he held Hillary.

But most of his team still had little use for her or her people. Part of it was residual bad blood between Plouffe and Mills, who had sparred over the retirement of Hillary's debt, filtering down. Part of it was a concern among the incoming White House team—warranted—that the Clinton folks wouldn't be able or willing to serve Obama first and Clinton second. They were all loyal to Hillary first. The best that Obama could hope for was that Hillary would make clear that loyalty to him was loyalty to her. Another part of it, as one of the president's aides said, was that "they really didn't hire any Obama people for the State Department." After Favreau's incident with the cardboard cutout of Hillary, the two sides had come together in mutual interest, but it would take years for some of Obama's other aides to warm to her. In other words, Hillary's us-and-them construct was no one-way street.

"It's like the Civil War. We're the North and we beat you," one Obama aide said in January 2013 of the attitude toward the Clinton contingent. "And that still was the feeling, like, years into the administration, by many, many people. I would say even today."

PART

FIVE

"Bloom Where You're Planted"

In the spring of 2009, Obama's vetting team gathered, as it often did, in White House counsel Greg Craig's wood-paneled corner office on the second floor of the West Wing. In lunchtime sessions, the small set of senior aides typically shuffled through the paperwork of as many as fifteen job candidates. On this day, one name conjured such searing memories from the campaign trail that it stood out from the others: Capricia Marshall.

The West Wing crew considered Marshall, a staunch Hillary loyalist, to be an enemy combatant. Like many of the women who surround Hillary, Marshall is graceful, disciplined, and down-home brassy. A brunette with a chic short haircut and highlights, the half-Croatian and half-Mexican Marshall, who favored rigorous P90X workouts, went way back with the Clintons. Marshall had been one of Hillary's closest confidantes in Washington since becoming the youngest White House social secretary in memory following Bill's 1992 campaign.

When Hillary suspended her own quest for the presidency in June 2008, she entrusted Marshall with running her political action committee, at a time when some Democrats feared that Hillary might make a final play for the nomination at the convention. Back then the animosity between the two camps had run so deep that Hillary's face was bulletin-board material in the Obama scheduling office. "They had all these unflattering pictures of her," said one source who saw the display. "Kind of the sports locker room mind-set." Even after the primary was decided, Marshall had been in charge of sensitive projects like recruiting staff to count late delegates from the Texas party convention to make sure Hillary won her fair share. But no single Marshall sin stood out in the minds of Obama's aides so much as a general view that she embodied the hated Hillaryland.

The president's team had acquiesced when Hillary chose Cheryl Mills as her chief of staff and, with even greater hesitancy, Philippe Reines as her senior adviser. They were members of Hillary's personal staff and thus entirely within her domain. But Hillary picked Marshall to be the nation's chief protocol officer, a position that carried with it the coveted prestige of an ambassador's rank and a reserved seat on Air Force One anytime the president traveled abroad. Not only would Hillary's gal pal have a lot of face time with Obama, she'd be taking up a high-profile spot in the administration that could have gone to a friend of the president.

There was another red flag on her nomination. Generally vetting issues run the gamut, from serious ethical lapses to DUI charges and, occasionally, embarrassing associations; one nominee had been photographed with Lisa Ann, the porn-film actress who played the title character in a *Hustler*-produced video called *Who's Nailin' Paylin*. Marshall's problem was less lascivious than that but troubling all the same: she hadn't filed a tax return in 2005 or 2006. She rectified the omission in the fall of 2008, around the time it became clear that Hillary might take a job in the administration. As it turned out, Marshall was entitled to refunds in those years. Still, tax issues had beset several Obama nominees, including Treasury Secretary Tim Geithner and Tom Daschle, and the White House had little appetite for another tax-cheat story line.

As a vetting attorney from the Justice Department read a three-page memo on Marshall aloud, White House deputy chief of staff Jim Messina and deputy communications director Dan Pfeiffer grew visibly agitated in their upholstered wingback chairs, as did other Obama campaign veterans around the room. By all rights, this job was a plum that should be going to an Obama loyalist—not to

Marshall, and not if it meant defending yet another nominee against questions about improper tax filings. Pfeiffer in particular thought "it was going to be a press problem at a time when we had been through a lot of confirmation issues with Daschle and Geithner."

They reacted viscerally. "Fuck no." "She was a complete bitch during the campaign." And worse.

Marshall's combination of experience with White House–level social planning and her closeness to Hillary made her a natural selection for the job, but Obama's aides didn't see it that way. No one in the room spoke up to defend her. Not legislative affairs specialist Sean Kennedy, who would have to get Marshall confirmed by the Senate if she was nominated. Not personnel director Nancy Hogan. Not ethics czar Norm Eisen. Not Greg Craig, who, along with Senator Richard Blumenthal, had been a study buddy of Bill Clinton and Hillary Rodham in the days when Bill cooked up his mama's fried chicken to serve to guests debating the Vietnam War in the future first couple's apartment near the Yale Law School. Craig's alignment with Obama had been a major betrayal during the campaign.

Aides close to Obama say it was less that they were against Marshall than that they wanted one of their trusted own in the high-profile role. "It was 'We should have our person. We need our person,'" said one senior White House aide familiar with the discussions on Marshall. "It would have been the equivalent of the roles being reversed if Hillary was president and us cutting a deal that . . . [longtime Obama friend] Desiree Rogers or Valerie Jarrett would be protocol officer," the aide said. "When you think of it that way, it's like why would they ever want one of us traveling with them?"

The vetting process worked in such a way that by the time a job candidate reached the team in Craig's office, he or she was the only hopeful under immediate consideration. It was up or down on Marshall. If Obama rejected her, another candidate would be lined up in the same way, a process that could take weeks or months.

Publicly the Obama and Clinton camps claimed they had put the primary behind them. But here, huddled in Craig's office, where the bookcases were still empty and the only personal effect was a Robert F. Kennedy poster on the wall, the truth poured out. The two sides didn't understand each other, they didn't like each other, and they didn't trust each other. The president's aides didn't have another candidate in mind when Messina asked his colleagues to cast their votes, but they were certain they didn't want Marshall.

One by one each aide extended a fist with the thumb pointing down. But then Messina, a strawberry blond Montanan whose soft voice takes the edge off his often-profane vocabulary, delivered some bad news to the team.

"I agree," he said. "But this is very clearly an HRC pick and needs to be raised with the president."

Typically, skirmishes over lower-level aides were resolved when either Mills or Obama's aides backed down rather than kicking the decision up the command chain. Obama's team tried to draw a line in the sand on Marshall, a proxy for Hillary. It was one of the rare occasions when a personnel fight ended up at Obama's door. This was a "test case" and a "watershed moment" in a brutal, months-long fight between the White House and State over Hillary's power to pick her team, according to one of the vetters.

Marshall had a secret weapon in another cousin of Valerie Jarrett, Ann Marchant, who had worked as a special assistant to the president in the Clinton White House. Marchant lobbied Jarrett on Marshall's behalf, describing her strengths and skills and encouraging Jarrett to prod the president.

Hillary went to bat for Marshall, too. The White House team didn't fully appreciate the role of a chief protocol officer and what went into it, she thought. It wasn't just some glorified advance staffer or a donor with little experience in Washington.

"There's nobody better to do this job," Hillary told Obama. "She's got the experience from the social office, she's got a great touch and feel for helping organize people. She'll be fabulous." Hillary had also gone rounds with the president's aides. "No, I'm telling you this is the best person," she had said. "You will know that I am right after you've worked with her for a month." And Hillary knew she held the trump card. "The president told me I could pick the people in the State Department, and this is my pick," she said. "So let's move forward."

In the end, Obama overruled his own vetting team, sending a strong signal to both camps that he would give Hillary the support he had promised in recruiting her. The dynamic infuriated Obama's foreign policy advisers, who were all but frozen out of State. Hillary blocked Samantha Power, an Obama campaign aide who had called Hillary a "monster," a remark that had cost her an official role with the Obama campaign. "You essentially had a merger, like a merger of two major corporations," recalled one senior White House adviser. "Beyond the ambassador stuff, Sam Power comes here instead of going to State, which she wanted to do."

Lingering bitterness and resentment over personnel choices colored the way the president's national security team interacted with the State Department during the first year of the administration and, for some aides, well beyond that. "The State Department was an island unto itself. I mean, no other cabinet secretary could plant people in the way that she could," one White House source said. "Her world, it was Clinton loyalists, where they could go without any fear of retribution for whatever sins or crimes against humanity they had committed during the campaign."

Obama's blessing gave Hillary tremendous leverage as her chief antagonists in Obama's camp—Messina, Pfeiffer, Robert Gibbs, and David Plouffe—learned the hard way. Of the various and sundry staff-level fights that roiled the relationship between the White House and State in Hillary's first year on the job, those over personnel were among the most hotly contested. Traditionally, the White House makes the bulk of the political appointments in any given cabinet department; the secretary is given the power to hire only a small handful of personal advisers. At State, the ratio was flipped because of Obama's promise.

So when Hillary first arrived at the State Department's headquarters, the Harry S. Truman Federal Building, as the new boss, she brought with her an entourage befitting an international icon. And she was greeted as a celebrity.

Her celebrity status came not only because she had the last name Clinton. It came, those who know her well say, because she is a woman who got up and fought every time the world knocked her down, from her failed health care reform effort and her husband's very public infidelities to the brutal slog of the 2008 Democratic primary. Time and again her personal tragedies and subsequent triumphs played out in real time for a global audience. Even though she had been first lady and U.S. senator, she retained an underdog quality. She had served as her husband's most valued adviser for decades but suffered accusations that she had ridden his coattails, unaccomplished in her own right.

When Hillary entered the atrium of the limestone and granite main State building on her first day on the job, January 22, 2009, she found it alive with anticipation. Lined with flags from around the world and filled with light pouring onto its black floors and square marble columns, the atrium of the building is an oasis at the center of a bureaucratic matrix remarkable mostly for the dim, drab, off-white hallways that suggest a 1950s-era junior high school that has never been renovated. That day sedentary bureaucrats navigated these hallways to come greet a boss whose very arrival promised to make their work more prominent.

The State Department is unusual within government in that it has a class of roughly fourteen thousand highly educated, highly trained foreign service officers who remain with the government from administration to administration, regardless of party, and who work overseas for most of their careers. They are complemented by a slightly smaller corps of civil servants—about eleven thousand in all—who support diplomacy, as well as forty to fifty thousand local employees in the roughly 270 American embassies and consulates around the world.

The foreign service officers are the heart of the department, and they traditionally come to State from Ivy League schools, though Georgetown, George Washington, and American University in Washington have also become major feeders. While State is actually a more diverse place now, the upper ranks of its foreign service still teem with adventurous do-gooders who grew up playing tennis at the club. They're difficult to impress, as part of their collective charm is a seen-it-all attitude, which, in turn, has been adopted by a civil service staff that increasingly includes high-level professionals who view themselves on a par with the vaunted foreign service officers.

But few of them had seen anything like Hillary Clinton's arrival at the State Department. "It was like a fucking rock concert," said one member of the civil service, who couldn't find an open spot on the jam-packed floor. He raced through the press briefing area and made his way to a narrow ledge above the landing where Hillary was set to make her remarks. He wasn't the only one with that idea: when he got there, the ledge was full. Government officials were almost literally hanging from the rafters, and finally diplomatic security officers prevented more people from cramming onto the ledge. The eager civil servant and the rest of the overflow crowd had to watch the speech on BNET, the State Department's closed-circuit television system.

Navigating through a buttoned-down sea of Brooks Brothers and Talbots as she made her way to the podium, Hillary was surrounded by applause, and by groupielike bureaucrats waving camera-phones. It was a historic moment, at least in the world of State. She smiled broadly and waved to familiar faces. When she spoke, she proclaimed a "new era for America" and said she planned to reassert the State Department's role in foreign policy.

Just behind her stood Bill Burns, the top-ranking foreign service officer who would spend much of the next four years within arm's length of Hillary. His presence signaled to the rest of the foreign service that they would have a voice in Hillary's State Department—music to the ears of a beleaguered corps of diplomats and policy analysts whose insights had often been ignored during the Bush administration.

If her debut was a rock concert, Hillary was Bono—a bona fide international celebrity, with credibility as a crusader for the disadvantaged. In that regard, she was one of a kind. She wasn't the first prominent political figure to reign at State. Six of the first fifteen

U.S. presidents had been secretaries first. Leading members of Congress, including Henry Clay and John C. Calhoun, also had held the post, as had two Supreme Court justices, John Marshall and Charles Evans Hughes. But it had been many decades since an elected official had become a heavy hitter at State, and never before had America's top diplomat been so instantly recognizable to, and admired by, so many people around the world. Her new army of apparatchiks at State didn't yet know what to expect from her leadership style, but they could be sure she would attract a crowd wherever she went.

Hillary's command of her troops that day obscured the fact that her last management job—as head of a dysfunctional campaign—had been a failure, and that she had never before run an organization anywhere near the size of the seventy-thousand-person foreign policy apparatus comprising State and the U.S. Agency for International Development. She was inheriting a department that had lost influence to the Pentagon and other national security agencies and whose diplomats had had to deal, on a day-to-day basis, with the fallout of a Bush foreign policy that had turned America into an international punching bag. It was hard to tell which was lower: the world's esteem for America, State's standing in the national security realm, or the morale of the folks at Foggy Bottom. With the Pentagon taking the lead in the major foreign policy issues of the day, most notably the wars in Iraq and Afghanistan, diplomats were relegated to defending America's actions to their counterparts in other countries.

As first lady and later as a member of the Senate Armed Services Committee, Hillary had met a lot of world leaders and thought about foreign policy on a macro level, but she had not spent much time on the details. "She was a bit of a novice at foreign policy. Even though she knew a lot of the personalities, there was a learning curve," one of her top deputies acknowledged. "This was somebody, much of whose passion was directed at domestic issues—at health care, and women's and children's issues domestically, veterans' issues. In our first year, we had to put a lot of time into the normalization of relations between Turkey and Armenia. That's not something she had spent a lot of time thinking about."

In addition, the centrist school of thought she subscribed to had evolved between Bill Clinton's last days in office and Barack Obama's election. She had become a devotee of the smart-power approach to foreign policy. But she still had to learn the intricacies of each country's interests to apply that mix of tools.

More important, Hillary had to deal with her new boss and all the anxieties around the most consequential shotgun wedding in Democratic politics since John F. Kennedy asked the reviled but politically indispensable Lyndon Johnson to be his running mate. Hillary is fond of saying "bloom where you're planted," an expression distilled from a story in the book of Jeremiah about the Jews, including Queen Esther's family, thriving in exile. Hillary has long cited Esther as one of her favorite characters in the Bible; not only is she one of the strongest women in Scripture, but her story of saving the Jews from annihilation by the Persians dovetails well with Hillary's own Middle East politics.

A big part of "blooming" at State would mean fully winning over Obama and his White House. The president was guarded in early interactions with Hillary, according to insiders who watched them. They might have developed a grudging mutual respect on the campaign trail, but they were hardly friends. Their new partnership was professional and polite but lacked depth. "They didn't have a close relationship in the first year," an Obama national security aide said. "At the beginning, it was perfectly correct," said a Hillary confidant. "Always very positive, even warm, but you know, just so. Not a lot of affection, not a lot of free-flowing conversation."

The relationship between Obama's staff and Hillary's, particularly those who worked on the campaigns, was anything but correct. Every disagreement was exacerbated by the aftertaste of the hard-fought primary, a dynamic that magnified petty fights and informed a series of clashes between Mills and McDonough, the senior national security aide who was very close to the president. "Stupid staff stuff like who's going to get credit for something. It was dumb, in retrospect, but we fought a primary campaign against them," the Obama aide said. "The first year you're not sure what the angle is.

What are these guys up to? I'm sure they thought the same thing about us."

When Obama took office, he brought with him a cadre of rambunctious and cocky late-twenty-somethings and early-thirty-somethings who had just come off the campaign of their lives. A number of early news accounts portrayed this group of mostly men as seemingly a bit too big for their britches; as they filled the desks and offices in the West Wing, reporters and other outsiders labeled it a frat house. Among the most aggressively anti-Hillary pledges moving into the White House was Pfeiffer, the snarky, fast-talking communications aide. (One Clinton aide referred to Pfeiffer as a "zero" who had ended up in the White House by happenstance and loyalty to Obama.) There was also the gum-chomping deputy press secretary, Bill Burton, son-in-law of Clinton backstabber Lois Capps, who relished being disliked and had dreams of taking over as press secretary once Robert Gibbs vacated the role.

The White House aides couldn't understand why Hillary's team still carried an air of superiority—after all, they had lost. In personnel fights, Mills kept laying down her trump card: Obama's promise to let Hillary hire. She never gave an inch. Reines liked to mock people to their faces, and, more often, over e-mail. And neither of them had risen—or wanted to rise—to embrace the high profile that Huma did. She once appeared on the cover of *Vogue,* violating the old Washington rule that staff ink stinks.

While their aides retained the nasty spirit of the campaign, Obama and Hillary tried to set a better example from the top. After one early television interview in the Oval Office, as the president talked with his communications team, including Gibbs and Vietor, one of his aides made a crack about Hillary, prompting the president to snap back, "Knock it off. None of that."

Obama made it clear from the moment he offered Hillary the job that he expected his team to put aside any sore feelings and treat her with the utmost dignity and respect, one of his top advisers said.

Similarly, in May 2009 Hillary reprimanded an adviser for

speaking ill of Obama behind his back. At the White House earlier that day, the president had asked Hillary to take on a minor task.

"Does he have nothing better to do?" the aide asked.

"Don't do that," Hillary said. "Don't ever do that. He's the president."

Hillary meticulously telegraphed proper deference to the president, both in public and in private. "She worked very hard at establishing, showing, that she was the secretary of state, not the president," said a former senior government official.

But the mutual distrust at the highest ranks below Obama and Hillary was poisonous enough in the first few months that an intermediary organized a dinner at Washington's exclusive Cosmos Club to try to defuse tension between Hillary's brass at the State Department and the high-dollar Obama donors who had been rewarded with ambassadorships over Hillary's picks for their jobs. "The Obama ambassadors to big countries were being shunned by senior State Department people," said a source familiar with the dinner, which featured a dozen of Hillary's top aides and a dozen Obama ambassadors. Among the ambassadors were Matthew Barzun, who would later factor prominently in the retirement of Hillary's campaign debt, and Don Beyer, a car dealer and former lieutenant governor of Virginia. "That dinner ended up being really important" in mending fences, the source said. "It was easy for these guys not to like each other in the abstract."

Unlike the scores of campaign loyalists who had landed jobs in the administration, Hillary was there not because Obama loved her or owed her anything. She was there because it all added up. By enlisting Hillary and Bush defense secretary Robert Gates, Obama backed up his lofty campaign-trail talk of creating a team of rivals. The Republican and the hawkish Democrat gave ballast to a fresh-thinking but wet-behind-the-ears National Security Staff at the White House.

Moreover, while Obama had put Hillary in a position in which she would have only as much influence as he wanted, he had also deprived her of a perch from which she could challenge him on the Senate floor, and he had made it next to impossible for her to run a primary campaign in 2012. Some, including longtime Clinton family strategist Mark Penn, could foresee Hillary mounting another run against Obama. Having her at State acted as an insurance policy against that.

For a new president who abhorred drama, there was a lot riding on their union. By the time she walked through the glass doors of the State Department's main lobby entrance that first day, Hillary already had shown Obama that she was a loyalist. Her ability to put aside her differences with him was now part of her own narrative as a politician willing to sacrifice her glory for a team. For his part, Obama put his faith in her to execute his policy.

The development of foreign policy within any administration is a complicated process in which various agencies have a strong hand. Depending on the president, one agency may win out over the others on a regular basis. The real power in the last half-century, though, has been the president's National Security Staff, which was originally formed as a statutory response to President Franklin Roosevelt's messy decision-making process. Over the years, that staff, responsible for coordinating the national security agencies—Defense, State, Justice, Homeland Security, the CIA, and others—has grown to a size of roughly three hundred people. Its leadership, the national security adviser and his or her deputies, is typically closer to the president, both in proximity and in personal relationship, than the cabinet secretaries. The old joke in Washington is that the only time the national security adviser and the secretary of state ever got along was when Henry Kissinger held both jobs.

Obama had to keep Hillary happy. On the off chance that she used her stature to fight him publicly—or worse, resigned in disgust—she could weaken his re-election effort. By appointing her special envoys and giving her free rein within the State Department, Obama allowed her some room to maneuver. But not a lot. It was Vice President Joe Biden who was given the Iraq portfolio, and the National Security Staff was at the forefront on Afghanistan,

Pakistan, and the Middle East. She had a seat at the table, but would have to find her own way into backroom discussions.

O n that first day in her new job, shortly after Hillary spoke in the lobby, Obama and Biden visited the ornate Benjamin Franklin Room, on the eighth floor of the State Department, for the ceremony at which Holbrooke was sworn in as special representative for Afghanistan and Pakistan and George Mitchell was sworn in as special envoy for the Middle East.

Obama framed Hillary's appointment in self-referential and almost terse terms. "It is my privilege to come here and pay tribute to all of you, the talented men and women of the State Department," Obama said. "I've given you an early gift, Hillary Clinton." That was it. His personal remarks about Holbrooke were also very limited. Ominously, Holbrooke drew a parallel between Vietnam and Afghanistan in his own comments, a comparison that annoyed Obama.

The brief remarks embodied the careful detachment with which he at first treated Hillary. He was respectful but not warm, willing to let Hillary have her department, her envoys, and her entourage without showing her much affection. Theirs was a professional relationship, limited to office hours. Bill and Hillary Clinton had lived at the White House for eight years, and as secretary of state, she would be there several times a week for meetings of the president's National Security Council and various other events. She had even made him promise to have a weekly lunch with her as a condition of taking the job. But it would be all work, and no play. The Obamas didn't invite the Clintons over for dinner; they didn't have them to the White House movie theater; and up to that point, Obama didn't ask Bill to join him on the golf course.

The Clintons had a full agenda anyway. While Hillary settled in at State, Bill was left to tend to the family business, especially the operation of the vast Clinton political apparatus. Hillary had several compelling reasons to limit her political activity as secretary. First and foremost, the law restricts what high-ranking administration officials can do in the electoral sphere. But just as important, it was helpful to Hillary to appear to be above the fray. On the campaign trail, she had been polarizing; but as America's secretary of state, she was popular. The prior February, during the heat of the Democratic primary, her approval rating had stood at 48 percent. As she battled Obama through that spring, it rose to 54 percent but jumped from there to 65 percent after she accepted the offer to become secretary. "The second she becomes political and partisan," one of her 2008 campaign advisers said, "she becomes a little bit more radioactive."

That was reason enough for her to focus on her rebuilding effort at State: to quietly and steadily reinforce her standing with the American public. It also meant that the burden of maintaining relationships and settling scores from the primary fell disproportionately to Bill. "He has to do all the politics for the entire family now," a source close to Bill said, while Hillary was at State. As part of the State deal, Bill had agreed to restrict his overseas activities with the Clinton Global Initiative. That left him more time to pepper his schedule with political events, some of which were helpful to Obama's cause while others were at odds with it. All of them were good for Team Clinton.

Bill was eager to get back to politics. Around Thanksgiving, he had stared down Jason Altmire at the Luke Ravenstahl fund-raising reception in Pittsburgh. But the time for retribution would come later. He focused first on repaying debts to tried-and-true friends like Terry McAuliffe, whose closeness to the Clintons obviated the need to keep track of the many ways in which he had helped them over the years.

Known as "the Macker" in Clintonworld, McAuliffe got his start chasing money as a fourteen-year-old in Syracuse, New York, where he created a driveway-sealing business. He ultimately became a big-time party moneyman and wrote in his own memoir of leaving his newborn child and wife in a car so that he could duck into a fund-raiser on the way home from the hospital. Over the years, his job titles included finance director for Jimmy Carter's presidential campaign, Democratic National Committee chairman, and cochairman of Hillary's 2008 campaign. But McAuliffe, who could sell a yacht to a camel, is mostly the Clintons' chief money guy. He even guaranteed a $1.3 million loan so that they could buy their home in Chappaqua.

Sometimes Bill's loyalty meant putting himself out there for someone who was destined to lose, and no one deserved that kind of support more than McAuliffe. Back in August 2008, during the Democratic National Convention, McAuliffe had approached Bill and Hillary to tell them he was thinking of running for governor of Virginia. He brought with him clips of local stories about a possible bid. "Do it," they said. Months later, as Hillary was interviewing job candidates at the posh apartment on Central Park South, Bill summoned McAuliffe to Harlem to talk shop. I'm a former governor, I know about the sets of issues that governors deal with, so why don't you bring your people up here? Bill had said. McAuliffe arrived in Harlem with half a dozen advisers. "Bill Clinton was fired up, and Terry was diligently taking notes," a McAuliffe aide said. The old Arkansas governor began rattling off policy prescriptions, supplementing McAuliffe's knowledge of campaign operations with substance. He was talking "nitty-gritty policy stuff, like turning chicken waste into alternative energy," the source said. After getting locked out of the early stages of Hillary's run, Bill was getting in on the ground floor of McAuliffe's race. The former president relished the roles of political consultant, fund-raiser, and campaign-trail surrogate. In February he headlined the state Democratic Party's annual fund-raising dinner, even though Virginia Democrats had given their primary vote to Obama. He barnstormed through the state, campaigning for McAuliffe in Richmond, Norfolk, and Roanoke through the spring.

Hillary kept her distance but checked in on McAuliffe's progress. At a March event for Vital Voices, she asked Mo Elleithee, a spokesman for her presidential campaign, how McAuliffe's race was going. When Philippe Reines was questioned over whether Hillary had talked to McAuliffe about it directly, he replied that any such conversations would remain private—a tacit acknowledgment that she had kept tabs on the race even while remaining publicly uninvolved.

Getting McAuliffe elected proved a tall order. Even in his home base, Washington's refined northern Virginia suburbs, he was looked on as a carpetbagger, more Clintonian than Virginian. Capricia Marshall, who had by that time been nominated by the White House for the protocol job, showed up at McAuliffe's election night party, representing Hillaryland. There was little to celebrate; McAuliffe had lost the primary.

Since the final days of Bill's presidency, Hillary had been the Clinton on the front lines of electoral politics, winning two Senate races and losing a presidential campaign. Under normal circumstances, she would have been right by McAuliffe's side, raising money and campaigning for him. But her new job meant that she had to keep her distance from McAuliffe's campaign and the rest of the electoral battlefield. Instead, she focused her attention on the international chessboard and Washington's own peculiar executive branch politics.

SIX

First Among Equals

Tim Geithner never stood a chance. Obama's new treasury secretary came into office with the charge of saving America's
financial system—and a fresh $700 billion bailout from Congress to
help him do it. He was Obama's handpicked guy on the biggest issue
facing the new president. But for all of Geithner's influence, a very
small symbol of Hillary's clout—an ampersand—spoke to her status
as the first among equals in the Obama cabinet.

At the beginning of any new administration, jockeying for power
is fierce among high-ranking officials in the White House, the cabinet, and the upper echelons of each of the departments. There are
countless signals, big and small, of who has power and who doesn't,
from which officials get the most face time with the president to
who wins early interagency turf battles. Aside from her formidable
reputation, Hillary enjoyed the advantage of knowing the federal
government inside and out. Between her stints as a staffer during
the Watergate hearings, chairwoman of the federal Legal Services
Corporation, first lady, and senator, she had acquired a lot of experience and insight into how the executive branch works. Many of her
peers in the Obama cabinet had never served at a high level in the
executive branch, having made their careers as governors, members
of Congress, or academics. For those who had worked in an administration, they mostly had been at much lower levels. Almost all of
them had more to learn than Hillary, both about their own agencies
and about the ways and customs of the executive branch.

Geithner was an exception. As a former undersecretary for international affairs at Treasury, he had served at a high level and knew his new building well. He was poised to be the big dog on China, through a series of talks called the Strategic Economic Dialogue. Under President George W. Bush and Treasury Secretary Hank Paulson, basic diplomatic matters had taken a backseat to the complex economic issues that made the world's two biggest powers either partners or adversaries on a wide range of topics with global consequences. Geithner, who had studied China at Dartmouth and spoke Mandarin, was positioned well to take over as the lead American negotiator with America's counterweight on the other side of the globe.

But Hillary already had set her sights on Geithner's turf. During the transition, she had talked extensively with Jim Steinberg and Bob Hormats, who later became an undersecretary for economic affairs, about the opportunities Asia presented for America to expand its influence. If Hillary could snatch a piece of the Strategic Economic Dialogue, she would give State new entrée into the most sensitive negotiations between any two countries in the world. Her decision to elbow her way into the dialogue pointed to Hillary's larger strategy of turning State into the lead agency on all foreign policy matters, except where an active war necessitated the Pentagon having the primary role. Many agencies, from Treasury to Commerce, had business overseas, but Hillary, who made "economic statecraft" one of the pillars of her agenda, wanted her ambassadors to function as America's CEOs, coordinating federal activities and branding the United States in whichever countries they served. In State's first-ever Quadrennial Defense and Diplomacy Review, published later, Hillary's view was laid out in plain language. "Today, given the wide array of U.S. agencies and actors and the corresponding need for coordination and leadership, it is essential that all ambassadors are both empowered and held accountable as CEOs," the report read. "They must be responsible for directing and coordinating coherent, comprehensive bilateral engagement that harnesses the work of all U.S. government actors in-country." In other words, foreign policy shouldn't be conducted by other agencies.

Geithner, the former head of the powerful New York Federal Reserve Bank, was hardly a pushover. But Hillary perceived that he had one hand tied behind his back because of the global economic crisis, and she used that to leverage her way into the discussion. "She knew that the Treasury Department, dealing with much more important things, was not in a position to fight over what, for most people, would seem like a smaller issue," one Treasury official explained.

By the time Geithner and Hillary discussed the China relationship face-to-face in February, their conversation was, according to a source familiar with Geithner's thinking, not about whether to make the change. It was, instead, about how to make the power-sharing arrangement work.

Geithner himself, the source said, supported elevating Hillary in the talks with the Chinese. But Team Geithner was incensed. Treasury officials thought Hillary was bulldozing her way in. At the staff level, they had spent years building up this structure to engage with China, even before the Bush administration, and now that it was under way, State was going to steal part of it. Geithner's inner circle grumbled about it, but there was little he could do. The view from Treasury: Obama didn't care much for turf wars, and Hillary was trying to take advantage of the president's desire to placate her.

"It did upset some people at Treasury," said a bemused senior State Department official who recalled Hillary's approach. "We're dealing with China here, and to have everything funneled—or to have the major dialogue with China focused only on finance and economics—was not considered a very strategic way of looking at things. That was one of the big changes she made. Paulson started this and it focused on economics, and then, from the get-go, she understood that this couldn't just be about economics, it had to be about foreign policy. So then she had this sort of tug-of-war—that's probably the wrong way—sort of a dialogue with Treasury and the White House. She insisted on it. She was not going to be denied."

Hillary spoke to Obama about it personally. "I'm working on a new concept to combine all these dialogues into one," she said.

"I've talked to Tim Geithner. He's fine. So this is what I want to do."
Obama gave his blessing.

The White House renamed the talks. The Strategic Economic
Dialogue was recast as the "Strategic & Economic Dialogue," changing the word *strategic* from a descriptor of the type of economic
dialogue the United States had with China to a term that gave foreign policy strategy parity with, if not primacy over, the economic
side of the talks. Treasury aides say it was a bitter early pill to swal-
low, but Geithner and Clinton enjoyed a good personal rapport, and
it wasn't worth a throwdown that the new treasury secretary was
bound to lose.

The move gave Hillary's team bragging rights abroad and in at
least one home. When the State Department's plane arrived for the
first Strategic & Economic Dialogue in China in 2010, Hillary's aides
wore fitted wool baseball caps with a gigantic white ampersand logo
on the front. Kurt Campbell, the assistant secretary of state for the
region and the husband of treasury undersecretary for international
affairs Lael Brainard, had distributed them as a reminder of State's
new prominence in America's relationship with China. Reines, who
like Hillary and Campbell loves an inside joke, could be seen wearing his ampersand hat in Washington years later.

Geithner's decision to acquiesce meant there would be no real
blowback from Treasury, but years later aides still fumed privately
about the episode. The quiet turf theft served as a marker for Washington insiders that Obama had Hillary's back. "That was kind of an
early sign to everyone in the administration that Hillary Clinton was
not your average cabinet official and was going to get her way on a
lot of things, and it was probably best to accommodate and play nice
[rather] than to try to pick fights, because you were probably not
going to win," the Treasury official said. "There was this overriding
sense that 'yes, we've given her the job, but we want her to be happy
in the job.'"

Hillary's star power gave her a leg up in the art of persuasion.
The simple truth is that others are more likely to say yes to someone

they admire, respect, or fear—and Hillary evoked all those feelings. And her moves inside the cabinet and within her own building demonstrated a rare skill in manipulating Washington's levers of power. Taken together, they represented an aggressive push to empower the State Department. Sometimes, as in the case with Geithner, that meant seizing turf. In other instances, she leaned on the president to get her more money, created alliances with other power brokers in the White House Situation Room, and found creative ways to bolster the beleaguered corps within the State Department.

Usually the people she dealt with, from low-level staff aides in her own building all the way up to the president of the United States, walked away with newfound respect for her. Often they found themselves liking her more with each interaction, even if they had been worked over. In that way, she proved herself to be the ultimate politician, a strategic power player whose hard work, command of politics and policy, and deft calculation produced more admiration than animosity. She was definitely someone other politicians wanted on their side.

"I sort of describe it as 'stages of Hillary,'" one member of Defense Secretary Robert Gates's inner circle said. "You know, you first dread the prospect of working with her, then you sort of begrudgingly begin to respect her, then you outright respect her and her incredible work ethic. You know, she's inexhaustible, she's tough-minded, and then you come to actually start to like her, and you just can't believe it but you actually like this person, and she's charming and she's funny and she's interesting and she's inquisitive and she's engaging."

Like Geithner, new budget director Peter Orszag was no match for Hillary. A wonk with a rap mogul's private life, Orszag had children by three different women and is now married to ABC television anchor Bianna Golodryga. The sleepy official name of his agency, the Office of Management and Budget (OMB), belies its power in the executive branch. Orszag held the key to every account at every federal agency; it is through OMB that the White House issues veto threats and federal regulations. He was considered a wunderkind in the Clinton administration, where he was a top economic aide in his early thirties.

With his short black hair and thick glasses, Orszag bore more than a passing resemblance to Lewis Skolnick, the lead character Robert Carradine played in the 1984 film *Revenge of the Nerds*. When OMB's staff held its annual variety show on the day of the public release of the budget in 2010, his minions serenaded him with a parody of the Rick James classic "Superfreak" retitled "Supergeek." When he put a framed picture of his new girlfriend Golodryga in a prominent spot in his office, OMB staff privately joked that he was bringing geeky back. At least one aide recommended that he take down the glam shot of Golodryga in favor of something a little more staid. The picture stayed. He was a nerd with a big ego and a lot of power.

Charged with putting together Obama's first real budget in 2009 and early 2010, Orszag had a great deal of autonomy in articulating the president's philosophy and policy through the thousands of pages of text and tables that constitute each year's federal budget proposal from OMB. He held the rank of a member of the president's cabinet, which technically made him a peer of Hillary and the rest of the top department heads. But his hold on the budget meant those peers had to beg him for cash.

Hillary knew, coming into the job, that she would have to fight for every dollar that came her way—and that she had to be creative to maximize what she did get. After all, the United States was fully engaged in two wars, the domestic economy had collapsed, and Obama had been plunged into an ocean of red ink from which dry land might not be visible for a decade or more. Even under the best of budget circumstances, it's hard to sell foreign aid funding to the American public. The basic question that members of Congress always hear from their constituents—and repeat to administration officials—is, why would the United States build a school in Baghdad when it could build one in Boston?

For most agencies, the funding request process was pretty simple. The department's staff spent months assembling a budget proposal and then in the fall submitted it to OMB. Ultimately, Congress had final decision-making power over the president's budget request for all the agencies, but the final request was a forceful statement of White House priorities. By late November, OMB would deliver its judgment on each department's initial request, often cutting back from an agency's desired funding level. An appeals period followed between Thanksgiving and Christmas, when minor adjustments might be made to placate a secretary or an administrator. But by the end of the year, all Orszag and his aides had to do was dot the i's and cross the t's. In early February of the following year, the budget was sent to Congress.

Few cabinet secretaries thought they could win a fight with OMB, mostly because the director was himself a cabinet-level aide to the president and because he typically had strong relationships with other senior advisers in the West Wing. That was certainly true of Orszag, at least at the start of the administration. Though Energy Secretary Stephen Chu and Commerce Secretary Gary Locke were known as frequent callers within the marble hallways of the Old Executive Office Building, the cavernous relic that houses OMB and other White House–run agencies, most didn't waste much time appealing to Orszag.

But Hillary Clinton had a lot more firepower in reserve than other Obama cabinet secretaries, as Orszag would come to find out. In late November or early December 2009, when OMB sent its first "passback" of State's budget to Foggy Bottom, the bottom line was a small cut in funding, according to a State Department source familiar with the numbers. Hillary, who was looking for a double-digit percentage increase, pulled out her "secret weapon" in response. Deputy secretary of state Jack Lew, the old Clinton budget director, told Orszag his number was unacceptable.

"Only a former budget director could get away with this," said one State Department source, who admired Lew's moxie. Orszag technically outranked Lew, but Lew's experience and credibility at the highest levels of government exceeded that of most of the cabinet. Hillary had recruited him for such missions.

Orszag and his bean counters made some minor concessions and came back with an upward revision that would have pleased most bureaucrats, taking Hillary from a cut to a small increase, maybe a little more than 1 percent. But from Hillary's perspective, Orszag hadn't gotten the message. It was time to go over his head. Now Lew went straight to Rahm Emanuel, one of many of Obama's new aides who had gotten their big political break from the Clintons. We can't live with this, Lew told Emanuel.

Again, Orszag came back with another number—one that Hillary found still too paltry. "We'll take it to the president," Lew assured her.

The budget request for the government's security functions, which included the State Department's funding, would ultimately be decided at a meeting of the National Security Council, where Orszag would have to argue against increasing Hillary's bottom line in a room full of people who dealt with her regularly and had reason to cultivate her as an ally. By the time the budget made it to the top level, the other members of the National Security Council—the heads of security agencies—had been working together on a strategy for Afghanistan and Pakistan for a year, and the Defense Department supported more funding for State. Gates lobbied appropriators on Capitol Hill to boost Hillary's budget, and he battled on her behalf within the administration. He once remarked to an aide that OMB was one constant from administration to administration: a Flat Earth society.

Orszag, an invited guest at the NSC meeting, stood no chance of beating Hillary in that arena. "Yes, we made a budget request that was turned down from the OMB. Yes, she went to the president directly," said a senior State official. "And yes, she got what she wanted."

In Hillary's first full fiscal year, the White House's budget request for State and aid programs grew by 10.6 percent to $56.6 billion. Hillary also won a provision, originally rejected by OMB, that protected money for embassies and consulates in war zones—Afghanistan, Pakistan, and Iraq, specifically—by funding them through a war-spending account. Congress wasn't likely to mess around with the new president's request to fund two wars started by his predecessor, though it did pare State's ask after Republicans took power in the House. But the new secretary understood that her budget figure was a representation of her clout within the new administration, and it reflected the latitude she would have to pursue her agenda.

She must also have understood that a roughly $50 billion budget for State and international aid programs didn't exactly give her the keys to the federal treasury. More important, it didn't make her the secretary of defense, who had almost $700 billion at his disposal. She wanted to be a player, not just a check-signer for do-gooder organizations in remote countries. That required forming strategic partnerships with other government agencies and private entities to amplify the State Department's resources.

Hillary's command of the levers of power, and her ability to seize unclaimed turf and resources, proved invaluable as she made the most out of the limited federal money available to State. As she had done with Geithner, she used her informal power as the first among equals in Obama's cabinet to assert herself and her department, maneuvering around her colleagues, straight through them, and preferably in coordination with them, to get what she wanted.

In the informal cabinet pecking order, the defense secretary is typically at the top because he controls an annual budget the size of all the other departments combined, commands American military forces, and comes from a massive agency that's been around a long time. But it is the secretary of state, because of the seniority of her department, who sits closest in line to the presidency and who is given the first chance to make her case to the president in meetings.

Other than Defense Secretary Bob Gates, who had served eight presidents, Hillary was by far the most experienced presidential adviser on the National Security Council by dint of the eight years she had spent informally counseling her husband. Her seat, either directly to the president's left or one seat down, depending on the list of attendees, spoke to the prominence of her post. Gates sat across the table from her, and the two made for an imposing pair for other members of the national security apparatus.

Even Tom Donilon, a longtime party operator who served as the president's deputy national security adviser and later as his national security adviser, was visibly unnerved by her presence. Donilon had a foot in each camp, having worked in political roles at the State Department during the Clinton administration and having helped Obama prepare for debates against John McCain and by serving as a cochair of Obama's State Department transition team. Along with fellow Clinton administration veteran Rahm Emanuel, Donilon was an important ally for Hillary, particularly early on in the administration when her connections in Obama's inner circle were limited.

Donilon had a little bit of a crush on Hillary—one he confessed to her and others privately. They were friends, but the intimidation factor went beyond the weak knees of a love-struck schoolboy. He described to others the way she would call on a Saturday morning at 7 a.m. and run through as many as ten different issues in task-master-like fashion. "Tom Donilon is scared shitless of her," said one official who worked on the National Security Council staff. "People would debate a certain issue, and he would kind of poke at them or probe them further or disagree, but he never did it with her because he was scared to death of her."

Donilon and Obama's first national security adviser, Jim Jones, ran Situation Room meetings from the same end of the table at which Gates and Clinton sat. From there, power dissipated quickly from seat to seat. "The national security adviser is there. Hillary is there. Gates is there. And then there's like all the other schmucks," said one aide who sat in from time to time. "Everyone else is like they're not there."

Depending on the president and the occupant of the office, the secretary of state can be a big-time player or an afterthought. Her budget is small, but she has a voice in the president's war council. That voice can be amplified if she makes sound arguments and has allies in the room.

But it can be easily diminished by the ever-growing National Security Staff, which is often mistakenly referred to as the National Security Council—a telling misconception because it points to the power that the legion of staff advisers have gained over the years. Technically, the national security adviser and his or her staff exist to coordinate policy among the various agencies and present the president with options for major decisions. In reality, they often guide the process and at times have even become policy makers on their own. "The National Security [Staff] has the gates to the kingdom in terms of getting information to the president," said former secretary of state Madeleine Albright, who worked on the National Security Staff during the Carter administration.*

Albright counseled Hillary about how to work the NSC process. "If you see it from the perspective of the secretary of state, you have to make sure that your voice is heard along with the others." That requires "finding allies and then making sure that the president gets your views, because what happens is the national security adviser is the one that puts the final memo on top and says 'This is what State says, this is what Defense says, this is what Treasury says, this is what I think,'" Albright said. "I did tell her that it was very important to have a strong relationship with the secretary of defense."

Indeed, Gates was really the only player on Obama's National Security Council who had more experience than Hillary in Washington's power game. Hillary pursued a much different strategy for dealing with him, cultivating an alliance that made it hard for either of them to be pushed around by the National Security Staff. Like Hillary, Gates had been an active Republican at a time of major liberal social upheaval in the mid-1960s—she as a "Goldwater Girl" in high school, and he as a member of the College of William and Mary Young Republicans. A career intelligence officer, Gates first made his way into the White House as a member of the National Security Council staff in 1974 and worked all the way up the ranks of the nation's spy community to the post of CIA director under President George H. W. Bush. President George W. Bush recruited him back into government to succeed Donald Rumsfeld as secretary of defense, and Obama asked him to stay on. Hillary and Gates were

---

* Then called the National Security Council staff.

the two people on Obama's national security team who didn't need a map to get around the West Wing. Unlike Hillary, who had been at least one step removed from the national security process as first lady, Gates had a lot of experience inside the Situation Room. "The next time you're in a situation with Gates, just think in your mind, 'How many seats did he sit in?'" one of Hillary's advisers recalls Albright saying. "He knows what everybody's going to say."

Between their common cultural roots, their proximity in age (Gates is four years older), and their status as the wise old hands on Obama's National Security Council, it was easy for Hillary and Gates to develop a certain kinship. They became so close so fast that there's a common misperception in Washington that they had been friends before, either when she was on the Armed Services Committee or perhaps during the Clinton administration. Several senior State and Defense Department sources offered up versions of the birth of their friendship along those lines. One had a more perceptive take: Hillary had made friends with a number of high-level flag officers—three- and four-star generals and admirals—during her time on Armed Services, and Gates had taken note from afar. Her reputation as a serious thinker on military issues preceded her. The Pentagon brass respected this Democrat who, to their surprise, was not only an ardent advocate of a strong military but also a careful student of their plans, their programs, and the way they went about securing funding. It wasn't just political positioning. She believed in all forms of American power, including force, even though those views had hurt her badly in the Democratic primary in 2008, when Obama invigorated the antiwar left by contrasting his opposition to the Iraq War with Hillary's vote for it.

The truth is Gates and Clinton had barely met before Obama introduced them as part of his national security team in early December 2008. More than fifteen years earlier, they had shaken hands in CIA director Jim Woolsey's office at a memorial service for officers killed in an attack on CIA headquarters in suburban Langley, Virginia. They didn't have a conversation then, and Gates didn't see Hillary face-to-face again until the Chicago press conference.

During the transition, they found that their policy instincts were similar. Gates, a moderate Republican, and Hillary, a hawkish Democrat, both saw the value of using all of the tools in America's foreign policy kit. Sometimes that meant a missive and sometimes it meant a missile. In a speech at Kansas State University in November 2007, Gates had embraced the smart-power approach favored by the Clinton wing of the Democratic Party's national security apparatus.

There was also a strategic imperative to their alliance. Hillary needed the defense secretary to ensure State's voice was heard on matters of war, diplomacy, and development and to reinforce her budget and policy requests. The purpose of the State Department is to conduct diplomacy and execute the president's foreign policy. Ideally, America's international footprint looks more like the sole of a wingtip than a combat boot. But during the Bush administration, the ever-growing Pentagon had taken over for State in global hot spots, most notably Iraq and Afghanistan. Both Gates and Hillary believed that the Pentagon was playing too much of a role in providing civilian aid, which both usurped the diplomatic role in foreign policy and distracted the military from its core defense mission.

When he had to make a case to a roomful of Democrats, the Republican Gates benefited from having Hillary on his side. "She was an influential voice in the administration," one Gates insider said of why Hillary was valuable to the Pentagon. "She had enormous political capital." Moreover, they liked each other, and they were outsiders at Obama's national security meetings, which were full of newcomers who had helped the president win election by promising to rock the status quo. In order to survive and thrive, they needed to function as a bloc as often as possible. "I think there was some strategy to it. When you have a secretary of defense and a secretary of state going into the interagency process united or going into the Oval Office together on an issue, they go in a much stronger position," said a high-ranking Pentagon source. "They often compared notes or coordinated in advance of some of those meetings to find common ground to allow them to influence or drive the direction of policy on a given issue."

Once or twice a month, Gates and Hillary ate lunch together, alternating between her office at State and his at the Pentagon. They also had a standing weekly lunch with the national security adviser in the West Wing. Most important, they kept an informal channel open to compare notes. "It was not uncommon for them to pick up the phone or have a pull-aside before or after a meeting they were both attending. They checked in with each other," the Pentagon source said. "In the cases where they disagreed, that was also useful to know early or to alert them where this was an area of disagreement." Major disagreements would come later, when Obama wanted to strike Osama bin Laden and when he weighed whether to intervene in Libya's civil war. But for the first two years of Obama's term, Hillary and Gates were on the same side in the Situation Room. "She and Gates were a pretty powerful tandem," said a former senior government official.

In October 2009 the unlikely pair sought to highlight their odd-couple status, appearing onstage together as part of a conversation series and rare joint interview at George Washington University. During the session with CNN's Christiane Amanpour and GWU's Frank Sesno, both cabinet secretaries spoke about their mutual admiration and drew contrasts between their relationship and that of their predecessors.

It was clear that they were not just being polite and politically correct. They had forged a kinship and a bond so tight that when they wrapped the hour-long interview that night, they went and grabbed dinner at the Blue Duck Tavern, a pricey Washington restaurant near Georgetown. "It was a good example of how they enjoyed each other's company," said one mutual acquaintance. "They wanted to go to dinner."

When he returned to the Pentagon the next day, Gates told aides he'd had "fun"—a term he didn't use a lot—at the CNN forum. That might have been in part because he came off a bit more relaxed and witty than his celebrity counterpart. But sources in both camps say their genuine affinity for each other strengthened a potent strategic alliance and sent a message to rank-and-file State and Defense employees that their bosses expected them to play well together. "He was always cognizant of how unusual it was that they got along so well," a senior Defense official said.

Clinton won the respect of Gates and the small circle of Bush holdovers at the Pentagon. Some of Obama's advisers—awed by her presence but still feeling the reverberations of the campaign—went through the same kind of progression, developing first respect and then warm feelings for Hillary. Shortly after she broke her arm in the summer of 2009, Tommy Vietor, one of Obama's fiery and loyal young press aides during the presidential campaign, ran into Hillary in a hallway at the White House. Vietor, who had recently dislocated his shoulder, noticed that Hillary's sling had a State Department seal on it.

"Oh, you're in a sling, too," said Hillary, who was accompanied by the ever-present Huma. "What did you do?"

"I hurt it playing basketball," replied Vietor, who was still scared of Hillary after having attacked her foreign policy chops on the record during the campaign. "Your sling is a lot cooler than mine."

Two days later, sitting inside the press office at the White House, Vietor received a white box from the State Department. Inside he found a sling with the logo. The gesture melted any lingering animus from the campaign days.

But because their suspicion of Hillary ran much deeper, some others in Obama's world, including Plouffe and Gibbs, never really warmed to her. With them, she didn't help her cause by lining up with Gates or backing Richard Holbrooke, whom the president could hardly stand.

While Hillary cleverly built power by working with, and sometimes around, the other luminaries in Washington, her unstinting loyalty to Holbrooke came at a price to her standing within the administration. It was a classic example of her belief in her people, and their wisdom, taking precedence over other concerns, for better or for worse.

Holbrooke was an innovator, a persistent operator, and a constant source of frustration for a White House that prized a kind of control that it couldn't exert over him. For his part, Holbrooke was obsessed with gaining access to Obama and his inner circle, and complained loudly and often about the president's national security team trying to freeze him out. He tried everything to get in, including hanging out at the Hay-Adams hotel because he knew White House aides were denizens of the bar there.

In particular, he sought out David Axelrod, the president's senior adviser. In the book *This Town,* author Mark Leibovich tells the story of Holbrooke standing next to a young Axelrod aide at a White House urinal to try to book an appointment.

"He wanted access and he wanted to talk through what his concerns were," said one West Wing aide. "He was vocally frustrated about his access to Obama. He was trying to ingratiate himself within the White House and he knew David was part of that."

Axelrod was a route around the people Holbrooke typically dealt with at the White House, and he worked Axelrod hard.

"He was very big about massaging people's egos," the aide said.

While Axelrod could certainly provide access to Obama, there was another reason to work the veteran operative: Holbrooke believed that the major impediment to his plan to use a surge of forces in Afghanistan to force the Taliban to the negotiating table was the fear of Obama's political team that a quagmire could damage the president's hopes of winning re-election in 2012. If he could demonstrate to Axelrod that a peace deal was better than a drawdown of U.S. forces without one, perhaps he could turn the president's thinking.

The biggest fight within Obama's National Security Council in the first term erupted over the Afghanistan "surge," a process that took until December 2009 to resolve. The president made an initial commitment of 21,000 more troops early in the year, a force that could hold back Taliban fighters until a bigger decision about whether to send as many as 40,000 more could be made later in the year. The debate over the number of troops and overall American strategy was so clamorous and acrimonious that Bob Woodward was able to write an entire book on the deliberations, called *Obama's Wars.*

The Gates-Clinton alliance was a threat to the power wielded by

Obama's White House aides in the early years of the administration, particularly as a narrative began to take hold that they, along with Central Command chief David Petraeus and other military leaders, were pushing the president into a surge in Afghanistan that he didn't want to order. It's hard for presidential aides to steamroll the top two cabinet secretaries if they are in lockstep. If they are divided, how-ever, each can be pushed around. In this case, Hillary left no day-light between herself and Gates. "The core objective was really to ensure that Afghanistan did not once again become a sanctuary for Al Qaeda or other transnational extremists as it was when the 9/11 attacks were planned there and the initial training was conducted there," said a former senior government official. Hillary "recognized that the only way to achieve that objective was to enable Afghans to secure themselves and govern themselves adequately, *adequately* being a key phrase there. And the only way to do that was through a comprehensive civil-military campaign that halted the momentum that the Taliban had achieved."

Fans of the twin titans of the Obama cabinet say they prevented the new team from steering American foreign policy off course. Obama was just coming off an election in which he had promised to end two wars and open direct diplomacy with Iran and Cuba, and the fear in the centrist Washington foreign policy establishment was that he might immediately pursue those objectives to the detriment of American interests.

Certainly the president's team sought to shrink America's foot-print in the region. Vice President Joe Biden wanted to ramp down in Afghanistan rather than deepening U.S. commitment, as did Chief of Staff Rahm Emanuel, Axelrod and the set of advisers who had worked on the Obama campaign. They distrusted the phalanx formed by the Pentagon's leaders and Hillary, though it was mili-tary leaders, not Hillary, whom they blamed for leaking frequently, making unhelpful public statements, and presenting unreasonable alternative options for the president in an effort to box him in on the surge. Still, Hillary's alliance with the pro-surge Pentagon camp did not help her standing with some of Obama's old campaign hands.

In an October 2009 Situation Room meeting on Afghanistan, Hillary spoke to the president of "the dilemma you face," a construction that caught the attention of Press Secretary Robert Gibbs, a member of Obama's brain trust since his Senate days. Gibbs jotted down her use of *you*—rather than *we*—in his notebook. Holbrooke later described it as a "Freudian giveaway" of Clinton's feeling of detachment, according to Woodward. Holbrooke, who was distant from the president and his advisers, had plenty of reason to portray Hillary as detached from the process. One of Hillary's aides, who conceded that Clinton's wording could have been better, described Gibbs's reaction as "the ultimate in parsing."

In the end, Hillary and the others supported Obama's decision to go with a hybrid plan that gave the Pentagon 33,000 more troops but also announced a timeline for drawing down after a year and a half. Once the strategy was announced at West Point in early December, Afghanistan policy moved off the front burner. That eased the relationship between Hillary and the White House aides.

To some officials with a foot in each camp, the idea that a cabal of top leaders at the Pentagon and the State Department had ever jammed the new president was laughable. "There was a very open, free-flowing, vigorous debate," said Jim Steinberg. "This is a president who never does anything he doesn't want to do." The review of American strategy gave Hillary an opening to enhance State by turning war into peace. Hillary, who had her own feel for the electorate as well as a desire to find a solution to the vexing Afghanistan problem, was willing to entertain the idea that the surge could put enough pressure on the Taliban to bring them to the table for a negotiated end to the war, according to sources who briefed her.

"The difference between her and the president on Afghanistan is she was more willing to complement a surge with diplomacy," said a senior member of Holbrooke's team. "I don't think the president was ever serious about diplomatic options in Afghanistan."

Hillary gave wide latitude to Holbrooke to see if he could find the sweet spot for a deal, but she was also clear-eyed about the obstacles. "She was very sober about the prospects for success, both if the Taliban would actually cut a deal or if the regional actors who all have their own interests would all line up behind a coherent diplomatic outcome," said one of her chief advisers. "Despite that sobriety, she was very intent on getting a serious muscular diplomatic process launched and executed, and she felt like as time passed, we were losing leverage and opportunity, the maximum opportunity, to make it successful."

In the mold of other savvy Washington operators, Hillary can be very good at keeping her motives to herself. That's why there is disagreement to this day about how much she truly believed that it was possible for Holbrooke, or anyone else, to put together a peace deal involving the United States, the Taliban, the Karzai government in Afghanistan, the Pakistanis, and other stakeholders in the region. But she kept bailing Holbrooke out every time he found himself in a deeper hole at the White House.

While everyone in the government would have preferred to strike the peace deal that Holbrooke sought in the region, few thought it was a practical possibility. The differences in the interests among the Pakistani government, the Karzai government, and the insurgents were too vast to close. With negotiation virtually removed from the table, the only space left to Hillary, and to Holbrooke, was to manage the civilian side of American efforts to help develop Afghanistan on the ground and negotiate with allies for more money, troops, and equipment. "The job of the State Department was not to negotiate peace," said Vali Nasr, who worked for Holbrooke. "It was to facilitate the war."

Holbrooke continued to bring up parallels between Afghanistan and Vietnam, and he wasn't shy about talking to the press, which infuriated the White House. Obama thought Holbrooke had walked out of another era. He quickly became the central point of tension between the White House and State on the war, the most pressing foreign policy matter in the first two years of Obama's presidency.

Obama's National Security Staff spent months trying to get Holbrooke fired, in part because he was abrasive and in part because he was a rival power center. For his part, Holbrooke was loyal to the presidency, but its new occupant flummoxed him. Privately, he complained bitterly to the people closest to him that Obama, lauded as a second coming of John F. Kennedy, didn't socialize with his own modern-day version of Camelot. And Holbrooke was his own worst enemy, providing ammunition for White House aides to undercut him with the president.

"It wasn't so much on the policy. So much of what Holbrooke did was about Holbrooke, and it did create a certain level of drama that the Obama team didn't appreciate," one source with a foot in each camp said. "It wasn't as much what he was trying to do. It was the way he was going about it. I think it was more a style thing, and obviously Holbrooke engaged a lot with the press. You felt like there was this other center of push that wasn't in sync with what the Obama team was trying to do."

After a September 2009 George Packer profile in *The New Yorker* painted the veteran diplomat as the last best chance for America in Afghanistan, a furious McDonough confronted Holbrooke in the West Wing. McDonough, too, was an avid player of the press game. The month before, when David Rothkopf wrote a piece in the *Washington Post* lauding Hillary's development of a foreign policy agenda, McDonough shot Rothkopf a terse e-mail. "Interesting choice for a profile," he chided, making clear he thought it was Obama, not Hillary, who deserved credit.

In February 2010, Jim Jones, the president's national security adviser, wrote a letter to Ambassador Karl Eikenberry suggesting that Holbrooke would soon be relieved of his post. The letter was transmitted in a way that made it available to many State Department employees, and of course, the contents of the letter leaked, undermining Holbrooke with foreign leaders and in Washington.

Hillary kept a file on such efforts to marginalize Holbrooke and turned her notes on Jones over to Donilon at one point. Furious with the backbiting, she went to Obama to tell him that he could either fire Holbrooke over her objection or get his squad to back down. Holbrooke remained in place. Holbrooke's aides lost count of the number of times his job was rumored to be on the line, and he was acutely aware that Hillary was the only person standing between him and an ignominious dismissal. "When you meet with Hillary, can you put in a good word for me?" Holbrooke asked Pakistani foreign minister Mehmood Qureshi. "Say I'm doing a good job."

Throughout, Holbrooke kept trying to work the Axelrod route. He even showed up at an event for Axelrod's charity, CURE, at real estate mogul and socialite Connie Milstein's house. And it wasn't a one-way street. While Obama found Holbrooke grating, "David had some admiration for him," the West Wing source said. "I don't think he disliked him at all. It was always an issue of time. But he thought it was appropriate to talk to him because he was handling some big issues."

Hillary's ability to protect Holbrooke—even if she couldn't get Obama and the National Security Council staff to respect him—spoke to her own standing. But no doubt it would have been greater had she not been forced to spend capital in his defense.

Over time, Steinberg, who had been close with Donilon for years, turned out to be another source of strain between the White House and Hillary's State Department. Donilon and Steinberg had come up together in the State Department, and they were both also close to Assistant Secretary Kurt Campbell. But Steinberg's relationship with both men frayed, according to senior Hillary aides. His tension with McDonough became so bad that when McDonough was promoted to deputy national security adviser in October 2010, Steinberg stopped going to the "deputies meetings" that McDonough ran, the aides said.

SEVEN

"We Did It, Buddy"

Hillary tapped Kris Balderston, the hit list author, to keep the Clinton political network humming at State. A longtime lieutenant to both Clintons, Balderston, who called everyone "buddy," liked to talk in salesman's terms about Hillary's "power to convene" and her commitment to making sure her partners could "do well by doing good." What he meant was that Hillary could use the Clinton Rolodex to focus private-sector money, government power, and the expertise at colleges and nonprofits to solve global problems. At best, they would do a public service and make a buck. At worst, they would make a powerful friend. Balderston became, for lack of a better term, Hillary's special ops guy at State.

He wrote Hillary the first memo on his concept for an office that would mirror Bill's Clinton Global Initiative on December 8, 2008, less than a week after she was named to her job and more than six weeks before she took office. Though she had to wait for some of her lieutenants to clear the Obama vetting process and a Senate confirmation vote, she had made it a priority to empower Balderston, the political fixer who could help her build unique networks connecting her State Department to other government agencies, the nonprofit sector, and the corporate world. While many Democrats believe that government is the answer to the world's problems, and many Republicans believe the same of the private sector, Balderston's office was the embodiment of Hillary's core Clintonian belief that government, business, and charitable organizations are all vital components of a thriving society.

"It's more than raising money," said one source familiar with the concept. "It's networking other people's intellectual property, networks, lists, that sort of thing. You need somebody who does more than just raise money." Just like the Clinton Global Initiative.

But intellectual property and network expansion would have to wait—Hillary needed cash. Balderston was still setting up the office when Hillary approached him at the end of February 2009. "I have the first project for you," she said. The job: raise more than $60 million from the private sector in nine months. In an era of billion-dollar presidential campaigns, that might not sound like much jack. But the government generally doesn't raise money from the private sector, in large part because of the potential for corporate donors to give with the expectation that they will get specific government actions in return. Moreover, Congress and the Bush administration had shunned the very initiative Hillary wanted Balderston to execute.

Hillary had just returned from China, the anchor stop on her first trip overseas, where she had been surprised to find that the United States didn't have a plan to build a pavilion at the world's fair the following year, the Shanghai Expo. Chinese officials were incensed at the insensitivity to a major international showcase event in their country, and they gave Hillary an earful. They had been complaining to American businesses, too. From China's perspective, America's failure to build a pavilion would be a little less insulting than a boycott of the Olympics but not much. At the time, Hillary and Obama were touting an American "pivot" toward Asia, a shift of focus away from Europe and the Middle East and toward China, Japan, and their neighbors, as a central part of their foreign policy agenda. The elevation of State through the Strategic & Economic Dialogue was but one example of the new emphasis on building a more comprehensive relationship with China. After all, the world's two most powerful nations had common interests in issues ranging from the world economy to fighting terrorism. Certainly, snubbing China at the encore to the 2008 Beijing Olympics would complicate those efforts.

So the expo held outsize symbolic importance in the new partnership Obama wanted to build. "It became important to [Hillary] because it was made clear to her by the Chinese senior leadership that it was important to them," said José Villarreal, a veteran Clinton fund-raiser with ties to China. "It was inconceivable to the Chinese that they could have a world expo and not have the United States there, especially not have the United States [be] virtually the only country that was not going to participate."

While she was in China, Hillary confessed that she hadn't been briefed on the fair—few politicians fail to blame their staff when necessary—and committed to looking into it when she got home. This impending diplomatic faux pas over the Shanghai Expo would be a serious affront to a country that the United States was in the process of courting. In addition to the downside risk, the expo offered Hillary two opportunities. First, she could draw a sharp contrast with the Bush administration, which had made clear that it wouldn't use government resources to raise money for a pavilion. "The Department of State is not now authorized, and does not in the future intend to seek authorization from the U.S. Congress, to provide funding for any aspect of the U.S. exhibition at the World Expo," the department wrote in a 2006 request-for-proposals for a private entity to try to build a pavilion on America's behalf. That effort had been going nowhere when the Chinese approached Hillary.

The U.S. government had soured on the world's fair idea after a scandal involving the American operation at the 1998 expo in Lisbon, and Congress had subsequently placed a nearly comprehensive ban on the State Department directly funding pavilions at future world's fairs. But lawmakers had left a loophole for staff to raise money from private donors, corporations, NGOs, and foreign governments. That loophole was just the right size for Balderston and his new shop to fit through. Under federal law and ethics regulations,

Hillary could even express her support to potential donors without making a direct appeal for money—a wrinkle in the law that would create great controversy when the secretary of health and human services, Kathleen Sebelius, helped raise private funds to promote Obamacare in 2013.

As a second bonus, setting up a fund-raising operation for the fair gave Hillary an invaluable early opportunity to strengthen and expand her network among top American business executives, a potential source of campaign contributions if she decided to run in 2016.

Balderston was a political operative but not a fund-raiser per se, and Hillary turned to two longtime Clinton money bundlers, Elizabeth Bagley and Villarreal, to jump-start the capital campaign. Bagley, a former ambassador to Portugal and a million-dollar donor to the Clinton Foundation, was named as Hillary's special representative for global partnerships, a role that Balderston would later take over. A former adviser to both Clintons and the treasurer of Al Gore's 2000 campaign, Villarreal had been a "Hillraiser," one of her big-time campaign cash bundlers. He was also a former member of the board of directors of Walmart Stores.

Villarreal had heard about the Shanghai Expo issue on a trip to China to visit his daughter a few months earlier, when Chinese Walmart executives gave him the same grilling on America's expected absence from the fair that Hillary would get from government officials. When he heard Hillary had been in China, he told Cheryl Mills he would be happy to help organize a U.S. pavilion— and Hillary tapped him to do just that as the U.S. commissioner for the expo.

In addition to the sheer magnitude of the fund-raising challenge, Villarreal, Bagley, and Balderston faced a set of rules that complicated their effort. They had to raise all the money from private donors, and Hillary couldn't solicit corporate contributions directly. To make matters worse, several of America's biggest players in China, including Coca-Cola and GM, were already building their own pavilions to safeguard their own relationships with the

Chinese. As a result, they were not likely to contribute money to the official U.S. pavilion.

Hillary had a lot riding on her ability to turn an international slip into a diplomatic coup that saved face for both the United States and China. The talk about her clout as an international celebrity was nice, but could she deliver? Her fund-raising commandos didn't have the luxury of time. They couldn't wait for the charitable-giving arms of major corporations to process requests. Instead, they went straight to CEOs, and they made it crystal clear that the ask was from Hillary.

"We knew how to get to the leadership of companies, and of course, being able to suggest that this was a project that was very, very important to Secretary Clinton really, really helped in opening doors," Villarreal recalled. Hillary even drafted a letter of support for potential donors, just in case they needed more proof than a name drop. Sources say she carefully walked on the legal side of the line, but there was no doubt that she was engaged. "She did a really good job of actually getting into the muck of raising that money," said one source.

In the summer of 2009, PepsiCo CEO Indra Nooyi, one of the world's most powerful women, according to *Forbes,* committed $5 million, a contribution that helped get the ball rolling. Chevron, General Electric, Honeywell, Microsoft, Intel, Yum!, the National Basketball Association, Pfizer, and nearly five dozen other corporations and foundations jumped on board. Just scratching the surface, the list included a who's who of major donors to the Clinton Foundation. In addition to Microsoft, Yum!, and Pfizer, common contributors to the Clinton Foundation and the U.S. effort at the expo included Bloomberg LP, Citigroup and its foundation, Dow Chemical, Procter & Gamble, and Sidney Harman. (Harman's company gave to the Shanghai Expo while his family foundation gave to the Clinton Foundation.)

"The Shanghai Expo," one Clintonworld fund-raising source said, "was a primary example of being able to tap into a base of people that Elizabeth [Bagley] was able to go after."

In November 2009, nine months after the Chinese chastised her, Hillary returned to Shanghai, where she made a personal pitch for more money. After visiting Boeing's new two-bay hangar at Shanghai Pudong Airport, where she spoke to a group of fifteen to twenty executives, including the heads of Boeing China, Caterpillar China, and GE China, Hillary made her way to the fairgrounds to take a look at the still-skeletal U.S. pavilion and make an ask.

"I know there are some in the audience who are still contemplating sponsorship or who may be in negotiations with the USA Pavilion team," she said. "Now is the time to join this effort." Boeing, the host of her earlier session with executives, doubled its contribution to the pavilion fund from $1 million to $2 million.

Hillary's personal effort paid dividends for Bagley, Villarreal, Balderston, and America's relationship with China. They had raised enough money at that point to ensure that America would be present at the fair, but the U.S. pavilion wouldn't be completed until the last minute.

Two days before the May 1, 2010, opening of the fair, Chinese president Hu Jintao, vice premier Wang Qishan, and state councilor Dai Bingguo toured the U.S. Pavilion, taking in what Hillary and her team had accomplished in less than fifteen months—under half the time it might normally have taken to complete such a project.

"We were still working on the finishing touches even after the expo officially opened," Villareal said. "Had it not been for her personal involvement in really lending her personal prestige, we just never would have been able to get it done."

In late May 2010, Hillary came back to Shanghai for a third time to get her own firsthand look as one of 7.36 million people who visited the carbon-neutral U.S. pavilion over a six-month period. The reviews were fair but not good. John Pomfret of the *Washington Post* called it "one of the singular successes" of her first year and a half in office but noted that the pavilion looked more like "a convention center in a medium-size American city than a national showcase—a warren of dark rooms with movie screens that pales in comparison to the ambitious pavilions of, among others, Saudi Arabia, which features the world's biggest IMAX screen, and Germany, festooned with hundreds of giant red balls."

Villarreal acknowledged that "we could have done much better" with two or three years to put it together. "We made the most that we could, given the limitations," he said. "At the end of the day, the question is 'Did ordinary Chinese enjoy it?' and the answer is 'Absolutely.'"

"I'm just relieved," Hillary said when she arrived, adding a lukewarm assessment of the pavilion itself: "It's fine."

Years later an iconic photograph of Hillary speaking in the rain at the construction site hung on the wall of the reception area outside Balderston's office, a testament to the first major project of the State Department's version of the Clinton Global Initiative. American and Chinese officials knew that it was a minor miracle that Hillary had been able to secure financing and build the pavilion in the first place, which was a major sign of respect for China. The Clinton family contact list had been invaluable for Bagley, Balderston, and Villarreal as they dialed angel donors directly. They "went to a lot of people in the network, the givers and funders network," said a senior Hillary adviser.

A hint of the Clinton network's central role was inscribed on the first page of Balderston's copy of the world's fair commemorative coffee table book: "As you would say, 'We did it, buddy.'" The signature: Bill Clinton.

The expo episode revealed a fundamental truth about Hillary's new job that she and her aides had to learn on their own: no matter how much planning and preparation they did, they would always be subject to the unpredictability of managing a world's worth of relationships and crises, including those within the State Department and within official Washington. Wendy Sherman, a former aide to Madeleine Albright and the cochairwoman of Obama's transition team at State, had tried to warn them before they took office. "The incoming is relentless," she told Hillary. But Hillary and her closest aides, confident after two decades of surviving the brutality of being a target in national politics, didn't quite get it.

"It's a different kind of incoming," explained one State Department official. "When you are running a campaign, you get up every day, and you have your schedule, and of course you have to respond to what your opponent's doing. But when you are here, the whole world—*the whole world*—comes at you every single day. . . . It is unlike anything else."

At one level, Hillary's first six months in office were a testament to the soundness of her strategy of keeping her head down while building up morale within State, strengthening her own position and the department's within the Obama administration, and beginning the process of repairing relationships with foreign governments. This building phase was familiar to anyone who had watched her closely in her early months in the Senate, when she kept as low a profile as possible and assiduously courted the chamber's living legends, humbly seeking counsel on how to do her job from lions like Robert Byrd and Ted Kennedy. She had shown her savvy in teeing up the Strategic & Economic Dialogue at a time, in early February, when most cabinet secretaries were still learning the names of their assistant secretaries; and in lashing herself to Gates, Petraeus, and other senior Pentagon officials.

On another level, though, that first half-year provided painful lessons in just how hard it would be for Hillary to meet the sky-high expectations for her tenure. She had to balance her own agenda with external demands, and it proved a tough act, in part because while she was adjusting to the role, national and international audiences were watching her every move. So even as Hillary was quietly gathering influence behind the scenes, the image of her among the Washington elite was one of a secretary struggling to find her place in Obama's sphere and the world.

Hillaryland couldn't quite shake the classic Clinton drama that had helped sink her 2008 campaign. Some of her aides had trouble adjusting both to the power and to the limitations of their new roles. They had inherited tremendous influence in a massive department, but were unaccustomed to the strict guidelines and decades-long protocol that helped keep American diplomacy on the rails. The upside was an ability to go around the bureaucracy or command it to move in a new direction. The downside was the risk that they were exercising power in areas they didn't really understand.

One trip in particular to Geneva in March 2009, on her second voyage abroad as secretary of state, demonstrated the exclusivity of Hillary's closed-off inner circle, its difficulty in adjusting to a bureaucracy, and its ongoing battle with Obama's White House team over primacy in foreign policy.

Hillary came to Geneva intending to telegraph a message of renewal to Russian foreign minister Sergei Lavrov. One of the few policy issues on which Obama had distinguished himself during his brief Senate career was reducing the global stockpile of nuclear weapons and thereby limiting not only the risk of the United States or Russia launching strikes but also the danger of weapons falling into the hands of terrorists or troublemaking smaller nations. During the campaign, he had used that work to promote himself as a big-picture foreign policy thinker, and in his first term, he was determined to chalk up a victory on the issue by signing a new Strategic Arms Reduction Treaty to replace the soon-to-expire pact. More broadly, he believed, a "dangerous drift" had pushed the two countries apart in recent years, preventing them from addressing a variety of common interests, from arms control to commerce and counterterrorism. From the outset of his administration Obama placed a high premium on bolstering the U.S. relationship with Russia, and Hillary's trip was intended to kick-start that process.

Philippe Reines, a lover of both gimmickry and iconic imagery, had come up with a plan to show the world a symbol of the "reset" mantra. Hillary would give Lavrov a gift-wrapped button emblazoned with the English and Russian words for "reset." It seemed like a clever way to draw attention to the message, one sure to be bounced across the globe on television and in newspaper pictures. But Reines had sidestepped the traditional protocol by not asking State's team of translators to help with the project from the start.

He later said he was unaware that such resources were available to him. He had asked NSC Russia director Mike McFaul for the word and both McFaul and State Russia expert Bill Burns had signed off on the spelling.

During a classic photo-op moment, as wire photographers' cameras clicked, Clinton reached into a yellow box to hand the gift to Lavrov. It represents "what President Obama, Vice President Biden, and I have been saying," she said, revealing the oversize button with the words *reset* and *peregruzka* on it. "And that is, we want to reset our relationship. So we will do it together," she said, holding up the red button for the cameras.

Presenting the button to Lavrov, she asked for approval: "We worked hard to get the right Russian word. Think we got it?"

"You got it wrong," Lavrov replied.

"I got it wrong," Clinton said, awkwardly echoing Lavrov's accent.

Lavrov pointed out that *peregruzka*—printed not in Cyrillic but in Latin script—means "overcharge."

Clinton let out one of her trademark laughs and slapped her hands together once. "Well, we won't let you do that to us, I promise," she countered.

Lavrov, smiling politely, promised to keep the button on his desk. But the moment caused some heartburn among career types back at the State Department and at the National Security Council, where, as one official put it, "I remember some moans and groans and slapping of the forehead."

Reines tried to correct the error, asking Russia's ambassador to Switzerland to give the gift back temporarily so that a new label—with the right word—could be printed and affixed to it.

"This is a gift from the United States. I don't think I can give it to you," the ambassador replied with a smile. "If I did, my minister would be very upset."

"If your minister doesn't give that back, my minister," Reines said, referring to Hillary, "is going to send me to Siberia."

Reines pleaded his case in good humor, even suggesting they

bring a label-maker into the room so that the Russian ambassador didn't have to let the gift—an emergency stop button that had been hastily pilfered from a swimming pool or Jacuzzi at the hotel—out of his sight. *Nyet,* the ambassador said.

Compounding the mistake, Reines then tried to pin the blame on McFaul, an Obama favorite, at a time when tension between the White House and State staffs was running high.

The gaffe overshadowed Clinton's trip to Geneva, as journalists pointed out in their stories. One Russian newspaper, *Kommersant,* highlighted the goof on its front page, stating "Sergei Lavrov and Hillary Clinton push the wrong button." Reines would have liked a do-over, but he felt that the main purpose of the button had been served. It was an ice-breaker for the two diplomats. And instead of getting angry and calling for heads to roll, Hillary and Lavrov found the moment amusing enough that they later signed a copy of *Time* magazine featuring the reset button on its cover and gave it to Reines. "Philippe, the Russians are pushing your buttons! (which is only fair since you pushed theirs!) As ever, Hillary," she wrote. But Senator John McCain, long considered a friend to Clinton, put a fine point on the public-relations goof. "If I gave him a reset button," McCain cracked, "I'd find someone in the State Department who understands Russian."

Reines's translation misadventures served as another reminder of how the wide latitude Hillary gave to trusted loyalists came at a price: there was blowback for her when they rubbed White House officials the wrong way, flubbed in foreign policy, or found themselves the subject of headlines for the wrong reasons. None of that reflected well on her, but it was very rare for her to cast someone out—and rarer still for her to turn a cold shoulder to him. When P. J. Crowley, the assistant secretary of state for public affairs, spoke critically of the government's treatment of Wikileaker Bradley Manning in March 2011, Hillary accepted his resignation, but she also called him the day his departure was announced. Crowley fielded the call at a Washington Capitals hockey game, and Hillary thanked him for his service. When Crowley asked her to give his best regards to Bill, Hillary put her husband on the line to offer his own words of consolation.

I n the first months of her tenure, small gaffes like the Russia reset button and the intermittent reports on infighting within the Obama administration often overshadowed the work Hillary was doing behind the scenes to bolster the State Department, advise Obama on foreign policy, and connect with the leaders and people of geopolitically important countries. By the first week of June, she had been to twenty countries, counting the Palestinian territories, and held innumerable meetings and phone calls with foreign leaders at the State Department. She backed up her rhetoric about engaging directly with the public in other countries to push for more coop- eration from their governments by giving speeches at universities, sitting for interviews with reporters wherever she went, and con- ducting town hall meetings in Tokyo, Seoul, and Baghdad.

She also made sure to connect with Americans involved in diplomacy and development, meeting with embassy staff in various countries. Hillary was working all the time—around the clock, and around the world—but she didn't have much to show for the brutal schedule, in part because diplomatic agreements take time to ripen and in part because Obama had empowered Biden and the White House national security team to take the lead on many hot-button issues. Folks in Washington began to wonder whether she could live up to the hype surrounding her selection. And then, in an instant, the insult was compounded by injury.

Shortly before five o'clock on a mid-June afternoon, as she walked from an elevator to her awaiting motorcade inside the base- ment garage at State, Hillary fell and landed squarely on her right elbow. She had been on her way to the White House with Hol- brooke, where they were scheduled to talk to the president about a number of issues, including an imminent trip that Melanne Verveer, Hillary's old chief of staff turned new ambassador for women's issues at State, was planning to take to Afghanistan.

The pain was so unbearable and excruciating that Hillary lay on the basement floor, wincing. Struggling to get back up, she asked Holbrooke to continue on to the White House and attend the meeting without her. "That's an order," Holbrooke recalled her telling him.

While Holbrooke would go on to meet with Obama, Hillary, her elbow throbbing, made her way back up to her seventh-floor office. She left a short time later for George Washington University Hospital, just down the street, where she underwent treatment for a fracture to her elbow. Later that evening, at around ten, now surrounded by Bill and Chelsea, who had flown into Washington immediately to be by her side, she fielded a check-up call from Obama.

Doctors told her that she would need surgery in the coming days, and Hillary—who rarely if ever took a sick day—holed up at her Embassy Row home. Unable to ever sit still, aides say, she spent her time reading briefing papers and making calls. During one briefing after the fall, State Department spokesman P. J. Crowley quipped that Hillary was figuring out "how well you can text with one arm in a sling."

The joke hinted that she was fit to be tied. Hillary knows one gear: overdrive. That had been a source of concern to her friends early in her time at State, who saw that the nonstop international travel, late-night briefing-book readings, and lack of exercise were already taking more of a toll on her than had past jobs. She had never missed a step in two decades of high-profile public service in Washington, but she admitted privately that she was running herself into the ground.

At a 2009 event for Vital Voices, Hillary ran into Mo Elleithee, a traveling press aide from her 2008 campaign, backstage. "How are you liking the gig?" he asked.

Hillary smiled and paused. "I love it," she said. "I absolutely love it. The work is great."

Then she paused again.

"But I am working so much harder now than I ever have in my entire life."

The remark was striking to Elleithee, who had watched her slog through a brutal primary campaign, moving at a dizzying speed and putting in "110 percent" without complaint.

Obama noticed, too. At a cabinet meeting, he decided to make an example of Hillary. It's a marathon, not a sprint, he told her and the rest of his top advisers. "Hillary was pushing herself too far or too hard," said one cabinet member, "and he basically said that she needed to maintain her stamina and her health, and he wanted to make sure everyone did the same." Now the fall was going to set her back. Before undergoing a two-hour early morning surgery a couple of days after her spill, Hillary was forced to scrap her public schedule, including an event for World Refugee Day that she had been set to attend alongside actress Angelina Jolie.

The fall came at an awkward time for Hillary. She didn't just lose her footing literally—she lost it figuratively, too. She had to cancel an upcoming trip to Greece and Italy, where she had planned to meet counterparts in the Group of Eight to discuss Afghanistan, the Middle East, and Iran. She also missed out on Obama's visit to Russia, where he and President Dmitri Medvedev negotiated a joint statement in support of continuing efforts to fight terrorism and drug trafficking in Afghanistan, creating a new START nuclear-nonproliferation treaty, and preventing North Korea and Iran from developing nuclear weapons.

The broken elbow became a metaphor for a gathering narrative that the boys in the West Wing were shoving her out of the foreign policy picture. It was clear that she still had a long way to go to prove herself to some of the folks in the White House, and the ongoing tension between Hillary's team and Obama's complicated her efforts to rebuild the State Department, the United States' image abroad, and her own reputation at home, because she was not regarded publicly as the central player on Obama's team.

The week after her fall, Ben Smith of *Politico* began working on a story headlined "Hillary Clinton Toils in the Shadows." The thrust of the article was that her grind-it-out style and staff-level fights with the White House had kept her on the back burner. As an example of her limited influence, Smith planned to single out Denis

McDonough's victory over Cheryl Mills in the fight over who had the power to appoint ambassadors. Reines reached out to a new friend on the White House team, Tommy Vietor, for help in tamping down the story. Vietor, responding to Reines's request, arranged interviews for Smith with McDonough and Tom Donilon, the president's deputy national security adviser. McDonough told Smith that a report of him going "mano a mano" with Mills was "not accurate" and that "one of the many blessings of this job has been working with and getting to know Cheryl."

Smith didn't buy it, personally, but dutifully reported the quotes. The White House and State had worked hard enough to dilute the story that for a few weeks other major news outlets declined to follow his smart lead. By the time Obama negotiated with Russian leaders in Moscow in early July, though, it became hard to deny the obvious contrast that Hillary was on the sidelines in a sling.

Her support network reacted as if her fall were somehow part of an Obama plan to marginalize her. "It's time for Barack Obama to let Hillary Clinton take off her burqa," Tina Brown wrote in a provocative article for the *Daily Beast* on July 13. "You could say that Obama is lucky to have such a great foreign-policy wife. Those who voted for Hillary wonder how long she'll be content with an office wifehood of the Saudi variety."

It wasn't just Hillary's cheerleading section that saw the White House diminishing her. Reines and Vietor may have delayed a pile-on after Smith's *Politico* story, but the narrative was taking hold nonetheless. A few days later, timed to Hillary's first major address to the salon of intellectual elites at the Council on Foreign Relations, the diplomatic correspondents for the Associated Press, the *Los Angeles Times,* the *New York Times,* and the *Washington Post* all wrote stories that cast her as struggling to regain lost influence.

Together the articles painted a secretary of state who chafed at being circumscribed by other powerful forces in the administration, led by Obama himself. One pointed to her special envoys, Holbrooke and Mitchell, as players whose portfolios took her out of the game on Afghanistan, Pakistan, and the Middle East, as well as Biden's prominent role as Obama's point man on Iraq. Another noted that Hillary's senior adviser on Iran, Dennis Ross, had just been reassigned to the White House; her pick to head the U.S. Agency for International Development was hamstrung in the White House vetting process; and Obama had selected a big-time contributor to become ambassador to Japan over her choice, smart-power advocate Joseph Nye.

Whether the stories were the result of Hillary supporters' frustration with the Obama team, a White House campaign to undermine her, or simply careful observation by reporters, private friction between the State Department and the West Wing had sparked into full public view. Within the State Department, some senior-level foreign policy experts strongly believed at the time—and still do, years later—that Obama's White House aides were a bunch of piker neophytes whose desire to keep a tight leash on foreign policy wasn't nearly as limited as their real-world experience. "These are not your Kissingers or Brzezinskis," one still-miffed former State Department official said.

In turn, many of the White House aides saw the Clinton network as part of a bipartisan Washington foreign policy establishment that kept getting it wrong, particularly in backing George W. Bush's decision to invade Iraq. Some of the exhibits in the case of Hillary's diminished influence were misguided, while others were more convincing. For example, Ross's move to the White House staff ultimately served as an end run around Mitchell, who resigned in disgust because he had been effectively boxed out of Middle East negotiations.

But the notion that the special envoys were a challenge to Hillary's power was off base. They had been her idea, she had picked them, and she continued to believe that the strategy of giving high-profile portfolios to the likes of Holbrooke, Mitchell, and others strengthened her hand. Reporters also missed the nuance between a "special envoy," the title given to Holbrooke and Mitchell, and a "special adviser," which was Ross's role at State. The envoys were expected to get into the muck of diplomacy and reported both to Hillary and Obama. Ross was basically Hillary's top counselor on Iran.

Moreover, the president always has more power than the secretary of state in setting foreign policy—and in most cases, so do his White House aides. It is a rare secretary of state—Henry Kissinger—who essentially runs foreign policy. Still, in this case, the gap between the story line and the reality threatened to damage the administration's efforts all around. Hillary's close associates say she is particularly well attuned to the effect that perception has on power, and halfway through her first year, the growing perception in Washington was that she didn't have much power. That was a dangerous counternarrative for a diplomat who relied to some extent on her celebrity—a status conferred by public perception—to do her job.

If the rest of the world were to think she had little or no influence with Obama, her star wouldn't shine as brightly when she reached out to foreign counterparts. The same was true at home, where she wouldn't have as much influence with colleagues in government if they perceived her to be weak. It might not have been apparent to everyone on Obama's staff, but Hillary's stature was important to the execution of the president's foreign policy. Some of the White House message men understood that dynamic, which helps explain why they put the president's top foreign policy aides on the record with *Politico*. "Once we're all in government together," said one White House official, "a story that is negative on Hillary is bad for the White House."

Hillary and Obama may have made an odd couple, but what Tina Brown didn't pick up on or didn't write—and what the White House aides might have lost sight of at times—was that Obama was better off with an empowered Clinton at his side. She provided a tremendous amount of political cover for him, and her successes were his successes. Her public blessings on his policy, which she conveyed without reservation, conferred added gravitas to his views. If she split from him on policy—or resigned—a good bit of his own party would second-guess every decision he made on the international stage. She was the rare Cabinet secretary with her own substantial national political following.

Six months in, it wasn't just Hillary who was hearing questions about her influence. Obama, too, was learning that a bar set high is hard to clear. He had promised other countries during his inaugural address that "we will extend a hand if you are willing to unclench your fist." But even with the groundwork being laid for a new START treaty, there had been no breakthrough in the first half of 2009.

Huma later confided to Wendy Sherman that the incoming fire had been more than Hillary's staff had anticipated. "You never told us how relentless it was," Huma said.

"Yes, I did," Sherman replied. "But you didn't believe me."

Sherman's point about handling the barrage of daily crises was so poignant because Hillary didn't have the luxury of choosing in which order she built her influence, promoted her agenda, and responded to challenges thrown at her from the White House and the world. And while other officials are required to pull off similar balancing acts—the president and the defense secretary, among them—secretary of state is high on the list of tightrope performers. Even as the media portrayed Hillary as a secondary player on Obama's national security team in those first six months, she continued to gather capital behind the scenes, not just within the administration but, importantly, within the State Department.

Any good politician knows that local politics are as important as geopolitics, and Hillary immersed herself in the issues that affected both the foreign service and the civil service, from setting long-term strategies to empower diplomats abroad, to fixing small quality-of-life problems that annoyed the folks at the department's Foggy Bottom headquarters.

She had walked into the State Department with a reputation for running a high-drama operation in which loyalty was rewarded over competence. The fact that Obama had given her nearly free rein to choose political appointees threatened to exacerbate fears that she would ignore the permanent structure of the department. Her unprecedented control over political jobs made it hard for her to counter the notion—and the reality—that most decisions would be made by an inner circle of longtime advisers whose ranks were almost impossible to crack. Those appointees, who generally came in and left with the secretary, were layered on top of the foreign service and civil service and given both formal and informal power within the bureaucracy.

In every agency, there's tension between the relatively small political set, which holds outsize influence with the secretary, and the much larger career staff. That natural clash between the two classes, combined with the dysfunction of Hillary's campaign, was cause for concern at the department, even among the small group of political appointees who didn't come from Hillary's own circle. "If you didn't work on the campaign, it was pretty clear where you stood," said one appointee who was outside Hillary's circle. "*Game Change* had come to the State Department."

That's why Hillary's emphasis on daily-life issues held a symbolic power as forceful as the substantive changes she made. She had to win "the building"—to get the career State Department folks on her side—and to do that, she knew it was smart to focus on the little things that made their lives better. If she was going to rebuild State's influence in the federal government and America's reputation abroad, she needed to invest in her people so that they would trust her and follow her. "She was clearly making a very authentic and really real effort in a very difficult circumstance because it's a huge bureaucracy, and it's very complicated to reach out to people and be part of the family," said one midlevel State official.

Just after she took office, Hillary ordered a review of same-sex partner benefits for members of the foreign service, a follow-up to Obama's direction that federal agencies look at ways to promote equality within their ranks. At best, disparate treatment of same-sex spouses amounted to extra inconveniences in traveling and living overseas for gay and lesbian foreign service officers. At worst, it meant that a State Department employee's same-sex partner could be left in a war zone during an evacuation in which the federal government took care of the families of foreign service officers in opposite-sex marriages.

"I view this as an issue of workplace fairness, employee retention, and the safety and effectiveness of our embassy communities worldwide," Hillary said on February 4, 2009, promising to determine what she had the power to change and to move forward on rewriting policy quickly. In May the *New York Times* reported on an internal memo detailing an emergent new policy for the equal treatment of same-sex partners of foreign service officers. The plan was formalized the following month, when new rights were codified in the State Department's manual. They included benefits such as medical treatment and housing expenses for same-sex partners and the children of same-sex couples.

Many of Hillary's new charges were surprised to find just how much thought and energy she put into empowering them. They also learned that they were dealing with a relentless campaigner who never failed to plot or execute a strategy for lack of personal effort. Her travel schedule, of course, became legendary, a function both of her commitment to backing up Obama's promise of a new American diplomacy, and of a public relations team that made sure the statistics were easy to track. The front page of the State Department website was turned into an interactive living history of her travels, which eventually covered 956,733 miles and 112 countries. Previous secretaries' aides had kept logs of their whereabouts but not with the zeal of Hillary's image-conscious PR team. It was an essential part of her narrative as secretary that she outhustled everyone. But within the State Department, both political aides and career officials were far more impressed with her diligence in drilling deep into arcane policy issues.

Dating back to her time in the Senate, Hillary started her day with a large packet of news clips that an aide began gathering at four a.m., in an informal competition with the staffer who did the same job for Bill Clinton. Hillary had been jealous of her husband's stack of news stories, and she instructed her staff to prepare a similar briefing each morning. At State, they included major news articles and stories about her husband and daughter.

Her day ended with a massive briefing book, as well as funny cat clips inserted by an aide. Rob Russo, who had sent out her thank-you notes following the 2008 primary, was responsible for making sure the book was in good shape each day. It included her schedule for the following day, memos on each meeting on the agenda, speeches and talking points for public events, and short biographies on people she would be meeting. The tabs upon tabs of information were sent in by staff around the building and compiled by two career officials. Often enough, aides were working on it as late as midnight.

While there's nothing unusual about a department head or member of Congress taking a briefing book home at night—most do—Hillary's command of each day's homework shocked her advisers. "She really read the memos," said one senior aide. "I worked on her Senate confirmation and also the first set of budget hearings that we had. I'd give her these big three-hundred-page things that I assumed would never be read, at least not the bottom fifty pages. And she'd take them home over the weekend, and on Monday she'd come back with them, page two hundred fifty folded over, highlighted with a note in the margin like 'This doesn't make sense' or 'Explain this to me.'" She gave the same attention to the stacks of personal notes that went out with her signature, often returning drafts with typos circled or small notes to add a recipient's nickname or fix some other detail.

Hillary's discipline and attentiveness were two of the ways in which she contrasted with her husband, who is famous for arriving late and multitasking. For those who know both of them, her style is as respectful as his is disrespectful. "Standing at the desk of the president of the United States while you're briefing him for a major meeting," Albright said, "and he's doing a crossword puzzle, and you feel like saying 'God damn it, listen to me,' and you never know, and then he'd say everything that you'd briefed him on, so you always knew that he had actually absorbed it. She, being a Wellesley girl, takes notes."

Even one of the most embarrassing episodes of Hillary's young life, when she failed the Washington, D.C., bar exam, didn't appear to result from a lack of discipline. She enrolled in a bar study class with a professor, Joseph Nacrelli, who had a reputation for knowing every nook and cranny of the D.C. test. But in 1973 the exam was in its second year of including a multistate portion that tested more generally on American law rather than just city-specific questions. Hearing the professor lecture on a topic they knew well, some of the students in the class determined that portions of the material he was teaching were wrong. Those students panicked because the bar would test them on subjects they hadn't taken in law school. So they began to study those subjects independently, in addition to continuing the class, and they passed. It's hard to know whether Hillary failed because she studied the wrong information—some of those who relied solely on the class made the grade. She was a great student but didn't have the vision to see the trouble some of her peers identified and adjusted for.

In her first weeks in office, Hillary set in motion a major initiative that spoke to her interest in building the institution and her penchant for preparation and planning, even as it alienated some of her in-house constituents. It was a project that she hoped would modernize the State Department at all levels, enhance its chances of securing big budgets, and ensure that diplomats were seen as the face of America in host countries. She invited several of her top aides to dinner on the eighth floor, where American treasures such as Thomas Jefferson's desk are housed in a matrix of marble columns, hardwood floors, and balcony that provides a stunning panorama of the city.

As she sat down to eat and plot with Cheryl Mills, Jake Sullivan, policy planning aide Derek Chollet, and Rich Verma, the department's lobbyist on Capitol Hill, Hillary began to talk about how effectively the Pentagon persuaded Congress each year to fund its massive budget requests, which had grown to more than $650 billion including supplemental spending for the wars in Iraq and Afghanistan.

As a member of the Armed Services Committee, she explained,

she had watched how the Pentagon brass had been equipped not just with the power of their special mission to defend the nation but also with planning documents that bolstered their case for funding increases. Every four years the Pentagon developed a report, called the Quadrennial Defense Review (QDR), that assessed longer-term strategy and priorities, including needs for weapons, personnel, and vehicles. Its basic function was to make sure that there was a directed, if sometimes vaguely stated, national defense strategy. But it also served as a reference point for military leaders who came to Capitol Hill with colorful presentations aimed at getting Congress to keep funding an old weapons system or to put out the seed money for a new one. The new ask could always be shoehorned into a strategy articulated in the last QDR.

But what the QDR gave the Pentagon, more than anything else, was a sense of long-range mission and purpose that integrated the needs of the department with the strategic vision of its civilian leadership. "I don't know why we don't do that here," Hillary told her aides. "It just doesn't make any sense."

State didn't "have a big-picture compelling strategic rationale why a given program is not only important in its own right but critical to the bigger-picture vision," said a government official familiar with the thinking behind Hillary's push. "It's not just the document that's valuable. I think it's more the process of articulating clear priorities."

Hillary listened attentively to her advisers' input, scribbling notes to herself. Then she wrote down the words *Quadrennial Diplomacy and Development Review.* She already had given a lot of thought to the QDDR by that point—she had discussed it with Jim Steinberg before she was confirmed—and the dinner was just a way of unveiling it to a wider circle of aides.

It turned out to be a long and painful process, nearly two years in the making, and many officials complained bitterly about the extra workload. Anne-Marie Slaughter, the head of the State Department's Policy Planning Office and the lead official on the QDDR, later wrote a piece for *The Atlantic* about the impossible demands on her time at State, headlined "Why Women Can't Have It All." Richard Fontaine, a senior fellow at the Center for a New American Security, which was originally cofounded by one of Hillary's assistant secretaries, noted that "even for those questions the QDDR does answer, implementation will be difficult." Even Hillary's top aides declined to sugarcoat the way the QDDR was received. "I assure you people hated it as they were going through it," one of them said. "But it was a really effective exercise."

In the end, they had a 242-page blueprint for elevating diplomacy and development as equal partners with military force in the conduct of American foreign policy. The first QDDR's goals included making ambassadors CEOs for American agencies in foreign countries; bolstering soft-power tools like economic assistance; improving the lives of women and girls around the world; reorganizing the department's bureaus to better reflect modern challenges; ensuring that diplomats had up-to-date computers and handheld devices; reforming the foreign service exam to bring in sharp new diplomats; increasing diplomats' direct engagement with the people of their host countries—not just their governments; and using technology such as social media platforms for diplomacy. The entire exercise was aimed at strengthening the institution, even if the medicine tasted bad going down. "The QDDR was a tough process, but it was about getting 'the building' right," said one veteran diplomat. "It was about affirming the work that got done here and trying to organize it in a better way."

It also reflected Hillary's modus operandi, for better and worse. She seized on someone else's idea, devised a plan for emulating it, and powered it through to completion. "She's not the most creative one, but she has the command of the substance, and she has the command of the strategic direction," one of her top advisers said. Her strengths were in executing on the good ideas that came to her and applying lessons learned from one problem to resolving another.

Hillary used her strength as a student, as well as her staff, to compensate for not being a fount of innovation. Insatiable for ideas, she solicited them from a wide range of people, and she imported a technique from her days in the Senate that was old hat for long-time Hillarylanders. Laurie Rubiner had been her Senate legislative director for about two months in 2005 when she was called into Hillary's office to find a pair of suitcases on two card tables. Inside were hundreds of pages of newspaper and magazine clippings with scribbles in the margins in the handwriting of Bill and Hillary Clinton. Rubiner could have been forgiven for thinking she had walked into the Unabomber's office. It was an old gambit that Hillary's previous senior legislative staff had discontinued. But with a new director now running the operation, Hillary renewed the game. Rubiner's task was to assign clips to all the junior legislative staffers in the office and get them to report back to Hillary on potential courses of action that could be taken to rectify a problem or take advantage of a new way of doing business. The practice spilled over to State, where Jake Sullivan ended up spending long hours going through clips with Hillary on her plane.

Much has been made of the nearly 1 million miles Hillary traveled around the globe over four years, and detractors have used the statistic to suggest she was vainly focused on setting records rather than on solving international problems. Her aides say she understood that her greatest value to the president was to physically represent the United States on his behalf. She's a natural diplomat, which is to say a politician who didn't have to win an election.

Hillary's celebrity creates a bit of an intimidation factor for many of the people she meets around the world, a dynamic she often breaks down with a compliment for a man's tie or a woman's necklace. "Oh my God, where did you get that purse?" Hillary exclaimed upon meeting one job applicant. "Oh, Huma, look at this purse!" The applicant, who got the job, saw Hillary use the same icebreaker time and again.

"This is a tactic I see her use with people all the time," the woman said. "She knows people are nervous around her, so she does this. . . . It's a calculatingly nice thing to do to somebody who is extremely nervous around you. . . . It's keenly self-aware."

And because Hillary was a demanding boss who would put State's career employees through the paces of painful internal changes like those outlined in the QDDR, her ability to connect with them—and demonstrate loyalty—mattered all the more. They were her constituents, and she had to find ways to serve them to win their support. In unveiling the QDDR in July 2009, she held a Senate-style town hall meeting in the State Department's ground-floor auditorium, soliciting questions both online and from the live audience.

Emily Gow, who worked in the Office of International Religious Freedom, presented Hillary with the perfect opportunity to demonstrate her command of constituent service.

At first, the audience laughed at Gow's question, which seemingly had little to do with the cultural change Hillary sought to implement through the QDDR. "It's about biking and running to work," Gow said, "and whether you would support an initiative to get us access to showers." Despite the prospect of embarrassing herself in front of her colleagues and her boss by asking about the most picayune of all daily details, the young woman pressed on. "First of all, it would save the government a lot of money because we wouldn't have to get our transit subsidies. I'd much rather bike to work than take the Metro. It would be green, and it would promote morale."

Like a seasoned political pro, Hillary took the request in stride and promised to look into the matter. No one thought much of the pledge, which sounded like a polite dismissal.

But the next week, at a daily eight-forty-five morning meeting with about a dozen top advisers, Hillary asked Pat Kennedy, the undersecretary for management, for an update. "Pat, what's the story on the shower?" she asked. She badgered Kennedy until the problem was resolved.

"I went to more morning staff meetings in these opening months," said a political appointee who was new to Hillary's world, "where we talked about, Were there enough showers in the locker room? Were there enough parking spaces in the garage? Were the computers and BlackBerrys working the way they should for staff? The kind of things that are not the big geopolitical thoughts. She was as focused on the stuff that matters to people who are kind of busting their tail every day for fifteen and twenty years. That stuff really mattered to her, and she got really mad when it didn't get fixed. Those were the days when I saw her lose her temper."

EIGHT

"Use Me Like an App"

Jared Cohen was sweating. The twenty-seven-year-old prodigy of the State Department's policy planning shop had a propensity to text as fast as he could think when he saw a solution within his grasp, and he seldom questioned his own instincts. Most high-end politicians follow the credo that it's better to seek forgiveness than permission. Bill and Hillary Clinton use a slight adaptation of the same idea: "Better to get caught trying." In that spirit, Cohen had just pulled off a behind-the-scenes coup using the American government to link Iranian revolutionaries with Twitter executives who could aid their cause. But in doing so, he had inadvertently set the State Department at odds with the president and put his own career at risk.

On June 13, 2009, in what would become known as the Green Movement, Iranian protesters took to the streets and the Internet to challenge the validity of Mahmoud Ahmadinejad's reelection. Two days later Mir Hussein Moussavi, the leader of the Iranian opposition, found out that Twitter was planning to shut down for scheduled maintenance for about ninety minutes shortly before one a.m. on the U.S. East Coast. That meant the Iranians wouldn't be able to use the social media platform, which had become a crucial organizing tool, to communicate with one another from about 8:45 a.m. to 10:15 a.m. in Tehran. Concerned that the movement could lose momentum as a result, Moussavi tweeted about it.

Cohen saw the Tweet and, without giving any thought to the

consequences, shot an e-mail to his buddy Jack Dorsey, the founder of Twitter. "Any chance you can do this at a time that's convenient for Iranians rather than Americans?" Cohen wrote. If not, the Iranian protesters could lose their ability to communicate with one another and the outside world.

"Let me look into this," Dorsey replied, promising to ask the Twitter team whether it could be done.

Thin, with curly black hair and blue eyes that come alive when he talks about a new idea, Cohen is a native of Weston, Connecticut, a wealthy New York suburb where the median income reaches nearly $200,000 a year. He graduated from Stanford and went to Oxford as a Rhodes scholar. A Condi Rice protégé at the tail end of the Bush administration, he showed such promise as a tech thinker that he caught the attention of two of Hillary's most influential aides, Anne-Marie Slaughter and Alec Ross, who were trying to implement for Hillary a vision of "21st Century Statecraft" in which the State Department would use tools of innovation in conjunction with, and sometimes instead of, traditional diplomacy. Cohen was certainly innovating on his own when he reached out to Dorsey. He had to wait a couple of hours, or two eons in tech time, for a response.

"It's not going to be as easy as they thought," Dorsey finally replied.

"Anything you can do would be very helpful," Cohen wrote back, emphasizing that the U.S. government was getting a lot of its information about what was happening on the ground from Twitter. "This is really important."

Long-standing unilateral sanctions on Iran meant there was virtually no American presence there and no embassy in Tehran. The United States has a small team of Iran watchers in nearby nations who gather intelligence by interviewing people when they leave the country. The Iranian protesters needed the Twitter network up and running, and so did the American Iran-watchers. A little while later Dorsey forwarded to Cohen a long internal e-mail chain from Twitter's tech team. The most important word was the one Dorsey had added at the top: "Done."

For Cohen, it represented a hard-earned victory and a step forward in the quest for innovative diplomacy. He had been quietly working with tech companies in advance of the Iranian election in hopes of finding ways to give support to the opposition. Dorsey, in particular, was something of a great white whale for Cohen and Ross, Hillary's senior adviser for innovation. They had been cultivating him for months. They had hosted him at the State Department. They had held a private dinner for him in Washington. They had even invited him to Iraq as part of a State-run business delegation that included Obama campaign consultant Blue State Digital. He was a blossoming ally, someone they thought could grasp the importance of the relationship between the business community's high-tech innovation and Hillary's goals for modernizing the set of diplomatic tools at America's disposal.

Tech tools can influence behavior and conditions at a lightning pace compared to the traditional levers of diplomacy. Sanctions and the promise of removing them offer the possibility of changing a foreign government's calculus over a time frame of weeks, months, even years, but tech tools work in real time. They can be used to organize or disrupt whole social and political orders overnight.

For a less-developed country, American tech assistance offers the possibility of building infrastructure, combating crime, improving communications, and defending against cyberwarfare. But it also carries risks: the people can use it as a weapon against the government, and as the Arab Spring would show, it can be a pivotal factor in toppling a regime. That means the United States can leverage a big tech company like Twitter, Google, or Facebook as either an incentive or a threat to a foreign government. Help us, and we'll help you. Hurt us, and we'll sit back and watch as revolutionaries use our tech tools to oust you from power.

In the wake of Hillary's primary defeat, she had become obsessed with the power of Internet-era innovation. Obama had used modern technology to organize, communicate, raise money, and market himself in ways that had left her campaign looking outmoded. She was intent on figuring out how she could apply the lessons from her failure to the new job—and perhaps beyond. "She asked in some cases, 'What could I have done better with technology' in this state or that state?" said a senior State official. "I know there was this curiosity from the campaign that existed. I think it's interesting that it then filtered over into an interest into how this could be leveraged for foreign policy."

Her desire to turn a weakness into a strength, as she moved from candidate to cabinet official, was exemplified by her successful pursuit of Ross, who had coordinated Obama's tech advisory group during the campaign. In the early days of Hillary's term, Ross and Cohen, bound by their enthusiasm for a new brand of diplomacy, had struck up a friendship, and together they assiduously courted executives at the nation's top tech companies, to enlist them in advancing America's foreign policy goals.

Because the tech companies operate in countries all over the world, they work hard to counter any perception that they might be pawns of the American government. But Cohen was about to give the world a peek behind the curtain and, in doing so, jeopardize his own job by putting State publicly at odds with White House policy. From his perspective, the ask that he was making of Twitter was so benign that he didn't bother to give a heads-up to his bosses in the Policy Planning Office. But that night he forwarded the e-mail chain to Ross, who dialed him back immediately.

"Jared, you realize you may have just contradicted the president of the United States' stated policy of noninterference in the election?" Ross asked.

"Oh, shit," Cohen replied.

On the very same day, June 15, Obama had said, "It is up to Iranians to make decisions about who Iran's leaders will be" and "We respect Iranian sovereignty." That is, the United States would not meddle in the Iranian election. Cohen hadn't been trying to undermine the president, and his stratagem might have been roundly well received if it had remained private. But when the story became public, it was suddenly just the kind of snafu that fueled White House suspicions about whether Hillary's empire at State could be trusted to execute the president's policy.

Cohen's chief advocate was one of the few Obama campaign advisers who had landed a job at State. Ross bears a resemblance to the actor Michael J. Fox in his *Spin City* days. A native of Charleston, West Virginia, and the grandson of an American diplomat, Ross had cofounded an international nonprofit aimed at closing the digital divide and had raised money for it by cold-calling top tech executives. He joined up with the Obama campaign before it was officially launched and took on a role as a conduit between the campaign and its advisers and supporters in the tech sector. By the end, he was coordinating a 509-person advisory committee of academics, executives, hackers, and techies who supported Obama. If the nerds in the Obama campaign's operations center wanted a new app, Ross would connect them to a tech company employee who backed the campaign and could help deliver it.

When Obama won, Ross, then thirty-six, was eager to find a job combining his two loves, innovation and foreign policy. There are other parts of government from which an aide can affect foreign policy, most notably the NSC and the Pentagon. But Ross, who had a lot of options after the election, found State appealing. When Obama appointed Hillary to take over, his friends told him he was out of luck, as it would be a hard place for any Obama campaign veteran to find work. But Ross had something Hillary wanted: he understood how the innovative tools that Obama had used to kick her butt on the campaign trail could be applied and expanded upon in service of American interests. Longtime Hillary adviser Maggie Williams had heard about Ross during the campaign, and during the transition in 2008, she and Cheryl Mills reached out to him. He sat down with the two of them and Hillary, and they discussed his view of the foreign policy challenges presented by the proliferation of information networks, essentially the diffusion of power away from traditional states and toward a variety of nonstate actors.

Hillaryland had been ignorant of the tools of modern campaign warfare and, compared with Obama, unaware of the ethos of the Internet generation. The concept of connectivity, however, wasn't at all foreign to Hillary. Long before Obama came along, she and her husband had been the masters of networking. By emulating what Obama did on the campaign trail—and using his adviser to do it—Hillary could quickly move from being a PC to a smartphone without stopping at Mac. Her desire to replicate Obama's domestic success in the global arena dovetailed well with Anne-Marie Slaughter's academic writings on the emergence of nongovernmental world networks. The Internet, more than any other single factor, facilitated the growing power of nonstate actors. That meant more influence over time for transnational quasi-governmental groups—like the United Nations and the G8—multinational corporations, and international social organizations. More imminently, political movements within countries could much more quickly be turned into revolutions. But it also meant the empowerment of terrorist organizations and crime syndicates. Power could increasingly be measured in terms of the ability to build your own network and disrupt someone else's, and that was an idea that Hillary could easily grasp.

Taken together, Hillary's investments in Slaughter, Ross, and Cohen could be seen as one of the clearest signs that she had learned from her loss in the 2008 campaign. For a woman whose operation was famously insular, she put a lot of faith in three outsiders—Slaughter from Princeton, Ross from the Obama campaign, and Cohen from the Bush administration—to develop and execute in an area where, just months earlier, she had been far behind the curve. Leaning in on innovation could serve her well not only in conducting foreign policy but if she ran for president again, and it showed that she had developed a deep understanding of the real power of technology as a political tool. "She never fell into that trap of 'let's just use technology for public diplomacy,'" one of her tech-savvy aides said. "She associated technology with grassroots organizing because of the campaign frame of reference."

But even within State, Hillary's emerging faith in the power of technology to transform diplomacy was a controversial proposition.

Ross had clashed with Jim Steinberg, the deputy secretary of state, over the balance of traditional diplomacy and the use of modern tools, particularly when it came to Ross's prediction that the world would see a leaderless revolution during Hillary's term as secretary. And while Slaughter provided a lot of the intellectual firepower behind Hillary's smart-power approach, she was marginalized by more savvy bureaucratic infighters as she took over the laborious process of compiling the QDDR. Even the set who appreciated Ross and Cohen viewed them as a lone-wolf unit. "They're both very hard to work with," said one longtime Hillarylander who worked at State. "They're not team players, which is why they're so good. They just go off and freelance and do creative stuff all the time. They're brilliant."

Cohen's mile-wide independent streak made him, the morning after his Twitter intervention, a hot topic of conversation among Hillary's senior staff. Hillary, who normally led the daily meeting, didn't attend that day, and neither did Cohen, who was far too junior to be included. But he did bring the episode to the attention of P. J. Crowley, the assistant secretary for public affairs, to make sure that the press team was aware of what had transpired. When Mark Landler of the *New York Times* asked about the incident, Crowley filled in the details, thinking Cohen's move would look good for State.

That was when Cohen's behind-the-scenes intervention suddenly became a public relations problem. Between the morning staff meeting and Landler's reporting for his article, the story was making its way around the building in double time. It was all anyone in the top offices could talk about.

Mills summoned Ross and Sullivan to her office; en route, the two men ran into each other in the secured part of the seventh floor, where national secrets are discussed.

"What Jared did is going on A1 of the *New York Times*," an exasperated Sullivan told Ross.

"What the fuck do you mean?" Ross replied. "P. J. just gave the *New York Times* Jared's intervention?"

"He gave it to him," Sullivan said. "It's going on A1."

Sullivan, Ross, and Crowley all gathered in Mills's office, where they brought in Philippe Reines by phone. Sullivan was agitated. This was a consequential decision, he thought, one that should have been carefully contemplated and messaged, not something done on a lark and then fed to the world's paper of record. Sullivan, who was becoming a powerful link between State and the White House, had a wider lens than Cohen on the administration's strategy in Iran. The Green Movement's leaders had been telling American officials to stay away from them publicly because U.S. intervention would only serve to discredit the revolutionaries with the rest of the Iranian people by fueling the regime's claim that the movement was led by American puppets. Mostly Sullivan expressed concern about State pissing on the White House. Obama was getting hit hard by conservatives who believed he should be more actively engaged in helping the movement along and Cohen's status as a Bush administration veteran sparked suspicion about his motives. The simple solution to save face for everyone would be to fire Cohen.

As the normally reserved Sullivan grew increasingly vocal, Crowley smiled and tried to calm him down. "I think you'll find that this is going to go well for us," he said, pointing to a long-term win for the United States in showing support for the revolutionaries in Iran.

"Why are we even discussing this?" Sullivan said. "He has to go."

Reines, who was much closer to Hillary than Crowley, began proposing ways to spin what Cohen had done. Motivation matters a lot to Reines, and he saw no malice in Cohen's actions. Others in the room thought he was looking for a way to save Cohen's skin by smoothing over the inherent conflict between the president's policy and Cohen's intervention. Reines's intensity matched Sullivan's.

But Mills repeatedly cut him off to tell him to stop talking. There was no good way to finesse this one.

They called Denis McDonough, the NSC's head of strategic communications. His directive: no one at State was to say another word about it publicly. They would sit back, wait for the *Times* story, and not help fuel a media firestorm by talking to other reporters about it. The best-case scenario would be a relatively positive

Times story that didn't embarrass Obama for taking a passive stance toward the Iranian protest movement.

Cohen was in a bind, his fate no longer in his own hands. The long knives were out not just for him but by extension for Ross, who was his patron in the department, and for Crowley, who had handed the *Times* a story about a midlevel State Department official conducting policy at odds with the president. Cohen hadn't meant any harm, but he now understood that his action could cost him his job and, perhaps worse, present a major setback to the work that he and Ross had been doing.

Operating largely outside the attention of the White House, Hillary had given the pair mostly free rein to explore the intersection of technology and diplomacy, not just in theory but in practice. In February she had sent Cohen to Afghanistan with Holbrooke and Admiral Mike Mullen, the chairman of the Joint Chiefs of Staff, where they saw that the Taliban had been smuggling iPhones to inmates at a prison there. Holbrooke then wrote Hillary memos about the role of technology in the war in Afghanistan, which further sparked her interest in deploying Ross and Cohen. At the same time, with Ross and Slaughter as her guides, Hillary was becoming a student of how technology interacted with foreign policy. She had built a little lab for innovation at State, and Ross and Cohen had been the tinkerers working in the shadows.

But now they were fast-blinking blips in the middle of the White House radar. Setting aside for the moment the question of whether what Cohen did was helpful or hurtful to the Green Movement, and the degree to which it amounted to insubordination to the president by either himself or Hillary, the imbroglio underscored a basic difference between Obama's worldview and Hillary's. At least as far back as her early days in the Senate, where she had represented New York's staunchly pro-Israel Jewish community, Hillary had been bellicose on Iran. When Obama had said during the campaign that he would be willing to sit down one-on-one with Ahmadinejad in his first year as president, Hillary suggested Obama had a naïve approach. "I don't want to be used for propaganda purposes," she had said.

Now her department, or at least Cohen, had taken a more forceful tack with Ahmadinejad than Obama's and had used social media to do it. For all of Obama's mastery of technology during the 2008 campaign, his team was notably much slower to embrace the power of new media platforms to transform the globe. Similarly, the old guard at State had little use for Ross and Cohen's new way of conducting diplomacy; the episode was a perfect example to them of the perils of 21st Century Statecraft, a term that seemed to come right out of the video-game generation and sounded a lot like *World of Warcraft*.

However Hillary reacted, it would be a major inflection point for a New Age diplomatic worldview that was still in its infancy but to which she had given early support. She had said many times privately that she wanted her team's errors to be those of commission rather than omission, but no one was quite sure that would be true when an error made Obama look bad, or potentially undermined U.S. efforts to get Iran to negotiate an end to its nuclear program. On the flip side, the White House refusal to explicitly back the Iranian protesters seemed at odds with American values. How could the world's leading democracy and its greatest power stand idly by while Iran crushed dissent? All these questions were swirling when the *Times* story popped online late that Tuesday.

By early Wednesday, with the story in indelible print in the newspaper that Obama trusted most, Hillary's top advisers gathered for their small-circle daily 8:45 a.m. meeting. They nervously waited for her word. If she was angry, they would know it quickly. Hillary can be sarcastic, even caustic, when she feels her aides have failed her. Her tone takes on an unmasked disappointment or she asks rhetorical questions that can't be answered without leading to further trouble.

The Cohen incident was a touchstone for so many points of tension. Was Hillary the kind of boss who would back her guy, or would she throw him under the bus? Was disrupting other governments just a clever theory or a real tool of modern diplomacy? Would she show backbone in a showdown with the White House?

The incident was clearly on Hillary's mind that morning when she walked into her conference room on the seventh floor, along the "Mahogany Hall" of wood-paneled executive offices, just across a narrow corridor from her own suite. It's highly unusual for her to carry a newspaper because she gets clips printed out and delivered. But on this morning, she held the *Times* in her hand. The story actually ended up on A12, not A1. Her aides watched closely for any signal of what she thought.

She put the paper down on the fourteen-seat rectangular wooden table in front of her and looked at her lieutenants. "This is great," she said. "This is exactly what we should be doing."

Hillary's commitment to innovation at State ran too deep to get sidetracked by the *mishegoss* over whether Jared Cohen had cleared his move with the right people or created momentary confusion over the administration's dovish policy on the reelection of Ahmadinejad. During the transition, Williams, Mills, and Hillary had discussed the need not just to catch up on innovation but also to get ahead of the curve. They wanted to turn a deficiency into an asset, and that mission wasn't something Hillary would give up on because of a little controversy.

In her first five months at State, she had poured mental energy and resources into making sure that her operation was far more forward-leaning in its use of technology as a political tool than her 2008 campaign had been. If anything, Cohen's Twitter-vention was a confirmation of the power of understanding and manipulating technology infrastructure. Not only was her innovation team a powerful tool at State, Hillary was keenly aware, according to associates, that technological superiority could become the force behind a second bid for the presidency. "The tools used to impact political movements abroad," one Hillary adviser said, "can be leveraged just as easily domestically."

▲

The innovation team eventually grew to number more than one hundred strong across the State Department's various bureaus; many of the aides simply incorporated 21st Century Statecraft activities into their existing jobs. They were a special forces unit of sorts for Hillary, and their efforts were directed at projects as benign as setting up social media accounts for State in various countries and as insidious as providing tech tools and training for rebels in Middle Eastern countries. She was taken not just with the possibility of affecting the rise and fall of governments or political candidates but also with the potential for technology to protect and empower the world's most vulnerable populations. Innovation, then, tied together her ambitions as a diplomat, her chances of running a successful campaign for the presidency, and her religion-inspired commitment to social justice.

Hillary turned to her tech team again in August 2009, during one of the most emotionally difficult periods of her first year as secretary. At a town hall meeting with Congolese students in Kinshasa, Hillary was asked what her husband thought about World Bank interference in Chinese contracts in the Congo. The question was an insult on top of a series of injuries to her stature: in Washington, Obama's team was still slow-walking her hiring decisions; journalists from Ben Smith to Tina Brown were writing about her perceived lack of influence; and Obama had even sent Bill to North Korea to negotiate the release of two American journalists who were being held there.

Now, sixty-five hundred miles outside the Beltway, on a trip that she had taken to empower women and combat abuses against them, some college kid had the nerve to ask what her husband thought about a policy issue. It was hot. The venue stunk of urine. Hillary was halfway through a twelve-day, seven-country trip.

She lost her temper. "My husband is not secretary of state. I am," she fired back. "If you want my opinion, I will tell you my opinion. I am not going to be channeling my husband."

Hillary's aides reached out to the White House, flagging what they knew would become the story of the day in the United States. One of Obama's top communications aides, who worked on the 2008 campaign, expressed sympathy for Hillary's reaction, which her aides had portrayed as the result of a bad translation or a poorly constructed question. "This is so infuriating," the Obama aide wrote in an e-mail to Reines. "She's flying to one of the most dangerous parts of one of the most dangerous countries on the continent to highlight the plight of women being put through unspeakable horrors and yet the press is still focused on psychobabble family bullshit from 1998."

The moment between two aides, former rivals and staunch loyalists, respectively, to Hillary and Obama, was a notable sign of the burgeoning solidarity between the two sides.

"I feel like a PUMA member right now," the aide wrote, referring to the "Party Unity My Ass" crowd that stuck with Hillary long after the end of the primary. "I'm calling Geraldine Ferraro immediately."

The video went viral. The *Today* show asked if she was jet-lagged or jealous of Bill. A little bit of both, NBC's Andrea Mitchell answered. The *New York Post* ran a picture of her under the headline "I'm the Boss." One of Hillary's aides said the moment was a reminder that she's a human being. "People think of her as some kind of automaton," the aide said, when she feels emotion just like anyone else.

The next day was even worse—and also much better, in a way that friends and advisers say defines Hillary. She traveled to the Mugunga refugee camp north of Goma, a godforsaken city on Lake Kivu filled with people who fled the Rwandan genocide, where she heard the detailed stories of two survivors of a rampant sexual assault epidemic. Through a series of seemingly never-ending conflicts in Congo and its neighboring countries, the sexual violence never stopped. Diplomatic security officials advised Hillary not to go to the war-torn region, but she insisted. The culture of rape, which had been perpetuated by Congolese soldiers and militias, "distills evil into its basest form," she said.

At a forum later that day, Hillary announced that the United States was pouring $17 million in aid into the country to prevent attacks and assist survivors. In meetings with top Congolese officials, she had raised the issue directly, telling them that the United States could not condone the government's tolerance of systematic rape. But she couldn't help feeling that she needed to do more. Shortly after her trip, Burns Strider, her 2008 faith adviser, e-mailed her to ask how she was doing. "I just came out of the Congo," she wrote back. "I cannot begin to tell you. Terrible. The pain, the atrocity, what's going on here."

The suffering gnawed at her, but she also drew strength from what she had seen and heard. "The thing that gives me hope," she wrote, "is that there are women who have escaped who turned right around and went back to help those who haven't escaped." Hillary doesn't cry much in front of other people, save for that famous moment in New Hampshire on the campaign trail, when she credited her supporters for helping her find her voice. In times of crisis during the campaign and at the State Department, friends and aides say, she kept her composure when others around her were losing theirs.

The way Hillary mourns, friends say, is to pour her emotion into healing and fixing, an approach deeply rooted in the teachings of John Wesley, the founder of Methodism. That's what she did when she returned from the Congo, even though she was supposed to have some downtime. She reached out to a wide circle of friends, aides, and spiritual advisers to see what could be done for the women of the refugee camps. "She was so mortified by what she heard, she was e-mailing everybody while she was on vacation," said one State Department source.

"She has something more driving her than just power. She has a very strong moral compass that she leans into," said one longtime friend. "So she doesn't wear [religion] on her sleeve, but I think if you had any length of conversation with her as a Methodist, and talked to her about her faith, she would be very insightful."

Hillary ordered Ross and Cohen to go to eastern Congo. They wanted to talk directly with soldiers and police to get a better sense of how corruption contributed to gender-based violence. But embassy officials refused to put them in contact with corrupt soldiers.

Figuring he couldn't come up with a solution unless he understood the root of the problem, Cohen seized on his first opportunity to circumvent the embassy staff. Riding in the midst of a long motorcade, he jumped out of his car, ran up to the front of the line of vehicles, and demanded to get in the front seat of the lead car, which was driven by a security officer. He didn't need an embassy translator because he spoke Swahili. He and Ross ended up talking to enough soldiers to get a sense of why government troops were participating in the systematic sexual abuse of women by local militias.

Soldiers took on extra work as muscle for the militias because the central government's cash payment system invited large-scale embezzlement. The government would send bundles of banknotes to generals, who were supposed to distribute them to their troops. Instead, the generals, who operated more like warlords than high-ranking military officers, pocketed most of the money.

If Ross and Cohen could figure out a way to ensure that soldiers were adequately paid, perhaps the troops would start protecting the women of eastern Congo instead of contracting with their assailants. They devised a plan for the government to pay soldiers through mobile technology, going around the generals. President Joseph Kabila threw his weight behind the idea, and the Congolese parliament passed a law allowing for mobile payments. But the law gave regulatory power to the central bank, which aligned with the generals and refused to set up the program.

Cohen and Ross also tried to create a text warning system for refugee camps that were in danger of being overrun by militias. The idea was to declassify intelligence on the militias' movements from a UN peacekeeping force and send it to the heads of the refugee camps, hospitals, and NGOs in real time. But it never got off the ground for two reasons: Ross and Cohen couldn't guarantee that the information wouldn't be intercepted by one militia or another, and alerting refugee camps about militia movements might create a "presumption of protection" that obligated the peacekeepers to intervene militarily.

Though Ross and Cohen came up empty in the Congo, Hillary never stopped looking for ways to reduce corruption and sexual predation there. At home, she launched an annual conference on ending sexual violence in the region. Both the enduring spirit of the Congolese women she met, and her failure to find a fix, stayed with her for years.

"She hears these stories, not just with her head and her intellect—stuff goes through her heart," explained a close friend who also has visited Congo and shared insights with Hillary. "What we discussed is how resilient the Congolese women are. Hillary's view is 'It's not difficult to go to the Congo. You are bearing witness, and you are giving them respect.' The women in the Congo hang together and give each other courage, and I think Hillary recognized that."

For someone who was considered a Luddite as recently as 2008, Hillary builds her own personal networks in ways that strikingly resemble the modern construction of massive political movements. She often finds ways to connect with people on levels that appeal to them—like a microtargeting program that synthesizes a Web user's friends, interests, and lifestyle, then markets back to them based on those preferences. To the extent that it is calculated, and a lot of it is, people tend to appreciate the effort. A lot of politicians are like that, but most of them aren't as good at it. Bill wins people over with his charm, but Hillary has to work harder to find commonality and develop relationships. As such, Bill's alliances have a more transient nature—his political friends come and go—while Hillary's tend to be more lasting.

One test of this may be the extent to which the new allies she made as secretary, from tech titans to Pentagon brass, stick with her if she runs for president. On the innovation front, her outreach to the top executives at big companies mirrored efforts she made to bring women leaders from around the world into State Department–backed initiatives to aid women and girls, as well as the public-private partnerships she created for the Shanghai Expo and an international "clean cookstoves" program.

In January 2010, a couple of weeks before she delivered a major address on Internet freedom, Hillary invited executives from Twitter, Google, Cisco, and the like to a private dinner at the State Department. I don't claim to be an expert on technology, she told them. I don't claim to be the most familiar person with this, but I know what all of you are doing is important. And I'm in a position where I can sort of help amplify the impact that you guys are having.

"Use me like an app," she said, eliciting a round of laughter.

The catchphrase helped Hillary communicate a nuanced message. She wasn't going to write computer code in the wee hours, but she was all in on both innovation and business. She believed that a partnership between the government and American companies could help both the execution of foreign policy and the expansion of American business opportunities. Moreover, American commerce could be used as both a carrot and a stick in foreign policy; most countries like the idea of a new American plant coming to their country and abhor the idea that the United States would force its businesses to move out.

A few months after the dinner at the State Department, Ross and Cohen led a delegation of five tech company executives to Syria. President Bashar al-Assad had raised the issue of American sanctions with Bill Burns, the undersecretary for political affairs, earlier that year. How could America talk about Internet freedom on the one hand, Assad said, while imposing sanctions that prevented countries like his from acquiring the technology that would allow for the free flow of information? If tech companies were granted waivers from sanctions, Assad figured, they would pour into his country and boost the economy.

At the time, the trip was reported as an effort by the United States to lure Assad away from his alliance with Iran by showing him what the American tech companies could do for his country. But that was a smokescreen; the actual story showed a different, more aggressive play, using tech to show Assad who held all the cards. According to a source familiar with the trip, Ross and Cohen really brought the executives—from Microsoft, Cisco, and Dell, among others—to Damascus to disabuse Assad of the notion that their companies were itching to get into the small Syrian market.

"The truth is they didn't give a shit," the source said. "What was really going on was the companies communicating to Assad that

Syria was no more important to them than Rhode Island. That they were fully supportive of the policies keeping them from doing commercial transactions in Syria." The companies would take their cues from the U.S. government about whether to push for waivers.

Then U.S. officials floated a bigger threat. "What we said, which enraged them," the source said, "is if you don't put in place a certain set of human rights reforms in your country, then not only are we going to deny sanctions waivers for these companies, but we are going to get sanctions waivers for other companies, which, oh, by the way, you don't want in your country."

In the end, after Assad failed to meet a ninety-day deadline for real human rights reforms, the United States quietly gave waivers to some of those companies, including Skype, in an effort to wreak havoc on Assad.

While he was there, Cohen tweeted that he had just enjoyed a world-beater of a Frappuccino at a Syrian university. Cohen, an international adventurer who had once sneaked into Iran, wanted young Syrians to know that the U.S. government was on the ground and interested in them. Senior State Department officials, most notably Steinberg, were furious. America was gently trying to get back in the business of engaging Syria directly, and Cohen's tweet didn't serve that purpose. Ross and Cohen could hear the executioners sharpening their swords again.

But a few days later, after they returned, Hillary sent a strong message to her own staff and the White House about where Ross and Cohen stood in her mind. During a speech to the U.S.-Russia Civil Society Partnership Program, she went off script to talk about her tech force. "I saw Jared Cohen when I came in. I don't know if Alec Ross is here or not. But who else—anyone else here from your team, Jared?" she asked from the podium at the Renaissance Marriott Hotel in downtown Washington. "We have a great team of really dedicated young people—primarily young people—who care deeply about connecting people up."

In case the message hadn't been received, Hillary crystallized it a moment later. "I'm very proud of the work they're doing. They have been everywhere from Mexico to the Democratic Republic of Congo to Syria to Russia and every place in between."

One of the lessons Hillary has drawn from decades on the public stage, for better and for worse, is that public criticism is not, in and of itself, a reason to stop pursuing a policy. Her newfound interest in the power of technology abroad and at home, as well as her reliance on aides who came from outside her inner circle, is a testament to her survivor's willingness to set a new strategy in the aftermath of failure. But they then became a sign of her commitment to following through on the new course, despite bumps in the road.

In four years, she was unwavering in her support of the 21st Century Statecraft concept. She demonstrated fidelity not only to the philosophy but to the people who implemented it, even when that meant pushing back on the White House or on her own inner circle at State. For Hillary, loyalty is a two-way street, and her defense of her innovation team bred the kind of loyalty that can't be purchased from a political consulting firm, and that will follow her out of State. She now has scores of loyalists who are poised to convert their expertise with data, social networking, mobile technology, and movement building into political work. Some of them joined her when she turned to philanthropic work in the spring of 2013. And some of the hundred-plus State employees who became the 21st Century Statecraft crew are certain to provide the building blocks for a next-generation presidential campaign, one that some aides suggest could make Obama's 2012 effort look archaic, if she runs again.

"She had people very, very close to her that are ready to go, as you can imagine," said a close Clinton friend who worked at State. "Those people that are supporters, and people like that, would actually put together a twenty-first-century campaign unlike the 2008 campaign. There's this new cohort of early-twenties to maybe thirty-five-year-old people, and they are just intellectually different than the people that ran [past] campaigns."

As secretary of state, Hillary, like an incumbent president, was able to flex political muscles under the cover of acting in America's interests. She couldn't attend campaign rallies or raise money for Democratic candidates, but the State Department offered countless ways to keep her friends involved, address deficiencies in her operation, and reach out to powerful forces in the business, government, and nonprofit worlds. In addition to the donor contacts for the Shanghai Expo and her focus on closing her own digital divide, Hillary built public-private partnerships around empowering women and girls; she sent corporate leaders around the world to act as ad hoc diplomats and seek new avenues for commerce; and she kept up her relationships with politicians of both parties in advancing State's interests on Capitol Hill. In those ways, she tended to the Clinton political machine.

NINE

Obama Girl

When Obama's top lieutenants met in the Cabinet Room of the West Wing of the White House on September 10, 2009, they came armed with concerns about the president's health care push. Tea Party Summer was in full bloom. Across the country, lawmakers had been under assault at town hall meetings during their August recess, and the rest of the agenda was getting subsumed into the maelstrom. Was it worth all that sacrifice? Not for much of the cabinet. As they settled into nameplated leather chairs around the oval mahogany conference table donated by Richard Nixon, one secretary after another complained that his or her priorities were getting crowded out by a health care debate that was also taking its toll on the Democratic Party's standing.

Hillary watched with concern from her seat directly to the president's right. She had lost her own battle to reform the country's health insurance system in 1994. As secretary of state, she had stayed away from weighing in on the president's domestic agenda with anyone other than Obama and a handful of his closest aides. Even many White House health care staffers weren't aware that she was giving back-channel advice to chief of staff Rahm Emanuel and deputy chief of staff Jim Messina, particularly on how to deal with members of Congress. She knew them, and the political complexities of their districts and states, as well as anyone in the West Wing.

"A member or two may have stopped and asked me what I

thought," Hillary said. "And I thought, 'You need to work with the president and try to get this done.' "

In small-group meetings, and sometimes in her weekly one-on-one sessions with Obama, Hillary played cheerleader. "I'm with you. I'm behind you," she told the president. But she generally was reticent. Any public whiff of engagement on her part could hurt the cause and throw into question whether she was crossing a traditional boundary that kept secretaries of state out of domestic politics. It was Bill Clinton who weighed in publicly on domestic policies. "The president's doing the right thing," he had said in an *Esquire* magazine interview that week. "It is both morally and politically right."

Now, at a critical juncture for Obama, with opposition to his plan playing out on national news broadcasts every night and some Democrats concerned that the issue would doom his presidency, the last thing he needed was petty infighting from his cabinet. Hillary knew this drill: it wasn't just Republicans who had killed her proposal—fellow Democrats had also left their fingerprints at the scene of the crime. With her party in control of the White House, the Senate, and the House for the first time since her health care push, she knew just how much was at stake in keeping Democrats, including the president's cabinet, focused on the task. "She used an anecdote or some sort of flashback to when she was first lady" to set up the thrust of her message, said one Obama aide who was present.

Then taking command of the room, she told her colleagues, as her husband had told *Esquire,* that it was the right thing to do. "This is the time to do it," she said. "We're all in it. Everyone in the room knows how important this is." The bitching and moaning ceased. It was a pivotal, if underappreciated, moment in the health care reform effort.

At the end of the meeting, Obama spoke briefly to reporters. "The time is right, and we are going to move aggressively to get this done," he said. "And every member of this cabinet is invested." That hadn't been true at the start of the meeting, but Hillary's sales job had been just what Obama needed to assuage the doubters.

"I thought, Look, the president had more support in Congress than my husband did back in '93, '94, so he could put together a majority," Hillary said. "If the Republicans stonewalled, which they were beginning to show they would, despite his best efforts, he could still put a package on the floor and get it passed in both houses, which doesn't come along every first term of a president."

"I believed strongly," she said, "that the president needed to forge ahead."

Her private efforts on behalf of the health care law—working with Emanuel and Messina behind the scenes, encouraging Obama and advising him on strategy, and now speaking up on his behalf at a key cabinet meeting—helped strengthen her bond with Obama. For all of his aides' suspicions, she was proving to be a loyal ally during the tumultuous first year of the Obama administration.

But Hillary felt that in some instances, the White House wasn't reciprocating on her priorities. In a rare break, she chided the president in the summer of 2009 for failing to move forward on a nominee to head the U.S. Agency for International Development, which fell under State. "The clearance and vetting process is a nightmare," she said at a town hall meeting with USAID staff. "It is frustrating beyond words. I pushed very hard last week when I knew I was coming here to get permission from the White House to be able to tell you that help is on the way and someone will be nominated shortly, and I was unable—it just was—the message that came back: 'We're not ready.'" Still, in general terms, the tension over personnel dissipated as jobs were filled, reducing the number of available flashpoints between Hillary's circle and Obama's.

Bill complemented her efforts by putting his shoulder into the health care reform push, both in his public comments and behind closed doors. In November, while Hillary was on a thirteen-day trip to Europe and Asia, he showed up at a private lunch meeting of Senate Democrats to urge them to put their differences aside and help Obama win on the centerpiece of his domestic agenda. As he chatted with reporters afterward, his cell phone rang. "It's my secretary of state calling," he said, offering a reminder of who he was acting as a surrogate for on his trip to Capitol Hill. A few hours later Obama finally announced the nominee to run USAID, giving Hillary what she had been seeking for months.

The first time she saw Obama after Congress passed the health care law months later, it was in the Situation Room. She told him she was proud of him, and she was uniquely positioned to affirm him. As first lady, as senator, as a candidate for president, and then as a shadow domestic policy adviser to the president and his aides, Hillary had poured so much of herself and her reputation into trying to provide access to health insurance for all Americans. It was the domestic issue with which she was most identified, and it was Obama who had muscled it across the finish line. They threw their arms around each other, and a photographer snapped a shot of the embrace. The image held such symbolic appeal in the White House that officials hung the framed picture on a wall near the Oval Office. Though such photos are routinely rotated every few weeks, the picture stayed in its spot for months.

It might have been a bittersweet conclusion for Hillary. After all, she'd put a lot of her mind, heart, and soul into health care reform but hadn't been part of the domestic policy team that put it into law. Still, Obama's victory, using a model that looked like her proposal from the 2008 primary campaign, left her satisfied if perhaps a touch wistful. "His political position in the Congress was stronger than the one that Bill had after he was elected," she said. "We—and Bill—had already put so much on the table with the deficit reduction, which passed with not a single Republican vote in either house, that was a huge lift. And then he also put a lot on them for the crime bill, and many members lost their seats because of the NRA. So, he didn't have the numbers. And he'd also really pushed them hard already. The stars aligned for President Obama and he took advantage of that. So I was thrilled about it."

Health care drew Obama and Hillary closer, but the big moment in their relationship, according to sources on both sides, came in December 2009, when they traveled to a UN-sponsored international climate summit in Copenhagen. The basic goal of the summit was to reduce greenhouse gas emissions worldwide, with special attention to making sure that "developed" countries agreed to specific limitations on their emissions and that "developing" countries could restrict emissions without hurting economic growth.

On the rare international trips they took together, Hillary made every effort to stand in his shadow, mirroring the deferential posture she struck at home. Despite her international celebrity, she played the role of the ideal staffer—well briefed enough to answer his questions, and well disciplined enough to take his directions. Humility may have been an acquired trait for Hillary, but she wore it well as Obama's diplomat. "In the first year, she was self-consciously deferential and wanted to debunk all the skepticism and doubt that she could be a team player," said a senior career official at State.

Hillary had a lot of personal capital riding on the Copenhagen summit because she had urged Obama to attend. But it was quickly turning into a disaster. It was poorly organized, and there didn't seem to be much hope for achieving a real deal among the key nations. At one point, American officials became aware that China was holding a secret multilateral meeting on the sidelines with Brazil, South Africa, and India—a meeting to which Obama had not been invited. He wanted to crash the party.

"Four against one," one official warned the president.

"No problem," he said, telling Clinton, "We're going in now."

"Absolutely," she said. "Let's go."

With Hillary as his wingman, Obama barged into the meeting, demanding to talk to the leaders of the four countries. Each of the countries had been dodging the United States at all levels—from Obama and Clinton on down—and this was a chance to address them all at once. The uninvited U.S. delegation of two caused quite a stir when they busted in.

"The Chinese diplomatic officer, he's really losing his shit in Chinese," said one Hillary aide who was briefed afterward.

"I don't know what he's saying, but I don't think it's 'Glad to see you guys,'" Obama joked to Hillary.

Ultimately they hammered out a watered-down, nonbinding

agreement that was not adopted by the full conference. The Americans proclaimed victory, but they knew they hadn't won much. What Obama and Hillary had gained, however, was a common appreciation for the difficulties of the nitty-gritty of diplomacy and the sense that they might actually enjoy each other's company. "We had fun in Copenhagen because we stormed the secret meeting," Hillary said.

"It was the two of them all day, improvising together, meeting to meeting," said a senior White House official. "That was the first time we saw them have to—no staff—just figure out 'What are we doing? What's our play? What are you going to say to X leader? What do I say here?' And they just had to improvise together for a full day in the most kind of chaotic environment possible, and that's when I started to see them kind of click in terms of just working more naturally together, so it wasn't this kind of formal relationship." Or as another White House aide put it, "They were real buddies after that."

One of Hillary's closest aides agreed that Copenhagen was a turning point. "They both basically walked out of that experience the same way, like 'You know what, this is really hard because there's a lot of voices out there in the world with their own ideas, and American leadership is herding cats. It's tough. It's a tough slog,' " the aide said. "They both had the same kind of sensibility about what it was going to take for us to succeed on the foreign policy front coming out of that experience. And I think it made a big difference in terms of the nature of their conversation from that point on."

They had already been working together for months on the hard question of committing more troops in Afghanistan and, in reaching a policy both could live with, had grown closer.

Just before Copenhagen, the Clarus Research Group released a poll of voters who described themselves as "news watchers." It found that 51 percent approved of the job Obama was doing, while Hillary's rating was 75 percent. Not only were her numbers with independents (65 percent) and Republicans (57 percent) better than Obama's, but so was her standing among Democrats (96 percent approval to Obama's 93 percent). It wasn't the first poll to show Hillary's numbers above Obama's but the contrast was stark, particularly at a time when Washington elites had concluded she had been pushed to the sidelines. After the heady days of his transition and inaugural celebration, Obama had been dragged back to earth by a series of controversial public fights over his stimulus, health care, and climate change plans, while any work Hillary did on domestic issues was completely behind the curtain. Gallup, which pegged Obama's approval at 49 percent among a broader set of Americans in the same time window as Clarus, had assessed it at 68 percent when he took office eleven months earlier. It didn't take a high-priced political consultant to figure out that by the end of their first year in office, Hillary Clinton's brand had become considerably stronger than Obama's.

Toward the end of 2009, she had begun to telegraph that she didn't expect to serve in Obama's administration for eight years if he won a second term. "Please," she had said when Glenn Kessler of the *Washington Post* asked her about it. "I will be so old." In January 2010 she told Tavis Smiley that "the whole eight" would "be very challenging" and, beginning to laugh, added, "I will be very happy to pass it on to someone else." She also told Smiley that she was "absolutely not interested" in running for president again.

But her approval ratings—and the fact that she didn't see herself as an Obama lifer—contributed to speculation in late 2009 and early 2010 that she might run a primary against the sitting president. Conservatives in particular liked to raise the prospect, since its mere discussion contributed to the idea that Obama was weak. Though it was fodder for political junkies and twenty-four-hour cable news programs, there was never any evidence that Hillary gave a thought to running against Obama.

It was really the second year of the Obama presidency in which Hillary's loyalty mattered. In the first year, she had just lost an election to him, and his star was bigger than hers. But by the beginning of the second year, they had essentially traded places in terms of public esteem. If anyone was familiar with the mercurial nature of public opinion and with the difficulty a president can have in keeping his lieutenants lined up behind his agenda when he's losing popularity, it was Hillary. She had watched Bill grapple with the same vagaries. Over the course of 2010, she and her staff threw themselves into delivering on Obama's agenda on a series of complex issues, from Haiti to the New START nuclear-arms-reduction treaty with Russia to the imposition of sanctions aimed at bringing Iran to heel.

While Obama and Hillary had grown closer in Copenhagen, their two staffs—along with Bill Clinton—forged stronger bonds in January 2010, when an earthquake measuring 7.0 on the Richter scale ripped through the heart of Port-au-Prince, Haiti, killing 316,000 people, injuring 300,000 more, and displacing 1.3 million. Cheryl Mills was the State Department's point person on Haiti and took charge of the recovery and relief effort, and the innovation team devised a text donation program for the Red Cross that raised $40 million in ten-dollar increments. It was a big moment for the fledgling 21st Century Statecraft crew because it demonstrated for Hillary and Mills the transformational power of technology for the poorer, less attended parts of the world that they cared so much about. "There was this kind of emotional connection to the work," said one State Department official.

Mills was on the phone around the clock, working with Haitian officials on every detail. To this day, she remembers which flights carried which orphans to adoptive parents in the United States, a product of poring over lists to figure out how to expedite paperwork for kids whose records had been destroyed or lost in the rubble along with their orphanages and Haitian government facilities. She and McDonough made sure that all the players on the president's national security team were on the same page in terms of search and recovery, military flights, and disaster aid.

In addition to directing the overall federal response, Obama summoned presidents Clinton and George W. Bush to the White House to announce a relief organization modeled after the fund established by Clinton and George H. W. Bush in the wake of Hurricane Katrina. As Clinton and George W. Bush waited for Obama in the Cabinet Room, they joked about being like brothers. After all,

Clinton and Bush are about the same age, and they grew much closer as a result of Clinton's partnership with the elder Bush.

Even their wives, who were not present for this meeting, had grown closer through a shared interest in two issues: empowering women and girls around the world and pressuring the Burmese military junta into adopting democratic reforms. The two former first ladies spoke privately with each other about Burma on more than one occasion, and as a courtesy, Hillary dispatched Kurt Campbell, the assistant secretary of state for the region, to give Laura Bush periodic briefings on developments in the Southeast Asian nation. The Bush and Clinton clans had found their comfort zone, a fact underscored by the demonstration of bonhomie by George W. Bush and Bill in the Cabinet Room, but Bill and Obama still hadn't hit that sweet spot.

The atmosphere changed when Obama walked into the room. Here was the new president, with his two immediate predecessors, one of whom he had trashed as the architect of a savaged economy on a daily basis and the other who had campaigned against him for months. It was clear, according to one observer, that while the Clinton-Obama relationship was getting better publicly, it was still awkward behind closed doors. "It was friendly but slightly stiff," the source said.

The Hall of Famer and the Rookie of the Year were still sizing each other up, trying to strike a delicate balance in which each man gained the most and lost the least from partnering on politics and policy. Sometimes their interests and beliefs brought the two presidents together; at other times, they drove them apart. More than any past president in memory, Bill remained wholly invested in electoral politics, a dynamic that surely owed both to the possibility that Hillary would run again and to Bill's own love of the game. Though he had two stents inserted at New York Presbyterian Hospital after feeling chest pain a few days before Valentine's Day, Bill went back to work within a week. He was eager to show that he was in fighting shape, and by April, with the midterm elections looming and analysts predicting that Republicans had a shot at taking control of the House and Senate, he began filling his political calendar. He cut radio ads to help Senator Blanche Lincoln of Arkansas fend off a primary challenge from Lieutenant Governor Bill Halter; showed up in western Pennsylvania to campaign for Mark Critz in a special election to fill the late representative Jack Murtha's seat; and even auctioned off a little bit of his time to help cut into Hillary's debt. At that point, she had whittled it down below $1 million, but its presence still bothered her.

At times Bill went head-to-head with Obama, proving that there were still defined Clinton and Obama wings of the Democratic Party. In Colorado, Bill backed Andrew Romanoff, a state legislator who had been loyal to Hillary, against Obama's candidate, Senator Michael Bennet, who had been appointed to succeed Interior Secretary Ken Salazar the year before. Obama's aides had tried and failed to push Romanoff out of the race with the offer of a low-level administration job, much like an effort they had undertaken—through Bill—to get Joe Sestak to bail in Pennsylvania. Obama recorded a message for Bennet, and Romanoff appealed to Clinton to counter it. Guy Cecil, a senior aide on Hillary's campaign who had become Bennet's chief of staff, didn't find out that the former president was going to weigh in until an hour before Colorado voters started getting phone calls with Bill's recorded voice on the other end. Obama won the proxy war, a fact that Cecil, who enjoys a strong relationship with the Clintons, wouldn't let Bill forget. "Your record's not perfect anymore," Cecil teased when Bill came out to do a general-election event for Bennet.

But with the 2010 primary season ending, Obama's political team was eager to get Bill out on the hustings for Democratic candidates. Patrick Gaspard, the head of Obama's office of political affairs, asked Doug Band to meet in midsummer to map out a strategy for using Bill to assist Democrats, particularly in highly competitive states and districts where an Obama visit might backfire. The magic of Bill Clinton on the campaign trail, according to both Clinton and Obama loyalists, is that he can "go anywhere." While Obama had done just fine with Democratic voters, he couldn't do much to help junior House Democrats who needed independents and some Republicans to win their districts. Bill had the capacity to sway middle-of-the-road voters and rally the party base.

Though it might have bruised their egos a little bit to admit the truth, each man was stronger when partnered with the other. For both, the pull of self-preservation was strong. Bill had inflicted enormous damage on himself during the 2008 primary, and joining forces with Obama was the best and fastest way to heal his image. As for Obama, the remainder of his first-term agenda depended on maintaining majorities in the House and the Senate. To the extent that Bill could help with that goal, it was worth bringing him back into the fold. They still weren't buddies, not in the way that Obama and Hillary were becoming closer personally, but mutual interest served as an adherent. And the budding friendship between Hillary and Obama couldn't help but reinforce Bill's relationship with Obama. The same dynamic replicated down the ranks at the White House and State, with aides reflecting the warmer rapport enjoyed by their bosses.

Most dead-end loyalists never achieved a full rapprochement, but by the second year of the Obama presidency, petty infighting about suspected leaks to the press and personnel matters diminished significantly. Obama himself drove part of that dynamic. After he fired the top commander in Afghanistan, General Stanley McChrystal, for comments made in a *Rolling Stone* article called "The Runaway General," Obama gathered his national security team in the Oval Office for a lecture. On the same day, the *New York Times* had reported the story of the cable, written by national security adviser Jim Jones and shared with a wide circle, suggesting that Holbrooke would soon be out of a job—a missive that, along with other slights, like efforts to exclude him from important meetings, undercut Holbrooke's standing in Afghanistan and Pakistan.

"The president said he didn't want to see pettiness, that this was not about personalities or reputations. It's about our men and women in uniform and about serving our country," a source told Lloyd Grove of the *Daily Beast*. Holbrooke remained a point of contention

The Women of Hillaryland in 2008

Front row:

Patti Solis Doyle, Hillary's onetime campaign manager who stepped
down from the post in the middle of the primary, and Ann Lewis.

Second row:

Neera Tanden, who would later join the Obama campaign; Melanne
Verveer, a longtime aide who would head up women's and girls' issues
at State; Capricia Marshall, a longtime Hillary aide who would become
chief of protocol; Minyon Moore; and Huma Abedin, one of her closest
aides and so-called second daughter.

Back row:

Cheryl Mills, a close aide to both Clintons who would go on to become
Hillary's chief of staff at the State Department; Tamera Luzzatto,
Hillary's Senate chief of staff; Mandy Grunwald; and Lissa Muscatine.

(Melina Mara, The Washington Post/Getty Images)

President Obama, Vice President Joe Biden, and Hillary Clinton share a laugh after she dropped her briefing papers on the Oval Office floor. *(White House photo/Pete Souza)*

President Obama and former president Bill Clinton speak outside the White House briefing room before addressing reporters in December 2010. *(White House photo/ Pete Souza)*

President Obama sits beside Secretary of State Hillary Clinton and Secretary of Defense Robert Gates in a cabinet meeting in February 2011. Clinton formed an alliance and friendship with Gates during her time at State. *(Mark Wilson/Getty Images)*

State Department aides Alec Ross and Jared Cohen helped Hillary ramp up her online efforts at the State Department. Many observers say technology was a major problem for Hillary during the 2008 campaign and one of the biggest lessons she learned in the campaign's aftermath. *(Michele Asselin/Contour/Getty Images)*

President Obama and Hillary Clinton pose for a photograph in November 2012 with Aung San Suu Kyi and her staff at the residence in Rangoon, Burma, where she had been detained for fifteen years.
(White House photo/Pete Souza)

Hillary Clinton talks to her speechwriter Dan Schwerin in Islamabad, Pakistan, in October 2011. She is also joined by top aides Huma Abedin, Toria Nuland, and Philippe Reines, along with Cameron Phelps Munter (*left of Schwerin*), the ambassador to Pakistan, and Ambassador Marc Grossman (*seated*), the special representative to Afghanistan and Pakistan. (*Diana Walker HC/Contour/Getty Images*)

Hillary Clinton watches the Osama bin Laden raid in the West Wing. The now famous photograph was particularly striking, observers said, because of Clinton's expression. Hillary described the time as "thirty-eight of the most intense moments." She later explained that she did not know what she, Obama, Biden, and other top officials were looking at when the photograph was taken. She also chalked up her expressive hand gesture to "my preventing one of my early spring allergic coughs. So it may have no great meaning whatsoever." (*White House photo/Pete Souza*)

President Obama receives a congratulatory hug from Hillary Clinton the day after the House passed the Affordable Care Act. Clinton, who had pushed for health care reform when her husband was president, supported Obama's insistence that the law be passed and spoke up on the president's behalf during a cabinet meeting. *(White House photo/Pete Souza)*

Hillary Clinton traveled to 112 countries, including this trip to the Philippines in 2009, during her time as secretary of state—more than any of her predecessors. At a cabinet meeting early in his first term, Obama looked at his tireless secretary of state and decided to make an example of her. She was working around the clock, flying around the world, and it showed. "It's a marathon, not a sprint," Obama said. *(Nick Merrill)*

Hillary Clinton, Defense Secretary Leon Panetta, and National Security Adviser Tom Donilon listen as President Obama and NATO Secretary General Anders Fogh Rasmussen speak at a NATO summit in Chicago in May 2012. *(White House photo/Pete Souza)*

Hillary Clinton watches her husband, former president Bill Clinton, deliver his speech at the Democratic National Convention. Hillary watched the speech from East Timor, after an aide downloaded the video. *(Nick Merrill)*

Hillary Clinton received a helmet from her staff upon her return to the State Department in January 2013 after a month-long illness. Clinton, who suffered from a stomach virus and later a concussion, also received a jersey with the number 112 on it. It referred to the number of countries she had visited as secretary of state. (*Nick Merrill*)

Hillary Clinton poses with first ladies Michelle Obama, Laura Bush, Barbara Bush, and Rosalynn Carter at the dedication of the Bush Presidential Library in April 2013. (*White House photo/Lawrence Jackson*)

between the White House and State, but as the rest of the respective staffs began to see threats as common—from international crises to news stories about the state of the Obama-Hillary relationship—Obama's aides and Hillary's developed respect for each other's abilities. "You are in the same foxhole," explained one of Obama's aides. "You build a bond with people that way, you just do."

The most surprising integration of the two camps came in the form of Capricia Marshall. It didn't take her long to become part of the furniture in the administration. "I've never been more wrong about anyone in my life," Dan Pfeiffer, who had tried to block her nomination, later told her. At a White House state dinner in the spring of 2010, Marshall led the Obamas out the door of the north portico to meet the Mexican president. As the first couple walked down a red carpet, Marshall, clad in a formfitting pink dress, gracefully peeled off onto a white marble landing.

As she reached the top of a small flight of stairs, her skinny Manolo heel caught. "Oh my God," she thought, "I'm going down!" The P90X routine paid off, however, keeping her core balanced. Rather than falling flat on her face, she bounced onto her backside and quickly got back to her feet, like an Olympic gymnast who had missed her dismount.

"Don't take that picture," the first lady admonished nearby photographers. "Don't take that picture," the president repeated, waving his finger, as the cameras audibly snapped in the background.

Michelle Obama made a last-ditch appeal for Marshall: "Don't print that picture."

It was too late. The pictures—and a full video—were captured for posterity and YouTube.

Marshall flashed a double thumbs-up, a fitting symbol of her rebound from the day Obama's aides had all put their thumbs down on her nomination.

At the next state dinner, the president teased Marshall as she waited to lead the Obamas out to meet a foreign leader. Standing directly behind her and adopting the hushed tone of a golf announcer, the president offered up a play-by-play.

"We are getting close," he said playfully. "Will she stay up or will she go down?"

Marshall had made it far enough into Obama's circle that he felt comfortable giving her a hard time. Still, the routine didn't impress Michelle Obama much.

"Oh, shut up, Barack! Stop it," she said. "Stop teasing her."

While Michelle Obama was defending Capricia Marshall from the president's gentle ribbing, Hillary Clinton was going to bat for Barack Obama on Capitol Hill. In June she invited Howard Berman and Chris Dodd up to a conference room on the seventh floor of the State Department to discuss a pending bill intended to punish Iran by sanctioning foreign companies that did business in the petroleum and banking sectors there. The basic concept was to force other countries to pull out of Iran and thus cripple its economy, which might persuade the Iranians to negotiate an end to their pursuit of nuclear weapons in exchange for the removal of sanctions.

Berman, a bespectacled veteran House Democrat with half a head's worth of curly white hair, was the chairman of the House Foreign Affairs Committee and as good a friend of the pro-Israel lobby as anyone on Capitol Hill. Dodd, the Senate Banking Committee chairman, had written a book about the letters that his father, Thomas Dodd, had written home when he prosecuted Nazi war criminals in Nuremberg after World War II. There was no question where they stood on Israel's mortal enemy, Iran. Each man had passed a version of a bill called the Comprehensive Iran Sanctions and Divestment Act, or CISADA, through his respective chamber with little or no opposition. Berman and Dodd had written slightly different bills, and they had had to convene a conference committee of House and Senate members to sort out their differences and send the bill to the president for his signature or veto. But in reality, the work of the conference committee was now being done by Hillary, Berman, and Dodd on the seventh floor because the White House had serious concerns about the consequences of the congressional approach; and with Democrats in control of both chambers and the presidency, Berman and Dodd wanted to find a path that would avoid an ugly showdown between the White House and Congress.

. For the most part, members of Congress always wanted to hit Iran with the biggest hammer available. Over the years, the United States had imposed every unilateral sanction imaginable on the Iranians—to little effect. Now the idea was to punish them further by sanctioning foreign entities if they did business with the regime. If all went well, the Iranian economy would plunge, and that could bring about the demise of the existing government or at least bring the Iranians to the table.

That would be all well and good if other countries also chose to stop doing business in Iran rather than face American sanctions. But the danger was that the other countries, particularly Russia, China, and Brazil, would decide it was better to suffer American sanctions and keep doing business with Iran. Aside from the question of which choice was economically better for each country, no leader would want to appear weak to his or her people by buckling to American demands.

In conjunction with the White House and the Treasury Department, Hillary was looking for a new approach that could provide incentives for foreign companies, some of which were state-run, to join in isolating Iran. One such angle, which flummoxed Iran hawks, was a State Department proposal to let companies evade sanctions by demonstrating that they were on a serious and irreversible path toward getting out of Iran. That way companies that wanted to cooperate with the United States wouldn't get hit with sanctions just because it took them a little bit of time to disentangle themselves from complex business relationships. While it sounded to many in Congress like the administration wanted to let bad actors off the hook, the top sanctions analysts in the executive branch thought that it was a creative way to produce a better outcome.

Nuance on Iran had never before been a specialty of Hillary's. As a senator from heavily pro-Israel New York, she had been among the hard-liners. In 2006, as she ran for reelection to the Senate and geared up for a presidential bid, she had blasted the Bush administration for "downplaying the threat." But as secretary of state, she worked for an administration that had concerns about the practical consequences of blunt-force sanctions. What her new perch taught her—or made it easier for her to accept—was that American efforts to coerce other countries into imposing sanctions might cause a backlash that ultimately hindered progress.

For months, her former congressional colleagues commented on her change of opinion. But Hillary told them it was natural that her perspective now differed from theirs. "You have a different position," she would say. "You work in a different place." The line allowed her to preserve some credibility as a hawk on Iran while suggesting to members of Congress that they might not hold the only reasonable point of view about the most effective way of putting pressure on the regime.

"She was always for turning up the heat on Iran," said a source who worked on Capitol Hill and at the State Department. "I think she just took a more nuanced view of it when she got [to State], which is that you get the Russians, the Indians, the Turks, the Europeans, to stop transacting business where that supports the petroleum sector in Iran, and you can't do that with a sledgehammer. You've got to do that through the careful art of diplomacy. If we just drive this kind of truck into the negotiations and say 'This is what we're going to do, take it or leave it,' they will leave it."

Despite pressure from hard-liners to move more quickly, Berman and Dodd already had bowed to an administration request to wait for the United Nations to impose its own sanctions before producing a final bill. On June 9 the UN Security Council voted 12–2, with Lebanon abstaining, in favor of a sanctions measure. The State Department and UN ambassador Susan Rice had assured Russia and China that if they cooperated in limiting Iran's weapons capabilities, any follow-on American law would give plenty of opportunity to companies in their countries to avoid U.S. sanctions. Now, two days later, Hillary had to make good on that promise by getting

Congress to agree to special waivers before voting for a final bill. Dodd, who had his hands full with the eponymous Dodd-Frank Wall Street reform bill, had mostly let Berman, an expert on foreign policy, take the lead, interjecting himself as a moderator between Berman and the administration when necessary over the course of more than a year of deliberations.

All sides had been in close contact with AIPAC, the American Israel Public Affairs Committee, which was the driving outside force behind the legislation. In general, members of Congress were eager to put the scalps of outlaw companies on the wall to impress pro-Israel voters and donors at home, and they were reluctant to do anything to soften the legislation. Berman had been "holding back AIPAC," according to one congressional source. The worst-case scenario for Obama would be to look like he was at odds with a nearly unanimous Congress on an issue affecting Israel in advance of a reelection effort in which he would need the support of pro-Israel donors and voters.

While the White House believed that its approach would likely be more effective in isolating Iran and forcing its leaders to the negotiating table, more discussion of provisions that could be interpreted as lenient presented a political risk. But Hillary and her aides took that risk. "I believed very strongly, as did she, that at the end of the day, it did not matter how far unilateral sanctions [went] if we didn't have strong international cooperation, because on an economic level and a political level, the thing that was going to make the biggest difference was for Iran to feel that it had no champions, no place to turn, no out," said Deputy Secretary Jim Steinberg, who has been credited with devising the "special rule" that let cooperating companies avoid sanctions. "This was a conversation that I was deeply involved in with the Hill and with outside groups like AIPAC—and with others—to demonstrate to them we were serious, that we were not just looking for excuses to let others off the hook."

Typically, House-Senate conference committees are conducted in the Capitol. Sometimes the administration has representatives observing the meeting with no official role. But in this case, Hillary became the de facto chairwoman of the conference committee, running the meeting from her own conference room with the two senior lawmakers responsible for writing the bill. The scene might have been a reminder that the separation of powers among branches of government is far narrower when a single party controls the White House and both chambers of Congress. Berman and Dodd were amenable to finding some kind of accommodation because Obama was a president from their own party and could benefit politically from signing an Iran sanctions bill. But there had been a total of twelve votes against the House and Senate versions of the bill in its first go-round, meaning the administration had little leverage to threaten to veto the bill or force changes like the adoption of a waiver for companies that promised to play nice.

For two Democrats who had been in Washington for so long—Hillary since 1993 and Berman since 1983—they hadn't spent much time together, apart from a congressional delegation trip to Kiev and Munich in 2004 and a few courtesy calls during her first year at State. Their lack of familiarity was one of the reasons Berman had felt comfortable endorsing Obama in 2008. For the moment, Hillary put that slight aside and dug into the policy at hand. Berman was struck by her command of the substance. It was uncanny, he thought, how well Hillary had digested the subject matter, given that she clearly couldn't have spent as much time on it as he had. "It was incredibly complicated. The sanctions aren't on Iran—they're on entities doing business with Iran," he said, ticking off the permutations of sanctions that she had nailed down. "At least on the major ones, she had learned them. She drilled down enough."

The negotiations came down to the wording of two provisions that State wanted Berman and Dodd to add to the final measure. One was called the "closely cooperating country exemption," which closed the loop on the assurances the administration had given to Russia and China in advance of the UN sanctions vote and clarified that the president could waive sanctions against a company if its home country was actively working to stop Iran from building its military capabilities. Technically, the president could waive the sanctions anyway, if he determined that it was in the national security interests of the United States to do so, but the language was something Hillary and Susan Rice could point to in discussions with the Russians and Chinese. The second provision, the "special rule," created the complex waiver authority in which the president could temporarily waive sanctions against a foreign company if the company could demonstrate that it was on a path to divest from Iran. As the bill was originally written, there was no incentive for a company with a lot of business interests in Iran to begin divesting.

Both provisions were added to the bill, with each side conceding ground on the particulars of the wording. Obama signed the legislation on July 1, 2010, and later used it as evidence of his support for Israel in his reelection campaign. His opponents cited waivers granted under the last-minute provisions as evidence that he wasn't tough enough on Iran—a line of argument that frustrated administration officials to no end because the waivers were a sign that the sanctions law had actually persuaded foreign companies to begin breaking ties with Iran. Hillary had taken up for Obama and cut a deal that preserved both his Iran policy and his ability to present himself as tough enough to pro-Israel voters.

In that way, she won on the substance. But by joking about how her new job gave her a new view on the issue, she also managed to convince her former colleagues that she was doing her duty more than her wont, reducing the political risk of her new position. "Hillary Clinton as a senator was a person I really liked because she was tough on Iran. Hillary Clinton as secretary of state had to do the bidding of the Obama administration," Republican representative Ileana Ros-Lehtinen, the former chairwoman of the House Foreign Affairs Committee, said. "You may think I'm excusing her, but I think in her heart of hearts she would have liked to have been as tough on Iran as possible."

The Iran sanctions deal came together just as Hillary was beginning to focus on two major unions in her personal life, the weddings of her daughter, Chelsea, and of Huma, whom the Clintons often referred to as being like a second daughter. Like many of the people closest to Hillary, Huma exudes one particular characteristic that is also central to Hillary's persona. Philippe Reines shares with Hillary an ability to anticipate political peril and a desire to be on the inside of the joke. Jake Sullivan is a government nerd, facile with both policy and the building of power within a bureaucracy. Cheryl Mills is the lawyer who ferociously represents her client's interests. Capricia Marshall breaks down interpersonal barriers by making other people comfortable. With Huma, the reflection of Hillary's own character can be seen in the perfection of the role of superstaffer. Hillary played that part for Obama on trips abroad, and for Bill as his right-hand political and policy adviser throughout his career in public life.

Whatever Hillary needed, Huma got it—often before Hillary had thought to ask for it. At the White House in the late 1990s, in the Senate, on the campaign trail, and in Hillary's first two years at State, Huma was seldom more than a couple of feet away from her boss and mentor. When iconic photos of Hillary were taken, Huma was usually just off camera, holding as many as three BlackBerry devices at once. Chelsea Clinton has said that Huma, less than four years her senior, is like a sister to her.

During the 2008 presidential campaign, Hillary intervened to help Brooklyn congressman Anthony Weiner secure his first date with Huma. As that relationship grew more serious, Huma again followed in Hillary's footsteps by falling for a politician. On June 30 the Clintons welcomed several hundred guests to their home for an engagement party for the young political power couple. "It was love at first sight," Hillary said, pausing for the punch line, "for Anthony."

Weiner choked up while delivering his own remarks, expressing his appreciation for his bride-to-be and his hosts. Bill, embracing Chelsea, said that if he'd had a second daughter, it would be Huma. It was a celebration, but there was an ominous undertone, according to one attendee. "Huma seemed like this aloof woman," the source said. "It was like 'how much Anthony loves Huma' and then it was like 'Anthony loves Huma.'"

Hillary often shows interest in the love lives of her many aides and advisers, including one who traveled with her frequently during the 2008 primary. "I was engaged at the time, and she was so interested in our wedding planning process," the aide said. "I was on this major diet at the time, and she was constantly concerned that I have diet-friendly food on the plane. She was really into it." Huma was much closer to the Clintons than the average aide, and they became heavily invested in the details of her wedding.

Bill presided over the ceremony on July 10, 2010, at Oheka Castle, a sprawling estate situated at the highest point on Long Island. He joked that their religious differences (Weiner comes from a Jewish family and Abedin from a Muslim family) were nothing compared with the difficulty of marrying a politician. It's "easy to distrust them, whatever their religion," he said. Oscar de la Renta, a friend of the Clintons—and of Huma—designed her dress, a flowing, cap-sleeved number embroidered in gold. Weiner, nearly ten years her senior, professed that he was "over the moon" about Huma.

The Weiner-Abedin nuptials whetted the public appetite for Chelsea's very private American version of a British royal wedding three weeks later, on July 31. For months, long before the actual wedding, reports surfaced that Chelsea was on the verge of tying the knot, which annoyed the Clintons to no end. "The press thought it was happening a year earlier than it did, when she wasn't even engaged, and they wouldn't accept it when the mother of the bride said it wasn't happening," griped one aide to Hillary. "One person, a wire reporter, was told by his editor, 'She's not a good enough source.'"

The last business call Hillary made before Chelsea's wedding was to Senator Johnny Isakson, a Georgia Republican and a pivotal player in the New START nuclear arms pact with Russia that was close to Obama's heart. Isakson had taken the text of the

complicated treaty up to his mountain home over the July 4 weekend, and sitting by the boathouse, with his grandchildren playing
nearby, he had gone through it page by excruciating page, scribbling
notes in the margin. Over the next few weeks, Isakson peppered
State Department officials with specific technical questions and
even spoke to Hillary repeatedly about it. With a committee vote
pending after the August recess, Hillary dialed up Isakson one last
time before Chelsea's wedding just to make sure he was getting all
the answers he needed.

It's not that she worried about the Foreign Relations Committee approving the treaty, thereby clearing it for consideration on the
floor. Because Democrats held 59 of the 100 seats in the Senate, and
thus a majority on the committee, the outcome of the panel vote
was a foregone conclusion. But on the floor, treaties require a two-
thirds vote of the Senate—at least 67 of 100—for ratification. So the
votes of Republicans on the committee would be an important indication, both to Democratic leaders in the Senate and to rank-and-
file Republicans who didn't serve on the committee, of the treaty's
viability on the floor. Indiana senator Richard Lugar, the top Republican on the committee, had worked on Russian arms treaties with
everyone from Ronald Reagan to Obama, and he was considered
more or less a mortal lock to vote yes in committee. For a variety of
reasons, most notably their openness to reason and to the nuclear
power industries in their home states, Hillary had targeted Isakson
and Tennessee Republican Bob Corker as possible supporters early
on in the process.

As in the Iran sanctions debate, Hillary became the point of
the administration's spear on Capitol Hill. In this case, rather than
playing defense with hawkish Democrats, she went on offense to
persuade a handful of Republicans that the dovish-sounding arms-
reduction treaty was in the national security interests of the United
States. She knew her way around the Hill as well as anyone in the
administration, save Vice President Joe Biden, and she understood
that it would take a lot of time and effort to get senators comfortable
with both the substance and the politics of the treaty.

"She started months before anyone else," said one official familiar with the administration's effort. Hillary focused most intently
on Isakson and Corker. Each had a home-state interest in nuclear
power, but each also had a political interest in denying Obama. As
a politician herself, she knew she had to assure them that the treaty
was not only the right thing to do but politically sustainable. That
meant making sure they could defend it back home.

But by May that was becoming increasingly difficult as conservatives, led by Senator Jim DeMint (R-S.C.), demanded that the
White House turn over a set of documents known as the "negotiating record" of U.S. talks with Russia. The dossier contained all the
offers, counteroffers, instructions, and side talks that had gone into
creating the treaty. Without the record, the conservatives argued,
how could they know that the Russians hadn't interpreted certain
provisions—particularly those relating to missile defense—one way
while the Americans read them another way?

The clash over the negotiating record created a bind for Corker
and Isakson, who were leaning toward voting for the treaty but
would have trouble justifying those votes if conservatives were saying publicly that they were voting without having all the information
provided by the negotiating record—that they were blindly trusting
Democrats. What if Obama had negotiated bad side deals? That, the
conservatives suggested, could lead to the Russians getting a leg up
on the United States.

Reagan had framed nuclear arms treaties with Russia with the
phrase "trust but verify"—meaning that for an accord to hold, the
two countries had to be able to inspect each other's weapons stock-
piles. Corker and Isakson were trusting, but they wouldn't vote yes
without being able to verify.

But the White House policy was to keep the negotiating record
private, in large part because discretion allowed for candor in negotiations with Russia. If the record were turned over to the Senate,
the details would surely show up in media accounts within a matter
of hours, if not minutes. Typically, the Senate had not been privy to
similar documents on past treaties. So the impasse was clear: the

White House didn't want to make the negotiating record available to senators, and the senators whom the president needed on his side wouldn't vote with him unless they felt they had all the information they needed.

Hillary devised a way to keep faith with the policy and at the same time satisfy Corker and Isakson. "We're going to have to give them something. We just can't say no, no, no," she told State Department lawyers and other aides involved in the process. "Go back and write a detailed summary of the points that they're most interested in that comes from the negotiating record. It can be a memo from me, or it can just be a summary of the negotiating record, and we're going to send it up there to the Senate classified space, and they can sit there and read it."

Corker and Isakson went to a secured space in the Capitol to review the summary. As she often did in international negotiations, Hillary had found a way to remove a major barrier with a small gesture. "This was personally a Hillary Clinton idea and solution," one of the aides said.

When the committee voted in September, Isakson, Corker, and Lugar joined Democrats in clearing the treaty to go to the floor. They weren't necessary for a majority vote, but their support sent a signal of bipartisanship that would be crucial to attaining a two-thirds majority of the full Senate. Still, the treaty was far from a done deal. Senate Majority Leader Harry Reid (D-Nev.) wasn't about to spend precious floor time on a treaty that might not be adopted. Worse for the administration, Republicans were going to pick up seats in the November election, and that meant an even tougher path for ratification—perhaps an impossible one—if it waited until the new year. If Democrats kept control of the Senate, a passel of new Republicans could still make it harder to reach a two-thirds majority; if Republicans captured the majority, the treaty was certain to die.

Arizona senator Jon Kyl, the lead conservative on nuclear arms issues, mounted objection after objection, and neither the White House nor the State Department ever got the feeling before the midterm election that there were enough votes. On November 2 the calculus shifted, but not as much as Kyl would have liked. Republicans delivered a powerful blow to Obama and the Democrats, picking up half a dozen Senate seats and more than five dozen House seats. Democrats had lost the House but narrowly held on to the Senate.

Kyl released a statement two weeks later saying the treaty was dead for the year.

But Obama was getting pressure from Russian president Dmitri Medvedev to finish the deal, an issue the Russian brought up when they met in Japan. Given Obama's stated commitment to renewing the relationship between the U.S. and Russia, prestige was on the line, both around the world and in domestic politics. With Republican opponents smelling blood in the water, the lame-duck session was his last chance to salvage a victory. Denis McDonough, who had been appointed deputy national security adviser, issued clear instructions to other administration officials: get it done before the end of the year.

Clinton met with members of the Foreign Relations Committee on November 17, the day after Kyl had pronounced a time of death on the treaty, and in a rare Capitol Hill press conference headlined by a cabinet secretary, she spoke to reporters along with John Kerry and Lugar. The lame-duck session was a time for the two parties to come together, she said. America needed to have inspectors on the ground in Russia. Moreover, she argued, "this is also a treaty that is critical to our bilateral relationship with Russia. We have enhanced our cooperation to the benefit of our country on Iran, on Afghanistan, on nonproliferation, on counterterrorism, and on counternarcotics." If America didn't consummate the New START Treaty, how could the Russians be expected to continue to support those efforts?

Hillary told associates that she thought the meeting with senators and the ensuing press conference created a major turning point in driving momentum toward a vote. Ellen Tauscher, Hillary's longtime friend and the undersecretary for arms control, had been hospitalized with esophageal cancer. She wished she could be in the mix on Capitol Hill, lobbying senators. Surely many Republicans hoped they wouldn't have to make the choice between helping Obama and voting against a deal that would reduce Russia's nuclear stockpile. If it went to the floor and they were forced to pick, Tauscher thought, votes would materialize from Republicans who had refused to say yes to Democratic vote counters. She could barely breathe, but she strained her voice to give well-wishers—including Hillary, Senator Dianne Feinstein, and Kerry—her strategic advice: "Make them vote!"

Meanwhile Hillary had made contact with more than half the senators, perhaps as many as two-thirds of them, according to a source familiar with her calls and visits. Biden, the former chairman of the Foreign Relations Committee, rushed to the Hill to help salvage the treaty. He called or visited half the members of the Senate in November and December. He and Hillary knew the worst outcome would be to put it on the floor and lose. Reid was still hesitant, unsure of the votes. But he finally scheduled a roll call for the week of Christmas. Senate Minority Leader Mitch McConnell (R-Ky.) said he would oppose the treaty. Worried White House officials held a conference call to discuss their next move. "We've got the votes," Biden said. "Period."

The truth is they didn't know how many. The evidence: in the moments leading up to the vote, Biden and Clinton huddled with Kerry in the ornate ceremonial Foreign Relations Office, just off the Senate floor, trying to seal the support of a few senators. "When we went to the floor, we didn't know how many votes we were going to get," said the source who had Hillary's contact list.

In the end, they got seventy-one—four more than the minimum. It was a full-scale effort by the administration on an issue that most Americans hadn't heard of, but that carried significant implications for Russian assistance in the war in Afghanistan and in isolating Iran. It was Obama's day—and Biden's, according to contemporaneous press accounts that hardly mentioned Clinton. But in the months-long full-court press on Capitol Hill, Hillary had applied steady pressure, snatched the ball, and delivered a no-look pass to the White House for the emphatic dunk. She had even managed to let Obama and Biden take public credit for the win.

Her diligent work on arcane matters like the New START Treaty and Iran sanctions, where failure would have gotten far more attention than success did, demonstrated Hillary's professionalism and dedication to Obama's policies. He liked that he could rely on her to do her job with little instruction necessary. "If he doesn't have to worry about you and the job that you're doing, that's the highest compliment he can ever pay you," explained one of Obama's closest advisers. "That was Hillary."

Her behind-the-scenes work on behalf of Obama that fall stood in stark contrast to her husband's turn in the spotlight. By late October, Bill had done more than one hundred political events in the 2010 cycle, most of them for candidates who had backed Hillary, and he kept her fresh in Democratic voters' minds. "I have to tell you, it's no secret that I did what I could to defeat President Obama, and I still like my secretary of state," he told voters in Battle Creek, Michigan, where he was stumping on behalf of freshman representative Mark Schauer.

He also handled a little bit of party dirty work for Obama, making national headlines when he tried to persuade Representative Kendrick Meek, a longtime family ally, to drop out of the Florida Senate race. Sunshine State Democrats were divided between Meek and Governor Charlie Crist, a Republican who was running as an independent. If Meek stepped aside, Crist might be able to take out Marco Rubio, a rising Republican star, who was seen as a GOP version of Obama—a young, attractive minority candidate who could stoke the party base without alienating its moderates. Crist had called Band, and Band had called Meek, and finally Bill thought he had gotten Meek to end the campaign early. But Meek changed his mind—or didn't interpret their conversation the same way Bill did—and Rubio cruised to victory over both Meek and Crist.

As the results rolled in on election night in 2010, it was clear that Obama and Bill would have at least one major parallel in the first two years of their presidencies: they had lost control of the House in their first midterm election. While Obama acknowledged that Democrats had suffered a "shellacking" at the polls, the same could almost be said for the state of his presidency. While he had passed health care reform, the economy was still in the toilet. His approval rating cratered in the mid-forties. And it was time to start thinking more intensely about his reelection. The Clinton brand, well polished over the two-plus years since the 2008 primary, was a good one for Obama to affix himself to.

Two years earlier it would have been virtually inconceivable for Obama to call on Bill Clinton for help publicly. Throughout the first term, aides say, Obama had talked to Clinton repeatedly but privately to pick his brain. On December 10, just a little more than a month after the election, Obama invited Bill Clinton to an Oval Office meeting. Obama, who had just struck a tax deal with Republicans that had the markings of a Clintonian move to the middle, thought it would be a good idea if Clinton would "share some of his thoughts" on the economy with the public.

He brought Clinton out to the White House press briefing room and told reporters that the former president would "speak very briefly." But "briefly" turned into a thirty-minute show from Clinton, who settled in at the podium and fielded questions from reporters he knew by name.

For most of the time, Bill was up there alone. Obama had told the press corps he had to run to meet Michelle Obama, who was waiting in the residence to attend a holiday party. "I don't want to make her mad," Clinton responded to Obama. "Please go."

And for the next half hour, it was as if the Clinton presidency had never ended. A reporter for the New York Times wrote that it looked as though Obama had "outsourced his presidency to Bill Clinton."

While Bill enjoyed his return to the spotlight in the wake of Obama's disastrous midterm, Hillary quietly tended to the wounds of friends who had fallen from office. Some of the recipients of her calls and notes, like representatives Dina Titus (D-Nev.) and Dan Maffei (D-N.Y.), lost in the 2010 midterm but would then make a political comeback two years later, positioned to help her if she ran for president again. These were people whose names remained in the virtual Rolodex of Hillary's friends and supporters.

"That's kind of an untold story," said one State Department official. "She made a lot of phone calls to people just to say 'thanks for your service.' It was a really interesting thing, just because she appreciated what they had done and probably knew it was a tough time for them." Of course, in politics, especially Clinton politics, "thanks for your service" is just another show of loyalty—delivered now and expected later.

The postelection period was an incredibly difficult time for Hillary, too. A few hours before Bill took the podium at the White House, Hillary had met in her office with Richard Holbrooke, his deputy Frank Ruggiero, and Jake Sullivan to handle the prospect of a negotiated settlement with the Taliban as the United States drew down its forces in Afghanistan, per Obama's decision to end the surge and transfer power to the Karzai government. Holbrooke still hoped that a deal could be cut with the Taliban, and he gave a spirited argument that the United States should pursue an agreement in which the Taliban broke with Al Qaeda, renounced violence, and abided by the Afghan constitution. For much of the rest of the administration, those outcomes were preconditions for even sitting down with the Taliban.

As he pressed his case with Hillary, Holbrooke heaved and then turned an unusual shade of red. Collecting himself, he told Hillary he was fine to continue.

"You've got to get to the hospital right away," Hillary said. "You've got to see a doctor."

Sullivan and Ruggiero helped him to the private elevator across the hall from her office, where other staffers arrived to assist him on his way to the State Department's medical office, while an ambulance made its way to the building. Holbrooke collapsed in the elevator. He'd had a heart attack—a ruptured aorta—and was rushed to George Washington University Hospital. Hillary had spent a lot of time over two years with Holbrooke's team; he had insisted on bringing everyone to his meetings with her, even though the department usually let senior officials bring only one or two assistants along.

Now, as doctors performed marathon surgical work on Holbrooke, Hillary embraced his tight-knit team again, appearing at the hospital repeatedly during their three-day vigil. On one of the nights, she took them to dinner, walking with them through Washington Circle, past the bronze statue of the nation's first president at the Battle of Princeton, to Mei Wah, a Chinese restaurant where signed pictures of politicians, including both Clintons, adorn the walls. It had long been Bill's favorite spot for takeout, and Clintonites have turned it into a lunchtime conference room over the years.

When Hillary received word that Holbrooke had died, she left Obama at a State Department reception and rushed to the hospital. Half a dozen members of Holbrooke's team congregated in the lobby.

Hillary found them there, crying. One by one, she hugged his aides.

"Let's go to the bar and have an Irish wake for Richard," she said.

The death of Richard Holbrooke turned into an opportunity for his advocates and critics to slug it out over his legacy in obituaries and at the numerous memorial services held in his honor. Much was made in Washington of the contrast between the Clintons' efforts to canonize him and the dry, impersonal eulogy that Obama delivered at Washington's National Cathedral. But on another level, Holbrooke's passing removed one of the final remaining points of tension between Obama's White House and Hillary's State Department. He was a reflection of the differences in their operations, a brilliant player with a flair for drama.

White House aides had soured on Holbrooke early on. Beyond his threats from the campaign trail, they had become convinced that he was the source of damaging leaks about sensitive negotiations regarding the future of Afghanistan and its president, Hamid Karzai, and then lied about it. "Those discussions can only work if they happen quietly and they don't get leaked, and he was leaking all the time," said one White House aide. "He would tell people at the White

House to their face, 'I haven't talked to a reporter in a year.' And the reporter would tell us, 'Holbrooke won't stop calling me.' And you go to his memorial and reporters were giving testimonials about how they had heard from him every day. It's not that people had any lack of respect for his intellect or his ability. . . . It's that he didn't tell the truth. And when someone lies to your face, that's frustrating."

With Bill emerging as an important validator for the president and Holbrooke no longer a flashpoint, the White House had little remaining reason to question Hillary's loyalty. Instead, after two years of working together, the prevailing view of Hillary at the White House was that she could be trusted.

PART

TEN

Promise and Peril

The Situation Room fell quiet on February 1, 2011, as President Barack Obama and the members of his National Security Council paused to look at a television screen on the far wall. Egyptian president Hosni Mubarak was speaking, and like millions of ordinary citizens around the world, America's highest-ranking officials wondered whether he was ready to give up power. Mubarak, whose government had clashed with prodemocracy protesters in Cairo's Tahrir Square, still clung to power, and the men and women in the Situation Room hung on his every word, because they had no better intelligence than the average viewer about what he would say.

For most of a week, the veteran foreign policy hands on Obama's National Security Council, including Hillary, Vice President Joe Biden, and Defense Secretary Robert Gates, had argued that the United States should give Mubarak as much operating room as possible. Hillary told reporters that Mubarak's regime was "stable" on January 25, and two days before Mubarak's speech to the Egyptian people, when she finally called for an "orderly, peaceful transition to real democracy" on *Meet the Press,* she didn't offer a timetable for starting that process. The old guard had personal ties to Mubarak, who was a rare ally in a tumultuous region and who had kept peace with Israel for more than thirty years. They also worried about the message it would send to other leaders in the region if the United States abandoned a longtime friend in his moment of crisis. Most important, they feared the unknown. There was no telling whether Mubarak's successor would be a friend or foe of the United States. But from the National Security Staff's perspective, indeed in Obama's own mind, those factors were outweighed by the simple truth that the United States couldn't do anything to save Mubarak, and it was better to get on the right side of the revolution as soon as possible.

Rather than stepping aside, Mubarak dug in. While he would not seek reelection, he said, he did plan to remain in power until the next election—certainly long enough for protesters to worry that he could rig the outcome or simply back down from his promise to move toward democratic reform. He cast his political opponents as thugs and criminals, commanding "censorship authorities and legislative authorities to carry out immediately every measure to pursue those who are corrupt and have been responsible for what has happened in all the destructive acts and looting and fires that have taken place in Egypt."

Inside the Situation Room, Obama knew that Mubarak's message would only inflame the revolutionary spirit in Cairo. The legendary New York congressman Charles Rangel has a saying, "I'll be with you as long as I can," meaning that he will stick with an ally up until the point that it becomes politically untenable. Obama had reached that moment with Mubarak. He called the Egyptian president to push for a swift exit.

Ben Rhodes, an adviser and speechwriter for the president on foreign policy matters, drafted a response statement for Obama to deliver from the White House that night. Because an NSC meeting had been under way when Mubarak spoke, the principals were all still gathered at the White House, and Rhodes circulated it on the spot, turning the normally complex process of formulating U.S. policy toward another major nation into an on-the-fly cram session.

The first version, reflecting Obama's view, called for Mubarak to get out in terms that neither he nor the nations of the world could possibly interpret as anything other than a full abandonment of the Egyptian president. But Hillary wasn't ready to go as far as Rhodes's original draft. Pen in hand, she began editing the text, as did Defense Secretary Robert Gates and other members of the NSC.

"Going beyond Mubarak was entering into an unknown. Everybody knew Mubarak; nobody knew what was going to come after Mubarak. . . . When you don't know what comes next, it's hard to call for somebody to go," said an Obama aide who was in the room. "The president's point was 'it's not as [though] if we didn't call for him to go, he'd be able to stay in power.' It was almost an analytical point, which was 'This guy has lost control of the country. What he's trying to do to stay in power is not going to work, so we just need to get to that reality faster.'

"The people around the table were a little more cautious about going that far," the aide added. Another White House source said they were "nitpicking Ben's statement." Obama sided with his speechwriter and delivered remarks nearly in line with the original draft. From the Grand Foyer of the White House, the president aimed his speech at the world community rather than a strictly American audience. "What is clear—and what I indicated tonight to President Mubarak—is my belief that an orderly transition must be meaningful, it must be peaceful, and it must begin now," he said.

Ten days later the NSC scene played out a second time in similar fashion, with some of the same officials watching a defiant Mubarak from the Situation Room and then group-editing a Rhodes statement. Again, the president was willing to go further than his top lieutenants. But even with Obama taking a more forward-leaning position than his NSC, he still seemed behind the times. Ten days were an eternity in Egypt's real-time revolution, and the tipping point had long since passed. But America, the leader of the free world, still didn't know what it wanted to say—much less do—in the face of a democratic transformation in a region that had long been home to a handful of America-friendly dictators.

While no one could have predicted the exact chain of events that transpired in the Middle East and North Africa, when the Arab Spring made its way into Egypt, the American foreign policy apparatus, informed by Hillary and like-minded officials at the White House and the Pentagon, proved slow to respond. It appeared to outsiders that the United States favored democratic reforms only if they didn't threaten to replace autocratic American allies with elected extremists. Of course, each country was its own case, each call complicated by complex political calculations. It was hard enough for a superpower, with a deliberative and democratic political process, to react to real-time revolutions. In Egypt, the conflicting impulses of promoting democracy, supporting a longtime ally, and preventing extremists from taking control of a geopolitically important nation compounded the paralysis.

Hillary "was reflecting a little bit her caution that every situation is different, and I think we learned in the last decade that just 'rah-rah democracy' in every situation is too blunt a sentiment," one of her advisers said. "She knew Mubarak pretty well. She knew some of the opposition figures and knew the military and was appropriately concerned about how this was all going to play out."

There was a personal element, too. The Clintons' relationship with the Mubaraks dated back as far as April 1993, when Bill had hosted the Egyptian president at the White House. "I really consider President and Mrs. Mubarak to be friends of my family," Hillary had said in March 2009.

As it turned out, Hillary's concern about trading out a moderate dictator for an untested but democratically elected Muslim Brotherhood president was warranted, as American officials would see two years later, when the new government was subjected to a counter-revolution that looked like a rerun of the movement that toppled Mubarak, aides to both Obama and Clinton said.

Still, of all the president's advisers, Hillary should have been the least likely to get caught behind the curve of the 2011 Egyptian revolution. She had long since recognized the emerging factors, primarily the power of technology to galvanize activists, which favored fast-sweeping political change. She knew that ideas, money, and power could be transferred from one place to the next in the time that it took to upload a YouTube video or hack into a computer. After all, it was Hillary who had said during her 2009 Senate confirmation hearing that "the promise and the peril of the twenty-first century could not be contained by national borders or vast distances." She had traveled to the region just weeks earlier to warn the leaders of the Middle East and North Africa that change was coming, whether they wanted it or not.

But it was far easier to topple a government than to create a new one. The modern leaderless revolution, accelerated by instantaneous electronic communication, could leave a country without anyone experienced in governance to establish a stable government. The writing was on the wall, but it didn't include instructions for how America could play a constructive role in encouraging both democracy and stability in a region where American interests had for so long depended on moderate autocrats suppressing popular extremism. So Hillary could glimpse the future, but she couldn't shape it—at least not yet.

In the first week of January, as the Arab Spring was beginning to stir, Hillary had summoned Dan Schwerin—who had risen through the Hillaryland ranks from junior press aide to speechwriter—and another wordsmith, Meghan Rooney, to her personal office, a small alcove with a desk, a short sofa, and three or four chairs. The tiny space connected to Cheryl Mills's office on one side and Hillary's much larger official reception room on another.

Hillary was heading to Doha, Qatar, the following week for an annual gathering of Middle Eastern leaders called the Forum for the Future, and she would have an unusually short window of five minutes in which to address the audience. She told Schwerin and Rooney that she was determined to make each moment count. "You know, we go to the Middle East all the time, and we give the same old message, and it never breaks through, and I am not going to do that this time," she said. "They are sitting on a powder keg. No one is talking about it. Find something fresh and interesting that we can say that's going to make them wake up."

Though the outcome wasn't yet clear, the seeds of revolution had been planted the previous month in Tunisia, where a street vendor had set himself on fire to protest the government's oppressive economic policies. That breathtakingly graphic act had touched off a wave of demonstrations that ultimately led to the downfall of the

Tunisian government. Schwerin, liberated by the reversal of a diplomatic speechwriter's typical assignment—it's not often they are told to shake things up—quickly reached out to experts within the State Department and at Washington think tanks to ask what they had always wanted to say about the Middle East but had not because of political sensitivities. The result was a prescient call for Middle East leaders to reform their own societies before others took charge.

"While some countries have made great strides in governance, in many others people have grown tired of corrupt institutions and stagnant political order," Hillary said in Doha. "In too many places, in too many ways, the region's foundations are sinking into the sand. . . . Those who cling to the status quo may be able to hold back the full impact of their countries' problems for a little while, but not forever. . . . Extremist elements, terrorist groups, and others who would prey on desperation and poverty are already out there, appealing for allegiance and competing for influence. So this is a critical moment, and this is a test of leadership for all of us. I am here to pledge my country's support for those who step up to solve the problems that we and you face."

Hillary aides still recall that members of the State Department's traveling press corps raved about her speech. "'Why doesn't she talk like this always? This is amazing,'" one aide remembered hearing. "And people in the audience were like 'Wow, we didn't expect to be talked to like this.' Some of them were offended. But some of them were inspired."

The Tunisian government fell the following day, putting a fine point on Hillary's warning. And within two weeks, Egypt was on the brink. It was one thing, in the abstract, to think about a revolution spreading from one country to the next across an entire region in a matter of weeks, not years or decades. It was another to watch it happening live on television. If the experience with Egypt proved anything, it was that the United States was too slow to respond to political dynamics that it could see coming thousands of miles away. Despite Hillary's prescience about the factors leading up to the

Arab Spring, her reluctance to throw Mubarak out exemplified the administration's equivocation.

But when the Arab Spring spread from Egypt to Libya, Hillary slingshot the United States, and the rest of the Western world, from trailing the moment to leading it. More than at any other time during her four-year tenure at State, she showcased her skills as a strategist, a diplomat, and a politician in building a coalition for a war against Muammar Qaddafi—a coalition in which the responsibility would be truly distributed among partners. Unlike many previous "coalition" wars, the drive to crush Qaddafi would not be a de facto U.S. operation dressed up with minimal participation by partner countries. The key was Hillary's ability to identify the policy sweet spot that satisfied the president, America's Western European allies, the Arab League, and the nascent rebel governing body in Libya, while helping win tacit assent from initial opponents, such as Russia and Congress. The mission required Hillary to balance the interests of the various players within the United States and of those around the world.

It was the same skill set—though applied on a much bigger stage and with much graver consequences for failure—as building a coalition for a bill in Congress among legislators, outside stakeholders, and voters. And of course, it's a particularly Clintonian talent to fashion a deal that everyone can live with to advance an idea supported by the Clinton in question. Libya's liberation, for better and worse, was Hillary's War.

On February 15, just a few days after Mubarak finally stepped down, protesters took to the streets in Libya, sparking violent clashes a couple of days later between Qaddafi's forces and a ragtag band of rebel militias. While Qaddafi conducted a vicious crackdown on demonstrators, the rebels quickly seized control of several cities in the eastern half of the country. At the urging of Libyan government officials opposed to Qaddafi's actions, French president Nicolas Sarkozy called for the United Nations to impose a no-fly zone over the capital of Tripoli, in the western part of the country, so that Qaddafi could not easily move troops and supplies to the rebel-held territory in the east or launch air strikes against his own people. Foreign policy experts have pinned a lot of possible motives on Sarkozy: altruistic concern for the Libyan people, a need to show strength in advance of French elections, a wish for redemption for supporting Egyptian and Tunisian despots for too long, and solicitude for the interests of the French oil titan Total. Whatever the case, he was first out of the box, and British prime minister David Cameron, who had also been criticized for a slow response in the other Arab Spring countries, soon joined Sarkozy's push for a no-fly zone.

Within the United States, a fierce two-to-three-week debate broke out between a small set of Obama administration officials who were eager to prevent Qaddafi from slaughtering his own people and a second group who, for various reasons, were dead set against the use of American military force in Libya. By that point, the issue hadn't risen to the president's level, at least not in any official sense. The first group, later portrayed along with Hillary as a set of mythological Valkyries—or Norse women of war—included UN ambassador Susan Rice and National Security Staff member Samantha Power. But there were men, too, among the minority voices that argued for a military response. Ben Rhodes and Tony Blinken, the vice president's national security adviser, joined them in making the case that the United States could not stand by and watch a genocide as it had in Rwanda in the 1990s.

But the second group, much more powerful on the surface, included Biden, Gates, White House chief of staff Bill Daley, and Joint Chiefs of Staff chairman Martin Dempsey. They told Obama's White House advisers that they were skeptical about whether America had any legitimate national security interest in Libya. They knew that the military was stretched too thin, and they worried about the prospect of starting a war in a third Muslim country when much of the Muslim world didn't draw a distinction between the American war on terrorism and a war on Islam. All of that added up to an overarching concern that France and Britain were dragging the United States into a military action that ultimately would be funded and executed by America. "One of the principal arguments against intervention was, we'd be doing it by ourselves," said a White House official who was in the room for the discussions. "Every time we do this, we have to hold the bag."

Hillary had been playing her cards close to the vest in the early deliberations but had begun to lean toward an intervention. In 1994 she had urged Bill to stop the Rwandan genocide, to no avail, and the arguments made by Power, Rice, Blinken, and Rhodes appeared to have an effect on her thinking. She was sympathetic to their view but very much worried that the intervention options on the table were too weak. The no-fly zone wasn't enough to impede Qaddafi.

"She understood the motivation to want to do something," said Jim Steinberg, who sat in on national security meetings. "She recognized that just kind-of gestures, futile gestures, were the worst of all worlds. You made it feel like you were doing something, but it wasn't actually going to make any difference. And much of what was being talked about in the early discussions about intervention were the kind of things we had already seen in the Balkans that would not make any difference—no-fly zones, safe havens, and the like. But those things were not going to transform the situation. And I think her perspective was 'If we are going to intervene, we have to do it in a way that will be credible and effective.'"

Obama wasn't formally briefed on his options until he had to make decisions about whether and how to intervene later in the process. But his leanings lined up with Hillary's—or hers lined up with his—according to senior administration officials.

As the debate intensified in Washington, so did the war in Libya. In early March, Qaddafi started to push forward, retaking cities that the rebels had captured in the early weeks of fighting. There were reports of air strikes from Qaddafi-controlled planes in Brega. His tanks began powering eastward along the coastal highway, on a mission to crush the rebel stronghold of Benghazi. "There wasn't a choice about time frames," said a senior administration official. "That time frame was forced on us by the movement of tanks across the desert on the doorstep of Benghazi."

By March 12, as the twenty-one-member Arab League huddled

at its Cairo headquarters, Qaddafi was on the verge of sacking the rebels. Some world leaders and human rights activists believed a slaughter of tens or even hundreds of thousands of Libyans might be imminent. After a closed-door meeting that lasted nearly six hours that Saturday, Amr Moussa, the secretary-general of the Arab League, announced that the Arab nations would support a no-fly zone. The Arab countries, which normally presented a bloc against outside intervention, were giving the go-ahead to Western powers to stop Qaddafi. Just like the Americans, they had to weigh whether to stand idly by while Qaddafi slaughtered his own people—fellow Arabs. Ultimately they preferred the rebels over Qaddafi, who had frequently thumbed his nose at his Arab neighbors over his forty-two-year reign.

Their interest in protecting the rebels from Qaddafi gave Hillary just the opening she needed to push for more aggressive military intervention than the ambiguous no-fly zone embraced by the British and the French. She believed the no-fly zone was a false solution because it would let Western powers feel good about taking action but wouldn't be forceful enough to stop Qaddafi. And it certainly wouldn't provide the power necessary to assist the rebels in toppling him. A no-fly zone meant allied forces would shoot down Qaddafi's planes; but by mid-March, it was Qaddafi's tanks that needed to be stopped.

Hillary told her aides she was convinced that Libya presented a unique opportunity for America to exercise a new kind of international leadership that relied on building a partnership in which the bulk of the might and money would come from other countries. Potemkin coalitions had cost America blood, treasure, and international prestige, and Obama wasn't about to commit the United States to taking the brunt of another war. Hillary's strategy integrated the desire of Rice, Power, Blinken, and Rhodes to intervene with the reluctance of Gates, Biden, and Daley to land Marines on the shores of Tripoli, and it added a much harder punch than a no-fly zone.

Libya was a particularly inviting crucible in which to test the theories of smart power, multilateralism, and democracy promotion that informed Hillary's philosophy of American leadership. The country was rich in resources, particularly oil and gas, and had a relatively well-educated population that, absent the repression imposed by Qaddafi, was positioned to build the economic, political, and civil institutions that she believed formed the heart of thriving democracies. With a little help at the margins, Libyans would have all the tools to build an inclusive democratic society. In addition, there could hardly be a more just cause than stepping in to prevent a massacre. In other words, the conditions were ripe for an American-backed intervention.

For some time, a coalition of the Friends of Libya had been discussing possible ways to get involved, but with no commitment from the United States, the plan for assistance was still, as one Hillary aide put it, "to be determined." When she flew to Paris for a March 14 meeting of the foreign ministers of the G8, a group of the world's wealthiest powers, Hillary was looking for evidence that would persuade Obama to back a war—essentially assurances that the Europeans would take the lead militarily, that Arab countries would participate in enforcing a no-fly zone so that it didn't look like the West was attacking another Muslim country, and that the Libyan opposition's government-in-waiting, called the Transitional National Council (TNC), could really create a democratic Libya. The United States had not yet given formal recognition to the TNC, a key indication that Washington remained skeptical of the organization.

On her first day in Paris, Hillary sat down with Sheikh Abdullah bin Zayed al-Nahyan, the foreign minister of the United Arab Emirates (UAE) and the head of the Gulf Cooperation Council (GCC), in the living room of her suite at the top of the Westin, just a few blocks from the three-thousand-year-old obelisk known as Cleopatra's Needle that, like Abdullah, had traveled to France from the Middle East. The couches in the room were soft, but Abdullah's tone was not. Having gained an audience with the American secretary of state, he intended to take full advantage of it, knowing that an American ask was forthcoming.

He gave Hillary an earful over what he saw as American meddling in Bahrain, one of the Gulf countries he was in town to represent. The day before, in a statement addressing a violent Bahraini government crackdown on demonstrators, White House press secretary Jay Carney had singled out the Gulf Cooperation Council for condemnation. "In particular," he had said, "we urge our GCC partners to show restraint and respect the rights of the people of Bahrain, and to act in a way that supports dialogue instead of undermining it."

Now Hillary was asking the head of the organization the White House had just slammed to join a partnership dedicated to intervening in Libya.

The room was uncomfortable. Abdullah was "not shy about expressing criticism about some of the things we had said publicly about Bahrain," said an American source who was there. But the important thing was that Abdullah got to make his point; he could tell officials in Bahrain and Saudi Arabia, another ally, that he had lectured Hillary Clinton. (In point of fact, during the tense early weeks of the Libya campaign, the United States softened its criticism of Bahrain and the GCC.)

The Libya portion of the discussion was much more agreeable. Abdullah confirmed for Hillary that Persian Gulf countries, including the UAE, would provide more than rhetorical support for a mission. Arab planes would fly. But it wasn't a one-way street. The UAE and other Persian Gulf countries needed to know that the United States wasn't just blowing smoke. It was one thing to say Qaddafi was a problem; it was another to remove him from power. If Arab planes were going to fly—and the GCC represented the rich Arab nations that would put up money and planes—Abdullah wanted to know that the United States was ready to take the dictator out.

If Abdullah was looking for a hawk, he had come to the right person. While European countries were still stuck on no-fly zones, Hillary was thinking about a comprehensive military action that included strikes on Qaddafi's ground forces—basically an all-necessary-means operation to give cover that the rebels needed to turn the tide.

The term of art at the United Nations, "all necessary means" authority, is, as it sounds, a blank check to go to war. "What the Gulf Arabs were looking for was American leadership on this, follow-through on the public statements about Qaddafi having lost legitimacy," said a source who was present at Hillary's meeting with Abdullah. "In that sense, he was reassured by what the secretary had to say, by her activist approach to it."

In the same room later that night, Hillary sat down with Mahmoud Jibril, the leader of the Libyan Transitional National Council. Deputy Secretary Bill Burns, U.S. ambassador to Libya Gene Cretz, and Chris Stevens, a Libya expert in the foreign service, were among the small group of advisers with Hillary.

Jibril, a low-key Benghazi native with a doctorate in political science from the University of Pittsburgh, had sneaked into Paris from the TNC's headquarters in Qatar to meet with Hillary. Passionate but also lucid and composed, Jibril told her that if the opposition didn't get military assistance, Qaddafi's forces would wreak havoc in Benghazi and likely kill the rebellion. That, he said, wasn't in anyone's interest. Qaddafi had called the rebels "rats," and his threat to destroy them was on the verge of coming to fruition. Jibril offered Hillary what the source called a "chilling reminder" that Qaddafi's past sins against his people "left no doubt that he was to be taken at his word."

But Hillary wanted to be sure that the United States wasn't getting dragged into a revolution that would replace Qaddafi with either chaos or another government that didn't respect the rights of out-of-power groups. She pushed back on Jibril, forcing him to detail his vision of a new Libyan society, a view that she would have to articulate to skeptics in Washington and elsewhere in advocating the use of military force.

"Part of the challenge was to get Jibril and others to lay out a clear sense of what they stood for, which was one of the things she pushed him on," said one source who participated. "She made clear that they needed to be clear and consistent in public about the kinds of things that they stood for, too, their vision of a post-Qaddafi

Libya, which was an important way to be inclusive, so that they were reaching out to people across Libya." Hillary told Jibril that his entreaties would be given full consideration but stopped short of making a commitment of support.

Jibril later confided to associates that Hillary's stern demeanor had made him feel like he'd blown his opportunity. He had not.

"I remember her being impressed afterward that this was a group of opposition leaders who were beginning to pull themselves together," said one of the officials who was present. "And then she used that not only in Washington but with other coalition partners to try and generate support from them, that the [opposition leaders] were pointed in the right direction, even though they needed a lot of support. She came away from it convinced that we had to plan actively" for an intervention.

In sidebar meetings with her French, British, and German counterparts, and in phone conversations with them later that week, Hillary pressed the case for the more robust intervention. "What she wanted to find out," Steinberg said, "was, were others prepared to take stronger and effective measures that would make it worthwhile—that is, going beyond no-fly zones to take the kind of forceful action that would provide protection for the people of Libya who were under threat by Qaddafi."

She left Europe optimistic that the United States could get support for a much broader UN resolution than the no-fly zone version the British and French preferred. If America led the way diplomatically, Britain and France would go along. Germany was still reluctant to sign on. But Hillary was putting together an ad hoc international military coalition that would, if everything went right, turn into a partnership for building a new and sustainable Libyan government. The alliance would rely heavily on other countries to bear the brunt of the work and the cost of pummeling Qaddafi, from airplanes to armaments. In an ideal world, the United Nations would sign off on a coalition action, giving it the imprimatur of the whole world, not just the West and the Gulf countries with an ax to grind against Qaddafi.

One politically inept administration official called the new model "leading from behind," a phrase that would benignly haunt Obama. But it would allow the United States to help shape Libya's future—to be on the side of a budding democracy movement—without being the face of an attack in another Muslim country and without asking Congress and the American public to support spending exorbitant sums to put more American troops in harm's way.

That formula required not just the support Hillary had sought from the wealthy Persian Gulf countries represented by Abdullah but also the backing of the broader Arab League, which spanned the Middle East and North Africa from the Persian Gulf in the East to Mauritania's Atlantic coast. The day after her meetings with Abdullah and Jibril, Hillary flew to Cairo, where her talks with leaders of the new post-Mubarak government there were not as pressing as her face-to-face meeting with Amr Moussa, a presidential candidate and secretary-general of the Arab League.

Moussa assured her that the Arab League would back a no-fly zone, but Hillary asked for more. She detailed for him the more extensive military intervention she favored. "She was quite direct with him," said one of her aides. You're calling for a no-fly zone, you're calling for us to get engaged, she said; this is what we're talking about doing, and you'd better be on board with it. The coalition was coming together.

Hillary called in to the Situation Room that night—it was still afternoon in Washington—to brief Obama and his National Security Council on what she had learned. European and Arab planes would be in the air over Libya; Britain and France would be on board if the United States could push a more powerful resolution through the United Nations than the no-fly zone; and the Arab League had given its blessing.

Susan Rice, linked up to the White House meeting by video-conference from New York, was ready to draft the "all necessary measures" resolution, in which the United Nations could basically give NATO its approval to pulverize Qaddafi with air strikes and a naval blockade. While NATO, comprised of Western countries, didn't need a UN resolution to go to war with Qaddafi, the administration considered the force of a world body that included many Arab nations an important element of building credibility for the attack in the Arab world. Later Moussa would complain publicly that he hadn't intended to green-light a full-scale bombardment of Libya, but he soon backed down from that line of argument.

Hillary's report addressed both the desires of those who wanted to intervene and the concerns of those who worried about over-extending the military and the optics of the United States committing to war in a third Muslim country. It wasn't a perfect solution, and it didn't bring Gates and the Pentagon around, but it gave the president the information he needed to move forward. Rice, armed with her own intelligence and Hillary's reporting, said she believed she could push the "all necessary measures" language through the UN Security Council. The meeting broke without a verdict, but Obama now had reason to be confident in both the moral argument to intervene and the likelihood that it could be pulled off with minimal risk and cost to the United States.

At a second meeting, which Hillary did not participate in because it was the middle of the night in Cairo and it was pretty clear that she was pushing for military force, Obama instructed Rice to seek a broad "all necessary measures" resolution from the UN Security Council, one that would be portrayed in the press as a no-fly zone but really meant that the world was going to stop Qaddafi with every available tool short of an occupation of Libya. Obama's one caveat: no American troops on the ground.

Any permanent member of the Security Council could scuttle a war resolution. The Russians preferred a much more modest call for a cease-fire. Working cautiously to avoid offending Russia, Rice said there was nothing wrong with the Russian resolution per se, but it didn't go far enough. "I think most members of the council [are] focused on the importance of the council taking swift and meaningful action to try to halt the killing on the ground," she said.

In Tunis the next day, as Rice continued to work for votes in New York, Hillary candidly discussed America's hope to do more than just protect civilians and rebels. "We definitely would like to see a democracy come to Libya," she said in a Nessma TV interview. "And yet at the same time, we know that unless the Security Council authorizes further action, it will be very difficult for the opposition."

When Hillary left the stage, she scrambled to a greenroom where Jake Sullivan was holding on an open phone line with Russian foreign minister Sergei Lavrov on the other end. In the two years since the "reset" button faux pas in early 2009, Hillary and Lavrov had developed a strong professional bond, in part during negotiations over the New START Treaty, according to a source who frequently watched them interact. Hillary didn't need Lavrov and the Russians to vote for the Security Council resolution, which was ultimately sponsored by France. She just needed them to refrain from vetoing it. She asked Lavrov to abstain, and he agreed. Hillary made another call to Portugal to wrap up a yes vote and departed for the airport.

As her plane headed back to Washington, reporters peppered Sullivan with questions about why the United States hadn't stopped Qaddafi from sacking Benghazi. Somewhere over the Atlantic, Hillary received word that the UN Security Council had voted 10–0 in favor of the "all necessary measures" resolution. China, Brazil, Germany, and India abstained. So did Russia. The coalition building had been a team effort—Obama and Rice had lobbied other nations hard for their votes—but it was Hillary who had done the on-the-ground work to put the puzzle together.

That Friday Obama informed a small group of relevant congressional leaders about plans to use American missiles and intelligence capabilities—described as "unique assets"—in support of the operation. Less than thirty-six hours later, American and British ships began launching scores of Tomahawk missiles at Qaddafi's forces.

After two years of learning her job, traveling the world, and marshaling her political capital in Washington, Hillary had become an ever more influential player on the president's team. She had cobbled together all the pieces needed to persuade Obama to intervene in Libya. Her international diplomacy had built confidence that America could lead an intervention on behalf of the Libyan rebels without alienating NATO allies or the Arab world. And on a question of using American force, she had split from Gates, the Pentagon chief whom she had courted from the beginning of the administration.

Hillary had come to the fore in Washington and Paris to create a war—promise, peril, and all.

ELEVEN

Below the Waterline

L eon Panetta had a secret. And it was time for the CIA director to let Hillary in on it. During a Situation Room meeting at the White House, he told her he needed to talk to her one-on-one. So, on March 7, 2011, Panetta paid a visit to Hillary at the State Department to inform her of an operation so delicate and highly charged that she didn't feel comfortable sharing it even with her husband. Panetta had a long history with Hillary, dating back to his days as a first-term chief of staff to Bill Clinton, when he had tried to keep her out of the decisions being made in the West Wing. Within Obama's no-drama Situation Room, the pair stood out as characters because they often behaved as old siblings—kindred spirits who could antagonize each other like no one else.

The kindred spirit part mattered most to Panetta as the two veteran policy makers settled into eagle-carved armchairs in the cozy James Madison Dining Room on the top floor of the State Department. The only other eyes and ears in the room belonged to a $70,000 marble bust of Daniel Webster. Over lunch, Panetta told Hillary that intelligence operatives thought they had located Osama bin Laden at a compound in Abbottabad, Pakistan. The president had been informed, and only a handful of his top military and intelligence advisers were in the loop. Panetta was telling Hillary because he needed her to make the case for action. There were doubters at the White House and the Pentagon—and the CIA couldn't say for sure that Bin Laden was actually at the compound.

But Panetta had become convinced that the opportunity was real, and he needed a strong partner in arguing that it was time to strike. "It was becoming increasingly clear," a senior intelligence official said, "that we were going to have to move on the intelligence, and any operation would require approval by NSC principals, and since it was in Pakistan, obviously, it would require buy-in from her. Second, I think he just thought that she would have a very good sense of how to finish the job against Bin Laden." Hillary and Panetta both believed that Obama could be too deliberative, too hesitant, too risk-averse. On the other hand, the official said, Hillary harbored a "huge bias for action."

As much as any top official in the Obama administration, Hillary had been personally invested in laying the groundwork for the moment when Bin Laden finally appeared again in American crosshairs. As the person responsible for direct negotiations with the Pakistanis on diplomatic and development matters, she was the velvet glove on the fist of American force in Pakistan. She brought to the debate the unique perspective of a senator who had represented New York when Bin Laden killed nearly three thousand of her constituents; a loyal Democrat who knew the risk the president would take if he let Bin Laden slip away; and a diplomat who had pulled every possible lever to ensure that the CIA, or Pakistani intelligence, would find Bin Laden. Others could debate the exact method and timing for a strike, but no one spoke with more authority than Hillary about the moral and political reasoning for launching an attack or the justification for violating Pakistani sovereignty. There was nothing more important than getting the top terrorist in the world, she thought. When she hectored David Petraeus at a hearing in 2007, she had framed her attack on President George W. Bush's Iraq surge in part on his failure to pursue Bin Laden.

Hillary was thrilled when Panetta laid out what he believed was a credible case for moving on Bin Laden. "Leon and I have worked together a very long time," Hillary said. "I think he knew from all kinds of conversations we had over the years that—especially since he was at CIA and I was at State—that if we had a colorable, creditable chance to get Bin Laden, we should do it, that it was a matter of keeping faith with the people that we represented in this country. For me, it was very personal because of what I'd lived through with what happened on 9/11."

She had been carefully weighing the need for seeking Pakistani cooperation against America's interest in pursuing and killing terrorists since before she started her job, at least as early as her first transition meetings in the fall of 2008. Hillary had named Holbrooke "special representative for Afghanistan and Pakistan" as part of a broader administration effort to acknowledge and deal with the truth that Pakistan, which remained a terrorist haven, was the real root problem in the region. To try to win cooperation from the Pakistani military and the government in fighting terrorism and possibly negotiating a peace in Afghanistan, Hillary and the rest of the Obama administration had showered new attention on the country, to make leaders there believe they were being shown as much respect as their rival India on the international stage. Prestige and American aid were the carrots. But there was plenty of stick on the other side of the equation.

In October 2009, on her first trip to Pakistan as secretary, Hillary wore a head scarf, a sign of respect for the traditions of modesty—and female inequality—in parts of the Muslim world. But there was nothing modest or veiled about the message she delivered. She accused the Pakistani government of harboring and abetting Bin Laden, his Al Qaeda brethren, and the leaders of the Taliban. "I find it hard to believe that nobody in your government knows where they are and couldn't get them if they really wanted to. Maybe that's the case—maybe they're not gettable. I don't know," she told a group of Pakistani editors. "As far as we know, they are in Pakistan."

It was no secret that Obama didn't trust Pakistan. "Let me be perfectly clear," he said in a private conversation in the first half of his first term. "We know the Pakistanis are lying whenever they're talking to us." And he had said during the campaign that he would authorize unilateral strikes against targets there if the Pakistanis couldn't or wouldn't help. Hillary had criticized him at the time—but only for being so candid. "It may well be that the strategy we have to pursue on the basis of actionable intelligence—might lead to a certain action," she said. "But I think it's a very big mistake to telegraph that."

But in October 2009, as Obama's top diplomat, Hillary was leaving unsaid exactly what Obama had articulated nearly two years earlier—that if Pakistan didn't step up its coordination in the war against terrorists, America wouldn't hesitate to act alone. Pakistanis shouldn't be under the false impression that there was daylight between the secretary of state and the president on that.

Hillary hadn't asked for permission to step up public pressure on Pakistan's leaders, and as her comments made international news, Jake Sullivan called back to Washington to check in with Ben Rhodes at the White House. Hillary wasn't asking for forgiveness, but she did want to have a better idea of what the president wanted her to do when she was asked about it again—which would surely happen the next time she was around a reporter. Was what she had said all right? Had she gone too far? Should she walk it back?

Rather than being upset, the president's adviser said he loved Hillary's candor and aggressiveness. If anything, Obama's review of American policy in the "Af/Pak" region had made him more distrustful of Pakistan. "Double down," Rhodes told Sullivan, prompting Hillary to repeat the charge later on the trip.

Bin Laden was the holy grail of national security for Obama. But where Pakistan was concerned, America had a delicate task. Aside from Bin Laden, the United States needed Pakistani help in prosecuting the war against the Taliban in Afghanistan and in striking other terrorists in the Pakistani tribal region along the Afghan border. American spies needed to be able to operate within Pakistani borders; the Pentagon needed to be able to coordinate with the Pakistani military; intelligence had to be shared; and the United States needed access to the supply route roads between the port city of Karachi and Afghanistan.

America had to maintain good enough ties in the short term with Pakistan—both its government and its people—to justify continued cooperation even in the face of unpopular American and NATO missions inside Pakistan, which were increasing in frequency and which sometimes killed the wrong targets. But at least at the start of the Obama administration, American officials were optimistic that they could build a better long-term relationship with the Pakistanis.

Hillary's diplomacy was, necessarily, aimed at both the short- and the long-term goals. In conjunction with Holbrooke, she was in charge of providing Pakistan with civilian aid, in terms of dollars and, more important, technical support for everything from agriculture to electricity to education. At home, she concentrated on building relationships between the State Department and the Pakistani American community in an effort to funnel donations to the right places and turn Pakistani Americans into informal ambassadors to their families in Pakistan. Like the other diaspora groups that Hillary connected with through Kris Balderston and his Global Partnerships Office, the Pakistani group offered both a way to strengthen America's relationship with people living in Pakistan and a way for Hillary to forge a bond with activists and donors in the Pakistani American community. Of course, the anger Pakistanis felt over American violations of their country's sovereignty—and the killing of civilians—would never be offset by the United States building roads and bridges, engaging the Pakistani people, or assisting in the modernization of the nation's electricity infrastructure. But it was Hillary's job to soften opposition to the American presence in Pakistan.

The United States had a good story to tell about the assistance it was providing in Pakistan, Hillary believed, but nobody there seemed to be listening. Every time the Chinese built a road or a bridge in Pakistan—a clear deliverable—they would get credit for it. But American aid, given through earthquake relief, small business assistance, and other lower-profile projects, earned little appreciation. Hillary focused on drawing attention to the good she felt the United States was doing. "If the American taxpayer is going to pay to do things in Pakistan because we're trying to curry favor and understanding and appreciation," she said, "let's do it right."

In Pakistan, she met not just with the top government officials but also with opinion leaders and the general public, another example of her belief in making direct contact with the people of a country—and their American relatives—to influence policy in the foreign nation. In a format that became familiar during her tenure, she met with Pakistani citizens and journalists in town-hall-style events reminiscent of those she had run as a New York senator. In one forum, a Peshawar University student drew a parallel between terrorist attacks on civilians and U.S. drone strikes. "In the United States, do you perceive both victims as victims of terrorism?" the student asked.

"No," Hillary replied. "I do not."

On the surface, and in reality, Hillary was the face of America's effort to build a better long-term relationship with Pakistan. But tacitly, she was also creating space for the CIA and the military to continue the short-run covert operations that infuriated the Pakistani people and made it more difficult for the Pakistani government to cooperate with the United States, according to sources in the intelligence and diplomatic communities.

"You have the above-the-water issues and below-the-water issues," said one senior administration official who worked on Pakistan. "Above-the-water issues are development, diplomacy, foreign aid, even security assistance. All those things had to be visible and seen so that you could do all the below-the-waterline things that could happen. And all those things were drones, counterterrorism cooperation, Pakistanis sharing intelligence."

On May 1, 2010, Faisal Shahzad, a Pakistani American working with the Pakistani Taliban, tried and failed to detonate a car bomb in Times Square. Thereafter, American officials redoubled their efforts to put agents on the ground. Days after the failed attempt, Panetta and national security adviser Jim Jones flew to Pakistan to deliver a stark warning. They showed Pakistanis information about links between Al Qaeda, the Taliban, Pakistani jihadists, and sectarian groups operating out of Pakistan. Your country is under siege, and you don't even know it, the American officials told their Pakistani counterparts, using the failed Times Square plot as a pretext for increased covert American activity in Pakistan.

"If this happens again, and it works—if somebody else bombs something in the United States—and it is linked back to Pakistan, we're going to do something," Panetta said, according to a source who was present. Pakistani president Asif Ali Zardari countered by saying Shahzad was an American and that the United States should be doing more to monitor its own citizens' ties to terrorism.

"I saw [Panetta and Jones] as trying to build the case for unilateral action through each of these kinds of mistakes that kept happening," the source in the room said, adding that the American attitude became one of pushing the envelope on covert activities in Pakistan under the guiding theory that Pakistani officials were abetting terrorists. "All of that process, I think, helped facilitate the investigation to where Bin Laden was. They were trying to create this environment."

Indeed, in 2010 the number of drone strikes within Pakistan, which required intelligence scouting on the ground, doubled, and that infuriated the Pakistanis, especially when they didn't feel that they had been properly informed or when the attacks killed noncombatants. That left Hillary with the delicate task of acting as a buffer for the military and intelligence communities. "She had done a lot of meetings, she had done a lot of town halls, she had done a lot of local press, she had done a lot of outreach, and it really just changed the whole tenor of the discussion," the intelligence official said. "It really paved the way for us to get the job done."

The tension between the two countries came to a head in late January 2011, when Raymond Davis, a CIA contractor bearing diplomatic credentials, shot and killed two Pakistanis who had approached his car on a motorcycle. Pakistani authorities found a camera in his car that contained pictures of military assets, and some believed he was trying to prove ties between the Pakistani intelligence service and the terrorist group that had carried out a deadly assault in Mumbai, India, in late 2008. It was a diplomatic nightmare for the United States: a spy carrying State credentials had killed two Pakistanis. Obama suddenly found himself in the position of arguing that the spy should be exempt from prosecution under international diplomatic immunity standards—even though it was obvious to everyone that he was no diplomat. Hot on Bin Laden's trail, a fact that was still known to only a handful of people in the American government, the United States could ill afford further complications in the relationship with Pakistan. But neither could the United States sit by as Pakistan prosecuted an American agent for murder. Hillary pressed Zardari to release Davis, and to signal displeasure with Pakistan's refusal to do so, the State Department canceled a planned meeting among the United States, Pakistan, and Afghanistan.

Fortunately for Davis, and for the United States, the situation was resolved on March 16 with a $2.3 million restitution payment to the families of the victims, negotiated in part by Senator John Kerry (D-Mass.), who was a central congressional player in providing aid to Pakistan, and by Panetta as part of a larger agreement involving Pakistan's long-standing demand that America identify its operatives working in-country. Hillary, speaking in Egypt during the trip in which she put together the coalition for the Libya intervention, denied that the United States had paid "blood money" for Davis's release, but that simply meant there was a way of laundering the transaction. "The understanding is the Pakistani government settled with the family, and the United States will compensate the Pakistanis one way or the other," a senior Pakistani official told *Foreign Policy* magazine blogger Josh Rogin.

There had been a substantial shift in America's approach to Pakistan since the start of the Obama administration. While some senior administration officials believe Hillary consciously used the soft-power tools of diplomacy and development to facilitate U.S. military and intelligence operations in Pakistan from early on in her tenure, others say she was forced by events to move the goalposts.

"At the beginning, there was a kind of theory that there could be this deeper relationship that could be developed with Pakistan," an Obama national security aide said. "The goals evolved from one of more ambitious elevation of the relationship to management of crises. . . . Whether that was a conscious 'this is their role' or whether that was more just 'events took us to that place' is hard to say."

For Hillary, there was no such confusion. The two sides were intertwined. "We did look at it that way," she said.

The Davis incident couldn't have come at a less auspicious time. for the United States, as a small circle of senior officials knew at the time that there might soon be a unilateral U.S. strike on Bin Laden. "It would have been that much more difficult to do the [Bin Laden] operation knowing that you had this unresolved situation," said a White House national security official. "That's not to say that we wouldn't have done it that way."

By that point, the CIA had identified Bin Laden's courier, followed him to a compound in Abbottabad, and spent months trying to figure out whether Bin Laden was living there, too. But the level of distrust between the Pakistanis and Americans was at a boiling point, and there was no telling if or when the Bin Laden hunt would be disrupted. Panetta believed it was time to act, and he believed Hillary would help press the case.

She kept the secret to herself, not even disclosing what she had learned from Panetta to top aides. But they knew something was up: She went to meetings that weren't on her public schedule. She disappeared for a few hours at a time, with no explanation of where she had been or with whom she had met. Sometimes she would show up at the White House without most of her State staff knowing how she had gotten there. The White House had instructed Hillary's highly trusted personal scheduler, Lona Valmoro, to list only "meeting" on the private schedule distributed to her aides. It was an unusual notation.

From mid-March 2011, when Libya was front and center, to the end of April, Obama chaired at least five National Security Council meetings on Bin Laden's whereabouts and options for trying to kill him, and there were about two dozen Situation Room meetings among top military, diplomatic, intelligence, and counterterrorism officials. Bill Burns, the deputy secretary of state for policy, was the only one of Hillary's lieutenants who participated in Situation Room meetings on Bin Laden. He and Hillary would be charged with negotiating with Pakistan in the aftermath of an attack, particularly if it went south. Even if the raid was executed perfectly, the State Department had to be ready for a backlash not just in Pakistan but in other countries. There had to be a plan in place for defending embassies and consulates against retaliatory violence.

The small-circle discussion in Washington revolved around two central questions: Should Obama order an attack even if intelligence officials weren't sure that Bin Laden was at the compound? And if he did order an attack, should it be carried out by bomb, raid, or perhaps an unproven small drone that could narrowly target Bin Laden?

Hillary typically left herself room to maneuver during Situation Room meetings. But it was clear from the first days of discussion that she favored a strike, whether by plane, drone, or SEAL team, according to Pentagon and intelligence officials involved in, and briefed on, the deliberations.

"Secretary Clinton was very focused on the fact that we had to move sooner rather than later," said a senior intelligence official, "that this was the best case we had against Bin Laden since Tora Bora, that we shouldn't in any way involve other countries, including the Pakistanis, or worry about them in any way, and that we had to get the job done. Initially the weight of the discussion was around an air strike, and my recollection is that it was something she was comfortable with."

Over the course of six weeks, various officials raised a litany of concerns and red flags, the most serious of which was that they still couldn't be certain that Bin Laden was actually in the compound in Abbottabad. In one of the meetings, Obama's advisers discussed whether to try to collaborate with the Pakistanis on a mission. The idea was dismissed pretty quickly because of the risk that the plans could leak—or that the Pakistanis could warn Bin Laden.

A question was then raised, rather harmlessly according to a source in the room, about whether the Pakistanis' honor would be offended by a unilateral strike. "What about our honor?!" Hillary exclaimed.

Another concern briefly preoccupied the small set of leaders who knew what was in the offing. As one official noted, the Bin

Laden raid was scheduled to go down the same night—Saturday—as the annual White House Correspondents' Association Dinner, a high-cachet black-tie affair that draws Washington's media elite, government bigwigs, and even a handful of Hollywood celebrities. There was a discussion of whether it would draw attention if the entire intelligence community skipped the dinner or if it would be worse if they all attended and the raid failed.

"Her view was that we had to do whatever we needed to do to preserve the discretion of the mission," said a source in the room.

When she'd heard enough of the back-and-forth about the optics, Clinton stated her position plainly: "Fuck the White House Correspondents' Dinner."

She had a more pressing concern. She believed that the circle of officials who had been "read in" to the plan had grown too large to keep it secret for much longer. If it leaked, Bin Laden could slip through American fingers, just as he had at Tora Bora in the aftermath of the American invasion of Afghanistan.

Over time the discussion had moved away from an air strike, which would have required too much ordnance to be certain of killing Bin Laden, and toward a special forces raid. Hillary supported either option, and she was persuaded that, as one aide put it, it was better to get Bin Laden up close than to have to "just peel DNA off some rock" after a bombing run.

Admiral Bill McRaven, the commander on the ground, was persuasive in bringing Hillary to the conclusion that a SEAL-team raid was the best option.

"Look, we know how to do this," McRaven said. "We've done so many in Iraq and Afghanistan. We are good at this now."

"But you're going deep into Pakistani territory," Hillary replied. "You've got to plan for everything."

They discussed every conceivable contingency, including the possibility that the Pakistani military might intercede in the middle of the raid. In the end, Hillary thought McRaven's planning was impeccable.

Vice President Joe Biden and Defense Secretary Robert Gates, two of the most powerful voices in the small set of presidential advisers, disagreed. Biden wasn't at all convinced that Bin Laden was at the compound. Gates worried about the wisdom of a raid. He remembered Operation Eagle Claw, the colossal 1980 disaster that had killed American servicemen who were trying to rescue Iranian hostages, and the Black Hawk Down loss of a chopper and American troops in Somalia during the Clinton administration.

That made Hillary's support all the more critical. Obama might go against the counsel of his vice president and his defense secretary, but all three of the highest-ranking members of his cabinet? If all three advised him not to do it and then he failed, it could irreversibly damage his credibility on national security matters heading into his reelection campaign.

The final meeting on the matter, held on April 28, was a "no plus-ones" gathering, meaning the national security principals were not allowed to bring aides with them. It has been reported that when it was Hillary's turn to speak, she did what top officials do in the Situation Room: she laid out the upside and the risk from her department's point of view, including the possibility of damage to the American relationship with Pakistan. But everyone knew where she stood. She would stand with Obama on this, come hell, high water, or political attack. She voted yes on the raid.

For the second consecutive time, following the decision to launch an assault on Muammar Qaddafi, Hillary broke with Gates— the defense secretary with whom she now had less of a strategic imperative to align—recommending again that Obama take military action. Her hawkishness also contrasted again with the dovish tendencies of Biden, who had argued against the Afghanistan surge, the Libya mission, and now the Bin Laden raid. In all three cases, Hillary and Obama were in agreement.

People in Clinton's inner circle say it was the president's call all along and that while Hillary was on the side that prevailed, her role was one of support for the view that he took. "When you're the president and you've got your senior military person [saying] that they are not comfortable, that makes it a pretty tough call," said one of

Hillary's closest advisers. "And I think her being on the side of 'Let's do it, let's do it this way' helped Obama and others in the room. I don't think the president needed her per se, but I do know other people in the room were either swayed or comforted by her confidence and her certainty."

That Thursday NSC meeting broke without a decision from Obama. The next day Gates called Tom Donilon with a message for the president. Two senior Pentagon officials involved in the planning, Mike Vickers and Michèle Flournoy, had helped persuade him that the raid was strategically sound. Tell the president I'm with him, Gates said. Obama had already given the order to go, Donilon told him. The raid was planned for Saturday, the day of the White House Correspondents' Dinner.

Obama's aides gathered in the Oval Office that Saturday evening, April 30, to go over his jokes one last time before the gala. They had to wait because he was on the phone with a general in Afghanistan. They didn't know that it was McRaven, the special operations commander who had been planning the Bin Laden raid, and that Obama was calling to wish him luck. When he hung up, Obama told his aides he wanted to revise his remarks.

"I think Bin Laden's played out and we don't need to talk about him," Obama said, referring to a line in the speech that joked about his potential 2012 rivals, including "Tim 'Osama bin' Pawlenty." Jon Favreau, Obama's top wordsmith, thought little of changing Pawlenty's nickname to "Hosni."

Obama asked him to add a "God bless the troops" line.

Hillary, who had made clear her assessment of the value of the White House Correspondents' Dinner during the discussion of the raid, skipped the gala to attend the wedding of one of Chelsea's close friends. There, over casual dinner table discussion and in the company of familiar faces, a coincidental question was raised. "Do you think we'll ever get Bin Laden?" one guest asked her. At that moment, Clinton knew what was soon to take place halfway around the world. She knew that Obama had already delivered the order to attack Bin Laden's hideout in Pakistan and that the SEAL team was preparing to execute it. She looked at the guest, smiled softly, and said, "I don't know, I have no way of knowing, but I can tell you this, we'll keep trying." She crossed her fingers behind her back, as she later told NBC. The next day, Hillary reported to the Situation Room to monitor the raid with Obama and his team.

"Those were thirty-eight of the most intense moments," Hillary later said of the raid. She had been photographed during the operation with her hand over her mouth but declined to say whether the picture was snapped when a helicopter went down in the midst of the raid. "I have no idea what any of us were looking at at that particular millisecond. When the picture was taken, I'm somewhat sheepishly concerned that it was my preventing one of my early spring allergic coughs. So it may have no great meaning whatsoever."

The truth is, she was awestruck. "We're all crowded in the little Sit Room," she said. "I'm sitting, holding my breath."

After the operation, Obama called Bill, who was at home in Chappaqua. "Hillary probably told you," the president started, according to a Hillary aide.

"I don't know what you're talking about," Bill replied. Hillary hadn't mentioned it.

Hillary's Politics

Hillary's campaign fix kicked in, if ever so briefly, on May 25, just a few weeks after the Bin Laden raid. It was early morning in London, and she had just been to a state dinner at Buckingham Palace, where she sat at the head table with Obama and Queen Elizabeth. The rest of the room was dotted with celebrities, including Virgin Group founder Richard Branson and Hollywood actors Tom Hanks and Kevin Spacey. Despite having spent much of her adult life in the salons of world power, there were still moments, like this one, that wowed Hillary. With footmen tending to her, and sleeping in a room near the royal family's famous balcony, Hillary felt like a princess, she later told her staff.

As night turned to morning, Hillary's attention shifted away from the bluebloods and movie stars at Buckingham Palace to Erie County, New York, and a Buffalo-born county clerk whom she just had to call. Kathy Hochul had run a surprisingly competitive race in the special election to succeed Representative Chris Lee in a solidly Republican district in upstate New York. The only reason a Democrat had a chance was that Lee, who was married, had abruptly resigned after having sent a shirtless picture of himself to a woman he met on the Internet. Scandal, as it often does, had presented a political opportunity.

The campaign quickly became a referendum on Obamacare and House GOP plans to cut Medicare. Hochul's success or failure would influence how Democrats, all the way up to Obama, handled the issue of health care in their 2012 campaigns. But Hillary had more than just a basic partisan rooting interest in seeing Hochul win. As county clerk, Hochul had endorsed Hillary in 2008. And on the eve of the March 24 special election, Bill Clinton had returned that favor by recording a robocall for Hochul in which he reinforced her health care attack on the GOP. "You can count on Kathy to say no to partisan politics that would end Medicare as we know it to pay for more tax cuts for multimillionaires," Bill said in a message that was dialed out across the district to some Republicans and independents as well as Democrats. With a lift from onetime Democratic congressional hopeful Jack Davis, who was running as a Tea Party candidate—and took more than ten thousand votes—Hochul defeated Republican Jane Corwin by 5,526 votes, likely less than the number that Davis siphoned from Corwin.

After celebrating her victory in upstate New York, Hochul checked her messages and heard Hillary's unmistakable voice. "I'm in London with the president," she said. "We are watching the results of your race, and we are so excited. I look forward to working with you."

It was a small gesture, one of thousands of similar calls, cards, and tokens of affection that friends and acquaintances of Hillary and Bill Clinton receive every year. That extra touch was the most glaring difference between the Clintons and Obama, who seemed cold and indifferent even to some of his biggest supporters. The Clintons know how to work a rope line, how to soften adversaries, and how much a personal contact means to a friend. They connect.

"I saved it. I treasured it," Hochul said of Hillary's voicemail. "Here she is with the president of the United States in London, obviously conducting business, and she takes the time to call me in Buffalo very late at night. She didn't have to do that. It wasn't expected. She made the extra effort, and it meant the world to me."

The Clintons go much further for the small circle of aides and friends closest to them. One aide after another can recount emotional stories of one of the Clintons intervening to help them during times of trouble, whether to arrange medical care, check in on a sick relative, or even attend a funeral.

So in June 2011, when a pregnant Huma Abedin found herself on the cover of all the tabloids because of her sext-prone husband, Anthony Weiner, the Clintons—especially Hillary—grew ultraprotective of her. Hillary, who had logged her own share of sleepless nights during the Monica Lewinsky scandal, counseled Huma and provided hugs and words of wisdom while the Weiner imbroglio metastasized.

More broadly, the Clintons are exceptional retail politicians, and Obama needed help with his common touch, particularly if he hoped to paint his likely 2012 opponent, Mitt Romney, as a mansion-bound elitist. The Clintons had survived and thrived in the wake of Hillary's 2008 defeat. Her approval rating was at 66 percent, and Bill's had moved back above the 60 percent mark a year earlier. Obama, stuck around 50 percent that spring, very much stood to benefit from standing next to the most popular power couple in Democratic politics.

Hillary's draw was so strong that she was rumored, throughout her four years at State, to be on the short list for a series of high-profile jobs, from Supreme Court justice to defense secretary to World Bank president. By the time Obama named Jim Yong Kim to head the World Bank in March 2012, many months after the rumor first surfaced in print, Hillary press aide Nick Merrill forwarded the *Politico* breaking-news alert to Philippe Reines, adding a prank sentence indicating that Kim would serve in the job only until January 2013, which Merrill expected Reines to read as an inside joke about the prospect of having to knock down a new set of Hillary-to-World-Bank stories in just a few months' time. Instead, a credulous Reines told Mills, who relayed to Hillary that Kim would be in the job only for several months, and Hillary mentioned it to the president in the Oval Office that day, touching off momentary confusion over Kim's intentions. "Who was the genius who did it to you?" Huma e-mailed Reines.

Some Democrats thought Obama would ice his reelection campaign with a switcheroo that put Vice President Joe Biden at State and Hillary on Obama's ticket. The Obama campaign even polled to see how she would fare, determining the numbers weren't good enough to pursue a change. Time and again the speculation was dismissed. But there was one post that Hillary's aides insist she was actually in the mix for, and though it was reported several months later, the rumor never seemed to have legs in the media, perhaps because other officials denied that it ever happened.

A Hillary aide, who cited the *Washington Post*'s reporting on the matter as gospel, told the story this way: In the summer of 2011, Bill Daley, then the White House chief of staff, visited Hillary at State to gauge her interest in taking over as treasury secretary. Tim Geithner, who held the job at the time, had put Hillary at the top of his list of potential successors, and the White House was taking the recommendation seriously enough to feel Hillary out about it.

She politely declined. It was "a nonstarter," one of her aides said.

But Daley said the reported incident never happened. "I never did that. That's bullshit!" he said while attending a Clinton Global Initiative event in Chicago in June 2013. "Not true. I never talked to her about it."

The whole story was overhyped, according to a source close to Geithner. Hillary's name appeared on a list that Geithner provided to the White House, but she wasn't his sole recommendation, the source said.

Surely, adding bona fides in the financial sector through a job at the World Bank or the Treasury Department to her work at State would have rounded out Hillary's résumé for a second presidential run, but the Treasury post would have carried the risk of a second economic collapse. Either way, Hillary never planned to remain in the administration for more than four years, according to her aides, and there was still a lot left for her to do at State.

At the time, Hillary was well aware of just how well she was polling, and at least one close friend warned her that her approval ratings were a function of voters seeing her as above politics, a perception that would be hard to maintain if she jumped back into the fray right after leaving State. In mid-September 2011, longtime friend Ellen Tauscher, the undersecretary for arms control, hitched a ride with Hillary from the Waldorf-Astoria to the UN building in

Manhattan during a General Assembly meeting. Bloomberg News had just published a poll showing that 64 percent of Americans viewed Hillary favorably, and Tauscher had heard the news on MSNBC's *Morning Joe*. The same poll also showed that 34 percent of Americans believed the country would be better off if Hillary, not Obama, were president, 47 percent believed things would be the same, and 13 percent thought the country would be worse off with Hillary at the helm. Major media outlets were reporting the news as a sign of voters' "buyer's remorse" over electing Obama and not Hillary. When Tauscher got in the car, Hillary was sitting in the back smiling, and Tauscher assumed it was because of the big numbers.

The stretch of streets between the Waldorf and the United Nations had been blocked off so that officials could move freely during the General Assembly, giving midtown an eerily empty feel as Tauscher cautioned Hillary to husband her popularity carefully. "What worries me is the reason that you have [high favorables] is that people have marked to market that you are out of politics and they can accept you now," Tauscher said. "If I have one more Republican tell me that they wish you were president, I'll just want to backhand them."

Hillary, who had been listening quietly, laughed at the backhand remark. But Tauscher still needed to make a serious point. She wanted Hillary to make sure her public standing remained strong after she left State. "You have to know what the downside of this is," Tauscher, the former congresswoman, said. "The moment you move back into politics, you go from sixty-six to forty-six to twenty-six faster than a split second. There is real political capital here. It's not conventional political capital, but it's real. How do you manage that in a post–State Department world?"

Of course, it was impossible for Hillary to completely escape politics, especially while her husband was settling three-year-old scores for her on the electoral battlefield. In August, Bill endorsed Representative Brad Sherman, a Democrat from Southern California's San Fernando Valley, for reelection. Sherman had been a loyal Hillary supporter until the very end, even cheering for her from the audience during her Building Museum concession speech. That Bill got behind Sherman would have merited little attention, except for the fact that the state's independent redistricting commission was expected to redraw Los Angeles–area political boundaries in a way that could induce Sherman and Representative Howard Berman, the thirty-year House veteran who led Democrats on the Foreign Affairs Committee, to run against each other in a primary. Berman was one of the most widely respected Democrats in Washington, and he had worked closely with Hillary on any number of thorny foreign policy issues, including Iran sanctions and aid to Pakistan. Sherman, on the other hand, would have had a hard time finding anyone in Washington, outside the people who worked for him, who thought he was a better congressman than Berman. But the district lines favored Sherman, and the calculus for Bill was clear: Sherman had endorsed Hillary early, and Berman had endorsed Obama.

Berman went into damage control mode, pushing every button he could to try to get Bill to stop at the endorsement and not campaign, or raise money, for Sherman. He dialed up Mickey Kantor, who had been Bill Clinton's trade representative, for help. He asked DNC chairwoman Debbie Wasserman Schultz to intervene. He leaned on friends at the State Department to make his case to Hillary. Berman heard back from the intermediaries that Bill understood which lawmaker was the better congressman but wasn't going to retract the statement he had given in support of Sherman. Moreover, the Clinton camp declined to say whether Bill would or would not do more for Sherman.

On one policy issue, in particular, Berman felt that maybe Bill Clinton owed him something. In the early 1990s, Berman had been a leading congressional advocate for Clinton's North American Free Trade Agreement, despite the political cost with labor unions that opposed the pact. Berman even hoped at one point that Bill might take the wind out of the Sherman endorsement by releasing a statement praising Berman for his advocacy on trade issues. In October 2011, as Hillary lobbied Democrats to vote for three Obama-backed free-trade agreements, Berman pressed her personally on Bill's support for Sherman.

"I pointed out the irony that she was asking me to vote for the free-trade agreements and alienate a significant base in my district while her husband was supporting my opponent," Berman recalled. "She gave that funny nervous laugh and said she wasn't involved in politics."

As Bill spent political capital rewarding Hillary's 2008 supporters, he also drew down on it in service of Barack Obama. But this was a calculated investment. If Obama won—and if Bill and Hillary, by extension, helped—the victory would enhance the Clintons' standing both within the Democratic Party and outside it. Back in 2008, as Obama began his steady march to the White House, his top campaign aides were hesitant to bring Bill Clinton into the fold for the final push, fearing that a halfhearted Clinton would show up on the trail and simply run through the motions with little feeling. And even as Clinton agreed to campaign that fall for Obama in key swing states—including must-win Florida—the decision to use him was met with some internal skepticism, aides confessed.

But as Team Obama began to map out the president's reelection bid in the summer of 2011, it became increasingly clear they needed a little Clinton magic. Bill was once again the patriarch of the Democratic Party, having regained his own broad popularity as Obama's had diminished over the course of more than two years in the presidency. It was the biggest irony heading into the reelection campaign, Obama's aides acknowledged. They needed the man who had once attempted to tear their guy down, the man some accused of race-baiting, to help win the second round.

Even though the relationship between the two presidents had grown from barely bearable to cordial, it would be a sensitive mission, asking Clinton to go all out for Obama. There was no love lost between Obama campaign manager Jim Messina and Doug Band, the self-important minder of Clinton's phone calls, calendar, and political favor file. So Obama's aides called on Wasserman Schultz, who represented Florida in the House, to play matchmaker between the two presidents.

During a blistering-hot Washington summer in 2011, Wasserman Schultz dialed up Band to start the dance of involving Bill in the campaign. Band, ever the savvy political operator who returns calls on his own timetable, knew why the congresswoman was calling. He was slow to call her back. Bill Clinton was playing hard to get—or at least Band was. "It's not like there was this enthusiastic rush to jump on board," said one Clinton ally.

Months went by, until Wasserman Schultz finally connected with Band in the late fall. Messina, chief Obama strategist David Axelrod, DNC executive director Patrick Gaspard, and pollster Joel Benenson wanted an audience with Clinton. They settled on November 9, just less than a year before Election Day, at Bill's Harlem office.

The meeting was a classic exercise in bonding, but it was also an opportunity for the Obama aides to roll out the full-court press and solicit advice from the former president. They needed Clinton solidly on their team, and to woo him, they were willing to play to his sense of importance.

Inside a conference room at the Clinton office, Messina presided over a PowerPoint slide show presentation, laying out the details of the Obama campaign strategy, state by state, and explaining in great detail the pathways to victory. As Messina spouted off statistics and numbers, Clinton—joined by Band and Band protégé Justin Cooper—carefully reviewed each slide and listened intently. Cooper, who would later take over Band's duties, had interned for Band in the Clinton White House, and he dressed like, spoke like, and committed the same grammatical errors as his mentor. When it was over, Bill offered up his thoughts on various states and counties. Few people knew the numbers and specifics of state-by-state politics better than Bill, who could easily tick off which counties in Colorado had the largest populations of college-age students to increase turnout and where Team Obama needed to set its sights in must-win Ohio.

Messina, who had left his deputy chief of staff job at the White House earlier in the year to head up the Obama campaign operation, had spent time reading books on reelection bids, including Clinton's 1996 victory. Going into the meeting, he was particularly interested in the strategy Clinton had used to define his opponent, Bob Dole, early on in the campaign, and he wanted Clinton's thoughts on how to replicate it in 2012.

Obama's top advisers were floating two ideas about Romney, the more clichéd theme of Romney being a flip-flopper, and another portraying Romney as an extreme conservative who held views aligned with the Tea Party. Clinton recommended that they focus on the latter. Donors in particular, he told the Obama crowd, would welcome such a strategy. Besides, he added, going with the flip-flopper tack didn't generally work.

The meeting was scheduled for an hour, aides said, but it lasted two and a half, as Team Obama mapped out the reelection strategy for Clinton. Bill savored the political talk, every second of it. The Obama folks, after all these years, were finally starting to speak Clinton's language back to him. It was always good to get political insights from the former president, but the gentle woo—soliciting his advice, talking to him in numbers, and getting him energized for the campaign—was more important for its power in creating buy-in from Clinton, who would go on to be Obama's most effective surrogate.

Obama's aides left the meeting feeling satisfied and grateful for Clinton's help. Back in Chicago and Washington, they bragged that the meeting went "really, really well."

"A lot of the advice President Clinton gave us was helpful and exactly right," said one of the Obama aides.

The Harlem power conference paved the way for a bit of business that would bind Obama and the Clintons in the way that most counts in politics: financially. Days after the meeting, Band dialed up Gaspard, executive director of the DNC. He was calling to relay an ask from Bill to Obama. The former president wanted Obama to take another crack at retiring Hillary's 2008 presidential campaign debt once and for all. The debt, which had once totaled more than $25 million, had fallen to $274,000, due in large part to e-mail pitches and raffles sent to donors from Bill. While Hillary crisscrossed the world as top diplomat, Bill sent several e-mails to donor lists, including one that stated that while her campaign was "so close to paying off the last of her debt—she's not there yet."

But nearly every dollar had been squeezed. Hillary's debt didn't seem like an astronomical number, but there were a lot of obstacles to getting it paid off. First and foremost, a lot of Democratic donors in both her camp and Obama's already had given maximum contributions either to fund the original campaign or to pay off the debt after the primary. The Clintons were desperate for new sources of cash. There were still Obama donors who had categorically refused to write checks to her, even after Obama appealed to them to do just that in 2008. Bill needed Obama to prod his elite set of givers a bit harder.

While some Obama donors still had hard feelings from 2008, others were now more willing to pony up. "It was significantly different because, number one, you were much further removed, and, two, you saw the work as secretary of state," said one Obama donor who subsequently gave to Hillary and called her the "number one team player" in Obama's cabinet. There was also a good back-scratching reason for Obama's team to step up its effort to pay off Hillary's debt: Bill agreed to do three fund-raisers for Obama in the spring.

A few weeks after Obama's aides visited Clinton in New York, the two presidents came together again in downtown Washington.

As the economy was beginning to awaken after a steep decline, Obama held an event on the twelfth floor of an environment-friendly building to announce a $4 billion initiative in federal and private green building investments aimed at creating jobs. He invited Clinton, who had worked extensively on the green building effort through his Global Initiative, to join him.

Even then, after Obama's campaign had courted Clinton and sought his advice on the reelection, the exchange between the two presidents seemed polite but perfunctory. "Work friends," one White House aide called them, adding that the two wouldn't necessarily be hanging out on a Saturday night recounting old tales over beer. Deep down, they had little in common—and said as much both publicly and privately.

But Bill Clinton tried his best to show the world that he was on Obama's side more than ever. "I never got to open for the Rolling Stones, so I'll try and do my best for the president," he said, before introducing Obama at the event in Washington.

The two presidents had spent some time earlier that fall on the golf course at Andrews Air Force Base, the first time Obama had invited Clinton onto the links. They golfed for four hours on a cloudy day, accompanied by White House chief of staff Daley and the ever-present Band. It was Band who had recommended to Patrick Gaspard that Obama invite the former president to play a round of golf as a means of bringing the two sides together. There, as they took swings, Bill offered his opinions to Obama. It was too much for Obama, who said he could only take Bill "in doses."

Two months later, around the time Obama aides traveled to Clinton's office to woo him, the former president continued to offer his opinions to Obama in a book he penned, *Back to Work*. The older president had been frustrated for quite some time, feeling as though Obama had lost his message. He would complain about Obama's loss of narrative to anyone who would listen: friends, former aides, and even those with ties to the president. The book was his way of explaining the policies, in classic Clinton style: simple and bite-sized.

Some White House aides privately grumbled about the book in the halls of the West Wing. But Axelrod, Obama's chief strategist, told the *New York Times,* "We appreciate his insights and his advocacy." Aides on both sides had always maintained there was little daylight between the two presidents on policy. And now at the green building announcement, Obama aimed to incorporate Clinton's presidency into his own narrative.

"When Bill Clinton was president, we didn't shortchange investment," Obama said. "We lived within our means. We invested in our future. We asked everybody to pay their fair share. You know what happened? The private sector thrived, jobs were created, the middle class grew, its income grew, millions rose out of poverty, we ran a surplus. We were actually on track to be able to pay off all of our debt. We were firing on all cylinders. We can be that nation again."

Incorporating Clinton into the fold was a mixed bag for Obama. It was smart to draw parallels to his Democratic predecessor, but it also served as a reminder of the good old days in the Clinton administration, while making Obama look more like the inexperienced leader he had been portrayed as during the 2008 campaign. Ultimately, Obama was willing to sacrifice a little pride in service of winning a second term.

Moments after Obama concluded his remarks, Ed Henry, the senior White House correspondent for Fox News, shouted a question for the president. President Clinton, that is. "President Clinton, do you have any advice for President Obama about the economy?" Henry asked. A smiling Clinton, who had rarely shied away from the cameras during his presidency, lit up, while Obama tried to bat it down.

"Oh, he gives me advice all the time," Obama said to laughter, as he shook Clinton's hand and tried his best to end the conversation there. White House press aides, always guarding against the risk of unscripted moments, began shouting for reporters to make their way out of the building. But as Obama shook the hands of the other attendees, Clinton, wearing a chocolate brown three-piece suit, slid up to the podium with its presidential seal and took a stab at the question.

"I just want to, I'll say again, this announcement today, the reason you should be encouraged by this, you can run the numbers and see how many jobs," the former president began. By then Obama was standing off to the side watching Clinton yet again commandeer the microphone. It was almost a repeat performance of the time a year earlier when an at-ease Clinton had taken the reins of the podium at the White House, fielding questions from reporters for nearly half an hour. Now as Obama looked on, Clinton settled in right at home, his elbow leaning against the podium and his right leg comfortably crossed over his left.

He never directly answered the question on what advice he would give Obama. Aides close to Clinton say he doesn't like to discuss the regularity with which he and Obama speak or what ground they cover. But Clinton gave his endorsement of the president's announcement.

"The president, by doing this, can trigger pools of investment so that you can have more buildings like this," he said. The nod may have seemed issue-specific, but what Clinton was really doing was giving his early endorsement to the 2012 reelection campaign and, more than anything, showing that the past was just that—in the past.

In mid-December, Hillary attended a baby shower for Huma Abedin at the Kuwaiti embassy in Washington. Huma's pregnancy had first been revealed over the summer as a coda to Weiner's texting scandal, with the news serving as a final outrage for those angered by his betrayal. A good number of them were present for the baby shower, which brought together what one participant described as a "great sisterhood" of Hillaryland. The guest list also included Alyssa Mastromonaco, the veteran Obama scheduler who had first contacted Huma to set up the meeting at which Hillary was asked to join the administration, and two of Hillary's most important rising-star allies in Democratic politics, New York senator Kirsten Gillibrand and Wasserman Schultz.

When Huma's friends offered toasts to her, Hillary was asked to give a speech. "Today is not my day. Today is Huma's day," Hillary demurred. "I love her, and I wish her the best."

"Huma is family to them," the participant said. Hillary "just wants her to be happy and have people leave her alone." But that would prove impossible when Weiner ran for mayor of New York in 2013, ensuring that Huma's personal life would be tied to Hillary's political narrative as the 2016 campaign season drew closer. "In a perfect world, she would not be with Anthony so that stuff would go away or come up to a lesser degree," one source with longtime ties to Clinton said. "He's an impediment. But the damage is done now. If she runs, it will be part of the narrative. Republicans are going to push it out in the press to remind people." Still, the source added, even with Huma's link to her husband, "she's more of an asset than a liability."

THIRTEEN

The HRC Brand

Hillary was just sitting down for an interview with CBS News in Kabul, Afghanistan, on October 20, 2011, when Huma Abedin handed her a BlackBerry to share the news that Muammar Qaddafi had been killed.

"We came, we saw, he died," Hillary crowed, laughing as she clapped her hands together. There could be no mistaking her glib reaction, the unseemly swagger of a victor who reveled in the demise of her vanquished foe. Hillary later said that she didn't know at the time the circumstances of Qaddafi's death—he had been captured by rebels, physically assaulted, and then summarily executed near his hometown of Sirte. But even days later, amid international calls for an investigation into whether the rebels had committed a war crime by murdering him without a trial, Hillary declined to say she regretted her initial boast.

She had wanted Qaddafi dead, and she took credit for his killing. Two days earlier, during a surprise visit to Libya, she had issued a decidedly undiplomatic call for him to be "captured or killed soon." Now, after rebels seized him, battered him, and shot him to death, Qaddafi had been both captured and killed. Seven months after Hillary had put together the coalition to stop his advance on the rebel stronghold of Benghazi, she was in the process of expanding American support for the nascent government, much of it through technical assistance rather than straight cash payments. Qaddafi's death marked a major milestone on what appeared to be a fast march to Libyan liberty and in the narrative of Hillary's tenure as secretary.

From the constant chatter about her taking another administration post, to Ellen Tauscher's advice about preserving her capital when she left office, to America's efforts to foster democratic reform movements in the Middle East and Asia, neither Hillary nor the rest of the political class could help but think about her future toward the tail end of 2011. At that point, Libya presented the best opportunity for a headline achievement—a "deliverable," in political parlance—that would ice her legacy as the smart-power secretary.

On the trip to Libya, just before Qaddafi's death, *Time* magazine and its photographer Diana Walker had been granted an unusual level of access to Hillary and her aides, for a cover story on her use of smart power. That was indicative of the State Department's confidence that Libya would be a signature achievement for Hillary, as she is typically very careful about which media get access to her and when. "There was a feeling that they had turned the page," said one adviser who traveled with the secretary to Libya. "It was an illustration of the smart-power approach."

On a military transport flight from Malta to Libya, Walker captured the most enduring image of Hillary in command. She was sitting in one of several business-class seats that had been installed in the middle of the plane when Walker began snapping photos. As usual, Hillary was surrounded by stacks of briefing papers held together by massive binder clips. Wearing sunglasses and a stone-faced expression, Hillary was looking at the screen of her BlackBerry. The photo conveyed an unmistakable countenance: She was in charge.

"You got this sense of power in her, and I think a lot of people gravitated toward that," said Stacy Lambe, who several months later would turn the image into the Internet sensation *Texts from Hillary*. "It captured her in a way that I think a lot of people hadn't seen."

▲

L ike an umpire in baseball, a diplomat is most effective when his or her work goes unnoticed. But that's death for politicians. To win elections and to have sway within government, they need visibility, the ability to point to what they've done. By the beginning of her fourth year, Hillary's own capital within the administration was at an all-time high, Obama's team was in hot pursuit of her husband's help, and nearly two-thirds of Americans approved of the job she was doing. Only the most hardheaded of Obama's aides still harbored a grudge against her from the 2008 campaign. As a token of his appreciation, Obama gave Hillary a black iPad case with "HRC" embossed in gold lettering on the cover and "Sec State" on the spine.

But most of Hillary's work had been behind the scenes. She had kept her head down for much of the first two years, but by the third year, she had emerged as a player who could tip the balance in internal White House deliberations on matters of war and peace. She had stood with Obama in going after Bin Laden—at no small political risk to herself if the raid went bad—and pieced together the coalition for war in Libya. Libya was truly Hillary's account, and it was on track to be the success that defined her legacy. The big knock on her was that she didn't have a major foreign policy breakthrough under her belt. As the *Time* cover spread showed, she had the confidence, and the political imperative, to start raising her profile. If all went right, Libya would be the jewel in her crown.

Legacy was clearly on Hillary's mind when she gathered her senior aides to her outer office in early January 2012. An aquamarine sofa and upholstered chairs sat around a small coffee table atop a gigantic blue and red Persian carpet. Hillary often met there one-on-one with visiting dignitaries such as Afghan president Hamid Karzai, sitting at one corner of the sofa while her guest took a pink-upholstered chair. Across the room, there was an old fireplace that no longer worked, and a midsize conference table with eight or ten chairs stood in the back of the room, near the entrance to Hillary's personal office.

On this day, with only a year left in their term together, Cheryl Mills, Jake Sullivan, Tom Nides, Bill Burns, Wendy Sherman, Harold Koh, and a handful of other aides gathered around Hillary, who had come prepared with one of her trademark long legal pads. She had written action items on page after page of ruled sheets. As she went around the world, frozen conflict by frozen conflict, to see what new approaches might be taken, what efforts might be redoubled to achieve a breakthrough, there was a collective sigh of exhaustion that was as real as it was inaudible. Three years after Burns had given her a presentation on the state of affairs all across the world in the transition space on the ground floor, Hillary was now delivering the same kind of country-by-country, issue-by-issue analysis from the comparatively ritzy confines of her seventh-floor office.

"There was a whole discussion about the Arab Spring fallout," said a source who was in the room. Beginning with Libya, the region offered the best chance to prove the wisdom of the smart-power approach. But there was still much work to do there—and in Burma, the best prospect for State to make its mark in the much-ballyhooed pivot of American focus from the Western world to Asia.

Hillary had just been to Burma the previous month, marking the first time an American secretary of state had been to the country in more than half a century and foreshadowing a smart-power success narrative in which the Burmese government instituted political and economic reforms and the United States responded by easing long-standing sanctions.

For decades, the United States and its international partners had ratcheted up pressure on the government of Burma—called Myanmar by its dictators—but had nothing to show for it by the time Obama took office. The American sanctions campaign, a bipartisan effort spanning four presidencies and attracting members of Congress as diverse as Senate Republican Leader Mitch McConnell and House Democratic Leader Nancy Pelosi, simply wasn't working. Hillary's view, at odds with many of her allies in the bipartisan push for Burmese freedom, was that there had to be a few carrots mixed in with the sanctions stick.

If Burma opened up, Hillary had been promising since 2009, the United States would respond by pulling back crippling penalties and fostering new relationships between Burma and the American business community. The United States had two primary interests in Burma—human rights and the balance of geopolitical power. The regime had systematically abused the human rights of dissidents, including Nobel Peace Prize–winner Aung San Suu Kyi, who had been under house arrest for most of the previous two decades; and the small nation was heavily influenced by China, America's leading rival for international power. In late 2010, the Burmese junta demonstrated its good faith by releasing Suu Kyi, and Hillary's visit a year later signaled America's continued interest in promoting democratic reforms. Burma's revitalized relationship with the United States, which would soon include the release of hundreds more political prisoners and the concomitant restoration of diplomatic ties between the two countries, represented a challenge to China's dominance in its own neighborhood. The small country, therefore, held outsize importance both for the smart-power approach to foreign policy and for America's focus on enhancing its influence in Asia.

Burma was on the path to becoming an unqualified success story for Hillary and for Obama, but when Hillary and her aides met in January 2012, many of America's larger foreign policy concerns were still unresolved. They talked about the democracy movement in Syria, the Russia reset, the Israeli-Palestinian negotiations (which the two sides had walked away from more than a year earlier), elections in Kenya, and even efforts to combat wildlife trafficking, which put cash in the pockets of warlords. Perhaps the biggest indication that Hillary was concerned with her legacy, though, was what one source at the meeting described as an emphasis on pushing her top lieutenants to find ways to institutionalize various changes she had made to the department during her first three years. She had developed the QDDR, articulating a vision for the department and restructuring it, created a series of public-private partnerships dealing with issues affecting women and girls, and pushed State onto better footing with the Pentagon and other national security agencies. Hillary was worried that if her aides didn't spend time and energy sewing changes deep into the fabric of the department, they could be easily undone by the next secretary of state.

After the meeting, Sherman, the undersecretary for political affairs, marched down the hall to her own spacious office, adorned with similar furniture and a gigantic old-school electric globe featuring outdated national borders. She summoned the assistant secretaries for the seven regions of the world to deliver the news that the last leg of Hillary's four-year relay would be a dead sprint. She opened up a bottle of wine and laid out snacks, all the better to soften the blow. "Y'all may think we're coasting for the last year," Sherman began. "Here's the agenda."

It would be a busy year—far busier and far more perilous than Hillary could have expected, and she was desperate to find a lasting legacy achievement before she left. As she built her policy portfolio in 2011 and 2012, she reaped a public relations windfall that her press team could never have concocted in its wildest dreams. Her image was about to get a surprise boost that would act as a sleeper agent in modernizing the public perception of her style as secretary.

On a quiet Wednesday night in early April, with Congress in recess, Stacy Lambe and Adam Smith, ambitious young public relations pros, were throwing back drinks at Nellie's, a pioneer in the cottage industry of gay sports bars where the big draws were drag bingo and buckets of chili-and-cheese onion rings.

Over cheap vodka and soda, the two men began talking about Diana Walker's *Time* magazine photo of Hillary, which was making the rounds in their circle of friends. Hillary looked like a total badass, Lambe thought.

"Who's she texting?" Lambe asked rhetorically. "What is she texting?"

He couldn't get the thought out of his head on the way home, and he started looking for pictures to match with the *Time* shot. He found one of Obama lying on a couch, looking at his BlackBerry, with David Axelrod and a "Change We Can Believe In" sign in the background. Bingo.

Lambe devised a fake exchange and posted the pictures to a page on Tumblr, a blogging platform on which photographs can be put together to create a story line. The page that Lambe shared with Smith would be used to spoof what Hillary and fellow celebrities in the worlds of politics and entertainment might text to each other.

"Hey Hil, Watchu doing?" Lambe wrote over the Obama photo.

"Running the world," he wrote over Hillary.

Just like that, at one a.m., a meme was born. Lambe, who went on to work at the media website *BuzzFeed* and at VH1, had tapped into a public desire to see more of Hillary's personality. The Tumblr page, called *Texts from Hillary,* quickly became a fascination in newsrooms in Washington and New York, then spread beyond to the point that it became a cultural touchstone for the political intelligentsia. Hillary's aides hadn't created the meme, but they recognized its capacity to help transform a leader who had been pilloried as the PC to Obama's Mac into a Technorati texter. During the 2008 campaign, Hillary had discovered that voters liked it when she showed her personality and her humanity. Any number of political and military leaders swore up and down that she was a riot behind closed doors. But as secretary, it was usually more tell than show.

Suddenly two guys outside her shop had given her lightning in a bottle. They had projected her as commanding, human, and funny all at the same time. Hillary told Chelsea that her favorite faux exchange was the one featuring Ryan Gosling.

"Hey girl . . ." the Gosling back-and-forth began.

". . . It's Madam Secretary," came the reply.

Chelsea couldn't believe her mother had even heard of the hunky movie star. Once Hillary was in on the joke, Reines invited Lambe and Smith to meet with her at the State Department. He even sent them a submission from Hillary, which they weren't certain was real. But they were convinced enough by the time they arrived at State to hit "publish" and send dialogue written by Hillary's staff out to the world.

Hillary met briefly with Lambe and Smith, took pictures with them, and autographed printed copies of her own post on the Tumblr page. "Love the site, 'Hilz,'" she signed.

"These last couple of years, she's been kicking ass, and this was a photo, regardless of our *Texts from Hillary,* that captured her in this moment, and I think that's why so many people were sharing it," Lambe said later. The Tumblr page ran updates for only a week, but it was one of the most memorable, and politically valuable, episodes of Hillary's four years at State.

Two weeks later, when she was photographed drinking a beer and dancing in a Colombian night club, the *Huffington Post, Washington Post,* and *New York Post* featured the photos on their websites. The revelry was quickly overshadowed by a Secret Service prostitution scandal arising from the same conference that she and Obama were attending, but Hillary would get another dance later that summer—this time captured on video—at a dinner hosted by the South African foreign minister in Pretoria.

Hillary, hair in a ponytail, followed the female singer's lead, shimmying low as she clapped and laughed.

"It was really sort of a magic moment in a way because we were all having such a good time," said Undersecretary Bob Hormats, who joined in the group dancing along with American ambassador Don Gips, and Export-Import Bank chairman Fred Hochberg. One of the songs they danced to was "Shosholoza," the Zulu laborers' folk song featured in the movie *Invictus.* Hillary didn't seem bothered by the title of the song, which means "move forward for the next man."

But the next day, after a trip to see Nelson Mandela, Hillary confided to Hormats that she couldn't understand why the video had gone viral. "I don't really know what to make of it," she said. "Why would people be so interested in my dancing in South Africa?" The buttoned-down "madam secretary" was becoming fun-loving Hillary to her fans. It was exactly the kind of image a politician would want to project in advance of a run for office.

▲

Hillary would have to continue to protect Obama's international blind side while he sought reelection because Republican nominee Mitt Romney was looking to exploit what his strategists believed was a softness in the marks voters gave Obama on foreign policy. "There's always a foreign policy strength when you're an incumbent. But we always felt like his numbers as an incumbent could have been higher and should have been higher," said Romney adviser Kevin Madden. "They were good, but they weren't fantastic. We felt we could still win persuadable voters."

Romney's attacks on Obama's foreign policy amounted to two main arguments: Obama had gone on an "apology tour" that lowered America's proud head in a bow to other countries, and Obama wasn't doing enough to promote democratic movements around the world. There was scant evidence to prove those claims when Romney started making them, but it was particularly important to Obama's reelection hopes to avoid new episodes that played into Romney's narrative. During the early stages of the campaign, Hillary was confronted with two crises that had the power to reinforce Romney's attacks: one that tugged at the theme of the government's competence in promoting democratic values and one in which the United States, through Hillary, actually issued an apology to Pakistan.

Late one night in April, Hillary got a call from Jake Sullivan. He was on his way to the State Department, he told her, where he would set up a secure conference call so that she could discuss a highly sensitive emerging issue with several of her senior aides. Chen Guangcheng, a blind Chinese dissident imprisoned for his criticism of forced abortions, had escaped from house arrest in Shandong Province, had broken his foot in a stumble during his journey, and was now in Beijing asking the American embassy for asylum.

There were risks to aiding him and refusing him. To give harbor to an escaped Chinese prisoner could badly damage relations between the two countries. But to turn Chen away would be a slap to human rights and America's rhetoric on freedom; that he was well regarded among anti-abortion forces in the United States raised the stakes even higher.

Sullivan and Kurt Campbell, the assistant secretary of state for East Asian and Pacific affairs, converged on State and conducted a series of secure calls with the American embassy and with a small group of senior officials including Hillary, deputy secretary of state Bill Burns, Cheryl Mills, and Harold Koh, the chief State Department lawyer and veteran human rights activist, who was, as one colleague put it, already "in the middle of nowhere in China."

There were two major questions that had to be resolved. First and foremost, could the United States admit Chen to the embassy under international law? Second, what rationale could America use to admit him that wouldn't result in a situation in which every political dissident around the world sought asylum on similar terms?

Hillary's team had confronted a similar conundrum in January, when Wang Lijun, a local official in the city of Chongqing, had sought asylum because he feared retribution when he accused a superior's wife of being involved in the murder of a British businessman. Wang was let into an American consulate long enough for him to secure assurances of his safety from Chinese officials, but he was not given more permanent asylum because the State Department determined his record of human rights abuses made him legally ineligible for safe harbor under American law. Still, the Wang incident gave State staff a useful trial run for dealing with the delicate negotiations surrounding asylum requests.

"Everyone who worked on [Chen] from the State Department side had worked on the Wang Lijun issue," said one State official.

Koh determined that there was ample precedent for giving Chen sanctuary, on a short-term basis, for the purpose of providing medical care. The broken foot, ironically, would allow Chen to walk into the embassy. But there were other complications, not the least of which was the diplomatic crisis that could ensue if the United States interfered in China's relationship with one of its own citizens. Hillary was about to travel to China for a round of the Strategic & Economic Dialogue and, her aides said, was very well aware of the potential for the Chen situation to roil the conference.

"This is actually kind of an easy one for me," said Hillary at one a.m. "We cannot turn this person away. I'm clear-eyed about the difficulties—we can manage them—but I feel very confident about this. Let's do it. And let the White House know we're doing this, so that they have visibility. Go get him."

Then she went back to bed, leaving her aides to work out the final details.

"It was another example of not running away from a problem," said a person who was involved in the discussion. "You could have lawyered that particular problem to death, because if you just dragged it out, inaction would have been its own decision, because he wouldn't have gotten in."

If the decision was an easy one, the nuts and bolts of executing it would prove more complicated. On a practical level, Chen was a fugitive. If he hitched a ride with a Chinese friend to the embassy gates, they could both be stopped and arrested. The way around that was for the United States to send a van to a rendezvous point where Chen, riding in another van, would be delivered. The American van would then bring him safely back to the embassy. Technically, he probably wouldn't have immunity just by climbing into an American car outside the embassy, but State officials determined that it was highly unlikely that the Chinese would create an incident by pulling over an American car.

In a car chase scene out of an action film, the drivers of both vans realized they had been tailed to the rendezvous point. One van turned into an alley, and the other pulled up alongside it, facing the other direction. The sliding side doors were opened, and American officials grabbed Chen by the lapels, yanked him into their van, and sped off to the safety of the embassy. The Chinese cars, in hot pursuit along the way, stopped once the van carrying Chen was inside the embassy gate.

Over the course of a few days, American ambassador Gary Locke, along with Koh and Campbell, who had converged on Beijing, worked to "find out what Chen wanted and then to cut a deal with the Chinese that gave Chen what he wanted," according to a source familiar with the discussions.

Chen, who was something of a celebrity within the tight-knit international human rights community but hardly a kitchen-table name, wanted to be treated at a hospital, be reunited with his family, and then be allowed to attend a university in China; he did not want long-term asylum at the embassy or in the United States. The Chinese signed off on the deal. Campbell called Hillary's plane, which was en route to Beijing for the S&ED session, and said the agreement was in place. The State Department, in dramatic fashion, had struck a blow for freedom. Or so it seemed.

A few hours later Campbell called back to say that Chen had balked and was still at the American embassy, unwilling to leave his secure spot for the hospital even with assurances from the Chinese government that he would not be seized. "Chen is a very jittery guy," said one American official, "and it's not because he doesn't have reason to be jittery." But he had a deal blessed by the Chinese and American governments in hand yet still didn't feel safe.

When Hillary's plane landed, she went to the opening of the conference, and Sullivan went to the embassy to help coax Chen into leaving for the hospital. Eventually, with an escort from American officials, Chen agreed to go. On the way to the hospital, he asked to speak to Hillary by phone. "I want to kiss you," he told her.

Hillary put out a statement, confirming that Chen had been transported from the embassy.

The Chinese, in an effort to save face, put out a harshly critical statement. The American intervention was an "interference in China's internal affairs, which is completely unacceptable to China," the statement said, and it called on the United States to "apologize for that" and "carry out a thorough investigation into the incident, deal with those responsible, and promise not to let similar incidents happen again." The public scolding was a small price for the United States to pay for having secured Chen's freedom.

But then the situation grew complicated again. The next morning Chen told American officials he had had a change of heart. He wanted to leave China for the United States with his family in tow, and he was about to start applying serious political pressure to Hillary.

As the Chinese and American officials watched their carefully or-chestrated deal unravel, Chen used his connections to human rights activists to call in to a Washington hearing of the Congressional-Executive China Commission, an organization set up by Congress to monitor the American relationship with China. With Representa-tive Chris Smith (R-N.J.), a leading conservative advocate for human rights and a critic of Hillary, chairing the hearing, Chen said he no longer felt comfortable with the deal.

Romney, who was wrapping up the Republican nomination for president, pounced on the unfolding debacle. He could slam the president for a major foreign policy snafu and try to drive a wedge between Obama and Hillary.

It is "apparent, according to these reports, if they're accurate, that our embassy failed to put in place the kind of verifiable mea-sures that would assure the safety of Mr. Chen and his family," Romney said while campaigning in Virginia. "If the reports are true, this is a dark day for freedom, and it's a day of shame for the Obama administration. We are a place of freedom, here and around the world, and we should stand up and defend freedom wherever it is under attack."

It was just the kind of story that could breathe life into the Rom-ney assertion that Obama was weak on democratic values. Romney had even used the word *freedom* three times in two sentences to ham-mer home the point. Some State Department officials were reading media reports from the United States that seemed to lay blame at their feet for being too trusting of the Chinese—even though it was Chen, not his government, that had reneged on the deal.

Sullivan and Campbell sat down with Cui Tiankai, China's vice foreign minister. Thank you for the hard work, Campbell told him, but we've got to change the deal.

That's not going to happen, Cui said.

Campbell tried to sell Cui on the idea that Sullivan was particu-larly influential with Hillary and Obama and was there to deliver a message directly from them.

Figuring they'd made it this far, Sullivan picked up the routine. The president and the secretary want these things for Chen, he said.

Cui, a veteran diplomat, was unmoved.

The Americans, who were starving after around-the-clock shuttle diplomacy, saw it as a particularly harsh rebuke when Cui had their food taken away.

As this minicrisis unfolded, Hillary was getting updates from her aides during breaks in the S&ED talks. At one point, she pulled a few senior State officials into a side room on the margins of the conference and delivered a pep talk.

"Our people did nothing wrong," she said. The State Department and embassy staff had "acted in good faith" and worked their tails off in trying circumstances. She wouldn't let Chen's change of heart reflect poorly on the people who had been working so hard to secure his release. There was still time to save the day.

"That struck me as being very protective of her staff," said an American official who was in the room.

Back in Washington, White House officials were paying close attention to the spiraling situation, which was now playing out in news reports and becoming a bigger issue on the campaign trail. Sullivan called Denis McDonough and reported that there were still some challenges to resolving the situation.

"Yeah, I see that," McDonough replied tartly.

In consultation with White House aides back in Washington, State officials decided that only Hillary herself stood a chance of getting the Chinese to agree to a second deal—and risked losing face if she failed.

"We knew we had one big play with her," said one American official who was in China.

The plan was to get Hillary into a room the next day with Dai Bingguo, the powerful state councilor, and let her make the case directly to him that it was best for both sides to right the situation. "We all agreed on a game plan, talking points, the whole nine yards," said a second source.

The next morning Hillary's aides sent word to their Chinese counterparts that Hillary wanted to meet with Dai privately on the sidelines of an official breakfast. The Chinese pushed back, but the Americans held their ground. It is a personal request from Hillary, they said, knowing that Dai would be hard-pressed to refuse what was basically a demand veiled as polite insistence. When Hillary got in the room with Dai, she told him that the Chen situation was blowing up in the United States. Chen had called in to a congressional hearing the previous day, Hillary said.

Dai's jaw dropped. Surely she had been mistranslated, he said. Chen didn't really call in to a congressional hearing, did he?

Hillary's power and prestige might have given her room to work, but she was also forced to put her personal credibility on the line. The United States had pulled off a caper of questionable legitimacy to give Chen asylum, negotiated his freedom with the Chinese government, and then turned back on a publicly announced deal. Chen might have been a little eccentric, but a lot was riding on this moment for her, for Obama, and of course, for the blind dissident who couldn't make up his mind.

Still, she boldly stepped farther out onto the limb. If China didn't play ball, shes intimated, the trust that had been slowly built up between the two countries through the S&ED and other inter-actions might just evaporate. Chinese and American officials were in the process of wrapping up a conference that produced fifty out-comes on issues ranging from climate change to international mari-time law; some of that progress could be jeopardized if there was no resolution to the Chen situation.

"She just, through kind of a piercing gaze and a stiff but calm tone, got Dai to see we were not kidding around—that this was a big, big deal," said one American official.

"If we do not resolve this, we're going to have a problem," Hillary said.

If it was a bluff, Dai didn't call it.

Hillary thought she had a solution that could work for all sides. If China declared Chen a free man and processed a passport request from him, he could travel to the United States. China could say they had dealt directly with their own citizen. The United States could be certain that its efforts to shield Chen had not been in vain. And Chen would be able to move his family to America. Dai liked the idea enough to task his aides to work with Hillary's team to put together the details of a plan that could be brought to Premier Wen Jiabao and President Hu Jintao.

Hu huddled with Dai and Cui at the end of his meeting with the American delegation, which American officials took as a good sign that serious consideration was being given to the plan. In the middle of the day, after working with their American counterparts, Chinese officials put out a statement indicating that Chen was eligible to apply for a passport. It would take another couple of weeks for everything to fall in line. But Hillary's face-to-face talk with Dai had turned a political disaster into a diplomatic success for the administration, and it had protected the Strategic & Economic Dialogue that she had worked so hard to build.

"She invests heavily in personal relationships," said one of her senior aides. "She spends huge amounts of time in these meetings, not just kind of going through her talking points but getting to know the person, asking them about things they care about. So she establishes a baseline level of credibility that she's not there just to transact but she's actually building relationships. With Dai, she had built up a relationship over a long time."

Rather than the "dark day for freedom" and "day of shame" for Obama that Romney had declared, Hillary's diplomacy had delivered a human rights coup. America liberated a Chinese political prisoner and did it with the assent of the Chinese. She had made the decision to go get Chen without asking for permission from the White House, and for at least a day, it had looked as if it would blow up in her face and cause some collateral damage to the Obama campaign. But ultimately the Romney attack was turned on its head. The Chen episode was a win for Obama.

Around the same time, Hillary was lobbying the White House on another issue with serious potential repercussions on the campaign trail. She wanted to issue an apology to Pakistan for a November 2011 NATO air strike in Peshawar that had mistakenly killed two dozen Pakistani soldiers. In late 2010 and early 2011, as her effort to woo Pakistani leaders with diplomacy and development assistance had taken a backseat to drone strikes and other U.S. counterterrorism measures, the relationship between the two countries had suffered, leaving little reason for the United States to keep a spotlight on it. The relationship had all but disintegrated when SEAL Team 6 raided Bin Laden's compound, and the NATO strike blew up what was left of it. Pakistan immediately ordered the CIA to stop conducting drone operations out of one air base, and—more important—it closed off supply routes from Karachi, the port city on the Arabian Sea, to Afghanistan, forcing the United States to rely on a northern route through Russia. That gave Russia more leverage in its politically delicate relationship with the United States.

Hillary argued that the United States should comply with Pakistan's demand for an apology—the mistake, after all, had cost Pakistani soldiers their lives; and at least as important as the question of whether it was the right thing to do, an apology was in the best interests of the United States preserving its tenuous relationship with a country that was both infested with terrorists and armed with nuclear warheads. Moreover, it was costing the United States money and time to use the Russian route. It didn't make sense for America to stand on ceremony when the refusal to issue an apology came with a price, both in terms of dollars and in conducting the war in Afghanistan, she thought.

But Hillary ran into resistance from the White House, the Pentagon, and the intelligence community. The Defense Department and the CIA felt that the Pakistanis owed the United States an apology for, at the very least, failing to prevent attacks on American soldiers. Some believed the Pakistanis were complicit.

"There was a lot of concern that these guys' behavior, the Pakistanis, they should be apologizing to us for some of the things they were doing to our soldiers in Afghanistan," said Deputy Secretary Tom Nides, who had succeeded Jack Lew.

With Romney accusing Obama of going on an "apology tour," it hardly made good political sense for the president to issue an apology to Pakistan, where Americans knew Bin Laden had been hiding in plain view for years. That could play right into Romney's unfounded attack that Obama liked apologizing for America. "When you go out and say that you're sorry, people like the Republicans jump on you and say, 'Oh, my God, why are you apologizing to the Pakistanis?" Nides said of a major undercurrent of concern in internal debates.

But Hillary thought it was vital to American interests to apologize, and she was willing to take it on the chin if there was a political backlash in the United States. "I have political capital. I'll expend it," she said. "If they attack me for saying that, I'm sorry, then so be it. I'm willing to do that."

She dispatched Nides, a veteran of Wall Street and domestic politics, to Pakistan, where he opened up a back channel with Pakistani finance minister Abdul Hafeez Shaikh. The Pakistanis were losing revenue from the closure of the supply route, and Hillary believed it was in their interests, too, to resolve the dispute.

Nides and Shaikh negotiated the language of a carefully worded deal in which Hillary issued a soft apology and Pakistan reopened the supply route. Hillary believed that "the ability to admit you're wrong is a sign of strength, not weakness," one of her senior aides said later.

Hillary's elevation of Pakistan, through her visits and direct engagement with both the country's leaders and its people, had helped make her the American official with the most credibility in the country. "I'm still shocked that the Pakistanis love her and hate Obama for the same damn policy," said one senior administration official focused on Pakistan. "That is a successful operation."

The pact was consummated in a July 3 telephone call between Hillary and Pakistani foreign minister Hina Rabbani Khar. "We are sorry for the losses suffered by the Pakistani military. We are committed to working closely with Pakistan and Afghanistan to prevent this from ever happening again," Hillary said in a statement.

"Foreign Minister Khar has informed me that the ground supply lines into Afghanistan are opening."

Romney, who had titled his precampaign book *No Apology,* chose not to jump on Obama for acceding to Pakistan's demands for an American mea culpa. When the subject came up in his debate prep, he told advisers he drew a distinction between blanket apologies for America and saying sorry in a specific instance. "As a country, you don't apologize for the country and your national stance and your point of view," Romney said. "Of course you make mistakes, but that's different than apologizing for who you are."

"It's one of those cases where he did not want to grandstand," one of the Romney advisers recalled.

Through Nides, Hillary had found a way to go around the fraught relationship between the two countries' military and intelligence communities to find a solution that benefited both the United States and Pakistan. Hillary's "artful apology," as her senior aide termed it, had opened up the supply routes but not a window for Romney to take advantage.

FOURTEEN

The Bill Comes Due

On April 29, 2012, more than five hundred donors packed into the backyard of Terry McAuliffe's seven-thousand-square-foot mini-mansion on Old Dominion Drive in McLean, the tony Washington suburb where Robert F. Kennedy's kids had grown up. Still bursting with the boyish enthusiasm that helped make him a great fund-raiser, McAuliffe was looking toward a second bid for governor in 2013. But he hadn't opened up his yard on this sixty-degree evening to fill his own coffers. The contributors were there to see two presidents—Bill Clinton and Barack Obama—at the first of several joint fund-raisers for Obama's reelection campaign.

Obama's courtship of Bill Clinton was working. The ice had thawed, even if Bill's response was a function of self-interest more than genuine affection. Raising money for Obama would unlock the door to the donors Hillary needed to pay off the last of her debt. But before that cash started flowing to her account, Bill had to prove himself a loyal field marshal in Obama's campaign.

He announced that night that he was lending support to Priorities USA, the flailing pro-Obama super PAC started by former White House aides Bill Burton and Sean Sweeney. The outfit had suffered a slow start in large part because Obama had spent so much time blasting super PACs publicly that many liberal donors didn't want to be associated with them. It had only been a couple of months since Obama finally blessed Priorities USA, and raising money was still a problem. Bill, having been a pioneer fund-raiser in the era of unlimited "soft" money, didn't have Obama's reluctance to squeeze small pools of donors for vast sums of cash.

The more important factor for Obama, who was still battling a sluggish economy and mounting debt, was winning a seal of approval for his policies from the last man to preside over budget surpluses. At this point, though, his praise for Obama was a little fainter than it would get later in the year.

Obama "deserves to be reelected," Bill said. "I think he's done a good job. I think he is beating the historical standard for coming out of a financial collapse and a mortgage collapse. I think the last thing you want to do is turn around and embrace the policies that got us into trouble in the first place."

Clinton was really just warming up, though. During a follow-up question-and-answer session, held under a tent for about eighty VIPs, the presidential pair grew more comfortable. Sitting side by side on stools, Obama and Clinton played off of each other, with Clinton taking on the atypical role of best supporting actor. The singer will.i.am asked Obama a question about education policy. When he didn't get a satisfactory answer, he pressed Obama a second time. Clinton jumped in to defend the president. And so it went for nearly an hour.

When the two-man improv act was over, Clinton went to the foyer of the house to say goodbye to Obama. Without a camera or a reporter in sight, the two presidents shared a private moment.

"Thanks for all your help," Obama said to Clinton.

"I'm here to do whatever I can," Clinton replied.

They didn't shake hands. They hugged.

"It was clear that night that, whatever issues they had had in the past, that event was a coming together," said a Democratic official who witnessed the physical and political embrace.

Shortly before Bill delivered on his end of the bargain to get behind the president, Obama fund-raising chief Matthew Barzun, who had attended the peace-pipe dinner for Obama ambassadors and Hillarylanders at the Cosmos Club in early 2009, put the word out to Obama's leading donors that it was time to retire the last of Hillary Clinton's debt. The joint fund-raiser at McAuliffe's house was held on April 29; in May and June, dozens of Obama's elite givers, including *Vogue* editor Anna Wintour, contributed to retiring Hillary's debt, helping her shave it from $245,000 to $100,000 by the end of June. None of Obama's big-time donors had given to her during the 2012 cycle before Bill's turn at the April fund-raiser for Obama. It was the payoff for Bill buckraking for Obama.

If the scars that the Obama and Clinton camps had inflicted on each other had not been forgotten, they had at least been forgiven. As the campaign season heated up in the spring and summer of 2012, however, the reconciliation between Obama and the Clintons created a delicious political irony. No sooner had he buried the hatchet with Obama than Bill Clinton dug it up for use on politicians who had backed Obama over Hillary in 2008, the names counted on the post-primary hit list. For his own political standing and for Hillary's future, Bill had to pursue rapprochement with Obama; but when it came to the betrayals of friends and associates, there was no forgetting and no forgiving. A full presidential-election cycle later, Bill was still determined to get payback. The once-a-decade redistricting process had seeded a bumper crop of high-profile Democratic primaries in which one candidate had supported Obama in 2008 and the other had backed Hillary.

Just a few days before the fund-raiser at McAuliffe's house, the Clinton bell finally tolled for Jason Altmire, the Pennsylvania congressman who had infuriated Hillary in 2008 by withholding his superdelegate endorsement. Earlier in the spring, Bill had gone into overdrive to help Kathleen Kane, a Hillary supporter, in a primary for the Democratic nomination for Pennsylvania attorney general. She was running against Altmire's fellow Obama-besotted pol Patrick Murphy, who had endorsed Obama early in the 2008 cycle and was now trying to make a comeback after losing his House seat to a Republican in 2010.

When Bill endorsed Kane in late March 2012, Altmire saw the writing on the wall. He called one of his leading advisers, Rachel Heiser, and told her he was worried that if Bill was willing to involve himself in a state attorney general's race to exact retribution for

2008, Bill's next step would be to target Altmire for defeat. At the time, Altmire was the heavy favorite to beat fellow Democratic representative Mark Critz in a redistricting-induced primary, because their new, shared district included more of Altmire's old turf than Critz's. But Bill had helped Critz succeed his old boss, the late representative John Murtha, who had backed Hillary in 2008.

On April 12, about two weeks before the primary, Altmire's fears were validated. "I am proud to endorse Mark Critz for Congress," Bill said in a statement. "I know that Mark will continue his work to create jobs, strengthen the middle class, protect Social Security and Medicare, and do what is right for western Pennsylvania and our nation."

Critz immediately turned the endorsement into a TV ad, and on primary election day he edged Altmire by 1,489 votes out of more than 63,000 cast. Critz won Cambria County, where Bill had campaigned for him in a 2010 special election, with 91 percent of the votes cast there. It's impossible to say how many votes Bill Clinton turned or turned out, but everyone involved in the race agreed that his endorsement of Critz had been pivotal. "It certainly had an impact," Altmire conceded.

On the same day, Kane beat Murphy, who had picked up an endorsement from Obama adviser David Axelrod, 53 percent to 47 percent. While Kane went on to win in the general election, Bill Clinton's aid to Critz may have resulted in the loss of a Democratic seat in the House: in November, Critz lost to Republican Keith Rothfus, the man Altmire had beaten in 2010, by less than four percentage points.

But the ledger had been balanced. Four years after Michelle Obama had wooed Altmire and Murphy, telling them how Barack Obama was going to blindside Hillary, Bill had blindsided them.

That same spring businessman John Delaney shocked Maryland's political establishment by defeating state senate majority leader Rob Garagiola in a primary in a solidly Democratic district anchored in Washington's wealthy Montgomery County suburbs. Garagiola and his friends in the legislature had drawn the district so that it would elect him to the U.S. House. He had picked up endorsements from Governor Martin O'Malley, House minority whip Steny Hoyer (D-Md.), and most of the liberal groups in the state.

But Delaney, who had raised money for Hillary, had Bill on his side. Delaney coasted to victory, helped along in part by a robocall Bill recorded for him. "Bill Clinton was as much involved and as much responsible for Delaney winning as anyone," said a former State Department aide familiar with Bill's activities.

In June, Bill went head-to-head with Obama in a New Jersey Democratic primary featuring Representative Bill Pascrell, a cigar-smoking seventy-five-year-old member of the tax-writing Ways and Means Committee, against Representative Steve Rothman, a fifty-nine-year-old member of the similarly powerful Appropriations Committee. Both men had first been elected to the House on Bill Clinton's coattails in 1996. Pascrell had jumped into Hillary's camp in 2008, while Rothman had gone with Obama. As president, Obama had been judicious—some might say stingy—in hitting the campaign trail for other candidates, particularly in Democratic primaries. On occasion, in his place, one of Obama's advisers would give an endorsement to a favored candidate, as Axelrod had for Murphy.

But when Bill showed up in Paterson to campaign for Pascrell, Obama countered personally. He invited Rothman to meet him at the White House, where pictures of the two men walking past the Rose Garden were taken. There was no guile in the act. "The president said he had invited me to the Oval Office because he wanted everybody to know that he supported my reelection to the Congress so I could help him with his agenda in his second term, as I have in the first," Rothman said.

But Obama didn't go all out for Rothman the way Bill did for Pascrell. In what had been expected to be a close race, Pascrell coasted, 61 percent to 39 percent.

Obama had plenty of reasons to stay out of intraparty feuds as much as possible and particularly to avoid appearing on behalf of other candidates at public rallies. By taking sides in other races, he would inevitably alienate some of his own supporters and would be seen as a partisan political operator, at a time when his own reelection hopes depended on his ability to capture the political middle ground. And of course, he didn't have a lot of extra time on his hands to campaign for other candidates. Bill wasn't constrained by the latter two considerations, but because Hillary might run again, he had to avoid angering her base with his activities on the campaign trail.

In an unusual twist, Bill backed off of Howard Berman, who had launched a full-scale campaign to persuade him not to raise money or campaign for Brad Sherman. Because of a new election system in California, Berman and Sherman were actually pitted against each other twice, first in a pivotal primary in the spring and then again in a general election in November. In May 2012, Obama lent his imprimatur to Berman by letting Berman ride with him to an Obama reelection fund-raiser at movie star George Clooney's house. But Bill, after releasing his August 2011 statement of support for Sherman, never reengaged with the race.

"I believe that effort kept him from doing anything more," Berman said. "He was mulling it. . . . He did not do fund-raising for Brad, he did not come into the district and do events for Brad. I didn't get the full treatment."

But the statement did enough damage. Sherman topped Berman by 10 points in the primary and by 21 points in the November runoff.

"I don't blame Bill Clinton for what he did," Berman said. "That's a certain loyalty. . . . I didn't like it, but it's not a source of hostility to me. That's the way politics is."

With Berman, Bill and Hillary scored a double victory. To Berman's friends, Bill had seen the wisdom of reason in the end. But Sherman's victory was touted in the press as another tally in Bill's column, feeding the perception among Democrats that it was dangerous to cross the Clintons.

There's no question that fellow members of the Democratic Party received Bill's message. There was a price to pay—sometimes an entire political career—for crossing the Clintons. "It has the desired effect," Representative Gerry Connolly (D-Va.), an admirer of Hillary's, said of the Bill Clinton payback tour. "Let us just posit that they're even thinking about Hillary running in 2016. In case she is challenged in the primary, a lot of people, after this, are going to think long and hard about supporting her opponent. It's not cost-free."

Even as Bill and Obama were fighting proxy wars through candidates like Pascrell and Rothman, they continued to plot Clinton's contribution to Obama's reelection. A few days after the New Jersey primary, Obama advisers Jim Messina and Axelrod paid a visit to Bill's suite at the top of the riverfront Chicago Sheraton. Clinton was in town for CGI's annual national conference and was joined by Doug Band, Justin Cooper, Jon Davidson, and spokesman Matt McKenna. John Podesta, who had served as Bill's White House chief of staff and as director of Obama's presidential transition team, was Switzerland.

It could have been a tense talk. Bill had just made two public statements that undermined Obama attacks on Romney: he had challenged the wisdom of letting tax cuts on earners making $250,000 or more expire, and he had come to the defense of Romney and private-equity firms when the Obama campaign criticized the Republican nominee's record at Bain Capital.

But Obama's aides, who were dealing with a lot of off-message surrogates, saw Bill's comments as rustiness rather than sabotage. "I don't think there was anyone on the campaign who thought he was intentionally trying to screw things up," one senior Obama adviser said. "He wanted to be an asset, and he was a big asset."

Messina, who could see the Obama campaign headquarters from the window of Clinton's suite, simply wanted to make sure that asset was being used in the right way. He began talking to Bill about polling information, voter data, and campaign infrastructure in minute detail. The rest of the room melted away as Bill and Messina spent an hour in the weeds of the campaign.

"The two biggest field data nerds I've ever met in my life, they're going over precinct-by-precinct data from '08 versus '12," said a source in the room who marked the meeting as the moment that Bill Clinton began to focus on reelecting Obama. "That was the day."

Messina found Clinton to be what he expected—a world-class

adviser and political strategist—while Clinton liked Messina's willingness to lay the campaign's cards on the table. Their discussion ranged beyond raw political data to messaging, policy, and the ways Bill could most be helpful on the campaign trail. Over the summer and fall, Clinton and Messina spoke frequently.

Bill had a particular expertise that only one other living man could claim: he had defeated a sitting president. In fact, the feat had been pulled off only three times since 1932—and one of the incumbents who lost was the accidental president Gerald Ford. Bill's 1992 victory over George H. W. Bush, and his reelection win in 1996 over Bob Dole, gave him special insight into what factored into voters' judgment of a sitting president. The common factor in lost reelection bids was a weak economy, and Obama's efforts to get America bustling again hadn't been as successful as he had hoped. If Romney won and the economy rebounded, as many experts predicted, it would be harder for Hillary to take the presidency in 2016. Therefore the best outcome for Hillary was an Obama victory followed by a booming economy. Ultimately, Bill had no reason to half-ass it for Obama and every reason to go full throttle.

Spurred on by his growing dislike for Romney, Bill hit the afterburners in Charlotte at the Democratic National Convention. The tipping point had come in August, when Romney tried to pin Obama for going back on the welfare reform law that Bill had signed as president. "The Romney people specifically sort of decided to cozy up to [Bill]. . . . They tried to drive a wedge between Clinton and Obama on welfare," recalled a source close to Bill Clinton. "That was one of their three biggest tactical mistakes of the campaign."

It was too cute by half in Bill's book, the kind of shenanigans that worked in a race for a town board but not in a presidential campaign. His professional sensibilities were a little offended. If the meeting with Messina in Chicago had gotten Bill invested in the Obama campaign, the welfare flap got him energized to bludgeon Romney. "Over time, more and more, it felt like he was part of the team," one Obama adviser observed.

Bill was eager to hit the trail not just for Obama but also for

Democratic Senate candidates—powerful players in future Democratic primaries. But he needed to turn his convention speech into the right springboard for that effort. Romney had been pounding Obama on the limp economy, and Bill's primary objective was to make Romney's worldview look like that of an insulated rich guy while wrapping the mantle of the Clinton economic success around Obama's shoulders. In 2008 everyone knew Bill had been a reluctant advocate for Obama's cause, but this time, when it came to the president's reelection, he strove to make sure there was no doubt where he stood.

In preparing for his dramatic turn onstage—a moment of redemption, catharsis, and political resurrection—Bill surrounded himself with a who's who of his presidency for a mighty thirteen-hour jam session. Paul Begala, Mark Penn, Joe Lockhart, Sandy Berger, Bruce Reed, and Gene Sperling served as the lieutenants in a new war room that looked a lot like the old one, only grayer and more grizzled. Lockhart had been Bill's White House press secretary, Berger his national security adviser, Reed the head of the Bill-driven centrist Democratic Leadership Council, and Sperling a top economic adviser. Reed and Sperling, both of whom now worked for Obama, were the connective tissue between the two camps. The Obama folks saw them as old Clinton hands helping the former president work his magic. The Clinton team regarded them as old friends who nonetheless were with Obama. The cast of characters rotated throughout the day, as Bill sanded a vintage speech full of clever contrasts, memorable for its delivery more than for its substance, and a bit too long.

Bill had begun collecting thoughts on the speech a few weeks earlier, but it was generally a souped-up version of the speeches he had already delivered for Obama. Like Sinatra warming up for a rendition of "New York, New York," Bill didn't need much of a rehearsal. He practiced the speech just once all the way through. Once he started the full run-through, his pals knew he would deliver onstage. The text was shuttled over to the Obama camp, where David Plouffe, David Axelrod, Jon Favreau, and Obama anxiously waited. They made a few edits. Then Clinton re-added some old material that hadn't been in the previous draft. News outlets would soon note that Clinton's remarks didn't quite match the prepared text they'd been given by the Obama campaign. Bill was satisfied with the speech by 9:45 p.m., and he took the podium half an hour later.

Romney's plan lacked an important component, Obama's team had been saying: math. But Bill said it differently. In the folksy tone that the lower-class son of Arkansas had used to connect with average Americans for more than two decades, he used a longer word to convey a simple concept that every American who had attended grade school could understand—particularly the older set that Obama was having trouble winning over. "Now, people ask me all the time how we got four surplus budgets in a row. What new ideas did we bring to Washington? I always give a one-word answer: Arithmetic."

Arithmetic, not math. It was classic Clinton, and the audience rewarded it with a rousing ovation. "If they stay with their five-trillion-dollar tax-cut plan—in a deficit-reduction plan?—the arithmetic tells us, no matter what they say, only one of three things is about to happen." He ticked through them, one by one: middle-class families would see their taxes go up, basic services would be gutted, or the national debt would pile even higher.

Then Clinton turned his attention to Republican vice presidential nominee Paul Ryan, who had been attacking Obama for slashing Medicare even though Ryan's budget used the same savings. "It takes some brass to attack a guy for doing what you did," Clinton said to laughter and applause. Sperling would later say privately that the "brass" line hadn't appeared in any of the drafts of Clinton's speech. One of the best lines of the night was ad-libbed—or at least held back from the Obama camp.

Obama watched the speech on a monitor from the wings. During the campaign, according to one of his top aides, he had sometimes found himself forgetting that he had his own speech to give while watching Bill spin text into narrative. He found Bill "very entertaining," the aide said, and swore to himself and others that he would give more freewheeling speeches when he was no longer in office.

There were a lot of ways to interpret Bill's newfound love for Obama, but they all boiled down to a simple defining trait of the Clintons' careers: loyalty. In the loftiest sense, Bill was showing loyalty to his country by promoting the candidate he felt was best positioned to lead it. From another perspective, he was demonstrating loyalty to the Democratic Party, as he had from his days as a driver for Governor Orval Faubus right up to that very moment.

But he was also loyally laying the groundwork for Hillary to run in 2016. If she hoped to capture the nomination and win the presidency, she would need a unified Democratic Party, one that was healed from the bitter 2008 primary. Bill mentioned her early in the speech. Obama, he said, had been wise enough to bring his rivals into the fold—he was of such sound judgment, Bill said, that he had hired Hillary to be his diplomat. Since that moment in 2008, in a political chess game played expertly by both sides, Obama and Hillary had bound together their own political fortunes as well as Bill's interests both in resurrecting his own image and in positioning Hillary for a second run. The Clinton-Obama political marriage had been more fruitful than any of them could have imagined four years earlier.

It was afternoon in Dili, East Timor, and Hillary had wrapped up meetings with the president, the prime minister, and the American embassy staff there. Before flying to Brunei for a dinner with the sultan, she settled into a chair in the ambassador's personal quarters to watch a recording of Bill's speech. Her aides had undertaken a minor operation to allow her to watch. First, after trial and error, they had determined that the ambassador's personal computer was the only one in the building equipped to download the recording that Philippe Reines had made remotely and accessed from the Slingbox in his Washington, D.C., apartment.

Then without warning, they kicked reporters off of the Internet to ensure that the connection to the ambassador's house would have enough capacity. With Hillary at the desk, her aides piled onto the ambassador's bed behind her to watch.

Nick Merrill, a press secretary who dabbles in photography as a hobby, tried to snap photos stealthily as Hillary sat glued to the monitor. His mission was complicated by the loud sound his Canon 7D camera normally made when it clicked away at eight frames per second. Merrill switched over to taking single frames, ducking behind an armoire between shots so as not to make Hillary aware that she was being photographed. Finally, he crept up close enough to capture a memorable image of her, smiling with her hand resting at the top of her sternum in a gesture of pride, as she watched. In the photo, a half-eaten sandwich sits on the desk. Hillary wore a look of satisfaction when Obama came out to the stage to greet her husband. Her aides later expressed mild surprise that Hillary was so enthralled, given the innumerable speeches she had seen her husband give over the course of more than thirty years.

When it was released by the State Department, Merrill's photograph was powerful enough to merit play on most major American news sites the following morning. Without uttering a word—without risking a controversial appearance or partisan jab—Hillary conveyed that she had her eyes on the presidential race and on her husband's role in it.

Even though she followed the tradition of most secretaries of state by declining to campaign for the president's reelection, Hillary closely monitored electoral developments, particularly in the battle for control of the Senate. During the 2012 election cycle, according to a Democratic source on Capitol Hill, she spoke to Senate Majority Leader Harry Reid, the Nevada senator, as many as five times about electoral politics. "It was like 'I just want to know,'" the source said. "She wasn't asking to do anything. We weren't asking her to do anything, obviously. But she wanted to have a little bit of the fix."

Hillary, who could watch Bill take care of her politics at arm's length, was largely focused on doing well in the job that she had. In a few months, she would leave the administration, and it looked as if she would do so with a spotless record.

FIFTEEN

Benghazi

When Hillary Clinton had met with Libyan opposition leader Mahmoud Jibril for the first time in the penthouse suite at the Westin Paris on March 14, 2011, as part of her campaign to build a coalition to fight Qaddafi, Chris Stevens was one of the handful of American officials in the room. Stevens was so taken with Jibril's presentation that day—the vision of an inclusive post-Qaddafi Libya—that he urged Hillary to repeat it to President Obama.

A model practitioner of the kind of expeditionary diplomacy that Hillary believed was essential to improving America's standing abroad, particularly in the Arab and Muslim worlds, the rangy Stevens had literally stood out from the crowd in his foreign service training class years earlier. Fluent in Arabic and French, he had spent much of his twenty-year career as a political officer in Middle Eastern and North African capitals, including Jerusalem, Damascus, Riyadh, and Tripoli, where he served in the roles of deputy chief of mission and chargé d'affaires for a two-and-a-half-year stretch ending in 2009. During his first tour in Libya, he had delivered blunt assessments of Qaddafi's eccentricities back to Washington, including observing at one point that the Libyan strongman "often avoids making eye contact during the initial portion of meetings, and there may be long, uncomfortable periods of silence."

The combination of his expertise in the region, his commitment to a view of diplomacy that emphasized on-the-ground engagement with the public and civil institutions, and his belief in Jibril's vision for Libya made him a natural choice to become America's liaison to the Libyan opposition in the weeks after the coalition began hammering Qaddafi's forces.

He arrived in Benghazi, the rebel stronghold, via a Greek cargo ship on April 5, 2011, with what he described as a mandate to "go out and meet as many members of the leadership as I could in the Transitional National Council."

Hillary's whole approach to conflict regions—articulated in the QDDR and demonstrated by the State Department's work with the Pentagon in Afghanistan, Pakistan, and Iraq—was to foster partnerships among government agencies that allowed diplomats to be on the ground in the most dangerous parts of the world. The risk, she believed, was necessary to protecting and advancing American interests. Released just a few months before Stevens landed in Benghazi, the first QDDR noted that "as we expand U.S. expeditionary capacity for conflict and crisis, we are building on the experience of innovative field officers at State and USAID who have set new standards for impact on the ground." The report argued that "these kinds of efforts must become a part of the 'new normal' for our personnel deployed to conflict and post-conflict environments." It also talked about how to "manage risk" in such places rather than avoiding it.

Stevens served in his Benghazi-based post until November 2011, left Libya, then returned in May 2012, this time to Tripoli, as America's ambassador to the fledgling government. Stevens was "famous for always maintaining his California sense of calm, even when he's up against the most challenging diplomatic crises out there," Hillary said at a State Department ceremony in honor of his promotion. Challenge was exactly what Stevens found. In March his predecessor, Ambassador Gene Cretz, had cabled Washington from Tripoli to ask for an alteration in the State Department's plan for transitioning from an emergency security posture to "normalized security operations." State was in the process of a phased withdrawal of three mobile security detachment (MSD) teams, groups of six specialized State security officers who coordinated closely with other agencies, including the Marine Corps and the FBI, and a sixteen-member

Pentagon site security team (SST). The plan called for replacing them with a combination of traditional diplomatic security officers from the State Department and local security forces.

But with the unstable security environment in Tripoli, during a political transition expected to last for a year beyond the June 2012 election, and with frequent visits from VIPs who needed security, Cretz requested in a March 28 cable that one MSD team remain in place to provide training for local forces through July 1, 2012, that Tripoli get an increase in the number of full-time regional security officers and that State provide a dozen traditional temporary-duty diplomatic security officers to replace the departing MSD teams. In addition, he requested that State maintain a force of five temporary diplomatic security officers, on rotations of forty-five to sixty days, in Benghazi.

In requesting more assistance, Cretz dealt primarily with Eric Boswell, the head of diplomatic security at the State Department's Washington headquarters. At the time, there wasn't believed to be a specific threat to American diplomats or assets in Libya, just a chaotic environment in which the new government had little authority to rein in the hundreds of militia groups across the country. Cretz said later that he did not bring up his request for more security with Hillary, Cheryl Mills, or anyone else in the secretary's personal office.

"To be honest, I felt that I could probably live within the gradual transition," Cretz said of his decision not to go higher up the chain of command. "If you had said to me 'Would you like more or less security?' of course I would have said 'I want more.' But given the fact that we really didn't have, to my knowledge, a credible threat against us, and we were facing what everybody else was facing [in conflict zones around the world], we had had at least sufficient resources to do what we were doing."

Before Cretz could get a reply to his cable, the Benghazi compound was hit with a small bomb, and in a separate incident, another improvised explosive device was thrown at an American diplomatic motorcade. When word finally came back from Washington on April 19, three weeks after his cable, Cretz was disappointed. The reply he received suggested that the original plan would remain in place.

"Whether that was a misjudgment or not, we had to live with the decision to basically go through as much normalization as we could, but we kept pushing for extensions," Cretz said. Instead of holding meetings in several locations, diplomats would now stay in one place and bring in other people to meet with them, as a means of reducing security force needs. "When faced with a situation, we saluted and we made the adjustments that we needed to make."

When Stevens arrived to replace Cretz in May, the situation on the ground was growing worse. But his requests to maintain a higher level of security met with similar resistance from Washington. Less than a month into the job, he sent an e-mail asking the director of the State Department's Mobile Security Deployment Office to allow two departing MSD teams to remain in place. The day before, an IED had blown a large hole in the outer wall of the Benghazi compound. But the informal request was denied.

In July, Eric Nordstrom, a regional security officer on the ground in Tripoli, was planning to send a formal cable requesting continued support from the sixteen-member SST and two MSD teams. Charlene Lamb, a deputy assistant secretary of state in Washington, responded angrily when informed of it. "NO, I do not [repeat] not want them to ask for the MSD team to stay!" she wrote in an e-mail to other State staff. Stevens and his security team ignored her admonition, sending a cable three days later expressing concern about a planned reduction from the existing thirty-four U.S. security personnel in Tripoli to only seven by mid-August. Specifically, the embassy asked for an extension of support from at least thirteen high-level security agents, through mid-September 2012. The conditions on the ground didn't meet the necessary benchmarks for a reduction in force, he argued, and the Libyan governing authority wasn't equipped to provide support, either for normal operations or in an emergency.

Pat Kennedy, the undersecretary for management, denied the request, according to a subsequent congressional investigation. There is no evidence that the request ever made it above Kennedy, who, as an undersecretary, was two levels below Hillary in the State Department power structure.

The brewing fight between Tripoli and increasingly senior State officials in Washington escalated over the summer. But the high-level security teams were stationed in Tripoli and seldom traveled to Benghazi. Indeed, while repeated requests for additional security were generally focused on Tripoli, in the western part of the country, the security situation in Benghazi, in the east, had been deteriorating badly throughout 2012.

In addition to attacking American facilities and personnel, terrorists fired rocket-propelled grenades at an International Red Cross building; Sudanese and Tunisian diplomats came under fire; and the British closed their consulate after their convoys were twice targeted by rocket-propelled grenade fire and possibly AK-47s. Despite the presence of a Libyan government police force, Benghazi was really a war zone dominated by competing militias, some of which were willing to provide protection for Americans for a price.

As State moved to normalize its security operations in Tripoli, it beefed up the physical compound in Benghazi—heightening the outer wall; reinforcing the facility with Jersey barriers, steel gates, and a steel door; and adding guard booths, safety grilles on windows, and an internal communications system. Technically, it was a temporary facility with a residence and workspace for the ambassador to use on visits to Benghazi, but State was preparing to turn it into a permanent consulate.

Stevens traveled from Tripoli to Benghazi for what would be his final trip on September 10, 2012, and attended a briefing at a secret CIA annex a mile or so from the compound. The number-two State Department official on the ground at the time, Greg Hicks, would later testify that Stevens went to Benghazi to prepare for a visit Hillary planned to make to Libya just before the end of her term.

"At least one of the reasons he was in Benghazi," Hicks said, "was to further the secretary's wish that the post become a permanent constituent post, and also there, because we understood that the secretary intended to visit Tripoli later in the year. We hoped that she would be able to announce to the Libyan people our establishment of a permanent constituent post in Benghazi at that time."

Stevens had told Hicks that Hillary personally conveyed that message just before he had arrived in Tripoli as the new ambassador that summer, and with the end of the fiscal year approaching, the State Department had only until September 30 to transfer funds from an Iraq reconstruction account if Hillary hoped to announce the transition during a trip to Tripoli later in the year, Hicks testified.

"Timing for this decision was important," Hicks told a House committee. "Chris needed to report before September thirtieth, the end of the fiscal year, on the physical—the political and security environment in Benghazi—to support an action memo to convert Benghazi from a temporary facility to a permanent facility."

B ut Benghazi was growing ever more dangerous, and when Stevens, the American diplomat most familiar with the area, set out for what was supposed to be a five-day visit on September 10, 2012, he knew it. Wary of potential violence on the anniversary of the September 11, 2001, terrorist assault on the United States, and believing himself to be a target of extremists, he decided to hold meetings and work inside the compound that day.

Early in the morning, before seven a.m., someone was spotted taking pictures of the compound, which was guarded by American security officers, local militia, and the government's ragtag police force. That morning Stevens sent a memo to Washington in which he detailed that in response to U.S. support for Jibril's candidacy for prime minister, local militia members were threatening to stop protecting Americans. In a meeting two days earlier, militia leaders had said that "very fluid relationships and blurry lines" defined membership in various militias, and many men were members of multiple militias. It was difficult to ascertain, at any given moment, who was fighting for what. Beyond that, there was a labor dispute with one of the major local militias.

Late that afternoon Hicks, the deputy chief of mission in Libya, sent a text message from Tripoli asking whether Stevens had heard about the attack on the American embassy in Cairo. Worried about mounting fury over an anti-Muslim video produced in the United States, the Cairo embassy staff had put out a statement around noon condemning "the continuing efforts by misguided individuals to hurt the religious feelings of Muslims."

The statement failed to quell the outrage, and several hours later a demonstration outside the embassy turned violent. Protesters stormed the grounds, lowered the American flag, and raised a black banner with Arabic script in its place. The State Department was consumed with the unfolding situation in Cairo and with fear that the protests—and perhaps violence—could spread around the region.

Up to that point, it had been a routine day in Benghazi, save for Stevens's decision to work inside the compound gates. He met with a Turkish official in the evening and walked his visitor to the main gate about 7:40 p.m. local time—or 1:40 p.m. in Washington. Two hours later, at 9:42 p.m., a local police car left its post outside the compound gate. That was when a pack of dozens of armed militants stormed the compound, quickly gaining access to the grounds. There were seven Americans inside at the time—five diplomatic security officers, Stevens, and Sean Smith, an Air Force veteran and information management specialist. The exact number of attackers remains unknown, but estimates ranged from a low of 20 to as many as 125. "FUCK," Smith wrote to a friend he was chatting with through an online instant-messaging service called Jabber. "Gunfire." The sound of explosions blasting the compound could be heard around Benghazi, all the way to the CIA annex a mile away.

The attackers set fires with petroleum, which emits cyanide gas. Within minutes, a diplomatic security officer in the compound's tactical operations center contacted the CIA annex, the embassy in Tripoli, and the State Department's operations center in Washington. Scott Wickland, a diplomatic security officer serving as Stevens's bodyguard, instructed Stevens and Smith to put on body armor. The three of them moved to a gated safe area inside Villa C, the residential space where Stevens lived when he was in Benghazi.

Stevens began dialing out for help. He tried twice, from two different numbers, to get Hicks, who was watching television in his villa in Tripoli and didn't pick up.

Hicks was alerted to the situation moments later, when a security officer stormed in. "Greg, Greg, the consulate's under attack," the officer blurted out.

Hicks looked at his phone, where he saw he had missed calls from Stevens's number and from a number he would learn was Wickland's. One State Department source later contended that Hicks had seen the incoming calls and declined to answer them. Hicks ultimately called Wickland's phone and reached Stevens.

"Greg, we're under attack," Stevens said.

The call abruptly cut off.

In the safe area, Wickland, Stevens, and Smith could hear that militants had broken into Villa C, where they were setting fires. Billowing smoke was cutting off the air supply, so Wickland, Stevens, and Smith dropped to the floor and crawled to a bathroom in the safe area. Desperate to find a source of fresh air, Wickland opened a window in the bathroom. Smoke poured through the opening, further depriving the three men of needed oxygen. The black smoke was so thick, they couldn't see even a few feet in front of them. Wickland decided the only chance to make it out was to leave the safe area.

He crawled toward an emergency escape window in the villa, banging on the floor so that Smith and Stevens could follow the sounds. He crashed onto an outdoor patio, convinced he was being shot at. Stevens and Smith hadn't made it out. He tried repeatedly to go back into the villa, but had to stop after he threw up and began to lose consciousness. With one officer still in the tactical operations center, communicating with the annex personnel, Washington, and the Tripoli embassy, the other three security officers made their way from another building to Villa C, where they found Wickland in dire condition. They made forays into the burning building to try to find Stevens and Smith.

The CIA force at the annex had heard explosions coming from the direction of the compound, and when they got word of the attack, they began preparing a rescue mission. But they waited, hoping local militias could be enlisted to join the fight at the compound with heavy machine guns mounted on vehicles. That didn't happen, and a little more than twenty minutes after the attack had begun, the annex team set out for the compound.

The State Department's Washington operations center, which monitors events around the world and connects the secretary to foreign leaders, sent out an alert to top State Department officials and the White House Situation Room at the same time the CIA team was leaving the annex—4:05 p.m. in Washington. "Approximately 20 armed people fired shots; explosions have been heard as well," the ops center message read. Stephen Mull, the executive secretariat, went into Hillary's office to inform her of the attack. Already the nation's security apparatus was on heightened alert because of threats to other embassies, particularly in Cairo. That was true not only at State but also at the White House.

"The first thing we were aware of was Egypt, Cairo protests turning violent," said a White House national security aide. White House staff held impromptu meetings on the Egypt demonstrations in the offices of Jack Lew, who had become Obama's chief of staff, and national security adviser Tom Donilon. "Everybody was really worried about Cairo because that is a huge embassy. We've got potentially hundreds of people [vulnerable]. . . . An embassy in Cairo is very different from the type of facility that is in Benghazi. We don't have the same kind of real-time communication." American officials believed the Egyptian protesters were reacting to the anti-Muslim satirical film produced by Coptic Christians in the United States and promoted by the Florida pastor Terry Jones, who had famously touched off violence in the Muslim world by burning the Koran.

When she heard Benghazi had come under attack, Hillary gathered several of her staff in her office on the seventh floor to get a full briefing on what was happening in Libya and give orders. Mills, Sullivan, Burns, Boswell, and an aide from the Near Eastern Affairs Bureau were among the group assembled.

In Benghazi, as the CIA annex team arrived at the diplomatic compound, they split up. Some went to the tactical operations center to retrieve the officer who was still there, and the others joined the search for Stevens and Smith. The security officers finally found Smith in the burning villa but were unable to revive him. He was dead. They still couldn't find Stevens. The five diplomatic security officers clambered into an armored vehicle and headed for the annex. On the way out of the compound, they took fire from people on the side of the road. The CIA team stayed at the compound to fend off a second-wave attack, a fifteen-minute barrage of gunfire and rocket-propelled grenades.

Around the same time, one of Pat Kennedy's subordinates told Hillary that Smith had been killed and that Stevens was still missing. Hillary's focus—and that of her department—was trained on finding Stevens and ensuring the safety of the Americans both in Benghazi and at the Tripoli embassy, where officials were concerned that they would also come under attack. Hillary called Donilon. We have an issue here, she said. We need you to be on it.

Bits of information were coming in fast and furious, by e-mail and telephone, and it was hard for officials at the various agencies to get a complete picture of what was happening in Libya in real time. Hillary was reminded that the CIA had an annex, the post from which the rescue mission at the compound had been launched. She called David Petraeus, who was now running the CIA.

"She essentially just wanted to touch base and ensure that the director was aware of what was going on, which he very much was," said a former senior government official, "and to get an assurance that everything would be done, with the resources available, to find and rescue the ambassador."

She also wanted to know in particular whether Petraeus had a surveillance drone available to provide intelligence on the unfolding attack. "Do you have any assets in the area?" she asked, according to a second source familiar with the call. The Pentagon, not the CIA, controlled the drones that flew over Libya at the time, and one was eventually rerouted to the area. "You let us know if you need anything," Hillary told Petraeus. "Let's stay in touch."

Leon Panetta, who had been promoted to defense secretary, and Martin Dempsey, the chairman of the Joint Chiefs of Staff, discussed the developing crisis with President Obama at a regular five p.m. Tuesday White House meeting. Panetta would later order a Marine antiterrorist unit in Spain to get ready to deploy to either Benghazi or Tripoli, and would also instruct special forces teams in Croatia and in the United States to prepare to travel to a staging base in southern Italy. Inside the State Department, Hillary and her aides discussed the delicate question of how to alert the public to the death of one American when another one was still missing. There was concern that if they released information on the death of Sean Smith, Chris Stevens's family might think the ambassador was safe.

By eleven-thirty p.m. in Benghazi—five-thirty p.m. in Washington—the CIA team and the survivors of the compound attack had made their way back to the annex, where they would shortly come under fire from RPGs. An American security team had also boarded a flight from Tripoli to Benghazi to provide reinforcement, if necessary. In Washington, the national security agencies, including the National Security Staff, State, the Pentagon, and the CIA, convened a "deputies meeting" via a secure video teleconferencing system. Deputy national security adviser Denis McDonough chaired the virtual conference, and all the other participants were the number two or number three person at their respective agencies.

"We had a rolling videoconference with all the various people all night," recalled one White House national security official. McDonough ran the videoconference from the Situation Room, with counterterrorism chief John Brennan, several of his aides, Tony Blinken of Vice President Joe Biden's staff, and Ben Rhodes and Tommy Vietor of the president's national security team at his side.

Kurt Tidd, the operations officer for JSOC—Joint Special Operations Command—joined from the Pentagon, and Mills represented Hillary from the seventh floor of the State Department.

At one point, Hillary walked to the operations center to participate in the meeting. The others on the call were surprised when Hillary appeared on their screens as afternoon turned to evening. It is very rare for a cabinet secretary to join a deputies meeting. "She wanted to talk it through," one of her senior aides said. "I actually remember her coming into the room when we're having the [video-conference] at the deputies level and sitting at the head of the table," the White House national security aide said. "This was all they were doing at the State Department, obviously."

Hillary briefed McDonough and listened to updates from the other agencies. "You can tell when someone talks—their tone—she was really concerned," a second White House official said, "really worried about her people. And she knew all the details and was on top of everything and briefing really pertinent, up-to-date information. She was as engaged as she could have possibly been."

At the White House, aides ran in and out of the Situation Room because they couldn't use their BlackBerrys to receive e-mail or make phone calls in the secured area. In Foggy Bottom, officials braced for a long haul.

For much of the night, Hillary shuttled between meetings in her outer office, the ops center, and a command center in a conference room where the senior leadership of the department had gathered. Hillary ducked out of the command center to make and take calls from her inner office to both foreign leaders and fellow American officials.

She didn't wait for Libyan president Mohamed Magariaf to call her. She called him and told him she needed his help—fast. She wanted him to help safeguard Americans in Benghazi and Tripoli. Magariaf pledged his support, but the coming weeks would demonstrate the logistical and political challenges of a partnership between the world's most powerful nation and its newest government. She placed similar calls to leaders in Egypt, Yemen, Tunisia, and other countries in the region, Deputy Secretary Tom Nides said. But it was hard to keep track of everything that was going on that night.

"It was both intensely piquant and a complete blur because so much was happening so fast," said a high-ranking State Department official who briefed Hillary that night, "and it was hard to grab hold of what was really happening in real time because there was chaos there. People got fairly frantic, particularly when we couldn't find Chris."

Around two a.m. in Libya—eight p.m. in Washington—Hillary and her senior staff called Hicks in Tripoli to see if there was any update on Stevens and what course of action Hicks planned to follow in order to keep the embassy staff safe, in the event Tripoli came under attack, too. Hicks said he wanted to evacuate to another facility, and Hillary approved.

At about the same time, a call came in to the Tripoli embassy from a cell phone number that Stevens had been using. The man on the other line, who spoke Arabic, said Stevens was at the hospital but wouldn't put him on the line. The embassy contacted Beth Jones, the acting assistant secretary for Near Eastern affairs, who told Sherman that they might have located Stevens. The news, delivered to Deputy Secretary Tom Nides on a slip of paper, created "a lot of euphoria in the room," Nides said.

But there was still no confirmation that Stevens was alive. American officials asked that the man with the phone take a picture of the man at the hospital. "It was impossible to know what was true, until we finally, among other things, suggested they try to take a cell phone photo of whoever was in the hospital," said a State Department official who declined to directly confirm that the picture was taken and relayed to Washington. "It was a really, really hard situation."

Hicks received a call at three a.m. from Libyan prime minister Abdurrahim Abdulhafiz el-Keib, who said that Stevens was dead. He passed the information on to Washington, and Hillary was informed around nine p.m. when one of her aides handed her a slip of paper. Stevens's death wouldn't be considered confirmed until American personnel made a positive in-person ID, but it appeared at that point that the only two non-security officials in Benghazi that day—Smith and Stevens—had been killed.

Meanwhile the CIA team and the survivors from the Benghazi compound were hunkered down at the annex. There they weathered sporadic RPG fire through the night as they waited for reinforcements from Tripoli, who had landed but took several hours to get to the annex because of a series of logistical problems. Then, just minutes after the reinforcements arrived, militants fired mortars and RPGs at the annex. Unlike the small-arms fire that had come into the annex through the night, this second-wave attack included heavy artillery. Five mortar blasts were counted in a period of ninety seconds, including three so precisely aimed that they hit the roof of one of the buildings on the annex property. Two CIA contractors, Glen Doherty and Tyrone Woods, were killed in the blasts.

In Washington, where the focus had been on finding Chris Stevens and securing American personnel in Tripoli and at other embassies in the region, officials were shocked by the second-round attack. Most Americans found out about the two attacks in one burst of news the following day, but for those who were trying to manage the crisis in real time, the storming of the compound and the loss of the ambassador had appeared for a time to be the end of the assault. "There's this gap of several hours," the White House national security official said. "From my vantage point, I did not know there was an ongoing attack of any sort." Administration officials didn't anticipate the second strike.

After the mortar attacks on the annex, a group of sympathetic Libyan militiamen escorted remaining American personnel as they evacuated to the Benghazi airport and a plane waiting to take survivors to Tripoli. Their flight to Tripoli departed at about the same time—roughly seven-thirty a.m. in Benghazi and one-thirty a.m. in Washington—that a second plane, which would carry the four dead Americans, arrived in Benghazi without a special forces unit that had been ready to go.

At first, special forces personnel in Tripoli had hoped to be on the flight to provide additional reinforcements. "The people in Benghazi had been fighting all night," Hicks later testified. "They were tired. They were exhausted. We wanted to make sure the airport was secure for their withdrawal."

But through the Pentagon chain of command, the special forces team was denied authorization to leave. "This is the first time in my career that a diplomat has more balls than somebody in the military," one of the special forces troops said to Hicks.

The flight departed without the unit, which included a medic, and did not arrive in Benghazi until after the firefight had ended. That is, despite the intense focus of congressional investigators on the questions of who told them to stand down and why, these special forces troops couldn't have done anything to mitigate an assault that already had happened.

Around seven-thirty a.m. local, wounded survivors of the attacks on the Benghazi compound and annex departed for Tripoli on the private jet that had brought the original team of reinforcements to Benghazi hours earlier. U.S. diplomats in Tripoli worked with Libyan officials to secure the use of a Libyan C-130 transport plane, and American security officers still in Benghazi contacted local allies to bring what they believed was Chris Stevens's dead body to the airport. He was positively identified at 8:25 a.m. local.

After one a.m. in Washington, Hillary left the State Department for her home on Whitehaven Street, where she stayed up to work until four a.m. She was there when she got word from Mills, at about two-thirty a.m., that Stevens had been confirmed dead.

Hillary had been an anchor for the team in the command center, said people who were there with her that night, balancing the emotion of the moment with the need to execute.

"She has this rare ability to be compassionate but also get stuff done," said Nides. "She's a really good executive. I saw it in real time, and she handled a real crisis. And you know, she wasn't mechanical, screaming at people, but she was emotional, she was firm in getting facts and getting the issues resolved."

In private moments that night, through the hours of crisis management and profound heartbreak, Hillary wore unmistakable anguish on her face. She had sent Stevens to Libya. This was on her.

The next morning she went to the White House to stand with Obama in the sunny Rose Garden as he delivered a mournful public statement. Before the address, he huddled with Hillary outside the Oval Office. He wanted to do more than just deliver remarks to reporters, he told her. He asked if he could visit the State Department, where she had planned to spend the morning with the men and women who served under her. Ben Rhodes, the deputy national security adviser for strategic communication, e-mailed one of Hillary's aides to make the arrangements. Rather than riding with the president, Hillary raced back to the State Department so that she could greet him when he arrived.

Together the once-bitter rivals made their way to the State Department's courtyard, which is surrounded by dark granite walls and features a massive Marshall Fredericks sculpture of a man astride a globe with a disc in each hand. Hillary instructed her staff to gather the people who knew Chris Stevens best in one spot. She had to push her tired voice to deliver brief remarks because her microphone didn't work.

Obama, who was given the working microphone, spoke for about fifteen minutes, without notes, to the hundreds of employees who had answered an invitation to come to the courtyard, and to those who listened from open windows above. There was no official transcript, but Obama personalized the moment by discussing his childhood abroad and the meaning the U.S. foreign service held for him. When he was finished, he found the throng of Stevens's coworkers and friends. Hillary introduced them to the president, one by one, name by name, as he shook their hands and offered his condolences.

Heartbreak permeated the State Department. It is an unusually close-knit group for a government agency, in part because of the common experiences and values of the foreign service officers who dedicate their lives to traveling the world on behalf of the United States. Bringing people together to focus on moving forward would be a delicate balancing act.

She didn't need to add the weight of televised interviews. The three networks all wanted her to appear that night on their broadcasts, but she agreed with Reines's recommendation that she decline the requests. Within a few hours of the president's visit—and within twenty-four hours of the attack on the annex—Sunday-morning television talk show producers began asking State and the White House whether Hillary would be available to appear that weekend.

Reines responded that he didn't think it was likely. A mythology has built up over time that Hillary never goes on Sunday-morning television. But during her tenure at State, she appeared on *Meet the Press* nine times. What is more accurate to say is that she doesn't like appearing on the shows. She is judicious about how often, and under what circumstances, she goes on, and there was no advantage to be gained from appearing on television to talk about Benghazi.

But the White House wanted her to go on. "Our thinking was, it made sense for a senior diplomat to go out and talk about the service of a senior diplomat. But it wasn't just that issue that day," said a White House official who was involved in picking someone to represent the administration on TV. "We also wanted somebody who could go out and talk about the Arab Spring, try to calm all the craziness about the video, deliver the message again that it was not a U.S. thing."

The White House was also anticipating questions about Iran and Israel because Israeli prime minister Benjamin Netanyahu was scheduled to be on TV that Sunday morning, and the White House had reason to be concerned, with only several weeks left before the election, that he might try to make Obama look bad on the subject of Iran's effort to develop a nuclear weapon. All in all, it added up to making sure that someone very familiar with foreign policy was sitting across from the tough interrogators on the five Sunday shows.

"We thought it made sense to have her or Susan [Rice]," the White House official said. Obama aides, conscious of how busy she was in the aftermath of the attacks, made a soft request to State for Hillary to go on. Reines declined on her behalf.

The White House had moved on to Rice by Friday morning, offering her up to all five of the Sunday shows—NBC's *Meet the Press, Fox News Sunday,* CBS's *Face the Nation,* ABC's *This Week,* and CNN's *State of the Union.* The feat of appearing on all of them on the same Sunday is known in Washington as the "full Ginsburg," a reference to Monica Lewinsky's lawyer, William H. Ginsburg, who pulled it off in 1998.

For Rice, the Sunday shows offered an outsize opportunity to audition for a bigger job in Obama's second term. For Hillary, they were a nuisance to be avoided unless she needed to get a message out, like when her presidential campaign started flagging or when newspapers were writing that she had been sidelined at State in her first six months. She didn't need the platform, it was a politically risky proposition in the middle of a crisis, and it was true enough that she didn't have extra time for the arduous preparation required of any guest on the big political programs.

As most of the State Department mourned, Capricia Marshall and her team worked through their grief. It fell to the protocol office to plan the somber Andrews Air Force Base ceremony at which Hillary and Obama would receive a military plane bearing the bodies of the four murdered Americans, which had since been flown to America's Ramstein Air Base in western Germany. Deputy Secretary Bill Burns, who had known Stevens, cut short a trip to Baghdad to accompany the remains home on the long, lonely flight from Ramstein to Andrews.

Marshall and her staff dug through their archives for precedents. They met with Pentagon officials and coordinated with the White House. The transfer of the bodies was scheduled for Friday, September 14, at Andrews. Marshall, the former White House social secretary, was a clinician when it came to pulling off major events. But she had just two days and so many arrangements to make.

Reines told Marshall that she should talk to the families of the men who had died. Even though the State Department had provided

grief counselors, it was important to walk them through the ceremony so that they could raise any concerns or objections before-
hand. On Friday morning, Marshall went to the Ritz-Carlton in
Georgetown to have coffee and juice with the families. Most were
fine with the plan, but one family broke down at the mention of
cameras and reporters. Marshall called Reines, who came up with
a solution: the press would be held back until all the families were
seated so that only the backs of their heads would be visible to television audiences.

Hillary arrived early for the afternoon ceremony at Andrews so
she could meet with the families. Marshall welled up as they shared
their stories, but Hillary did not.

"It was almost as if they were pouring their grief out upon her,"
said a source who was in the hangar. "Bodies were slumped and
hanging, and children were all around. I did not see her tear up. I just
saw her feel it. The face of 'I'm here.' I think a bit of it is her Methodist roots and her belief in the Lord and her faith, and then it's
this kind of 'What am I here to do? I'm here to be that person.' She
believes in service to country and government, and part of her role
is that—being that compassionate person." Marshall had planned
to introduce Obama to the families, but when the president arrived,
Hillary took on that job.

This was the darkest moment for Clinton and Obama. At the
home of Air Force One, where Obama often played golf on the weekends, they stood together to bear witness to a horrific homecoming.

The flag-draped coffins containing the remains of the four
dead Americans were unloaded from a military jet for the formal
transfer back to U.S. custody. During the opening prayer, Clinton
and Obama stood as mirror images, heads bowed, hands delicately
crossed in front of them.

As if speaking to her own resilience, Hillary issued a call for
fortitude. "We will wipe away our tears, stiffen our spines, and face
the future undaunted," she said. Her voice cracked and the exhaustion and emotion of the week were evident on her face. She had lost
a new friend, the man she had sent to Libya as a special envoy, and

administration critics and journalists were already asking tough questions.

When it was his turn to speak, the president quoted the book of John: "'Greater love hath no man than this, that a man lay down his life for his friends.' Their sacrifice will never be forgotten."

With the election looming, pressure was mounting—on State Department staff, who had just lost four of their own; on Hillary, who ran the agency; on Obama, the man who had sworn the most solemn oath to defend the country; and on a policy of supporting certain revolutions in the Arab and Muslim worlds that suddenly looked less wise. Both Obama and Clinton had a lot on the line—they would be judged by whether this policy ultimately made America safer or more vulnerable to volatility and hostility in the region. This moment required resolve, Hillary said at Andrews. "The people of Egypt, Libya, Yemen and Tunisia did not trade the tyranny of a dictator for the tyranny of a mob," she said. "Reasonable people and responsible leaders in these countries need to do everything they can to restore security and hold accountable those behind these violent acts."

It was still striking to see Obama and Clinton, once fierce political adversaries, standing and speaking in unison. But over the previous four years, whenever the nation had had an international inflection point—from the surge in Afghanistan to the Bin Laden raid to the Arab Spring and its aftermath—they had stood within arm's length, physically and substantively. Hillary had served as the dutiful executive of Obama's policy. But in the previous few days, he had demonstrated a political loyalty uncommon for him. He had brought Hillary to the Rose Garden for a public statement the day after the attack. He had gone that day to the State Department to address the beleaguered staff, and he had put his arm around her as they received the bodies of their fallen compatriots. When their speeches were finished, Hillary reached out for Barack and grasped his right hand in her left hand. He had been there for her during the most deeply emotional period of her four years at State. She whispered in his ear, "Thank you."

▲

While Obama and Clinton were at the service at Andrews, the president's national security team was in the early stages of a tussle over talking points. At a private briefing, Maryland representative Dutch Ruppersberger, the top Democrat on the House Intelligence Committee, had asked CIA director David Petraeus to provide talking points about the Benghazi attack that lawmakers could repeat in television, radio, and print interviews. It is not uncommon for members of Congress, particularly those of the president's party, to seek guidance on what should and should not be said publicly when matters of national security are at stake. Running afoul of laws prohibiting the unauthorized disclosure of classified information happens all too easily, even by accident.

The CIA's career staff worked up a batch of talking points for the committee members to use. The original draft asserted that the Benghazi attack was "inspired by" the assault on the embassy in Cairo earlier that day; there had been a crowd outside the compound before violence erupted; militants with ties to Al Qaeda participated in the attack; an extremist group called Ansar al-Sharia had not denied participation; the easy availability of weapons in Libya contributed to the deaths of the American personnel; previous terrorist acts had been carried out in Benghazi; and the intelligence community was working with Libyan officials and other American agencies to find the perpetrators.

But some CIA officials were unhappy with the draft because it didn't mention warnings the agency had given to State about a possible disturbance at the Cairo embassy. In an internal CIA e-mail time-stamped 4:42 p.m. that Friday, a new version of the talking points deleted the specific mention of Al Qaeda. The previous version had referred to the "attacks" in Benghazi as being inspired by the protests in Egypt and evolving into a "direct assault" against the compound and the annex. That didn't make sense—it said the attacks evolved into an assault. The word "attacks" was changed to "demonstrations" in the internal CIA edit. There were also two new lines added. "On 10 September we warned of social media reports calling for a demonstration in front of the Embassy and that jihadists were threatening to break into the Embassy," read one of the new bullet points. The other said that the CIA had "produced numerous pieces" about the threat of Al Qaeda–linked terrorism in Libya.

Surely it didn't take a world-class intelligence agent to know Benghazi was a dangerous place full of armed extremists. The additions were the equivalent of saying the CIA monitored Twitter and read the newspaper, but they were also a signal that there would be a fight between the CIA and State in avoiding blame. Had the CIA failed to predict and prevent the attacks on the compound and the annex, or should the State Department have taken more precautions, given the intelligence provided by the CIA?

On a separate track, Dag Vega, who headed up broadcast bookings for the White House, confirmed at 6:16 p.m. that Rice would be appearing on all five Sunday shows. In an e-mail to the producers, with whom he had negotiated a common set of rules, Vega outlined the lineup of in-studio interviews, which would be pretaped on Sunday: CNN at 7:15 a.m., Fox at 7:45 a.m., ABC at 8:15 a.m., NBC at 9:00 a.m., and CBS at 9:40 a.m.

"Each interview should be no longer than ten minutes," Vega wrote. Neither the State Department nor Rice's team at the United Nations had been looped into the e-mail discussion of the talking points for the House Intelligence Committee yet.

Toria Nuland, the State Department spokeswoman, was the first to get a copy early in the evening, after the CIA and White House had been tweaking them for a few hours. Nuland wondered why the administration would give members of Congress talking points that could prejudice a probe by the FBI, which, under standard operating procedure, was investigating the crime on the American soil of the Benghazi consulate. She also caught on to the danger that the CIA's additions created for her department.

"The penultimate point could be abused by Members [of Con-

gress] to beat the State Department for not paying attention to
[CIA] warnings, so why do we want to feed that either? Concerned,"
she wrote at 7:39 p.m., copying Sullivan and another State Department official, David Adams, into an e-mail chain.

"I'm with Toria," Adams replied. "The last bullet, especially, will
read to members like we had been repeatedly warned."

The CIA revised the talking points but did not delete the references to threat assessments. "These don't resolve all my issues or
those of my building leadership," Nuland wrote in an e-mail she
later forwarded to Sullivan with the letters FYSA (for your situa-
tional awareness) to ensure he knew that there were still red flags for
the State Department. "They are consulting with [National Security
Staff]."

Republicans would later use the phrase "building leadership" to
suggest that Clinton was engaged in the editing of the talking points.
Hillary has said she was not. But Sullivan, according to the publicly released e-mails, was acting in the interests of his boss and her
department by making the case to Vietor and Rhodes—members
of the National Security Staff—that the CIA's additions should be
dropped.

"Talked to Tommy," Sullivan wrote back to Nuland at 9:32 p.m.
"We can make edits."

At 9:34 p.m. Rhodes called a halt to the discussion. The issue
would be taken up at a "deputies meeting" in the morning. Among
other things, that ensured that any decision making would be done
face-to-face, without the risk of e-mail chains being leaked or later
made public in archives or through press requests under the Freedom of Information Act.

Under political pressure to clarify the origin of the talking
points, the White House would eventually release what it touted
as one hundred pages of Benghazi talking-points e-mails. But the
document was puffed up by the repeated inclusion of long e-mail
chains from messages that were replied to and forwarded. More
important for anyone attempting to do a forensic analysis of the
decision-making process, the e-mails represented only a slice of the

conversations that were going on within and between agencies on phone calls and through other forms of communication.

"Needless to say, there were other exchanges on other systems," said one senior government official familiar with the debate over the talking points.

In the end, the talking points sent to lawmakers—and to Susan Rice—the next day were pared to three bullet points. The language that had bothered State was removed. The exercise had started out as an effort to answer the request of a single lawmaker involved in national security issues. It then morphed into a set of talking points vetted by the public relations folks, and more-senior officials, at the various agencies involved.

At some point deputy CIA director Michael Morrell had made similar edits without sharing them among the agencies, according to the White House. Petraeus, his boss, was not pleased with the outcome. "No mention of Cairo cable, either?" Petraeus wrote to officials at the agency, referring to the CIA's effort to make State aware of the planned protests in Egypt. "Frankly, I'd just as soon not use this, then. . . ."

Rice went out on the Sunday shows and delivered talking points drawn from the set sent to Capitol Hill. The difference was that she drew a straight line from the anti-Muslim video to the Cairo demonstration to the Benghazi attack, and she erroneously stated that a protest had morphed into the assault.

"Putting together the best information that we have available to us today, our current assessment is that what happened in Benghazi was in fact initially a spontaneous reaction to what had just transpired hours before in Cairo, almost a copycat of—of the demonstrations against our facility in Cairo, which were prompted, of course, by the video," Rice said on *Meet the Press*. "What we think then transpired in Benghazi is that opportunistic extremist elements came to the consulate as this was unfolding."

But there had been no demonstration in Benghazi. Rice gave slightly varying versions of the same talking points to all five of the programs. There's little doubt that anyone representing the administration in that hot seat would have said something similar. Hillary had sidestepped a political minefield—or so it would seem later, when Republicans focused in on Rice's appearances on the Sunday shows as evidence of an Obama administration cover-up. At the time, it was Obama, in the stretch run of a campaign against Romney, that Republicans hoped to score points against. All the better to hit him through Rice rather than the still-popular Hillary. Rice would pay a stiff price for the talking-points fiasco, and for not showing expected deference to senators, when she lost out on the nomination to succeed Hillary at State.

"Susan just got fucked," said one White House official.

F our days later, on September 20, Hillary organized separate classified briefings on the Benghazi attack for the House and Senate. Along with deputy defense secretary Ash Carter, vice chairman of the Joint Chiefs of Staff Sandy Winnefeld, director of national intelligence James Clapper, and other senior administration officials, Hillary delivered a presentation to the House members in a cavernous auditorium in the Capitol Visitor Center and sat for a question-and-answer session. The meeting was both uneventful— save for Hillary shooting Representative Michele Bachmann a death stare after one question—and long.

That meant senators had to wait for the caravan of Hillary and deputy secretaries and deputy directors from various agencies to arrive on their side of the Capitol. The senators, unaccustomed to waiting for anyone, much less administration staff and a former colleague, were growing antsy, and Hillary's Senate legislative affairs team sent word ahead to the staffers with her that Majority Leader Harry Reid was on the verge of disbanding the group.

When Hillary walked in, she and her aides could feel the tension. Reading the room, she said she would dispense with her prepared remarks and just answer questions. Clapper told the senators he'd better get started because he knew from delivering the remarks to the House that they would take up a little less than fifteen minutes.

Reines noticed Senator John McCain (R-Ariz.) growing increasingly irritated. "Watch him," Reines told Mills. "He's going to blow."

When Clapper wrapped up, Carter began speaking in his painfully deliberate style, adding to the feeling that senators in the back were beginning to express, in just-audible-enough comments, that the administration officials were wasting their time. McCain, a former Navy pilot and longtime Armed Services Committee bull, interrupted Carter, telling him he didn't need an assessment of U.S. naval assets. When Carter resumed speaking, McCain stormed out of the room. Winnefeld seemed to take the hint and quickly dispensed with his opening remarks.

"They went right to questions, and it was pretty bad," one State Department source said. "It was the moment they decided that Susan lied."

Senator Lindsey Graham (R-S.C.) quarterbacked the GOP assault, dispensing questions for colleagues to ask. Finally he stood up to make his own point. "Every time we ask you a question about something you don't want to answer, you tell us you can't talk about the investigation or you don't know the answer," he said. "But every time there's a fact you want us to know, you sit here and make us listen to it for twenty minutes."

Senator Susan Collins (R-Maine), for whom Hillary had once thrown an engagement party, asked the panel how five diplomatic security agents had made it out of the compound alive when their protectees were killed.

During the briefings, lawmakers later recalled, Hillary had distinctly suggested that the attack had been staged by terrorists, a marker that contrasted subtly but importantly with Rice's account of the events.

Soon afterward, as administration officials appeared in classified briefing after classified briefing for various committees on Capitol Hill, partisan lines broke down, and Rice became the focal point for members of Congress. "In subsequent hearings, if you closed your eyes, you couldn't tell friend from foe. Mostly because there were no friends," the State source said. "What's most notable about those briefings is that we volunteered them. Nobody asked for them. We said, 'Let's go up there and brief the entire Congress,' and it was effectively kicking a beehive."

In the short run, Rice got stung. Obama had planned to make her secretary of state, but the talking-points flap cost her any chance of winning Senate confirmation. Moreover, the Benghazi attack deprived Hillary of the ability to point to Libya as her crowning achievement. And once the 2012 election ended, Republicans were intent on making sure it cost her much more than that.

PART

SIXTEEN

"Road Warrior"

Down the home stretch of the 2012 election cycle, Bill Clinton checked in regularly with two men: Obama campaign manager Jim Messina and Democratic Senatorial Campaign Committee executive director Guy Cecil. With each man, Bill had bonded over the nuts and bolts of politics. Cecil, a gay former Southern Baptist minister and high school teacher, had kept Clinton engaged during the early phase of the 2008 campaign, when much of Hillaryland had wanted the former president as far from the day-to-day operations as possible. Cecil was close enough to the Bill wing of the Clinton political operation that he had briefly gone into partnership with Mark Penn after the primary, before landing a job as Senator Michael Bennet's top aide. Messina had given slide show briefings to the data-munching Clinton in Harlem at the end of 2011 and in Chicago in June 2012, and they spoke regularly by phone.

Now Messina and Cecil were facilitators of a dual-track political mission that fall that promised to build more capital for Bill and Hillary within the Democratic Party, one that would allow the Clintons to help Obama *and* continue to take care of Clinton family priorities. "They didn't necessarily schedule him only to have his travel coincide for Obama," said one Democratic official familiar with Bill's campaigning in 2012.

After the final debate between Obama and Mitt Romney in late October, Messina hopped an early morning flight from Boca Raton to Chicago, where he met with Bill on the 34th floor of the Hyatt

Regency, high above the Chicago River. There were just two weeks to go before Election Day, and it was time to map out Bill's last dash for Obama. The two men agreed: no interviews, all hustings. "Time on the stump made more sense and was a better venue for him," said an Obama campaign source.

"We want him to go talk to voters, not you guys," one Clinton camp source said of reporters.

Messina came up with what he thought was an aggressive travel schedule for Bill, but the former president was insatiable. He called back time and again with the same message, according to an Obama campaign source familiar with the calls. "More, more, more," Bill said. "I want more than this." The only thing Bill wouldn't do for Obama was break a date in Washington to watch his nephew Zach Rodham's final high school football game for Maret against Chelsea's alma mater, Sidwell Friends, three days before the election. Even better for Bill, a lot of the Obama stops were twofers, where he could validate the president and also ask voters to help House, Senate, and gubernatorial candidates, who might return the favor for Hillary in a few years' time.

The *New York Times* counted thirty-seven campaign rallies that Clinton did for Obama over the last seven weeks of the campaign, many of them backloaded in the final weeks. Bill offered help that no other surrogates could. In addition to being what Messina called the Obama campaign's "economic validator" because of his record of governing during a time of surpluses, he could rally Democrats of all ideological stripes.

"He's a great surrogate in campaigns because you can send him to both base areas and swing areas," said one senior Obama campaign official. It was Bill who insisted on adding events in Minnesota and Pennsylvania in the final days of the campaign, both states where Obama was doing well but where Democrats had other candidates who could use a little boost. For the party, the benefit of having Bill out there stumping outweighed the risk that it might look like Obama was worried about states he was thought to have already locked up. If it gave false hope to the Romney campaign that they might expand the map and thus push them to spend money, all the better.

Presidents who leave office on good terms are generally loath to sully themselves with the nitty-gritty of partisan politics for fear of hurting their own standing with independents and members of the other party. For Bill, the imperative was the opposite, and he was unhesitant in attacking Romney. After 2008 it was good politics for him to reinforce his place within the Democratic Party. He had cut a video for the Obama campaign in mid-October in which he looked at the camera and directly accused Romney of lying about his own economic plans. On the stump, he was even harsher. "This guy ran Bain Capital and is a business guy, and he's hiding his budget?" Bill asked at a stop in Parma, Ohio, in mid-October. "That ought to tell you something. He—well, he's hiding his taxes, too. He's hiding everything."

His efforts as a surrogate became even more vital to Obama as Hurricane Sandy bore down on the East Coast and Obama was forced to cancel his own campaign appearances so that he could monitor events from Washington and not seem overly political in the face of an unfolding tragedy. In the early morning hours of October 28, Obama met with Bill in a room at the Doubletree in Orlando to ask him to continue with a planned rally in a part of Florida that was pivotal for Democratic turnout even as Obama flew back to Washington to attend briefings in the Situation Room. The White House released a photo of the two men, Obama with his sleeves rolled up and Bill in jeans and a lavender shirt literally leaning into the conversation, in a room illuminated only by a desk lamp breaking the darkness of the early morning sky outside. Obama's feet are curiously cut out of the shot; he wasn't wearing shoes, according to one of his aides.

Wherever Bill went, from New Hampshire to Virginia, Colorado, Florida, and Ohio, he reminded voters, as he said at one stop, that Obama has "a heck of a secretary of state, too." But the Obama people couldn't have asked for more from Bill on the campaign trail, and they continued to raise money to retire the last of Hillary's debt.

"He became an absolute road warrior for us," said a grateful top Obama campaign aide.

The election period was fruitful for Hillary's 2008 treasury, but a mythology built up that Obama gave her the parting gift of paying off her debt at the very end, when, in fact, his biggest contribution was actually over the summer of 2012. After having raised more than $200,000 for Hillary between May and July—eighty-five new donors gave the maximum of $2,300 to her over that period, and other Obama supporters wrote smaller checks—Obama also rented a list from Hillary's campaign in October at a cost of $62,782. Pollster Celinda Lake and candidates such as Elizabeth Warren, Joe Kennedy, and Christie Vilsack rented donor lists from her at lower prices, and Bill sent out a fund-raising solicitation in late November that reaped $63,284 over eight days, putting the finishing touches on the debt-retirement effort. In fact, Hillary was technically in the black by the end of September; she had more cash on hand then than the $73,000 she owed at that time. The most interesting nugget from her campaign finance records is that while Obama raised cash for her from top donors in the spring and summer of 2012, the highest number of contributions came after the election. There were only 238 individual donors to her campaign before the election, and 1,026 after it, suggesting an energy among grassroots Democrats to make sure her balance sheet was in good shape. She would end up with more than $200,000 on hand at the end of December and close out her campaign account in early 2013.

In the stretch run, Bill made stops that helped a handful of House candidates, including Kathy Hochul, the New York congresswoman whom Hillary had called from London after a 2011 special election. Bill showed up for a joint rally in Rochester with Hochul and Representative Louise Slaughter, who had been among Hillary's most vocal advocates in 2008. Hochul was in the fight of her life—one she would lose by a little more than one percentage point—but Clinton insisted on trekking to upstate New York.

"They weren't just showing up as the icing on the cake in easy races," Hochul said. "Afterward, I thought he'd be running out to the plane. He stuck around and gave me advice on my race. . . . My daughter, who was twenty-three, couldn't make it, so he wanted to write her a note on a poster. It's that genuine personal touch that separates the Clintons from the people that run for office that I've encountered in my time in public office."

Bill's late-campaign visit to Minnesota had the national press wondering whether Obama was vulnerable there. He wasn't, but Rick Nolan, who was bidding to return to Congress for the first time in thirty years, was in a tight race. Bill had endorsed Nolan's primary opponent, Tarryl Clark, who was a Hillary supporter in 2008, but Nolan needed all hands on deck in the general election. The trip to Duluth—unnecessary at the presidential and Senate levels—assuaged any lingering resentment on the part of Nolan, who ended up winning.

Moreover, Bill, who was losing his voice from the string of stump speeches for Obama, jammed in a series of robocalls for Democratic candidates who had been loyal to Hillary. Representative Steve Israel, the chairman of the House Democrats' campaign efforts, began to worry about turnout in his own Long Island district in the aftermath of Hurricane Sandy. He put in a call to Bill's team to ask for help, and Bill quickly recorded a robo-message for him.

While Messina plotted Bill's schedule for the Obama campaign, the former president was mapping out his own set of side trips and political tasks. Many of them were for Senate candidates. His main point of contact for that was Cecil, who had immersed the president in Hillary's New Hampshire strategy when the rest of her campaign was busy in Iowa in 2008.

At one point during that campaign, Bill had been told that the governor of North Carolina, Mike Easley, a Hillary supporter, had endorsed Obama. He called Cecil, who was in the shower at the time, and left a message. "God damn it! How the fuck did this happen?" Bill yelled into the receiver. "Someone just told me that the governor of North Carolina just endorsed Obama. I'm going for a walk. Call me back at home."

Cecil scrambled to find out if it was true. It wasn't. He called Bill back. "Just so you know, it wasn't the governor," Cecil said, explaining it was Lieutenant Governor Bev Perdue, who was running for governor.

"All right, good job," said Bill, cooling off. He called back the following day to mend fences.

The two men had remained friendly despite Bill's support for Andrew Romanoff in a Colorado primary against Cecil's then boss, Michael Bennet. During the latter half of 2012, Bill checked in with Cecil a little more than once a month to strategize about helping Senate candidates who had been Hillary loyalists. The DSCC had a clear sense of Bill's priorities. "We weren't asking him to go and campaign for people who were hard-core Obama supporters," said a Senate Democratic source. "He did events for people that endorsed and supported Hillary."

The only place he was asked to go that he declined to visit was Massachusetts, where Elizabeth Warren, an Obama acolyte, was running for Senate. Bill would offer his support in the form of an e-mail fund-raising solicitation, but he would not appear with Warren, who is often mentioned as a potential progressive rival to Hillary in 2016. And while he had forgiven Claire McCaskill, Bill Clinton also stayed out of her skin-tight reelection campaign in Missouri. He did hit the trail for Bill Nelson in Florida, Joe Donnelly in Indiana, Tammy Baldwin in Wisconsin, Sherrod Brown in Ohio, Amy Klobuchar (who didn't need the help) in Minnesota, Shelley Berkley in Nevada, and Heidi Heitkamp—twice—in North Dakota.

"He loves the politics," the source said. "The Obama folks—he was doing more for them than any other former president had done in an electoral contest, maybe ever. So a lot of it was just working out with the Obama folks when they didn't need him or when they would be willing to give up dates so we [could] do stuff."

As Bill barnstormed the country, Hillary was very much in the spotlight herself because of the ongoing fallout from the Benghazi attack. On October 15, the day before the second presidential debate, she insisted that the buck stopped with her, that Obama and Vice President Joe Biden didn't run the State Department.

"I take responsibility," she told CNN on a trip to Lima, Peru.

Given the timing, it seemed like she was diving on a political grenade for Obama, but her remarks set up the president to field a question about his level of culpability the following night at a debate in Hempstead, New York. The Obama team saw a vulnerability for Romney in discussing Benghazi, in part because he had put out a statement the night of the attack that had garnered significant political backlash.

"While we were still dealing with our diplomats being threatened, Governor Romney put out a press release trying to make political points. And that's not how a commander in chief operates. You don't turn national security into a political issue, certainly not right when it's happening," said the president, who had himself sought to capitalize politically on the killing of Osama bin Laden. "When I say that we are going to find out exactly what happened, everybody will be held accountable, and I am ultimately responsible for what's taking place there, because these are my folks, and I'm the one who has to greet those coffins when they come home, you know that I mean what I say. . . . Secretary Clinton has done an extraordinary job. But she works for me. I'm the president. And I'm always responsible."

Around the same time, the research team at the Republican National Committee (RNC) was putting together a forty-two-second video that blended a clip of Hillary's famous three a.m. phone call ad from the 2008 primary with the Benghazi attack. Hillary had suggested Obama wasn't ready to deal with a middle-of-the-night crisis, and aides at the RNC thought Benghazi might have proved her right. Over images from Hillary's original ad and of the burning American consulate, white block letters asserted that "the call came on September 11, 2012." In the background, a phone rang repeatedly. "Security Requests Denied. Four Americans Dead. And an Administration Whose Story Is Still Changing," the script read. The ad ended with the sound of a busy signal.

The RNC didn't have the money to run the ad on television stations, but aides there thought that journalists would give it a free ride by reporting on it if it were posted to the Internet and the link distributed. In a regularly scheduled messaging meeting shortly after the second debate, the RNC pitched it to the Romney campaign. But it just wasn't fertile ground for Romney, who had botched Benghazi twice already—first with the ill-advised statement the night of the attack, and then during a debate, when the moderator took Obama's side in an argument over whether the president had called the attack an act of terrorism. The RNC aides were told that Benghazi "is not what the message is this week" by Romney campaign aides, who were trying to keep the focus of the campaign on the economy, according to a source familiar with the discussion. That source did not dispute the notion that Romney's own flubs on Benghazi made it virtually impossible for him to effectively hit Obama on it.

Romney's failure to make Benghazi into a campaign issue was good for Hillary—at least for the moment—and so was Bill's work on the trail for Obama and other choice candidates. Democrats' success in Senate races meant that, despite a handful of losses in primaries and the general election, Bill's batting average in the big contests looked pretty good.

On November 6, Obama won reelection, becoming only the second Democratic president since Franklin Roosevelt to perform that feat. (Bill was the other.) Sixty percent of voters identified the economy—the issue on which Bill acted as a validator—as the most important matter facing the country. So even with unemployment at 7.9 percent, Obama had managed to persuade voters that he was better than Romney on the economy. After his victory was secure, Obama spoke briefly with Romney. Then he called Bill Clinton.

SEVENTEEN

Please Don't Go

High above the jungles of Southeast Asia on November 19, 2012, in the president's private cabin aboard Air Force One, Barack Obama and Hillary Clinton had a one-on-one sit-down. They reminisced like longtime friends about their last five-plus years together, dating back to the 2008 campaign. But as they sat in the cabin, ringed with leather chairs and couches and a big wooden desk for the president, Obama had a serious question about Hillary's future, too.

It had been about a year since Hillary told Obama she wasn't going to stick around for his second term.

I'm confident that you'll win reelection and my camp will do everything in its power to help you, she had told Obama. But I'm ready to take a break from public life. She was giving him fair warning—plenty of time to pick a successor.

Obama had put her off, telling her that they could discuss it after the election.

Now Obama had won that second term. On Election Day, Defense Secretary Leon Panetta surprised Obama by confiding that he was ready to leave the Cabinet. "That hit him like a ton of bricks," said one source familiar with their discussion.

Susan Rice, Obama's preferred pick to succeed Hillary, was running into such heavy criticism from Republicans on Capitol Hill that it had become obvious to all but her most ardent supporters that she couldn't win a confirmation fight. Obama was facing the prospect of losing the top two members of his war council and struggling to find a replacement for one of them. Hillary had proved herself a vital ally during the first term and the pair of onetime rivals had gotten into a good rhythm. Why end a good thing?

Would you reconsider? Obama asked, perhaps stay another year?

No, Hillary said. It was time for her to leave public office.

Even though he had refused repeatedly to take no for an answer in getting her to take the job in the first place, Obama pressed just once more, lightly, asking if she might stay just a little longer.

That didn't suit her, either. Obama gave up.

Hillary hadn't been able to turn down a call to serve in 2008, but after four years in the job—and with the 2016 election looming—her calculus had changed. Part of that was Obama's understanding that she had done her duty.

"He didn't put the screws to her," said one source who was briefed on the conversation. "If he put the screws to her, she'd still be there."

When Obama had asked her to be his secretary of state back in 2008, his top advisers wondered aloud how such an arrangement could possibly work, given the acrimony of their primary campaign against each other and the suspicion they held about her ability to faithfully execute his directives. Now, four years later, Hillary was as close to indispensable as any member of the president's cabinet, and she was in the midst of a ten-day trip in which she would showcase both her skills as a smart-power strategist in bringing about democratic reforms in Burma and her willingness to dive into a crisis as a Middle East peace negotiator.

During this swing through Thailand, Burma, and Cambodia, on their last trip together as the president and secretary of state, Obama and his team were feeling a deep nostalgia for their onetime rival. As a sign of gratitude, Obama's aides even made sure to manifest time on Air Force One for Hillary's staff. Hillary wasn't the only one at State who got an offer to remain in office during that trip to Southeast Asia. By the end of four years, it was almost unthinkable that Obama's aides had nearly blackballed Capricia Marshall's nomination to be the nation's chief protocol officer. Over time the Hillarylander had become an honorary member of Obama's foreign policy clique, developing a strong bond with the boys on Air Force One through her hard work, charm, and sense of humor.

On one trip, Marshall and Obama's younger, mostly male foreign policy aides had settled in to the staff section of the plane, farther back from Obama's cabin, to watch the 2011 movie *The Sitter*. With Ben Rhodes next to her and Tommy Vietor across the aisle, Marshall's jaw dropped as the film opened with a scene in which actor Jonah Hill performs oral sex on the actress Ari Graynor. Marshall, who shares Hillary's sometimes-bawdy sense of humor, seemed to be both amused and a bit mortified. Just as the scene ended, Obama emerged from his cabin and walked through the staff portion of the plane. Marshall shared a knowing glance with his aides, who had become two of her strongest advocates. "Fuck," one of the aides thought. "Thank God he didn't see that." Marshall didn't say a word.

While Obama remained unaware of what was happening around him on the plane at that moment, he was very aware of the work Marshall had done to prepare the White House for visits of foreign dignitaries and to make sure things ran smoothly when he traveled abroad. He tasked Valerie Jarrett, his closest personal friend among his team of White House advisers, to approach Marshall about extending her tour of duty.

"The president would like you to stay," Jarrett told Marshall one day on the trip.

"Yes," Marshall replied, without hesitating.

Obama and Clinton spent the entire hour-long flight from Rangoon to Phnom Penh holed up in the cabin, looking back at their time together and discussing an emergency trip Hillary was about to make to the Middle East to negotiate a cease-fire between the Israelis and Palestinians.

A few days before she met up with Obama in Thailand, at the front end of his three-day trip to Southeast Asia, Hillary had been in Australia, where she heard the news that Israel was planning to launch a counteroffensive into Gaza to respond to rocket fire from Palestinians. The Israelis and Palestinians had broken off direct peace talks two years earlier, after an Israeli moratorium on building new settlements in the West Bank and East Jerusalem expired in September 2010. The Palestinians had conditioned a peace deal on Israel ceding land, including areas in which the settlements were being built. For all the internal wrangling in the early days of the administration over who would be the lead U.S. negotiator in the Middle East—George Mitchell, Dennis Ross, Joe Biden, or any number of other players who wanted to solve foreign policy's Gordian knot—the situation had been stagnant for most of Obama's first term because the United States couldn't forge a lasting peace in the Middle East if the Israelis and Palestinians refused to negotiate with each other.

But now, rather than standing still or moving toward peace, the two sides were falling back into a familiar routine of Palestinians firing missiles into Israel and Israel responding militarily. Ehud Barak, the Israeli defense minister, called Defense Secretary Leon Panetta, who was attending a conference in Perth with Hillary and other senior administration officials, to give him a heads-up that Israel planned to strike the Palestinians. The phone line went dead before Barak could finish delivering his message, and when he called back, he reached Panetta's chief of staff, Jeremy Bash. Wanting to make sure there was no confusion, Bash took careful note of the additional details. He then found Panetta, who was with Martin Dempsey, the chairman of the Joint Chiefs of Staff, and Hillary.

Panetta and Hillary, allies on the Bin Laden raid, had lately been squabbling again in National Security Council sessions. The first ugly clash came in the summer of 2011, when Hillary backed up U.S. ambassador to Pakistan Cameron Munter's demand that he get a heads-up in advance of American drone strikes in Pakistan. "No, Hillary," Panetta fired back, "it's you who are flat wrong." Even toward the very end of Obama's first term, they fought like they were jockeying for position at the dining room table. Several days before they arrived in Australia, Iran fired a missile at a U.S. drone. Inside the Situation Room, in a meeting that Obama did not attend, Panetta pressed the other heads of national security agencies to agree to issue a robust statement to send a message to Iran that the United States didn't take the act of aggression lightly.

"That's ridiculous," said Hillary, who had recently sparred with Panetta on another matter by videoconference. "Why would we do that? It's unnecessary."

The two of them yelled back and forth at each other for a few minutes, creating a palpable tension in the room. Then Hillary broke the moment.

"Wow, Leon, this is really nice to be yelling at you again," she said. "Last time you were on the screen, and it was just not as fun as yelling at you to your face." The whole room, including Panetta, burst into laughter.

Now, a few days later, they were standing together with Dempsey when Bash delivered Barak's message. Israel was planning to hit back with an operation targeting militants in Gaza, called Pillar of Defense, Bash told them.

"We've gotta support Israel one hundred and ten percent here," Hillary said. "They're in the right, and they have a right to defend themselves."

At first, Israel responded with limited air strikes, but in the ensuing days, it became clear that the Jewish state was considering sending thousands of ground troops across the border into Gaza, a move that Obama hoped to prevent. "An Israeli ground incursion in Gaza could have set everything on fire in the region, in terms of Egypt, in terms of Palestinians, in terms of blowback on us," a senior White House official explained.

Hillary, who had already been traveling for a week, met up with Obama in Thailand on November 18 for a series of meetings with Thai officials and a dinner at the government palace in Bangkok. That night their two staffs began discussing whether it would be wise to send Hillary to the Middle East to see if she could broker a cease-fire. Typically, a secretary of state would be dispatched in such a situation only if there was sufficient reason to believe a breakthrough was in the offing; otherwise the secretary, and by extension the president and the American government, risked looking ineffectual.

On that Sunday night, there was no sense yet among State Department officials or their White House counterparts that a deal between the Israelis and Palestinians was imminent. "Even then," said a White House official, "the potential for the situation to go off the rails was such that we might need her to go anyway, even if there wasn't a possibility of succeeding." Jake Sullivan, who so often spoke for Hillary, was adamant that she should go, even if the effort fell through, but others at the State Department and the White House felt that her very presence could cause more harm than good.

"It was a really tough call because you don't want to go at the wrong time, and there's a very legitimate point of view that says 'If we go in here, it will set back the cause of the cease-fire because they'll be posturing around us in a different way,'" said a source who was traveling with Hillary. "She and her husband both have this saying they like, which is 'Better to be caught trying.' . . . Her instinct is 'I'm going to step into it.'"

Obama told his aides that he was leaning toward sending her, but he wanted to see if the Palestinians and Israelis could get closer to a deal before he chanced embarrassment by sending his secretary of state into the mix. We'll give it another twenty-four hours or so before making a final decision, he told his aides. So by the end of that night, the Sunday before Thanksgiving, there was still no decision on whether she should break off from the president and gamble on mediating a cease-fire.

On Monday morning, Obama and Hillary flew to Burma, where Hillary had tallied her clearest success as an advocate of smart power, using both hard and soft power to coax the military regime into adopting democratic reforms.

For four years, Hillary had used Burma like a lab to demonstrate that America could pull different levers to affect the thinking of leaders in other countries. "Clearly," she had said during a February 2009 trip to Southeast Asia, "the path we've taken in imposing sanctions hasn't influenced the Burmese junta." Instead, she mixed carrots with the sanctions stick: if Burma made reforms, sanctions on its military regime could be lifted or eased, and American companies could begin doing business in Burma.

The promise of removing sanctions—and of opening up a commercial relationship between Burma and the United States—proved influential in persuading Burmese dictators to change their behavior. Aung San Suu Kyi, the Nobel Peace Prize winner, was released from house arrest in late 2010, and President Thein Sein signaled his desire to restore diplomatic ties with the United States by releasing other prisoners, decensoring certain Internet sites, and calling for new elections. The Obama administration responded by easing American sanctions, and Hillary visited both Suu Kyi and Sein in late 2011 during the first trip of a secretary of state to Burma in more than half a century.

The unfolding success story infuriated China, which had long been the dominant outside force in Burmese politics. "They think we're trying to pull Burma away from China, that it's all a plot basically to contain and isolate China and keep China down," said a senior American official in the region.

By January 2012, when Hillary discussed Burma with her top deputies as part of outlining her final-year agenda, Suu Kyi was thinking about a run for president, and the United States was on the verge of announcing it would restore full diplomatic ties with Burma.

Suu Kyi traveled to the United States in September 2012, just after the Benghazi attack, to collect a congressional gold medal and to lobby American leaders to lift the remaining sanctions against her country. On the morning of the ceremony, Suu Kyi met with Laura Bush one-on-one, in a private suite at the Ritz-Carlton on the cusp of Georgetown. Bush and Suu Kyi talked for nearly an hour, but Suu Kyi delivered the thrust of her message to American leaders in just three words.

"The sanctions worked," she told Laura Bush, according to a source familiar with their discussion. From the Obama administration's perspective, the sanctions had indeed worked—but only because lifting them was mixed with the possibility of opening up a commercial relationship between the two countries. And the White House was happy to pat Hillary and her State Department team on the back for a job well done.

"There were absolutely times when she brought something to the president, like Burma, and said 'We really think there's an opening here,'" said a White House national security aide. "They deserve a lot of credit for that."

That week NBC's Ann Curry asked Suu Kyi if she would rule out running for president of her country, and Suu Kyi responded with an answer that could have served as an insight into Hillary's thinking.

"No," she said. "If you're a politician, you never rule out such a possibility."

In terms of Hillary's legacy, Burmese democracy was an issue that she had identified early, worked on methodically for several years, and then brought gift-wrapped to Obama. When her Libya narrative fell apart in Benghazi, Burma was the backup testament to smart power. "It's just a symbol of things going right. It's an important demonstration of [how] working together and political pressure can cause change without having to drop a bomb, and it's a good news story," said a senior official who remained at the State Department after Hillary left. "It's a great example for the rest of the world."

While Hillary loyalists see the victory there as a validation of her theories on foreign policy and as a model for how she would approach democracy building if she were president, critics view the notion that Burma was Hillary's tour de force as evidence that she had an unremarkable tenure as secretary of state. Brit Hume of Fox News said in January 2013 that successes like Burma "add up to a case for her competence" as secretary. "They do not add up to a case for greatness."

Likewise, Republican operatives scoff at Hillary's "deliverables." "Burma?" one laughed. "Really?"

Once they arrived in Burma, Obama and Hillary went to the government palace, a famous Buddhist pagoda, and finally to Aung San Suu Kyi's house, where she had been held prisoner for so many years. Hillary lingered in the limousine as Obama greeted Suu Kyi with a small bow and a handshake. They both turned back toward the limo to see Hillary emerging. Hillary had visited Suu Kyi nearly a year earlier, and the two women hugged and held hands as they walked toward the house.

In his remarks following the meeting with Suu Kyi, Obama credited Hillary with her work in Burma.

"I could not be more grateful, not only for your service, Hillary, but also for the powerful message that you and Aung San Suu Kyi send about the importance of women and men everywhere embracing and promoting democratic values and human rights," he said. Then he and Hillary boarded Air Force One for the flight to Cambodia and the long one-on-one in his cabin in which they discussed her decision to leave office and the prospect of her jetting into the escalating crisis in the Middle East.

All the while, Obama's aides and Hillary's aides had been in discussions among themselves and with Anne Patterson and Dan Shapiro, the American ambassadors to Egypt and Israel, respectively. The Egyptians, who talked directly with the leadership of Hamas in Gaza, were key intermediaries in the cease-fire negotiations.

That night Obama excused himself early from a dinner in Phnom Penh to call Egyptian president Mohamed Morsi. Obama began to get the sense that a deal could be struck and urged Morsi to get back to him with any developments. "You can call me back as late as you want," Obama told him, "if you think there's information you need to let me know about."

A few hours later, around one a.m. in Cambodia, Ben Rhodes roused a slumbering Obama in his hotel room. Morsi was on the line. The outlines of an agreement were coming together. Obama told Morsi that he was considering sending Hillary to the Middle East because he thought she could help bring Israel toward a cease-fire. But, he said, he was only willing to do that if Morsi vowed to meet with her personally. He couldn't send her there to get a cold shoulder. Much of statecraft is stagecraft, and Obama wanted to make sure Hillary had a solid script in hand before she left. Between the two calls with Morsi, Obama had spoken with Hillary, and he was increasingly leaning in the direction of sending her.

By the next morning, he was sure. In a holding space at the Phnom Penh convention center, where they were attending an Association of Southeast Asian Nations summit, Obama huddled with Hillary, Jake Sullivan, and White House national security aides Rhodes and Tom Donilon.

"Let's definitely do this," Obama said.

For all her strategic planning, Hillary is often at her best and most decisive when faced with an emerging crisis. Like a veteran hitter who remains even-keeled under pressure, her steadiness is born of her experience. She's been through a lot of situations where it seemed like the world was crashing in on her. The plan, heading into Obama's Asia trip, had been for Hillary to get credit for an impressive bit of long-term diplomacy in Burma. But it was the worsening conflict in Gaza and Israel that quickly became the focal point of her last major overseas voyage.

Part of the reason Hillary made sense as the intermediary in the first place is that she had a good relationship with the Israelis, certainly better than Obama had. "Of everybody in his shop, she's the right one to be there," Representative Ileana Ros-Lehtinen, the Florida Republican who ran the Foreign Affairs Committee, said at the time. "I'm sure the Israelis feel like I do that she was a better senator in terms of pro-Israel feelings than a secretary of state. But you know, you work for your boss."

On the flight from Cambodia to Israel, though, Sullivan began having second thoughts about the wisdom of the mission. He had been a strong advocate for making the trip, but there had been a difference of opinion among Hillary's advisers. The risk that she would fail to get a cease-fire—or worse, that a full-scale war would break out while she was on the ground in the Middle East—was real enough that Sullivan couldn't shake from his mind images of Israeli soldiers pouring across the Gaza border.

They landed in Jerusalem shortly before ten p.m. local time on Tuesday, November 20—about forty-eight hours before guests were scheduled to arrive for Hillary's annual Thanksgiving dinner in Chappaqua. She and her team went directly to meet with Prime Minister Benjamin Netanyahu. Advisers to Netanyahu and Hillary crowded into his small personal office, dragging in extra chairs. Shapiro, David Hale, who had succeeded George Mitchell as the special envoy for the Middle East, lawyer Jonathan Schwartz, and Jake Sullivan joined Hillary to form the American contingent. It seemed to the Americans that the entire Israeli leadership was in the room. In addition to Netanyahu, Defense Minister Ehud Barak, Foreign Minister Avigdor Lieberman, national security adviser Yaakov Amidror, and Miami-born Netanyahu adviser Ron Dermer were among the Israelis who participated.

Hillary planned to spend an hour with the Israeli leader, but the meeting dragged on into the early morning hours, as advisers shuffled in and out and noshed on fruit and cookies. Rather than a two-sided debate, the Americans and Israelis were trying together to come up with an offer of concessions that Netanyahu could live with and that would satisfy the Palestinians enough to bring about a cease-fire agreement. Some of the Americans were struck by the Talmudic style of discussion among the Israelis. Netanyahu would suggest a possible solution, and one of his advisers would challenge his thinking directly in a manner that contrasted sharply with the deferential treatment the president of the United States expected in meetings with foreign guests.

The free-flowing discussion made little progress, even though both sides had the same goal. "Everybody was just trying to figure out how to crack the nut," said one of the participants. But there remained a huge gulf between what the Palestinians wanted from the Israelis and what the Israelis were willing to give. It wasn't going well.

"I'm not sure we should have come," Sullivan told a colleague during a break in the marathon session. "It's going nowhere. This is probably a big mistake."

Hillary, who was due in Ramallah the next day for a talk with Palestinian Authority president Mahmoud Abbas, left Netanyahu's office with nothing in hand.

"It wouldn't take but one direct rocket hit somewhere to lead to a ground assault. Things were hanging on the knife's edge," a meeting participant said. "When we left that night, it was not clear to me that we had a way forward."

But overnight, Netanyahu's aides called Hillary's team and asked for another meeting in the morning. She agreed to see Netanyahu after her session with Abbas, and Sullivan and Schwartz headed back to the prime minister's office to try to lay groundwork. By the time she returned to Jerusalem, Netanyahu had found concessions he felt comfortable with. He gave Hillary enough "in her pocket to be able to go to Cairo and get the deal closed," said one of her aides. Essentially, in exchange for an end to Palestinian rocket shots into Israel, Israel would halt its strikes and would agree to open up crossings on the Gaza border, which would allow Palestinians to move freely and reengage in commerce.

In Cairo, Hillary sat down with Morsi, Foreign Minister Mohamed Kamel Amr, and Essam al-Haddad, the top national security adviser to Morsi. Because the United States did not negotiate directly with Hamas, the Islamist military group in power in the Gaza Strip, Egypt, which had a relationship with Hamas, was the key to getting the Palestinians to agree to, and observe, a cease-fire. From Cairo, Hillary spoke to Netanyahu by phone. Obama also placed calls to Netanyahu and Morsi. Hillary, according to sources close to her, kept emphasizing that Thanksgiving was fast approaching. She had to leave soon if she was going to get home to her family.

Finally, she told the Egyptians the pot wasn't going to get any better. The Israelis had signed off, and it was time for Morsi to do the same.

Hillary was playing hardball. "This is the deal, and we are announcing it tonight," she told Morsi, Haddad, and Amr, according to a source who was present. "It's happening."

The Egyptians were risking an Israeli invasion of Gaza, Palestinian lives, and the international embarrassment of pulling out of a deal. For Morsi's fledgling government, that amounted to a big gamble. Eager to show he could be a serious player on the international stage, Morsi agreed to the terms.

Hillary and Amr held a press conference in Cairo that night and distributed the points of what was, in the end, a pretty straightforward formal cease-fire. It was clear from later releases by the White House that some side deals had been cut, but the important part, from the standpoint of Hillary and Obama, was that the Palestinians had agreed to stop firing at the Israelis and vice versa. Suddenly, in addition to the expected victory lap in Burma, Hillary had a second trophy from her trip.

One aide likened the mood to the aftermath of liberating Chen Guangcheng. "We had been in a very unpredictable, difficult situation where at several points along the way it didn't seem like it was going to work out, and then it did at the last minute," the aide said.

One of her aides congratulated her as she boarded her plane for the long trip across the Atlantic.

"Well, let's see," she said, knowingly skeptical of the shelf life of any peace in the Middle East. "Has it broken yet?"

EIGHTEEN

Four Dead Americans

Darrell Issa, the high-energy chairman of the House Oversight and Government Reform Committee, was at the White House for, of all things, the signing of a whistleblower protection act, when he bumped into Hillary in a West Wing stairwell. It was November 27, about three weeks after Obama's reelection, and Issa had been fighting with State Department officials for a raft of information on the Benghazi attack, including various memos and cables. An olive-skinned, black-haired, Toledo-born grandson of Lebanese immigrants, Issa was positively disposed toward Hillary after more than a decade of occasional interaction. She was always polite, remembered his name from his earliest days in Congress, and deferentially answered yes to most routine requests. If their relationship wasn't warm, it was at least cordial.

Shortly after the Benghazi attack, Hillary had called Issa to offer assistance in his investigation. "I was in the Senate—I get it. You have an obligation," she had said then. "I would feel the same way, and I want to cooperate. I will give you as much as I can. But I want to underscore that this should not be politicized."

She had also offered to provide witnesses above and beyond the number the committee sought and had helped ensure that Issa had access to an early briefing for congressional staff on Capitol Hill. Before Benghazi, she had brought him up to the State Department, along with other members interested in foreign policy, for a series of private lunch briefings. He was always impressed with her ability to dive right into substance, picking up a conversation where it had last left off.

So when they ran into each other in the stairwell and pulled off into the quiet atrium of the West Wing basement, Issa wasn't the least bit surprised that Hillary was prepared to answer questions about the status of his sundry requests of her department. One by one, she told him she was working on each question. He began to get the sense—perhaps a confirmation of the bias he had against an administration that had fought him on a set of investigations—that it was the White House, not Clinton, that was impeding him. In his view, the White House had "lawyered up" and taken the position that it would provide only the documents and testimony that White House officials believed were necessary to his investigation.

Issa challenged her on Undersecretary Pat Kennedy's refusal to hand over materials. Without throwing Kennedy under the bus, she said she grasped why Issa was upset. She understood his frustration, she said, and was working to get him more information. Fair or not, he perceived Hillary as an honest broker whose hands were tied by an administration for which transparency was more of a talking point than a way of doing business. He thought she had negotiated the treacherous waters of Washington politics better than other secretaries of state, including Republicans Colin Powell and Condi Rice, and was therefore his best hope for getting Obama to accede to his requests.

That helps explain the question he asked just before they parted ways.

"Hillary, are you going to stay on until this is resolved?" Issa asked.

For Hillary, it was the only truly tough question he had posed in their brief chat. She answered not with her typical laugh of avoidance but with a subtler smile. Then she was gone.

Their exchange was a telling snapshot of a time when Republicans were much more focused on Obama than on Hillary. There was a renewed focus on investigating the administration and proving that it had covered up scandals in service of the campaign. For example, House Intelligence Committee chairman Mike Rogers (R-Mich.) charged that the president might have known about the Justice Department's probe into CIA director David Petraeus's affair with biographer Paula Broadwell, which had prompted his resignation just after Election Day. (Hillary showed Petraeus her gracious side in the aftermath of that scandal, writing him a note and calling to express her sympathy. "I have a little experience," she joked, referring to her husband's infidelity.)

Even three weeks after the election, while she was still secretary of state, Hillary had utility to Issa. She could prevail, or at least try to prevail, on the president to be more cooperative. In a December interview in Issa's House Rayburn Office Building committee suite, as he got ready to go to the White House Christmas party, he called Hillary a bright spot in the administration.

"The front end of it, Hillary's part of it, was very good. By the time you got to Undersecretary Kennedy, he came in with the Obama standard playbook," Issa said. "I don't think she'd lie to me. In that sense, I trust her like any politician and particularly any diplomat—every word within a statement has to be carefully made sure you heard it correctly. But no, when you look at Eric Holder, I do not trust him. I do not believe he is trustworthy. I do not believe he is honest. In the case of Secretary Clinton, I think her personal standing—her legacy of tough but honest, diplomatic but not disingenuous—I think it's important to her."

Issa blamed Obama, not Hillary, for what he viewed as an inadequate response to the attack. "When the call came in at three o'clock in the morning, the failure wasn't viewed, at least as of today, as Secretary Clinton's," he said. "It was really an Obama failure."

He even said that "her legacy is mostly intact for 2016, if she chooses," but he stopped short of saying that Republicans wouldn't go after her on Benghazi, and his investigation would increasingly focus on how high up the chain security decisions in Libya went at State.

The dynamics on Benghazi were shifting, even as Issa spoke. Republicans weren't about to let Hillary coast out of the State

Department—and possibly into a 2016 bid for the presidency—
without making her answer Benghazi questions under oath. The
investigations, launched by more than half a dozen committees in
the House and Senate, gave Republicans the dull tools they needed
for a drawn-out process that would keep Benghazi alive in the headlines well into the start of the presidential election cycle.

With her shift back to private life imminent, and her name
already bandied about as a 2016 front-runner, Hillary was now the
main target of Republicans who were thinking about the next election. In addition to the regular congressional committees, several of
which had jurisdiction to investigate aspects of Benghazi, Representative Frank Wolf of Virginia and Senator John McCain of Arizona
called for the formation of a "special committee" to look into the
attacks. Even if some of the lawmakers didn't think Hillary was at
fault, many of their constituents did, and so did right-wing commen-
tators and opinion writers.

This was nothing new to her. She and her husband had spent
eight years fighting congressional committees over Whitewater,
Travelgate, and ultimately the Monica Lewinsky affair. Given the
history, she wasn't about to make herself an easy target. While she
had a penchant for finding ways to give members of Congress access
to information to which she believed they were entitled, there were
hard limits to the ways she would make documents available. For
example, members of Congress were allowed to look at certain State
Department files "in camera," meaning they could view them but
not distribute them or make photocopies of them—and while they
reviewed the material, a State Department minder would sit a few
feet away, taking notes. A similar strategy had appeased senators
Isakson and Corker when it came to reading the negotiating record
on the New START Treaty.

But it didn't fly with the House Republicans investigating Benghazi. One lawmaker familiar with the records made available to
Congress said there were actually 25,000 e-mails related to Benghazi, far more than the one hundred pages of talking-point-related
e-mails the White House later released. The two sides were in a

high-stakes political dance that could shape whether the attack would cripple a presidential campaign, make Republicans look embarrassingly hyperpolitical, or both. Hillary had more to lose than Republicans in Congress, few if any of whom would be punished by voters in heavily Republican districts and states for going after her.

Signs of overreach began popping up that December, when a health scare for Hillary turned into fodder for extremists in the Republican Party to accuse her of dodging accountability for Benghazi. The list of people who thought Hillary worked too hard included her boss. Obama had made an example of her at the 2009 cabinet meeting, but the one person who didn't get the message—or chose to ignore it—was its intended target. Hillary spent 401 days on the road, traveling nearly a million miles to a record 112 countries, sometimes to godforsaken parts of the world. Her time at home could be just as grueling, as the agenda often required her to step off of an international flight and go straight into another day of meetings in a different time zone. Remarkably, she rarely lost focus.

On one occasion, in July 2010, she flew overnight from Hanoi to Andrews Air Force Base so that she could attend a staff retreat at Blair House, the nineteenth-century yellow row house across from the White House that is used as an inn for visiting dignitaries, from Queen Elizabeth II to Afghan president Hamid Karzai. Each member of her senior staff was instructed to prepare a two-minute briefing on the status of issues in his or her area of expertise. It was hot and the room was crowded, but that didn't stop Richard Holbrooke from going on six and a half times as long as the time allotted for him. Deputy Secretary Jim Steinberg took up ten minutes. By noon, after nearly four hours, most of the staff had checked out mentally, and some were openly scrolling through messages on their BlackBerrys.

The session dragged on for another five hours after that, but Hillary never seemed to lose interest or focus. "She did not look at her BlackBerry. She had questions. She looked intently. She listened to everything. She focused the entire day," one participant said. Then her aides were invited to her house on Whitehaven for a reception. Hillary shifted from work to life, greeting spouses in the kitchen and the living room and asking about their children.

When the gathering began to wind down, a little before nine p.m., one Hillary aide was getting into his car to go home when he caught a glimpse of her sneaking away from the party at her own house. She was loading bags into a sport-utility vehicle that would take her to the airport so she could spend the weekend in Chappaqua.

"I was like 'How did she do that? How did she stay awake all day? How did she stay focused? How did she stay so gracious? And, my God, she's getting on another plane,'" the aide said later. "She's obviously not bionic. Her ability to focus all day long through all these people—and she's laughing, she's paying attention, she's reacting to stuff."

By the tail end of her tenure, Hillary joked with friends that she was looking forward to the time when her schedule was filled with nothing but "beaches and speeches." But before she could escape to a seaside resort or the friendly environs of the paid lecture circuit, her unrelenting work ethic caught up to her and gave her a health scare that began to color discussions of a 2016 presidential run. Of the few major asterisks surrounding a potential bid, perhaps the largest is whether Hillary, who will be sixty-nine on inauguration day in 2017, can physically sustain the demands of both a modern presidential campaign and the presidency, back-to-back. It was at the end of such a six-year stretch of unrelenting campaigning and governing that Hillary suffered a sobering series of ailments, one of which could have killed her.

She had been bouncing around the world on both sides of the Thanksgiving break—Australia, Singapore, Thailand, Burma, Cambodia, the Middle East (the hastily scheduled trip to broker the cease-fire), the Czech Republic, Belgium, Ireland, and Northern Ireland—when she caught a nasty stomach virus. By the time she got home from Andrews Air Force Base late the night of Friday, December 7, she was feeling awful. Over the weekend, as she battled dehydration, Hillary fell in her bathroom and hit her head. The stomach bug was bad enough that the State Department initially pushed back a planned trip to Tunisia, Morocco, and the United Arab Emirates by a day, and then canceled it altogether. That meant Hillary missed important meetings of the Friends of the Syrian People, the committee of nations supporting reforms in that country.

In the summer and fall, Hillary had joined David Petraeus in a private internal campaign to get Obama to sign off on arming the Syrian rebels—but opponents of their proposal, concerned about the possibility that arms would end up in the hands of extremist enemies of the United Sates and its allies, won out in the short run.

It wasn't until a few days after her fall, when she saw a doctor, that Hillary learned she had suffered a concussion.

She was supposed to testify on Capitol Hill in conjunction with the release of an Accountability Review Board (ARB) report on Benghazi. Under a system that had been in place for decades, Hillary had appointed the quasi-independent board to review what had happened; to determine who, if anyone, had failed to do his or her job before, during, or after the attack; and to make recommendations about how the State Department could avoid a repeat of the tragedy. Led by retired admiral Mike Mullen, the former chairman of the Joint Chiefs of Staff who had befriended Hillary in their early days together at National Security Council meetings, and former ambassador Thomas Pickering, a well-respected veteran of the foreign service, the board was technically independent but also very much stacked with people sympathetic to the notion that the secretary wasn't directly responsible for the failings of her underlings.

While she worked from home, Hillary's stomach issues dissipated, but the effects of the concussion remained.

Hillary had been scheduled to testify on Benghazi in the House and Senate on December 20. But after she sustained the concussion, doctors told her not to work. Her aides planned to announce on Friday, December 14, that she would have to cancel her planned appearances on Capitol Hill. But because of the unfolding Newtown, Connecticut, school shootings, they held off a day. On Saturday, Mills called Representative Ileana Ros-Lehtinen and Senator

John Kerry, the chairs of the two panels, to inform them, just before a public announcement was made.

Republicans and right-tilting media accused her of inventing an injury to elude investigators. On December 18, the *New York Post* editorial page called it a "head fake." The night before, during an appearance on Fox News, John Bolton, the ambassador to the United Nations under President George W. Bush, accused Hillary of concocting a "diplomatic illness." Representative Allen West of Florida gilded the lily, calling her affliction "Benghazi flu." It wasn't the first time, during her final year at State, that charges of duplicity had been hurled at her and her inner circle: over the summer, Representative Michele Bachmann, the wild-eyed Minnesota Republican on the House Intelligence Committee, had accused Huma Abedin of having ties to terrorists. But after Hillary's fall, the old anti-Clinton conspiracy machine really kicked into high gear. To her critics, the timing of her injury seemed all too convenient, just as the State Department was releasing the ARB findings.

The attacks on Hillary's character brought out the aggressive side of her staff in response. On Christmas Eve, Bolton received a lump of coal in his e-mail inbox. Reines had written Bolton the first of several e-mails, sent over the course of a month, expressing outrage over the "diplomatic illness" remark and providing updates on Hillary's health. The final missive was sent on January 23, just after Hillary testified before the Senate and House committees. "J—have not heard back from you, and I'm honestly getting concerned," Reines wrote sarcastically. "I hope you haven't come down with anything. Something's definitely going around. The CDC says influenza activity is high across most of the United States. They have a very useful FluView report posted here." Helpfully, Reines included a link. "But who really knows these days what's made up and what's not—could be millions of people across the country faking it," he wrote. "Anyway, I promised to keep you updated, so I want to make sure you have the transcripts of the secretary's testimony before the Senate Foreign Relations Committee and the House Foreign

Affairs Committee. Best, Philippe." He pasted the full transcripts of both hearings—each ran several hours—into the body of the e-mail, copying Bolton's assistant. Bolton never responded, but his assistant sent back a reply about an hour later that subtly signaled her boss had gotten the message. "Thanks," she wrote.

On December 19, two days after Bolton's initial remarks, Obama attended the State Department's annual holiday party, which Hillary missed because she was still recovering. Obama, who had spent so much time in close quarters with Hillary on their recent trip to Southeast Asia, had already called, in the wake of the injury, to express his concern for her.

When he arrived at State for the holiday party, Capricia Marshall greeted him.

"How's my girl doing?" Obama asked.

"She was so touched by your call," Marshall replied.

Obama stopped and looked Marshall in the eye to make sure his message sank in.

"I love her, love her," he said. "I love my friend."

State had released the ARB report earlier that day, and Hillary sent an accompanying letter to Congress outlining her instructions to the department to begin implementing all twenty-three of the board's recommendations for actions that might prevent similar lethal attacks in the future. The review board came down hard on senior State Department officials several rungs below Hillary but didn't implicate her.

"Systemic failures and leadership and management deficiencies at senior levels within two bureaus of the State Department resulted in a Special Mission [consulate] security posture that was inadequate for Benghazi and grossly inadequate to deal with the attack that took place," the board found. "Certain senior State Department officials within two bureaus demonstrated a lack of proactive leadership and management ability in their responses to security concerns posed by Special Mission Benghazi, given the deteriorating threat environment and the lack of reliable host government protection. However, the board did not find reasonable cause to determine that any individual U.S. Government employee breached his or her duty."

Four State Department employees were immediately put on leave in response to the ARB. Eric Boswell, the assistant secretary for diplomatic security, resigned from his post as assistant secretary—though, as it turned out, he did not quit State altogether, as he held another position within the department. Charlene Lamb, who had testified before Issa's committee that the security posture in Benghazi was appropriate, and two others were moved out of their jobs pending further review of their cases. Three of the four worked in diplomatic security. The fourth, Raymond Maxwell, who was a deputy assistant secretary of state for Near Eastern affairs, later told Josh Rogin of the *Daily Beast* that he had "no involvement to any degree with decisions on security and the funding of security at our diplomatic mission in Benghazi."

Maxwell appeared to be a fall guy for security decisions made above his pay grade. But, unbeknownst to him, the board found that he had not been reading his classified material—which incensed Mike Mullen—according to a senior State official.

Deputy secretary of state Bill Burns later testified before the Senate Foreign Relations Committee that cables from Tripoli advocating greater security "would have been reviewed up through the assistant secretary level, and it may be that some of my colleagues on the seventh floor saw them as well." The top executives at the State Department, including career officials and Hillary's personal staff, work on the seventh floor.

In August 2013, Hillary's successor, John Kerry, would reinstate all four of the employees who were put on administrative leave; in explaining the decision, a State Department spokeswoman cited "the totality" of their careers and the ARB's finding that their actions did not amount to a "breach of duty."

The question of responsibility presented a Scylla-and-Charybdis dilemma for Hillary. If she accepted blame for failing to respond to security requests, the admission would damage both her legacy as a manager and the narrative of strong leadership she would present if she ran for president. But if she shirked responsibility for what had happened in her own department, that would also be politically damaging.

Hillary tried to navigate a narrow channel to avoid both beasts. On the one hand, she had been saying publicly for more than two months that she took responsibility for the tragedy. But on the other, she had an official government report in hand that laid the blame at the feet of career State Department employees far removed from her—a report created by people she had appointed. It placed fault for denying an extension of high-level security teams at least three steps below Hillary. She was responsible, but not to blame, according to an ARB narrative that neatly matched up with her own story.

The details of the ARB's findings on particular personnel were not contained in the unclassified report released to the public but appeared in a classified version. The report had spared Kennedy, the career foreign service officer whom Hillary had kept on to manage the sprawling agency's resources, but House investigators, displeased with his level of cooperation, targeted him.

Kennedy had gotten pressure from the Pentagon to give back security officers on loan in Libya, but declined to throw Defense officials under the bus to help himself, the senior State official asserted.

Burns and Nides testified in Hillary's place in December, and it was revealed on New Year's Day that her condition was much worse than previously thought. Doctors had treated her for a blood clot in her head. Still, Republicans clamored to put Hillary under the scrutiny of white-hot congressional hearing lights and television cameras. Issa's admonition that Benghazi was a "developing scandal" proved prophetic. The old reality of a GOP focused on pinning Benghazi to Obama had been replaced by a new focus on Hillary. Sure, they were interested in hearing what the secretary had to say. But they were just as interested—if not more so—in creating a made-for-television moment that would haunt Hillary if she ran in 2016. Hillary thought Issa was succumbing to pressure from his own party and couldn't help himself as the investigation turned from Obama to her.

Over the course of more than a year, in testimony that was both public and in closed session, congressional investigators broke the Benghazi tragedy into three phases.

The first dealt with the deteriorating security situation in Benghazi, where armed militants—some of whom had links to major terrorist groups such as Al Qaeda and Ansar al-Sharia—were filling the power vacuum left when Qaddafi was toppled. The main questions centered on the decision by State Department officials to reduce the number of military security officers in Libya and to start transferring responsibility for security to diplomatic officers and local militias at a time when violence was rising. In particular, investigators wanted to know why State Department officials in Washington had denied requests from Americans on the ground in Libya, including Chris Stevens, to maintain a Pentagon presence, and they wanted to know how high up the chain of command that decision went. Specifically, had it come from the career foreign service officers who were blamed for it, or did it reach up into the political ranks of the department, perhaps as high as Hillary?

The second phase was the attack itself. The investigators never seriously tried to argue that Hillary had not responded quickly and correctly to the assault. There was ample evidence that, of all the major national security principals in Washington, she had been most on top of the situation. She had been on the phone or videoconference with Libyan officials, ministers in other countries where Americans might be at risk, the White House, the Pentagon, the CIA, and others.

Instead, the investigators looked at whether Defense Secretary Leon Panetta, Joint Chiefs chairman Martin Dempsey, and Obama had done enough to save the Americans in harm's way. Republicans were particularly incensed that jets and special forces teams weren't deployed to protect the CIA annex, since there had been no telling, at the time, how long the attacks would last.

The third matter that consumed investigators' time was whether the administration had covered up the nature of the attack in its aftermath in order to protect Obama and other officials, including Hillary. Republicans believed that the administration had misled the public about whether the assault was a "terrorist" attack on the watch of a president who was seeking reelection at the time.

"It was five days after the Democratic National Convention, where President Obama stood up and said 'Al Qaeda's on the run, we killed Osama bin Laden. We're pushing back on the terrorists.' Nobody wants to get caught and be embarrassed like that," Representative Jason Chaffetz (R-Utah), the chairman of the Oversight and Government Reform Committee's subcommittee investigating Benghazi, said. "It was all political. It was political trumping reality. And the casualty was the truth."

That part of the investigation explained the obsession with Susan Rice's talking points—the exclusion of the names of terrorist groups in their final version, the omission of references to generic warnings issued by the CIA to the State Department, the insertion of a protest that had never happened, and the extent to which top officials in the White House and the State Department were involved in revising the intelligence community's assessment. Hillary, of course, had an interest in several elements of that part of the probe, not the least of which was the question of whether the State Department should have been more ready for the attack, based on CIA warnings about protests at the Cairo embassy and the possibility of violence on the anniversary of September 11, 2001.

All those questions were swirling shortly after eight a.m. on January 23, 2013, when reporters, spectators, and Senate staff began filling the cavernous main hearing room on the second floor of the Senate's Hart Office Building—where a special committee had investigated Hillary's role in the Whitewater scandal more than fifteen years earlier. Used for high-profile moments, including the confirmation hearings of Supreme Court justices David Souter and Sonia Sotomayor, Hart 216 is a favorite space because of its combination of size and modernity. On a mezzanine a few feet above the main floor are openings on either side for television cameras and their operators.

Senators sit in a U-shape, with the senior members of a committee in front of a gigantic white-marble wall bearing the Senate seal and junior members flanked on their sides below the camera bays. The witness sits alone at a small table about ten feet away, facing the senators, with reporters and other visitors behind her.

R and Paul, the fifty-year-old first-term Kentucky Republican, walked through the Capitol complex from his Russell Senate Office Building suite to the hearing with Rachel Bovard, his legislative aide for foreign relations matters, at his side. It would be the libertarian-leaning Tea Party favorite's first hearing as a member of the Senate Foreign Relations Committee, and he had met with his staff the day before to go over the Benghazi timeline. As Paul made his way to the Hart Building, Bovard briefed him on Hillary's prepared testimony, which the State Department had sent over the night before.

For the rest of the ten-minute walk, and for a few minutes in an ante space behind the hearing room, Paul detailed his grasp of the timeline, the flow of memos and cables on security between Tripoli and Washington before the attack, why Hillary wouldn't have been apprised of those interactions given the high threat level in Libya, and why State Department officials had been placed on leave or moved to other jobs rather than being fired in the wake of the ARB report. Instead of asking a long list of questions, Paul laid out his understanding of the essential elements of the Benghazi story, giving Bovard a chance to correct him if necessary. If he planned to go hard at Hillary during the hearing, he didn't share his strategy—or the specifics of his questions—with his aides ahead of time.

Paul was one of two Republicans on the committee who were widely considered to be interested in running for president in 2016. The other, Marco Rubio, a telegenic forty-one-year-old Cuban American from Florida, had been following Benghazi intently for months as a member of both the Intelligence and Foreign Relations Committees. Unlike Paul, Rubio leaned heavily on his national security aides to generate questions for the hearing. He had been present for both public and closed classified hearings on Benghazi and was determined to use his time with Hillary to press for the answers to questions he had been asking of the State Department privately. The posture he hoped to strike was that of a serious investigator, eager to plug gaps in the information he had gotten from the State Department and to get to the bottom of answers he didn't think made sense.

Hillary's own preparation for the hearing included reading transcripts and summaries from more than thirty separate Capitol Hill briefings and hearings over the four and a half months since the attack, both sessions in which she participated and those at which other administration officials appeared without her. She suspected that she would be asked questions about what other departments and agencies had done, and she wanted to be ready to answer them—even if they had nothing to do with her role as secretary of state. She had also met behind closed doors with top aides in the days before the hearing to go over questions she might get from various senators. Her staff expected that Paul and Rubio would take shots at her.

They went over the story line of the talking points that Susan Rice had used on the Sunday shows and a wrinkle that had become a focal point for Republican critics of the administration. Because the FBI had interviewed survivors of the attack at Ramstein in Germany before Rice went on the shows, Republicans were convinced that the White House and State should have known definitively that there had been no protest outside the gates of the consulate before the attack. The State Department's response was that officials in Washington had waited to talk to survivors because they didn't want to create any appearance of interfering with the FBI's investigatory interviews, and the FBI hadn't disseminated information about its probe to other agencies until after Rice's Sunday-show appearances.

During her prep session, Hillary expressed frustration at Senate Republicans' focus on the talking points Rice had used and the question of when the administration started calling the assault a terrorist attack. While she had cast the assault as terrorism in the twin

House and Senate briefings the week after Benghazi, determining the motivation of the attackers was secondary in her mind to finding them and bringing them to justice.

"I just don't understand," she told her aides. "Why don't they get it?"

"Everyone who has briefed or testified has wanted to stand up and scream 'What the hell difference does it make?'" Reines said, unwittingly planting a seed.

Indeed, late in 2012, James Clapper, the director of national intelligence, had become so irate with questions along that line from the House Intelligence Committee that when one lawmaker asked him what he had learned from Benghazi, he finally lost his temper. "I learned that it will be a cold day in hell before we ever give talking points to you people again," Clapper had said.

One Republican getting worked up over the talking points was Ron Johnson, a first-term Wisconsin senator who, like Paul, would be interrogating Hillary in his first hearing as a member of the Foreign Relations Committee. Johnson, who came from a business background rather than the world of politics and public policy, required staff briefings to get up to speed on most issues. But he usually developed his own questions while a hearing was going on, rather than coming with preprinted notes on what to ask. No one, save perhaps Ron Johnson, was prepared for him to create the most memorable highlight of the hearing.

Hillary arrived on time for the inquisition and emerged from a holding room behind the marble wall wearing a new pair of glasses with a thick black frame and lenses covered with a thin film designed to help her with the bouts of double vision she had been suffering since her fall. She quickly found her old Armed Services Committee chum John McCain and hugged him. Then she gave a hug to California Democrat Barbara Boxer, whose daughter was once married to Hillary's brother. Ben Cardin, the Democratic senator from Maryland, got a handshake and a kiss on the cheek before

Hillary posed for pictures with Bob Corker, the top-ranking Republican on the panel, and Bob Menendez, who was chairing the hearing because Foreign Relations Committee chairman John Kerry was the president's pick to succeed Hillary.

After the demonstrative pleasantries, Hillary rounded the side of the dais and whispered something to Reines, sat down, and laid a big, white three-ring binder on the table in front of her. Reines took a seat in a row of chairs directly behind Hillary and to her right. Mills, who held her own copy of the binder, sat next to him.

When Menendez opened the hearing, many of the senators had not yet arrived. Paul and Johnson were among the early birds, while Rubio was one of several senators who filtered in once the hearing was in full swing. Everyone in the room was waiting to see just how far the Republican senators would push Hillary, and how hard she would push back. Reporters listened intently for the kind of exchange that could be sent out in a breaking news e-mail alert or typed into the crawl across the bottom of a cable television feed.

In her opening remarks, Hillary choked up as she talked about making phone calls to the families of Sean Smith and Chris Stevens, but she revealed no new information about the attack or the State Department's response to it. Idaho senator Jim Risch pressed Hillary on the administration's characterization of the attack.

"I called it an attack by armed militants," Hillary offered.

"Well done!" Risch interjected, his tone sopped in sarcasm.

Surprisingly, as the press and Hillary's team were prepared for a fistfight, Rubio took a pass on going toe-to-toe with Hillary. It was important to Rubio to stay focused on the facts, not political grandstanding—a posture that in and of itself spoke to his careful cultivation of a narrative in which he was a serious player on national security issues. Perhaps he also saw too much risk of hurting his own political chances if he ended up on the losing side of a caustic one-on-one exchange.

But Johnson, the political newcomer who had swept to victory in Wisconsin on Tea Party power in 2010, displayed none of Rubio's reticence. He was locked onto the question of whether the administration had lied to the public about the nature of the attack, and he was pretty sure he knew the answer.

"I appreciate the fact that you called it an assault, but I'm going back to Ambassador Rice, five days later going on the Sunday shows, and, what I would say, purposefully misleading the American public," Johnson began.

"Well, since . . ." Hillary started, but Johnson cut her off.

"Why wasn't that known?" he asked, pushing Hillary to explain why State hadn't simply interviewed the survivors of the Benghazi attack to find out what had happened.

Mills reached forward from the row of seats behind Hillary to hand her boss a slip of paper. Hillary read from the note, which reminded her of the essential element of the administration's timeline—the FBI's intelligence on what had happened on the ground wasn't available to other federal agencies at the time the talking points were devised.

"I would say that once the assault happened and once we got our people rescued and out, our most immediate concern was number one taking care of their injuries. As I said, I still have a DS [diplomatic security] agent at Walter Reed seriously injured. Getting them into Frankfurt Ramstein to get taken care of, the FBI going over immediately to start talking to them—we did not think it was appropriate for us to talk to them before the FBI conducted their interviews.

"And we did not—I think this is accurate, sir—I certainly did not know of any reports that contradicted the [intelligence community] talking points at the time that Ambassador Rice went on the TV shows," Hillary said, adding a politically helpful—if a bit too late—defense of Rice. "And you know, I just want to say that people have accused Ambassador Rice and the administration of misleading Americans. I can say, trying to be in the middle of this and understanding what was going on, nothing could be further from the truth." But, intentionally or not, there could be no doubt that Rice had mischaracterized the chain of events in Benghazi.

Hillary was getting the better of the exchange, but Johnson wasn't ready to give up. He was going to score some points.

"We were misled that there were supposedly protests, and then something sprang out of that—an assault sprang out of that. And that was easily ascertained that that was not the fact . . ." Johnson started.

Reines had told Hillary that other senior administration officials, in closed-door briefings, when confronted with this line of GOP criticism on the talking points, had boiled over.

Hillary jumped in and she and Johnson jousted to be heard, with the senator finally getting out his point.

"The American people could have known that within days, and they didn't know that," he said.

If the Republicans wanted a made-for-TV moment, Hillary gave it to them—on her terms. "With all due respect," she said, slowing down to emphasize each word in the rest of the sentence, "we had *four dead Americans.*" Her pitch rose with the volume of her voice. As he heard the change in her tone, Reines, seated behind Hillary and to her left, craned his neck to see who she was addressing and was surprised to see Johnson, whom he knew little about.

"Was it because of a protest?" she went on. "Or was it because of guys out for a walk one night and decided they would go kill some Americans? What difference at this point does it make?

"It is our job to figure out what happened and do everything we can to prevent it from ever happening again. Senator, now honestly, I will do my best to answer your questions about this, but the fact is that people were trying in real time to get the best information. The [intelligence community] has a process, I understand, going with the other committees to explain how these talking points came out. But, you know, to be clear, it is, from my perspective, less important today looking backwards as to why these militants decided they did it than to find them and bring them to justice, and then maybe we'll figure out what was going on in the meantime."

For the many administration officials who thought Republicans wanted to make political hay out of a tragedy rather than learn lessons that might prevent another successful attack, Hillary's response was a bravura performance. For Republicans, there was now a video clip of Hillary losing her cool under questioning on Benghazi.

"Okay," Johnson replied. "Thank you, madam secretary."

But the fusillade was only half over. Paul, sitting several seats down from Johnson, took note of Hillary's charged response and decided that when his turn came to ask questions, he would pick up on his Wisconsin colleague's aggressive line. Speaking without notes, Paul intimated that Hillary's imminent departure from the department was related to Benghazi and then dropped the bomb that if he were president—a job he planned to seek in 2016—he would have fired her.

"Ultimately, with your leaving, you accept the culpability for the worst tragedy since 9/11," he said. "Had I been president at the time, and I found that you did not read the cables from Benghazi—you did not read the cables from Ambassador Stevens—I would have relieved you of your post. I think it's inexcusable."

Paul was fashioning a highlight-reel moment of his own, but he was working a shaky point. More than one million cables are sent to the State Department each year from diplomats across the globe; if any secretary reads one, it is typically because an underling has brought it to his or her attention. Still, Paul's aides blasted the video out to reporters.

"You know they practiced that when they were shaving in the morning," one of Hillary's closest friends said. "I could see that Rand Paul going over it three times as the shaving cream disappeared."

All the major players had what they wanted from the hearing. Rubio cast himself as above the partisan fray; Johnson put himself on the map by pushing Hillary into a testy exchange; Paul conjured the image of himself as president; and Hillary defended Obama, Rice, and herself in a way that questioned the motivations of junior senators from the Tea Party wing of the GOP. Her exchange with Johnson was the move of a veteran witness, one who understands how to wait for the right moment and then use the weight of her adversary's thrust against him.

"She has a full range of emotions," said one former senior

government official. "They were always a full range of emotions, but very carefully controlled. . . . I think she's very savvy, and I don't think anybody laid a glove on her frankly. There may be a video clip or two that perhaps may be unhelpful later on, but so be it."

In her most comprehensive remarks on the topic of Benghazi, over several hours of hearings before the Senate Foreign Relations and House Foreign Affairs Committees that day, Hillary laid out her view that it would be far more dangerous for the United States to pull back from violent parts of the world than it was to maintain and build a presence. The United States, she said in essence, is a beacon of good and cannot cede ground to terrorists and other perpetrators of violence and oppression. The QDDR had articulated her philosophy of making expeditionary diplomacy in conflict areas the "new normal" and "managing risk" rather than averting it by avoiding it.

When American outposts came under attack in countries where radical brands of Islam flourished—as at the Peshawar consulate in 2010, an attack that she had watched images of in a meeting with her top deputies—Hillary's response was to make sure her team at the State Department knew the risks that diplomats were taking, to work to reduce them, and to redouble public diplomacy efforts in those regions.

"We've come a long way in the past four years, and we cannot afford to retreat now. When America is absent, especially from unstable environments, there are consequences. Extremism takes root; our interests suffer; our security at home is threatened," she said. "That's why I sent Chris Stevens to Benghazi in the first place."

A source who had worked closely with Hillary on implementing the recommendations of the ARB report said she wanted to make sure that "we don't overcorrect" in the wake of the attack.

"I think she believes, accurately, that we will never get to zero risk," the source said. "Her notion of expeditionary diplomacy, which is very much a part of the QDDR, is important to her. . . . Diplomacy is not just about government-to-government relations anymore. Especially ambassadors and their diplomatic staff need to be out with the NGOs, with the nonstate actors, with the businesses, and she very much believes that. I think she wants to address any shortfalls that were there, any systematic issues in how diplomatic security does its job. But she also doesn't want to overlearn this lesson, and I think she wants to remind members of Congress and other people that we're going to have a lot of risk out there, and we're going to have to figure out how to manage it. . . . That's the picture of modern diplomacy."

Jason Chaffetz, a boyish-looking forty-six-year-old Utah Republican and a critic of Hillary's view of expeditionary diplomacy, had quickly become the engine behind the House Oversight and Government Reform Committee's investigation into Benghazi in the fall of 2012. A onetime pal of former New York representative Anthony Weiner, Chaffetz had actually been to Hillary's Washington home for the engagement party the Clintons threw for Weiner and Huma Abedin in 2010. Bill Clinton, Chaffetz thought, had been a little overzealous in greeting visitors with a "two-minute man-shake," consisting of a handshake and a firm arm grasp. He had also met Hillary during his first term, at a reception the State Department threw for freshman members of Congress.

Chaffetz's aw-shucks manner and natural charm make it easy to underestimate him. Reines once sought to play down his importance by referring to him as "Jeremy Chaffetz." But the media-friendly former placekicker for Brigham Young University's football team is a sharp political operative who beat Representative Chris Cannon in a 2008 primary despite not living in the district at the time. Before that, he ran Jon Huntsman's victorious campaign for governor of Utah in 2004 and served as Huntsman's chief of staff.

When Chaffetz traveled to Libya in October 2012, a State Department lawyer was assigned to shadow him in meetings with General Carter Ham, the head of the military's Africa Command, during a stop in Germany and with U.S. officials in Tripoli. Because Chaffetz served on two committees that were already investigating the Benghazi attack—Issa's panel and the House Intelligence

Committee—his trip was regarded as part of an investigation rather than a typical congressional delegation visit to a foreign capital. Though Chaffetz didn't like having the State Department lawyer at his meetings—he complained to the lawyer but not to the State Department in Washington—the lawyer was allowed to stay in the briefings until one with Gregory Hicks, the deputy chief of mission in Tripoli, turned toward classified information. The lawyer didn't have high enough security clearance for the topic and was forced to leave.

Hicks later got a call from Cheryl Mills. "She was unhappy that the lawyer that came with Congressman Chaffetz was not included in that meeting," Hicks testified. "The statement was clearly no direct criticism, but the tone of the conversation—and again, this is part of the Department of State culture—the fact that she called me and the tone of her voice—again, we're trained to gauge tone and nuance in language—indicated to me very strongly that she was unhappy."

From State's view, Mills was providing standard legal protection for the department and its employees. In Chaffetz's eyes, the lawyer was there to intimidate those same officials. "That's highly unusual, to have a babysitter/note-taker in there the whole time, watching my every move," he said. "I think it was intimidating for the people who wanted to talk to me. It made me feel uncomfortable. I think it suppressed information that should've been shared."

While the sprawling set of congressional investigations into Benghazi generally suffered from an abundance of zeal and a lack of focus—the obsession with Susan Rice's talking points and whether the president had called the assault an act of terrorism diluted the Republican message—Chaffetz was in the process of developing a more coherent narrative that placed blame on Hillary for her belief in expeditionary diplomacy.

More than any other member of Congress, Chaffetz questioned whether Chris Stevens's death was the result of a flawed philosophy. He was struck by a conversation he had with the major leading a Marine fleet antiterrorism security team (FAST) in Tripoli. The two men were looking over the south wall of the Tripoli embassy into the rural outskirts of the city, and the Marine pointed to a modest home sitting on about half an acre not too far away.

"Before we got here, they had a ladder, and the ladder from the home was leaning up against our embassy wall," the major told Chaffetz. "There's no barbed wire. Every day they'd come out and they'd take their garbage, and they'd dump it on our embassy grounds. You go over there, and there's fishheads and all kinds of garbage and crap, When we got here, we had to go tell 'em, 'You take that ladder down. In fact, if you go up on that wall, I will kill you.' They got the message, and they don't dump garbage on the embassy grounds anymore. But before we got here, that was just the attitude: 'We don't want to offend anybody. We don't want to make anyone feel bad about us.'"

To Chaffetz, the diplomatic dynamic reflected a problem with an approach that left Americans too vulnerable to attack. The Marines were willing to use—or at least threaten to use—lethal force against people who disrespected America's post, while diplomats let it go in a way that could embolden potential attackers. "We had trees growing right next to the embassy wall. All you do is scurry up the tree and jump over the embassy wall. It would be easy," Chaffetz said later. "Any high school kid could do that. The Marines were so frustrated, but that was just the cultural approach that the State Department had."

Chaffetz, who opposed Obama's decision to go to war in Libya, blamed Stevens's death on Hillary's desire to see the intervention prove wise. "Prior to the attack," he said, "I think toppling Qaddafi and building a strong presence in Libya could have been her swan song. It really could have been her major achievement, but the whole deck of cards fell out from underneath her. I'm not blaming her for the fact that we were attacked. I just think her push for normalization [of diplomatic relations] at the sacrifice of security cost people their lives and that was a cultural push from this administration, and I think from her, personally."

Obviously, the terrorists were to blame for the attacks. But Hillary was anxious to build Libya into an enduring success story, and, according to Hicks's testimony, Stevens went to Benghazi in September at least in part because Hillary wanted to upgrade the facility there to a permanent post as soon as possible. At the same time that the State Department brass sought to demonstrate progress in Libya by normalizing security operations, the country was becoming more dangerous by the day. That was particularly true in Benghazi. But Washington didn't heed the warning calls from its agents on the ground in Tripoli, from Gene Cretz to Chris Stevens. While there's no evidence that their requests ever made it past the desk of Undersecretary Pat Kennedy and up to Hillary's inner circle, it is perfectly legitimate to ask why. The Accountability Review Board found that security was inadequate both in Tripoli and Benghazi and that folks on the ground in Benghazi felt certain that their security needs were not a high priority in Washington. In the end, Chris Stevens died doing what he had signed up to do: venture into one of the most dangerous parts of the world with a small enough security footprint to avoid intimidating the very people he hoped to create partnerships with. But the ARB found that the State Department was too willing to let him operate without a fully functioning net. Hillary had sent the message throughout her department that she believed the risk of putting diplomats in dangerous areas was worth it, but in this case, the ARB strongly suggested that the calculation of risk and reward had been out of whack. "The Department should urgently review the proper balance between acceptable risk and expected outcomes in high risk, high threat areas," the investigators wrote. "While the answer cannot be to refrain from operating in such environments, the Department must do so on the basis of having: (1) a defined, attainable, and prioritized mission; (2) a clear-eyed assessment of the risk and costs involved; (3) a commitment of sufficient resources to mitigate these costs and risks; (4) an explicit acceptance of those costs and risks that cannot be mitigated; and (5) constant attention to changes in the situation, including when to leave and perform the mission from a distance."

Regardless of the philosophical questions, Hillary earned high marks for her response to the attacks. David Petraeus had fought a tug-of-war with State over the Benghazi talking points, but he said Hillary's response demonstrated her leadership skills. "Like a lot of great leaders, her most impressive qualities were most visible during tough times. In the wake of the Benghazi attacks, for example, I thought she was extraordinarily resolute, determined, and controlled," he said. "And her speech at Andrews Air Force Base, when the flag-draped caskets brought home those killed in Benghazi, conveyed those qualities, as did various other actions that she took and directed."

If the Benghazi investigation had proved anything, it was that Hillary, the putative front-runner for the Democratic presidential nomination in 2016, was no longer above the partisan fray that Hillary, the secretary of state, had so deftly avoided for most of four years. In the context of presidential politics, the relationships she had built up with Republicans during her tenure held less meaning. Less than a week after she testified before the Senate Foreign Relations Committee in January 2013, Lindsey Graham, the on-again, off-again moderate Republican who was entering a reelection cycle in ultraconservative South Carolina, said on Fox News that Hillary "got away with murder."

The old RNC Benghazi ad, the one the Romney campaign chose not to use in the final weeks of the campaign, was distributed just as House Republican investigations were heating up in the spring. The script had flipped sometime in December, when Republicans shifted their focus from Obama to Hillary. Hillary, in turn, had put up her political defenses. If she wanted to run for president, she would be dealing with the likes of Darrell Issa, Jason Chaffetz, Lindsey Graham, Rand Paul, and any number of other Republican antagonists for the next four years—and if she was lucky, for the four years after that. It was clear by the spring of 2013 that she would hear about Benghazi time and again. Sean Spicer, RNC spokesman, put it bluntly: "If she runs, she might as well get used to seeing that ad."

NINETEEN

"Out of Politics"—For Now

E ven though Hillary hadn't picked a formal end date, which would depend on when the Senate confirmed her successor, she gave indications to her friends and aides that she was more than ready to move on from State. In addition to her joke about filling her time with "beaches and speeches," one of her longtime advisers observed that she had dropped one of the hallmarks of her industriousness even before her fall.

"I noticed she's no longer taking notes," the aide said shortly before she left. "She walks into those meetings now, it's like 'Tell me what's going on?' No more follow-up. 'I'm coasting out of here.'"

When she fell in December, aides had been in the process of planning at least one more trip across the Atlantic. But at a follow-up examination later that month, doctors discovered that a blood clot had formed inside her skull, in a sinus cavity behind her ear. The clot could have killed her, or caused severe brain damage, if it had gone untreated. Hillary was immediately admitted to New York Presbyterian Hospital. She was placed on blood thinners and remained at the hospital for several days, so doctors could keep an eye on her. Those close to her say Hillary, hardly accustomed to standing still, had a bad case of cabin fever as the New Year approached. It wasn't the first time she had suffered from a blood clot. In her memoir, *Living History,* she wrote of the clot she developed in her leg and the blood-thinning medication she had taken for several months after its discovery. It had been caused by "non-stop flying around the country," she wrote. Now her doctors advised her to stay on the ground while she recuperated. Flying around the globe, with very little sleep, would interfere with her ability to recover.

To the great disappointment of some of her closest aides, Hillary was finished traveling. Reines and Sullivan had a running competition over which of them would make it to the most countries during her tenure (Sullivan won by one—Reines had missed Hungary). Others "were relieved" because, before the fall, stops kept getting added to her final planned trips, according to one adviser, who termed the process of scheduling her victory lap "ridiculous."

While Hillary was recovering from her illness and concussion, her successor was chosen. On December 13, Susan Rice, who had poisoned the well with senators first through her Benghazi talking points, and later in a round of one-on-one sessions meant to smooth her path to confirmation, withdrew from consideration for Hillary's job. Speculation in Washington quickly centered on John Kerry, who had taken on sensitive diplomatic assignments for Obama during the first term, and on December 21, Obama announced that he would appoint Kerry. Hillary's exact end date wasn't yet clear, but there was little doubt that Kerry, the chairman of the Foreign Relations Committee, would sail through the confirmation process. Suddenly the length of her tenure could be measured not in years or months but in weeks.

The notebooks and the odometer were no longer necessary, but Hillary's staff thought she would need one piece of essential equipment to get through her final month at State. On January 6, the day she returned to work, Clinton showed up for a 9:15 a.m. assistant secretaries meeting, resplendent in a hot pink blazer, the new hipster glasses, and a freshly trimmed and highlighted coif. State Department spokeswoman Toria Nuland declared Hillary was "in the pink."

More than seventy people, from deputy secretaries to special envoys, had packed into a conference room to greet Hillary. When she walked in, they stood and applauded. For weeks, over the holiday season, her friends and advisers, frightened by the fall, the concussion, and the blood clot, had traded e-mails and texts on the latest on her condition. They knew she hadn't fully recovered. She was, after all, still on blood thinners. But seeing her walk in the room smiling brought some comfort. "I was relieved," said a top aide who attended the meeting. "You never know who's giving you the right information, even in our world. And she looked like she had taken three weeks off, which she did, whether she liked it or not."

After Hillary took her seat at the head of the table behind her "S" placard that Monday morning, Deputy Secretary Tom Nides presented her with a box. "As you know, Washington is a contact sport," he told her, handing the box to her. He added that while it can be "dangerous" at the State Department, "it can also be dangerous at home."

Clinton opened the box to find a football helmet with the State Department seal as well as a football jersey that read CLINTON on the back. The number 112, representing the number of countries she had visited, was on the front. Hillary let out one of her classic hearty laughs. She held up the helmet and the jersey as her all-smiling staff applauded.

A moment later it was back to business. Aides in the room say she was particularly focused on Afghan president Karzai's trip later that week and that she wanted the ARB recommendations implemented, to the degree possible, before Kerry arrived to take over. When she quizzed her staff about what was going on in various parts of the world, they all began by saying how good it was to see her back at the table.

Later that day, during the daily briefing for reporters at the State Department, Nuland was asked if the secretary was back to her normal routine. "She's planning to work as hard as she always does?" the question came.

"I would guess, judging by the way she was this morning, yes," Nuland replied.

For Hillary's admirers, her relentless travel schedule had not just been a sign of her drive to outwork everyone else; it had represented a genuine belief that she should use her platform as both secretary and an international icon to spread positive messages about the

United States as far and wide as possible, and to as many different audiences as she could. The statistics on miles traveled and countries visited were the most quantifiable way of measuring her dedication to achieving that goal. Politicians who enter public office often talk about "deliverables," the successes they can point to at the end of their term to recommend them for higher office. The very nature of her job tended to militate against "deliverables." Much of what she did as a diplomat was to head off emerging crises before they exploded and to manage them when they did. The same was true of her role as an adviser to Obama on national security matters. To the extent that he had foreign policy successes, including the killing of Osama bin Laden, she was one player on a large team, and he was the quarterback. Had there been a major peace deal during her tenure, she would doubtless have had to share the glory with—or more likely, give it up entirely to—Obama. The story of Libya continues to unfold, and the murders of four Americans in Benghazi may end up being either a sign that chaos will reign there or a tragic exception to a successful transition from repressive autocracy to inclusive democracy. In either case, Hillary proved her ability to focus a fractious international coalition on a singular objective. In Burma, she demonstrated that a smart-power approach can work.

But even her most ardent admirers discuss her legacy as a stateswoman in terms of less visible deliverables than, say, a lasting Middle East peace accord. Nides, an ardent defender, framed her work to integrate the national security agencies as a major accomplishment. "The legacy of Hillary Clinton at the State Department will, in fact, be in the dramatically better relationships between the State Department and Department of Defense," he said. Before she arrived, "the personalities were such that the buildings wouldn't talk to each other because everyone thought the DOD was basically trying to take over the legislative authority of the State Department. And the whole thing turned totally on its head when Hillary Clinton came in. . . . We have more joint programs now in DOD and State than we've ever had in the past, where we use their money but we use our authority."

One of her undersecretaries pointed to Hillary's work to rebuild America's brand abroad as a key to opening foreign markets to American businesses; her insistence on talking about women's issues as a game changer in getting foreign leaders to elevate women in their societies; her focus on smart power as a key to transforming Burma's government; and her emphasis on using technical training as a tool of development, rather than just money, to strengthen civil society in other countries, thereby reducing the chance that they would become threats to American national security. That under-secretary boiled it all down to this: "Secretary Clinton reintroduced America to the world, and they liked what they saw. They wanted to be a part of it."

There's certainly evidence to suggest that the world approved more of American leadership during Clinton's tenure than it did in the years before she took over at State. How much of that is attrib-utable to her, how much to Obama, and how much to other factors is hard to know. But in the last two years of the Bush administra-tion, Gallup measured world approval of American leadership at about one-third, a figure that trailed well behind Britain, France, Germany, Japan, and China. In 2009 and 2010, the American rating leaped to the head of the pack, spiking to one-half in 2009, then set-tling back to 47 percent in 2010, seven points higher than any other country. In 2011 America fell into a tie for first place with Germany at 41 percent.

But in January, as the inevitable legacy stories began to appear in newspapers and foreign policy journals, Hillary faced criticism from a variety of outside experts who portrayed her as a strong advo-cate for the United States but one who fell short of piling up major accomplishments. "Even an admirer, such as myself, must acknowl-edge that few big problems were solved on her watch; few victories achieved," the centrist scholar Michael O'Hanlon wrote, concluding that her term was "more solid than spectacular."

Indeed, some critics even took aim at her work ethic as more self-glorifying than effectual. In a column entitled "Hillary Clinton's Ego Trips," Michael Kinsley of Bloomberg wrote, "Clinton looks awful and has looked worse for years. I don't mean to be ungallant. It's just that she clearly has been working herself to death in her current job as well as in her past two, as senator and first lady. And for what? Despite all the admiration she deserves for her dedication and long hours, there is also a vanity of long hours and (in her current job) long miles of travel."

Yet Obama left little question about how valuable he found Hillary's efforts. In the fall, he told Ben Rhodes he wanted to do something special for her, to show how much he appreciated her work on his behalf. Rhodes, in turn, began discussing with Hillary's aides various options for the president to give an interview to a major newsmagazine.

"The original idea was *Time* magazine, a wrap-up piece on her that he would very much cooperate with," said one of Hillary's aides. The conversation was put on pause when Hillary was sick around the holidays. But when she recovered and headed back to the State Department in the new year, the discussion picked back up.

And soon the idea shifted to one with even greater visibility. Reines, who prefers the imagery of television to print, thought the idea of having the two sit together for a magazine or newspaper interview seemed lame. "We were like, 'If we're gonna do it, do it right, let's put them on TV together,'" said a senior State official. "The image of them together is what would be powerful."

Rhodes and Reines brainstormed what show would be best. They ruled out the morning shows and the evening news because they would only get five to seven minutes of airtime. Likewise, they thought the Sunday shows wouldn't be the best way to illustrate their relationship because the shows, while an obsession in Washington, were "silly," the senior State official said. They settled on *60 Minutes* because it has "no peer in terms of ratings," the aide added.

In a joint White House prep session before the interview with *60 Minutes*'s Steve Kroft, Rhodes broached the topic of Obama's personal relationship with Hillary. "They're going to ask a lot about what it took for you two to get past disliking each other," he said.

"I never had that problem with Hillary," Obama said.

"I think a lot of this was staff," Hillary said.

"Yeah, I think that maybe it took some of the staff longer to get over the primary," Obama said, looking directly toward Reines as he spoke. Reines, always quick with a one-liner, made everyone in the room laugh with a self-conscious joke.

Obama made one further effort to make sure it was clear there was no ill will toward either Hillary or her staff. When State Department colleagues held a going-away party for Cheryl Mills, Obama dispatched his chief of staff, Jack Lew, to deliver a note saying that his team of rivals had become an "unrivaled team."

In the actual 60 Minutes interview, Obama told Kroft why he had decided to give her the parting gift of a joint television appearance.

"Hillary's been, you know, one of the most important advisers that I've had on a whole range of issues," Obama said. "Hillary's capacity to travel around the world, to lay the groundwork for a new way of doing things, to establish a sense of engagement, that our foreign policy was not going to be defined solely by Iraq, that we were going to be vigilant about terrorism, but we were going to make sure that we deployed all elements of American power, diplomacy, our economic and cultural and social capital, in order to bring about the kinds of international solutions that we wanted to see."

When asked whether Obama's endorsement of Hillary's work as secretary would carry over to a 2016 presidential run, they both dodged. "I was literally inaugurated four days ago, and you're talking about elections four years from now," he said. And Hillary, less than a week from leaving office, wasn't ready to give up the political cover provided by her job. "I'm out of politics," she said, "and I'm forbidden from even hearing these questions."

The exaggeration spoke to an obvious fact: it wasn't in her interests to talk about politics. Moreover, she needed a rest from policy, too. Even those closest to her knew that the rigors of the job had taken more of a toll on her than past posts had. She had redefined the job of first lady as an active participant in government, only to watch successors Laura Bush and Michelle Obama take on more traditional and less visible roles in their husbands' administrations.

Michelle Obama's war on childhood obesity wasn't quite the same as taking a health system overhaul up to Capitol Hill.

"I won't lie to you. I'm tired," Hillary told Kim Ghattas, a BBC reporter who wrote a book about her travels with Hillary. "My friends call and e-mail and say 'Oh my gosh, I saw you on television. You look so tired!' To which I reply, 'Gee, thanks a lot!'"

Even Hillary knew it was time to back off a little bit. Her friends said she was leaving public life behind at a perfect time, when she could rebound from the concussion and take the time off that she needed so desperately, time she had never had in a twenty-year run as first lady, senator, and secretary of state.

On February 1, 2013, in a bookend ceremony in the atrium of the State Department's main building, with all the pomp of her arrival four years earlier, Hillary addressed her troops before she exited the big glass front doors one last time. Most of Hillary's closest advisers were leaving with her, but Marshall and Mills would remain at the State Department well into 2013, and many other Clinton loyalists remained marbled into the bureaucracy as Kerry struggled to fill political jobs with his own people.

"I'm proud of the work we've done to elevate diplomacy and development, to serve the nation we all love," she told the crowd, "to understand the challenges, the threats, and the opportunities that the United States faces, and to work with all our heart and all of our might to make sure that America is secure, that our interests are promoted, and our values are respected."

At a farewell party at her house that week, aides reminisced with Hillary about the last four years. Marshall joked about Jon Favreau's cardboard-cutout groping incident way back in 2008. "You're still talking about that?" Hillary asked, her amusement evident. The old injuries were forgiven, if not entirely forgotten.

Despite the criticism that she had struck no major peace deal, the last Gallup poll before her departure, taken after Benghazi in November 2012, found that 63 percent of Americans approved of the job she was doing, three points below her peak as secretary but nine points higher than she had stood during the 2008 Democratic

National Convention. It was within the margin of error of her standing when she was sworn in as secretary, which was 65 percent, suggesting that, at the very least, she had served her four years without doing any damage to her prospects for the presidency in 2016. Already, perhaps inevitably, her interest in running was a hot topic in the national press, and clues about her viability were piling up.

In her final days at State, Hillary sent out 811 individualized, typed thank-you notes. Delivered in special envelopes with cardboard inserts—so they could be preserved as keepsakes—the notes were sent to cabinet officials; senior members of the military; national security staff; House and Senate leaders; and State Department employees who were political appointees, members of the foreign service, and members of the civil service. No doubt some of the recipients viewed the letters as possible presidential mementos.

TWENTY

Ready for Hillary

Hillary Clinton's 2016 campaign for the presidency had already begun—without her—on November 6, 2012, the day Barack Obama won a second term.

That night Allida Black and Adam Parkhomenko, veterans of Hillary's 2008 campaign, began e-mailing each other about plans to construct a virtual national campaign called Ready for Hillary. They knew Hillary had been on the sidelines of politics for four years and hadn't been able to build her list of volunteers, activists, and donors as aggressively as an overtly political figure could, at a time when the rapid advancement of social media had revolutionized the art of developing a national constituency. They wanted to build Hillary a grassroots organization while she decided whether to run.

Black, a George Washington University professor with a background in social and political activism dating back to the 1970s, had traveled to fourteen states for Hillary's 2008 campaign, attending more than five hundred house parties and knocking on more than five thousand doors by her count.

Part of her allegiance to Hillary stemmed from the fact that after Black's mother, Anna, suffered a heart attack, Hillary had called Anna at the hospital and had been the last person to talk to her. "I'm really sorry that I haven't met you," Hillary said. "But I want you to know that you must be a wonderful woman because you raised a wonderful daughter." Then Black's mother died.

Black and Parkhomenko, who had worked under the deposed

Patti Solis Doyle on the 2008 campaign, both had strong ties to Hillaryland's central nervous system. After Parkhomenko left the campaign following Doyle's departure, he and Black worked on a petition drive called Vote Both, organized around the hope of a Clinton/Obama or Obama/Clinton "dream ticket." And when Parkhomenko ran for a seat in the Virginia House of Delegates in 2009, his small donor list was packed with people who had worked for Hillary or contributed large sums of money to her campaign. He reported receiving donations from Elizabeth Bagley and José Villarreal, the pair who raised money for the Shanghai Expo; Beth Dozoretz, a longtime big-dollar Clinton family donor who would later be appointed head of the State Department's Arts in Embassies program; heavy-hitting Texas megadonor Alonzo Cantu; and a who's who of Hillary aides starting with Capricia Marshall, Harold Ickes, Burns Strider, Minyon Moore, and Jonathan Mantz, the national finance director for Hillary's 2008 campaign.

Black, who knew Maggie Williams, Melanne Verveer, and Marshall well, believed strongly that if Hillary didn't like what she was doing, someone high up in Hillaryland would call and say "Allida, shut this down!" That call never came, and over time an increasing number of high-profile Hillary loyalists jumped on board to give the fledgling super PAC a boost in credibility and fund-raising prowess.

Hillary's supporters weren't the only ones champing at the bit to run the 2016 race. The day after the election, at *Politico*'s headquarters in Rosslyn, Virginia, editors slated a story about a possible Hillary Clinton–Jeb Bush 2016 matchup for the top of the website the following morning. The story, which began "American politics may be headed back to the future," posted online at 4:34 a.m. on November 8, less than thirty-six hours after Obama was declared the winner of the 2012 race, and it carried the bylines of the paper's A-team of political reporters, Jonathan Martin and Maggie Haberman.

Not too long after that, the RNC researcher who dealt with foreign policy issues was assigned to full-time Hillary 2016 duty. While the Republican Party kept tabs on other potential Democratic candidates—Vice President Joe Biden, New York governor Andrew

Cuomo, and Maryland governor Martin O'Malley, among others—Hillary was what RNC communications director Sean Spicer called the "eight-hundred-pound gorilla" in the Democratic field.

Even former House Speaker Nancy Pelosi, who had angered mutual supporters by claiming neutrality while tacitly helping Obama in 2008, jumped on the bandwagon in mid-December, presaging a trend in which women politicians who opposed Hillary in 2008 treated the prospect of a 2016 run as a chance to get back into the good graces of Hillary and her loyalists. "I hope she goes," Pelosi told NBC's Andrea Mitchell. "If she decided to run, and I think she would win, she would go into the White House as well prepared or better prepared than almost anybody who has served in that office in a very long time."

The depth and breadth of the list of prominent leaders who thought Hillary would make for a capable candidate and commander in chief were impressive. David Petraeus, once mentioned as a possible GOP opponent to Obama, is among those who think she's more than up to the task. "She'd be a tremendous president," he said.

Everyone in the political world, it seemed, was ready for Hillary to start the 2016 campaign—everyone but Hillary.

After she left State, Hillary took a breather. Though she was the subject of countless headlines, she said very little publicly in her first six weeks as a private citizen. In mid-February she announced that the Harry Walker Agency would manage her lucrative turn on the lecture circuit—the "speeches" part of her "beaches and speeches" mantra. She persuaded Bill to take her out on a triple date with her friends Meryl Streep and Esprit founder Susie Tompkins Buell, and their husbands, to see the play *Ann* on Broadway. Hillary already had seen the show, a one-woman act about former Texas governor Ann Richards, and she desperately wanted Bill to see it with her the second time. The couples topped off the evening with a dinner at Cafe Luxembourg on the Upper West Side, the kind of outing she had rarely had time for in years past. She was spotted a handful of times in New York and in Washington, where she continued to live part-time and where she set up a small postgovernment operation on Connecticut Avenue called Hillary Rodham Clinton Office, or HRCO in the e-mail convention her aides used.

Then in mid-March, prodded by the timing of the arguments before the Supreme Court on a pair of gay marriage cases, Hillary jumped back into the domestic policy debate, in an area in which public attitudes had shifted most dramatically during her time away from the political battlefield. While at State, she had pushed forward on gay rights in ways that she felt fit within the four corners of foreign policy, but she hadn't addressed her own position on gay marriage in the United States. "She and Cheryl mapped out an agenda," said one of Hillary's aides, that boiled down to "We're going to do, within our field, what we can do, we're going to do things internally to help our own people, we're going to put it on the diplomatic agenda, and that's how we're going to work on this issue."

Hillary's strong support for gay rights in the diplomatic sphere was overshadowed by her reticence in the domestic political debate, which garnered far more attention among the general public. Still, she had rewritten the department's rules so that same-sex partners of diplomats posted overseas would get the same benefits as husbands and wives; incorporated the protection and advancement of gay rights abroad as part of the core mission of American diplomats; and given a December 2011 speech to the UN Human Rights Council in which she compared the minority status of gays and lesbians to that of racial, religious, and ethnic minorities, declaring, in an echo of her famous women's rights speech in Beijing during the Clinton administration, that "gay rights are human rights, and human rights are gay rights." What she said to the Human Rights Council, in advocating for the rights of lesbian, gay, bisexual, and transgender people, went much further than an endorsement of gay marriage. She said that all human rights should apply to them, including international legal protections against violence and discrimination. Beyond the international audience, said one Hillary friend who has worked on gay rights around the world, "it says to American diplomats, 'You can't fuck this up, because I'm gonna hold you accountable,' and that's pretty stratospheric."

She also hinted at the domestic debate in the United States, asserting that "my own country's record on human rights for gay people is far from perfect." And on a personal level, Hillary celebrated the weddings of same-sex friends. "At long last," she wrote in a note when Allida Black married her longtime partner, Judy Beck, on April 25, 2012.

But within the United States, as the general public and many politicians came to favor gay marriage, Hillary's last known position was the one from her 2008 campaign: she opposed it. Joe Biden had thrown his support behind gay marriage in an interview on *Meet the Press,* pushing Barack Obama to follow suit earlier than he wanted to in an election year. Hillary may have been ahead of the curve in the international human rights sphere, but she was behind it in terms of domestic politics. Like many other politicians, including Ohio Republican senator Rob Portman, she thought the oral arguments before the Supreme Court offered an opportunity to weigh in on the issue in a meaningful and timely way.

So in early March, she conducted a conference call with some of her aides, including speechwriter Dan Schwerin, to map out what she wanted to say in a video clip recorded for the Human Rights Campaign (HRC), the venerable Washington-based gay rights organization. Hillary wanted to make two main points: she supported gay marriage, and she respected the views of those who didn't. For years, friends of Hillary's had seen her struggle with the question of whether legalizing gay marriage could infringe on the rights or beliefs of religious groups, and she told her aides that she wanted to be respectful of their views even as her public position shifted. "There was not a what-should-my-position-be kind of conversation," said a source involved in the discussion. "She was pretty clear. But she was equally clear that she was not going to demonize people who disagreed with her on this."

On March 18, the week before the oral arguments at the Supreme Court, HRC released Hillary's taped remarks. "LGBT Americans are our colleagues, our teachers, our soldiers, our friends, our loved ones, and they are full and equal citizens and deserve the rights of citizenship. That includes marriage," she said, looking directly into the camera. "That's why I support marriage for lesbian and gay couples."

Reporters seized on it as a politically motivated shift. "Hillary Rodham Clinton's embrace of gay marriage Monday signals she may be seriously weighing a 2016 presidential run and trying to avoid the type of late-to-the-party caution that hurt her first bid," Chuck Babington of the Associated Press wrote.

Despite the obvious political advantage of moving quickly on an issue on which public opinion polls showed metastatic growth, Hillary's aides insisted that her decision had nothing to do with electoral politics. "Anything we did would be perceived politically," one aide said, "and obviously that's not why she wanted to do it."

Regardless of her motivation, the video was a signal that she felt comfortable weighing in directly on domestic issues again, after four years of accruing the political benefits of remaining above the fray. Republicans were already determined to bring her back down into partisan political warfare. Three days earlier Senate Minority Leader Mitch McConnell trotted out what would become the GOP's mainstay argument against both Hillary and Biden, that they were too old to be president. "Don't tell me the Democrats are the party of the future when their presidential ticket for 2016 is shaping up to look like a rerun of *The Golden Girls*," McConnell said to roars from the audience at the annual Conservative Political Action Conference in Washington. National Republicans set out to contrast their crop of younger rising stars—Marco Rubio, Rand Paul, Texas senator Ted Cruz, and New Jersey governor Chris Christie—with Democrats born in the 1940s.

The battle for the White House was in full swing, and Hillary's vacation was over. Around the same time, she began calling advisers and a tight-knit circle of friends with a clear message. "I've rested now," she told them. "I'm ready to work."

As with the possible presidential campaign, the groundwork for Hillary's return to the private sector had been laid by others. Over the course of more than two years, first Chelsea and then Huma had spent time cleaning up the freewheeling Clinton Foundation and its spin-offs, including the Clinton Global Initiative. Shortly after her summer 2010 wedding, Chelsea, who had worked in business consulting at the firm McKinsey & Company, jumped into analyzing how her father's office was run. The younger Clinton, thirty-one years old at the time, felt the foundation was in need of some serious housekeeping, if not housecleaning, sources familiar with the situation said, and an internal audit was ordered up.

"Chelsea was involved in that effort," said one foundation insider, "but rumors that have circulated that Chelsea was gonna come in and clean the place out and get rid of persons X, Y, and Z are inaccurate. I don't think her behavior was any different than any kid who sees their parents' business in need of some reorganization."

During the restructuring of the foundation, Chelsea also recommended that the foundation take a look at bringing aboard her friend and former McKinsey colleague Eric Braverman as chief executive, a move that later came to be.

But Chelsea's arrival seemed to signal a more dramatic shift in Clintonworld. Not only was Chelsea, who would become the vice chairwoman of the foundation board, for the first time owning her role as heir to the family political and philanthropic dynasty, but this transitional period was also the beginning of the end for Doug Band. Chelsea grew concerned that Band's business ties were tainting the Clinton brand her father had worked so hard to build. While Hillary is said to have very much appreciated Band's work to raise money for the Clinton library and to help pay off her campaign debt, Band's bad-cop role as gatekeeper to Bill also rubbed some of her advisers, and certainly other Democrats, the wrong way.

Band made Bill notoriously difficult to access and was often hard to pin down himself. Even Obama's emissaries had to pursue him for months to set up the November 2011 meeting in Bill's Harlem office that set the stage for Bill's involvement in the 2012 campaign. By then, Band was already transitioning out of the foundation empire that he had built for Bill. He had started an international consulting company with two other partners, called Teneo

Holdings, that hung its hat on having Bill Clinton and former British prime minister Tony Blair as paid advisers. Teneo expanded rapidly, counting two hundred employees in thirteen global offices within two years of its launch. More than anything, the firm built its reputation on access, boasting on its website that it worked "exclusively with the CEOs and leaders of the world's largest companies, institutions and governments" and solved problems by "leveraging . . . deep global relationships."

One of Band's partners, Declan Kelly, had been appointed by Hillary to be America's economic envoy to Ireland before starting the company. The State Department cleared Bill Clinton's role as a paid adviser to Teneo, but the whole idea left a bad taste in the mouths of some Clinton loyalists. Wasn't there at least the appearance of a conflict of interest if the secretary of state's husband was being paid to advise a company with international clients? Some Clinton allies thought Band was putting Bill and Hillary in an awkward position to help line his own pockets and theirs.

But the Clintons have a blind spot when it comes to their closest aides, including Band and Huma Abedin. The Clintons' loyalty to those two aides would come back to haunt Hillary.

Still, the arrangement of Band working for Teneo and CGI didn't last long. In February 2012, *Politico* reported that Bill had severed his financial ties to Teneo. Around the same time, Band was pushed out of his role as the linchpin for the global initiative, reportedly at the urging of Hillary loyalists. "You can do CGI or Teneo, but you can't do both," Bill Clinton had told Band, according to a *New York Post* source. "Doug chose Teneo."

The former president responded to news stories about Band's departure with a misty statement nearly twice as long, at a whopping 362 words, as the one he had released when Mother Teresa died in 1997. "I couldn't have accomplished half of what I have in my post presidency without Doug Band. Doug is my counselor and a board member of the Clinton Global Initiative, which was created at his suggestion," Bill said. "He tirelessly works to support the expansion of CGI's activities and my other foundation work around the world. In our first ten years, Doug's strategic vision and fund-raising made it possible for the foundation to survive and thrive. I hope and believe he will continue to advise me and build CGI for another decade."

The cherry on top for Band, who remained involved with Clinton's domestic operation, was that Bill didn't cut his ties to Band and Teneo but rather flipped the flow of money so that he became a client of Teneo rather than a paid adviser. "I felt that I should be paying them, not the other way around," he said.

But those in the Clinton sphere who were uncomfortable with the whole deal had reason to worry that the Band bond could end up hurting Hillary. In December 2011, Huma Abedin gave birth to a son, Jordan Weiner, and decided she could no longer work as a full-time State Department employee in Washington. So that she could remain as an adviser through the end of her term, Hillary allowed Huma to become an outside consultant to the department on June 4, 2012, an arrangement under which she could legally earn income from other sources.

"My understanding is Huma is doing some work for Teneo ... and has been," said a Clinton Foundation source in January 2013. At the same time, Band's relationship with the Clinton Foundation was ending. He "don't work here no more," the source said.

Abedin's dual relationship with the secretary of state and Band's international consulting firm came to light in May 2013 when *Politico* reported it, sparking a new round of questions about possible self-dealing in Clintonworld. In a July letter bearing her new Park Avenue address, Huma told Republican senator Chuck Grassley that she provided "strategic advice and consulting services to the firm's management team" but did not provide "insights about the department, my work with the secretary or any government information to which I may have had access."

At the time of the letter, she and her husband, former New York congressman and mayoral candidate Anthony Weiner, were dealing with the fallout from the disclosure that he had continued to have sexually explicit extramarital electronic chats after he was forced to resign from Congress. The damaging investigation into Huma's business practices didn't factor in the mayoral race because the new round of stories about Weiner's sexual proclivities already had sunk his chances of winning. But it did threaten to blot Hillary's legacy at State and raise questions about her judgment in letting one of her top State Department advisers make money working for an outfit with international clients. At best, it just looked bad. At worst, it presented a conflict of interest.

The appearance questions raised around Band and Abedin—the aides physically and emotionally closest to Bill and Hillary, respectively, for more than a decade—spoke to a tough bind that the most competent and trusted Clinton loyalists faced. If they were willing to earn good money, they'd always have a job at the heart of the operation. But if they wanted to get rich, they would lose access, suffer accusations of trading on the Clinton name, or both. When that happened, it inevitably reflected poorly on either Bill or Hillary, whichever Clinton the staffer was closer to. In Abedin's case, it was Hillary.

Grassley fumed at the responses he got to questions from Huma and State about her status in the department's "special government employee" program. "So far the State Department and Ms. Abedin haven't provided a single document that I requested," he said in response to Huma's letter. "Putting up a stone wall raises a lot more questions about how the program is being used than it answers."

Huma had taken on another role in the summer of 2012, working to help set up Hillary's post-State integration into the Clinton Foundation, which was renamed the Bill, Hillary and Chelsea Clinton Foundation when Hillary left State. Former Hillary aide Tina Flournoy took over the reins in February, as Band exited for good. When Hillary reemerged from her post-State respite to cut the video for the Human Rights Campaign, her long-planned absorption into the Clinton Foundation was just one part of an ambitious—perhaps overly ambitious—agenda for the future.

TWENTY-ONE

The Last Glass Ceiling

The question facing Hillary in 2013 wasn't whether she would run for president but rather whether she would stop running for president. She had built and maintained a political network that kept open the option of running for higher office, and in her case, there was really only one worthwhile rung left on the ladder. In early April she began reconnecting with old political friends, and Bill started reaching out to new ones, even as Hillary focused much of her attention on her publicly advertised gigs for 2013—diving into charitable work, giving speeches, and writing her latest memoir.

On April 4 she gave her first speech in two months at the annual gala for Vital Voices, the international women's leadership organization she had launched from the White House in 1999. Two days later Claire McCaskill, who had said in 2006 that she wouldn't let Bill Clinton near her daughter and then had slammed Hillary in support of Obama in 2008, appeared at Bill's invitation at CGI's college conference at Washington University in St. Louis. McCaskill had changed her tune on Hillary, having said on February 1, the same day Hillary departed the State Department, that she would "work my heart out" to elect Hillary in 2016, if she ran. McCaskill and the Clintons hadn't completely mended fences by the time Clinton Global Initiative University rolled around in April, according to a source close to the Missouri senator, but they were starting to get along a lot better. "You had a professional division and a personal division, and both of those faded," the source said. "The personal division was never meant to be as such, and the professional division was just that—it wasn't personal."

Many of Hillary's close friends and aides rolled their eyes at McCaskill's sudden love for the early front-runner for the 2016 Democratic presidential nomination—McCaskill was so enthusiastic about letting everyone know her choice that she reendorsed Hillary in June after her initial statement, reported by the *St. Louis Beacon,* didn't get much national attention. Hillary seemed willing to have one more person on the bandwagon—not having to deal with the same obstacles she faced in 2008—but she was also busy tending to the folks who had been on it for years.

By the time McCaskill and Bill appeared together at CGI, Hillary was scheduling one-on-one sessions in Washington and New York with an elite set of her political supporters, including members of Congress and big-time donors. These breakfasts and dinners were not explicitly political, but the men and women who found themselves sitting across the table from Hillary had no illusions about what amounted to the reacquaintance phase of the political courtship ritual.

"She talked about how she was very specifically not being political this year," said one of the people who met with Hillary early in 2013. "That she was focused on giving speeches, being involved with CGI, writing her book, catching up with her family, relaxing, and that she would turn to politics, you know, speaking at Jefferson-Jackson dinners and doing the things that were more overtly political during 2014.

"I came away with the sense that she was probably, not definitely, going to run for president," the person said. "The whole conversation just led me to believe that she is going to go through a deliberative process and a deliberate process that will get her increasingly engaged politically, and I got the sense that she would be in a position to be able to pull the trigger if she decided to."

For the time being, Hillary was, as Ellen Tauscher had advised back at the UN General Assembly in New York in September 2011, marshaling her hard-won political capital. If she hadn't brokered any major peace accords in her time at State, neither had she committed many unforced political errors. It made strategic sense for her to stay out of politics for as long as she could, with the caveat that she would find a way to help Terry McAuliffe, who was again running for governor in Virginia's off-year 2013 election.

While she put out the word to her top-level supporters that she wouldn't be hitting the campaign trail or raising money for other candidates until at least 2014, some of them began to advise her about 2016 anyway. Kirsten Gillibrand, the forty-six-year-old rising star who had taken Hillary's seat in the Senate, was one of the first guests at a series of one-on-one breakfasts to give counsel that Hillary had been hearing for years. Hire new people to run your campaign, said Gillibrand, who had worked on Hillary's first campaign for the Senate.

Clinton insiders sought to make clear in the summer of 2013 that Hillary wasn't explicitly laying out plans for 2014 in these meetings, and that any political activities she engaged in during the midterm election cycle would be expressly for candidates on the ballot that year. But they also noted that her expected reemergence on the political scene would be a sign that the option to run for president was still alive and well in her mind.

"There's no plan, but she's going to do more politically next year than this year, defined primarily by work on behalf of other candidates," one of her longtime advisers said in July 2013. "If she was to do nothing, that would be a pretty interesting sign. Doing something is a sign that she's continuing to keep her options open."

On April 23, Hillary summoned the team for her first philanthropic project to the house on Whitehaven Street. The sliding French doors of the dining room were usually open, but for this meeting they were closed, a sign of her desire to shut out the outside world and get down to business.

Already it looked as if Hillary might have bitten off more than she could chew in designing an agenda for her post-State life in the private sector. In addition to the cattle call of meetings with political supporters, she was writing another book, for which she had reportedly received an $8 million advance; she was about to give the first of her paid speeches, to the National Multi Housing Council, the next day; and she was planning to launch three separate charitable projects—one focused on women and girls, one on economic development issues, and the one being discussed at this meeting, on promoting early childhood development.

That might have been a small set of tasks for the seventy-thousand-person State Department staff to pull off, but Hillary now had a much smaller corps to call on. Mills, who was still working on Haiti issues on a part-time basis at the State Department, remained Hillary's consigliere and the de facto head of Hillary's fast-sprawling post-State operation. Maura Pally, a Mills protégée whose distinctive black-framed glasses with silver-frosted edges stood out as particularly retro in Clintonworld, had been hired as Hillary's chief of staff at the Clinton Foundation. Huma, who had so contorted her professional relationship with the State Department to live in New York seven months earlier, was named director of Hillary's new Washington operation.

In Washington, Hillary had moved more than half a dozen aides into the HRCO office. Jake Sullivan, at the urging of Hillary and Obama, moved on to become Joe Biden's national security adviser. But Reines, who was busy planning to open a consulting shop with former Panetta chief of staff Jeremy Bash, used the office a little bit as he handed off many of his day-to-day press duties to Nick Merrill. Dan Schwerin, Rob Russo, Lona Valmoro, and Shilpa Pesaru also jumped from State to HRCO. Hillary's remaining staff was competent and loyal but not equipped to get half a dozen major projects up and running smoothly in the time frame Hillary envisioned. She added consultants into the mix, but even then it was hard to focus an amorphous start-up.

Anxious to have something to roll out at CGI's annual national conference in Chicago in June, Hillary prodded the team of aides and consultants gathered around her dining room table to find a way for her to elevate early childhood development as an issue and persuade parents, businesses, and child care workers to use the best practices identified by scientific research to promote healthy brain development in children under the age of six.

"We're not doing enough," she said. "What can we do to leverage my name, my standing, and my time to actually improve the health and well-being of kids?"

Hillary already had created a partnership for the project, which was originally the brainchild of Ann O'Leary, a legislative director in Hillary's Senate office who had moved on to work at a San Francisco nonprofit called the Center for the Next Generation. Hillary would operate her early childhood development project in conjunction with the Center for the Next Generation, which was cofounded by Jim Steyer, who had been a mentor to Chelsea. His brother, Tom, who had made a fortune as a hedge fund manager and had long been a leading source of campaign cash for Hillary, poured money into trying to elect McAuliffe in 2013, fortifying the ties between the Clintons and the Steyers.

In addition to Mills and O'Leary, Hillary had invited Karen Dunn, a former aide who was also working with the Center for the Next Generation; Alec Ross, her innovation adviser at State; and Tom Freedman, a former Clinton White House aide who had served on Obama's innovation transition team. Several other familiar faces in Hillaryland peered at her from around the table.

But even deep into April, there still wasn't much meat on the bone. O'Leary's original idea, first broached in November 2012, called for Hillary to engage in the public policy debate over early childhood development. But Hillary made clear to her aides that she wanted to stick to the private and nonprofit sectors. The group was sharp enough that Hillary didn't have to tell them why she wanted to avoid political land mines in Washington. Lobbying Congress or the White House would inevitably turn her year out of politics into nothing but politics, and by making it difficult for Republican politicians to support the issue, she might cause more harm than good. "You don't need to be that explicit," said a source in the meeting. "Nobody in that room is on training wheels."

Two days before the June 13 opening of the CGI conference, Hillary launched a new Twitter account. She was one of the few non-incumbent potential presidential candidates in history who had no need to raise her profile, but she had developed a new understanding of the power of social media, particularly Twitter, as a political organizing tool. She chose the famous *Time* magazine photo that had launched *Texts from Hillary* as her avatar, even nodding to the Tumblr's creators with her first Tweet.

"Thanks for the inspiration @asmith83 & @sllambe—I'll take it from here . . . #tweetsfromHillary," she wrote. Her Twitter bio tantalized those who hoped she would run for president: "Mom, wife, lawyer, FLOAR, FLOTUS, women & kids advocate, author, dog owner, hair icon, pantsuit fashionista, U.S. senator, ceiling cracker . . . TBD . . ." In sloppy fashion, her aides showed just how much attention she pays to every minute aspect of her own brand by making six changes to the bio on the first day. *Wife* was put before *mom, pantsuit fashionista* was changed to *pantsuit aficionado*—ensuring that she wouldn't be confused for a South American sartorial socialist—and several other words were moved around or added. While *BuzzFeed* popped a quick story on the changes, Hillary racked up new followers. She had 493,000 of them in the first five days, more than the much older Twitter accounts of Joe Biden, New Jersey governor Chris Christie, Florida senator Marco Rubio, Kentucky senator Rand Paul, New York governor Andrew Cuomo, Maryland governor Martin O'Malley, or Virginia senator Mark Warner, all of whom were, by the summer of 2013, leading suspects to run for president. First Lady Michelle Obama even gave Hillary a "forward Friday"—a call to her own followers to start following Hillary.

But a few days later the ramshackle staff work in assembling her Twitter bio proved to be a harbinger for the rocky rollout of her first philanthropic project. The seat-of-the-pants rush to patch together an early childhood development initiative, organized mostly through conference calls and e-mails, produced a dud when Hillary gave the first public hint of her plan at CGI in Chicago on June 13. Hillary's advisers confessed that a few hours before she took the stage in the main ballroom at the Sheraton, they still weren't 100 percent sure that they were ready to launch. Rather than announce the initiative, Hillary told the audience that she would have something to unveil the following day. In a video released the next morning, Hillary announced the Too Small to Fail program—a clever title that had already existed at the Center for the Next Generation before Hillary became involved—which she said would "promote new research on the science of children's brain development, early learning, and early health" and "help parents, businesses, and communities identify specific actions" that would contribute to giving children under the age of six the resources and tools necessary to thrive.

Several people involved with the project jumped on a conference call with reporters that morning but spoke much more about the general aims of the program than about any specific work that Hillary planned to undertake. Only a few reporters bothered to ask questions. When Hillary took the stage at CGI later that day to announce commitments of money from partner organizations, she did so in competition with the loud clinking of glasses and silverware. The renaming of the Clinton Foundation to the Bill, Hillary and Chelsea Clinton Foundation earned far more media coverage than the new child development initiative, even though the name change already had been announced in April.

That week she broke away from the CGI festivities to appear as the keynote speaker for CURE's annual gala, not too far from the Sheraton. In the years that David Axelrod worked for Obama, Hillary didn't attend the CURE dinners, but she often asked the Axelrods about their daughter and the foundation.

It was clear on that June night, as Hillary took the stage at the Navy Pier Grand Ballroom, beneath an eighty-foot dome ceiling with sweeping views of Lake Michigan, that she was regarded by everyone in the room, except perhaps herself, as a candidate for the presidency.

Nick Merrill, Hillary's baby-faced spokesman, fidgeted in his seat, firing off e-mails on his BlackBerry as his boss spoke; he repeatedly got up to confer with event organizers and Huma, who was waiting in the wings. Speechwriter Dan Schwerin leaned forward in his seat and watched Hillary approvingly from a press area on the sidelines of the dinner floor. Reporters from the *Washington Post,* Associated Press, and *Bloomberg News,* already assigned to Hillarywatch 2016, typed away on their laptops as she spoke.

Hillary gave them copy, using her speech to dip back into politics by launching an attack on sequestration, the automatic spending cuts agreed to by the president and congressional Republicans in 2011. With the caps in place, she argued, research dollars for epilepsy would be harder to come by. At the time, fellow Democrats, including Obama and Biden, were trying to convince Republicans that the limits should be replaced with a mix of tax increases and spending reductions. But Hillary's attack on sequestration could also be taken as a soft shot high across Biden's bow; after all, he had cut the deal with Senate Minority Leader Mitch McConnell that created the budget-slashing mechanism.

The coming months would test Hillary's belief in her capacity to bring attention to a wonky policy issue without the benefit of a high-profile role in government and the hungry press corps that came with it. But the time would also give her the opportunity to activate and add to her political network while she stayed out of the partisan fray. For example, in November 2013, she was scheduled to headline the Chicago Mercantile Exchange's conference in Naples, Florida. The head of the CME, Republican Terry Duffy, raised six figures for Hillary in the 2008 election and would be expected to bundle money for her again in a 2016 run. Associating herself with such financial titans was a double-edged sword: sure, she could count on them to raise money for her, but the Democratic primary electorate doesn't hold financiers in high esteem, whether they operate from Wall Street or Chicago's Wacker Drive. As for her charitable work, the formula was similar to the way Hillary built her capital at State: focus on a topic that doesn't inflame partisan tensions, reach out to the business and nonprofit communities, and engage people directly through carefully selected media, such as video messages and Twitter.

For the second time in eight years, if Hillary chose to run, she would begin a campaign as the front-runner both for the Democratic primary nomination and for the general election. Where many voters had once seen her as a creation of her husband's, a coat-tail rider who had made it into the Senate on the strength of Bill's popularity and figured she could waltz back into the White House, the way she handled the ultimate reversal in the 2008 primary and stepped up when Obama asked gave her greater credibility as a success in her own right. She would run as a former secretary of state, a former senator, and a philanthropist on the mom-and-apple-pie issues of improving the lives of women, kids, and American workers. She would run as someone who had been told repeatedly what she needed to do to avoid a repeat of the cluster-fuck campaign she ran the last time: hire staff based more on competence than on loyalty and personal comfort, and position herself as the transformational candidate that she would be as the first woman to hold the presidency. She would run as a Clinton-style centrist who believes that government, business, and the nonprofit sector must all thrive. She would run as a shrewd manipulator of the levers of government who understands how to maximize dollars with public-private partnerships and how to get agencies that seem always to be at odds on the same page. She would run as an advocate and practitioner of smart power, the use of all forms of America's influence, from persuasion to pulverization. Most of all, she could run right up to the moment—if it ever came—that she decided not to. She would even run as a candidate who, despite getting knocked down, was answering the bell for one last round.

The X factor was Hillary's health. Her concussion and the ensuing blood clot were no trifles. Friends who visited with her in the spring and summer of 2013 were struck by how relaxed she was but also how much older she looked after four years at State. Spending time in the Dominican Republic could do wonders for the soul, but it couldn't roll back the clock. But her aides said, perhaps unsurpris-ingly, that she was fine, another indicator that they were doing every-thing they could to preserve her political standing. "She got back to it faster than anyone anticipated," said one of her senior advisers. "She said her motto is 'Rest, not rust.'"

Short of health concerns, her aides said personal and family considerations could stop Hillary from jumping into presidential politics again. "Not wanting to spend another thirteen million dol-lars out of your pocket," the adviser said. "Not wanting to subject yourself to it. Feeling you can do what you want to do in other ways. Being entirely content that you tried and gave it your all and it didn't work. There are as many reasons to do it as not to do it. If you're one of the few people who can run and actually be president, it's a much more serious proposition, and I think it's at once a more compli-cated and normal decision than we mere mortals think. Maybe she doesn't want her daughter subjected to more scrutiny. Maybe she doesn't want her daughter to walk around with nine agents."

If she were to run for president, she would need to marshal every last bit of goodwill, because her poll numbers were already drop-ping back to earth. On June 10, Gallup released a poll showing her approval rating had dropped from 64 percent in April to 58 per-cent. "Once Clinton left the State Department, it was inevitable that Americans would start to view her again in a political light," CNN polling director Keating Holland said, noting the parallel drop in her approval when, as first lady, she began to campaign for a Senate seat. "This has happened to her before."

Around the time of CGI, Cheryl Mills invited Guy Cecil to breakfast. Cecil, who had become close to Bill on the 2008 campaign and gone on to a successful run as the executive director of the Democratic Senatorial Campaign Committee, served as chair-man of the board of the charter school that Mills's kids attended. So they talked about charter schools for a little while.

Then the conversation turned to the what-ifs of a 2016

presidential campaign. Cecil, who was the subject of much Washington speculation about who might run that still-hypothetical campaign, couldn't imagine saying no if he were asked to do it. "It was about her, what's she going to do next, and then it was like if she ran, who should be the manager?" said a source familiar with the conversation. "A lot of the discussion was about 'Will there be the right changes in place?' I think everybody's interested in that piece of it." Mills became the de facto chief of informational interviews for political operatives who wanted to get in on the ground floor of Hillary for President 2.0. Her involvement almost certainly precludes a campaign manager selection as disastrous as Solis Doyle in 2008, but the challenges facing anyone who lands the job will be formidable.

A modern presidential campaign has more than just one primary. In addition to courting votes for the nomination, candidates wage a "shadow primary" to win high-dollar donors and top campaign operatives. Hillary's formidability reversed the power in the market for operatives. Instead of Hillary wooing them to come to her, several of the rising Democratic stars seemed to be auditioning for the role of her campaign manager. In addition to Cecil, pegged by many Democratic politicos as the man with the inside track, his good friend Robby Mook, another veteran of the 2008 campaign, latched on as manager of McAuliffe's 2013 gubernatorial bid. In early 2013, Stephanie Schriock, the head of EMILY's List, an organization dedicated to electing women who support abortion rights, started a campaign called Madam President to build support for a female candidate for the Oval Office. Jen O'Malley Dillon and Jill Alper, two veteran Democratic operatives, also earned mentions from Hillary insiders as possible campaign managers. Dillon, who was deputy campaign manager for Obama's reelection run, has done work for the Children's Defense Fund, the nonprofit where Hillary got her start in public policy.

More than three years before the election, some of Hillary's closest advisers openly discussed the characteristics she would look for in a campaign manager, without adding the caveat that she might not run. "The one thing about a campaign manager as a political strategist, that is the most personal decision you can make," said one Hillarylander. "Part of what she has to look at is whether or not she and the campaign manager have chemistry. . . . They have to be able to bring almost as much to the table [as the candidate] in terms of being able to talk to your donors, being able to talk to your field staff, putting together infrastructure."

Hillary would also look for a manager who understands how to highlight her gender as a positive. "You have to put a strategy in place that supports that vision of her being a woman," the adviser said. "It has to be a person that uniquely understands that [it] will be as much history as Obama was making. . . . You either lean into that history or you kind of put the history under the carpet, and I would suggest you lean into it."

In any case, Mills would likely be the behind-the-curtain power in a second Hillary run. But there are a lot of entry points into Clintonworld, and even staffers on, and donors to, Anthony Weiner's mayoral campaign thought they could better position themselves for jobs or status in a 2016 campaign by helping Huma's husband. But by July 23, when Huma stood by his side at a torturous press conference in which he acknowledged having text-messaged other women after his resignation from Congress, Weiner's campaign looked like a dead end; as *Politico*'s Maggie Haberman put it, his scandal was "proving to be another stress test of the Clinton infrastructure in a year that was supposed to be relatively quiet for them."

Not only was the Weiner episode an ugly reminder of the scandal-plagued Clinton years, it appeared that the Clinton camp hadn't learned much from "no-drama Obama" about how to suffocate a bad story. In the aftermath of the revelation, Clinton sources talked to reporters, usually on background, to send the message that they were angry with Weiner—and with Huma for allegedly drawing parallels between her own situation and Hillary's decision to remain with Bill through the Monica Lewinsky affair. Some began suggesting that Huma had to choose: Hillary or Anthony. Rather than trying to force Huma out of Hillaryland, they were trying to get her to dump

her husband, one explained. Reines even gave an on-the-record interview to the *New York Times* for a story about his role in successfully
encouraging Huma to distance herself from her own husband to preserve her status.

Whatever the aims of their advisers, none of it looked good
for Bill or Hillary Clinton. "If that's the game they're playing, then
Hillary's campaign has already started behind the eight ball," said a
senior operative from another candidate's 2008 primary campaign.
"What's going to happen to the campaign is the same fucking thing
that happened last time."

Whether the Weiner scandal would turn out to be a bad omen
for 2016 or simply an ugly blip, the Hillary Clinton for President movement was otherwise firing on all cylinders by the end of
July. Over the first half of 2013, the Ready for Hillary super PAC
transformed from a shoestring outfit to a credible operation. While
it grew in size and visibility, Hillary insiders moved to provide what
one source called "chaperones" for the organization. Harold Ickes,
James Carville, and Ellen Tauscher all signed on in advisory roles.
The PAC hired Craig T. Smith, who had been a White House political director under Bill. Smith, who approached Allida Black about
integrating into Ready for Hillary, started running the day-to-day
operations. George Soros, the liberal billionaire who had long
funded progressive groups and causes, eventually signed on as a
major donor. Hillary allies who checked in with top advisers to see
whether they should support Ready for Hillary were given tacit
approval to do so. "They did give me the yellow light," said one
major Hillary donor. "I got the feeling that if I wanted to do it, they
thought it was a good idea."

The PAC's organizers reached out to Clinton supporters with a
triple ask: join the group's contact list, ask your friends to join, and
be ready to write a check later. Several of Hillary's closest friends and
top donors, including Susie Tompkins Buell and Jill Iscol, agreed to
lend their names and some start-up cash to the effort after checking

with Hillary's advisers to make sure it was kosher. The money was less important to Black and her small staff than the buy-in. In fact, as they built the grassroots organization, they generally asked for relatively small checks. There was a $25,000 maximum, according to sources familiar with the fund-raising structure, but even multi-millionaires were often asked to give $5,000 or less. "If people were writing million-dollar checks, that might be a problem," said one Ready for Hillary donor who is capable of writing a seven-figure check. "If they were taking big checks, that really taints it. We have much more credibility this way."

The move by Hillary's friends to integrate into the fabric of Ready for Hillary was taken as a sign by insiders that Clinton wanted to protect her brand in service of a presidential run. "We're all look-ing to see how these groups or efforts are being professionalized and by whom," one veteran Clintonworld political operative said in May. "People that have been tacked onto these things are typical Hillary people. They're more senior folks, and they're respected. . . . Now they're starting to reach out to people that clearly have networks." In July the group reported having raised $1.2 million in the first half of 2013—a modest sum for a super PAC, but enough money to suggest legitimacy, particularly given the fact that, unlike other super PACs, Ready for Hillary capped donations.

In more than one way, Ready for Hillary was becoming a reflec-tion of the characteristics likely to define a fourth Clinton bid for the presidency. It wasn't just the sudden infusion of familiar Clinton-world faces. Black, the ground-level organizer, and the top-dollar donors like Buell and Iscol who invested their time and money in the operation were part of what one Clinton insider called the "army of women" waiting for marching orders in Hillary's next campaign.

If it seemed like the Hillary 2016 campaign was beginning to warm up in Chicago in June, it had reached a fever pitch by early fall when the Clintons convened the annual international CGI confer-ence in New York.

The confab, held to coincide with the United Nations General Assembly each year, always has the feel of a Clinton reunion. That was particularly true in the fall of 2013, as Bill and Hillary's friends, philanthropic partners, and political operatives roamed the hallways of the Sheraton near Times Square. With Hillary weighing whether to run again, her political contingent was out in force. Huma, Capricia Marshall, Melanne Verveer, and Harold Ickes were all there to see and be seen.

Doug Band was there, too, seemingly eager to prove his continued relevance in Clintonworld in the days after *The New Republic* published a highly unflattering nine-thousand-word opus on how he "drove a wedge through a political dynasty" in his handling of Bill's postpresidency and his own pursuit of wealth and power. It suggested that Band wouldn't be able to get much closer to a Hillary candidacy than writing a check to her campaign. Because his business model at Teneo is built on access to the Clintons, the narrative was dangerous not just to Band's ego but to his bottom line.

"There are a lot of people jockeying for position, and Doug is a little bit on the sidelines," a former White House associate of Band's told the story's author, Alec MacGillis.

At CGI, in a pattern he repeated, Band circled the lobby of the hotel, chatting up reporters, longtime Clinton friends, and other attendees before letting them know he had somewhere else to be. Then, almost an hour later, he would turn up again, coming through the hotel's giant revolving door and go through the same song and dance. One attendee noted that if Band was still close in Bill's orbit, "he would have been backstage at the meeting, not in the hotel lobby."

Band's efforts at rehabilitation served as a sideshow when Hillary wasn't front and center that week. It was her debut as a full partner in the foundation's main annual event. She emceed events, moderated discussions, and even announced a new initiative to combat elephant poaching in Africa—an issue that isn't likely to factor prominently in the 2016 presidential campaign. At each event, it was as though Clinton already had a full campaign press corps.

Everywhere she went, and the reporters followed, Hillary got a version of the same question. During one panel discussion, on women and girls, she almost went the full hour without being pressed to address her potential candidacy. But then CNN's Sanjay Gupta, who had been moderating the panel, took a stab.

"How important is it for there to be a woman president in the United States?" Gupta asked Hillary, as an audience packed into one of the Sheraton's smaller ballrooms laughed and cheered.

Hillary, prepared to answer that question in whatever form in which it came, had her response ready. "That is a question I will answer taking myself completely out of it," she said. "We have a lot of challenges," she continued. "Electing one person, a woman, is not going to end those challenges. But it provides a kind of boost to the efforts that so many of us have been making for so long." The short answer, she added, "is that I think it would be important. . . . I think it would be a very strong statement that would be made to half of our population and half of the world's population and someday, I hope it happens."

In the same discussion, Hillary also made news. She waded publicly into domestic politics, which she had done ever-so-briefly at the CURE dinner in Chicago in June. Clinton was asked about the looming government shutdown, something her husband had to face when he was in office nearly twenty years earlier. Clinton slapped congressional Republicans, saying that they "ought to go back and read history, because I would just say it wouldn't be the worst thing for Democrats if they tried to shut down the government. It didn't work out very well for those who were so obstructionist.

"So I hope that our friends on the other side of the aisle—and it's a minority, but it's a noisy one—understand that this is not right to do and this is bad politics for them to do," she said.

Throughout the three-day conference, even when she talked about poaching, Hillary's potential run was the real elephant in the room. During one dinner in the main Sheraton ballroom, Clinton got the biggest nudge to enter the race from Malala Yousafzai, the Pakistani teenager who was shot by the Taliban in 2012. Yousafzai, who was being considered at the time for the Nobel Peace Prize, told the packed ballroom of bigwigs and celebrities who hung on her every word, that "even in America, people are waiting for a woman president." The cameras in the room immediately panned to Hillary, who was smiling broadly, amid roaring applause.

Clinton aides balked at the notion that the presidential campaign had ostensibly started that week. She was simply taking on a bigger, more public role at the foundation. And she was just focusing her attention on initiatives like elephant poaching, her aides insisted. But there were constant reminders of the big question all week and there was tension created—arguably by the Hillary press corps—when the vice president and second lady Jill Biden stopped by the dinner that evening. They sat beside the Clintons at a round table in the front of the ballroom, trying to ignore the buzz around them.

On October 2, 2013, Quinnipiac University released a poll showing Hillary with a 61 percent to 11 percent lead over Biden among Democrats in a hypothetical 2016 primary matchup. From the perspective of Biden supporters, it didn't make sense that he wouldn't do better with a Democratic electorate. After all, he had carved out a serious role in foreign and domestic policy, from helping Obama wind down the wars in Iraq and Afghanistan to spearheading the administration's effort to enhance background checks for gun purchases. He had been first out of the box in supporting gay marriage, even before Obama had been willing to embrace that position. He could credibly argue that he played a significant role in the Obama administration's major accomplishments. In sum, there was a lot for a Democratic primary voter to like about Joe Biden, but it was all seemingly eclipsed by Hillary's star power.

For much of the past year, Biden had been courting fellow Democrats in early caucus and primary states. He invited New Hampshire governor Maggie Hassan to the swearing-in ceremony for his second term as vice president in January 2013 and attended a preinauguration party thrown by Iowa Democrats that week. In mid-September, Biden visited Charleston in the early primary state of South Carolina on technically official vice presidential business and appeared as the headliner at Iowa senator Tom Harkin's annual steak fry, a ritual for Democratic candidates for the presidency. Hillary, having committed herself to staying out of electoral politics in 2013, did not attend.

Biden hadn't made a decision about whether to run by the time of the steak fry, sources close to him said. "He's doing things that would put him in the conversation if he chose to run," said one. Team Biden insists he'll make a decision with his family about whether to run, regardless of whether Hillary's in the race.

"Obviously, who he's going to run against is a big issue, but it's one of a lot of big issues that you're going to have to sit down and work out in real life before you run for president," said Ted Kaufman, who served as Biden's chief of staff and later succeeded him in the Senate. "If she runs," he said of Hillary, "it's a different set of questions."

While Biden built a record as a progressive on domestic issues and a dove on national security matters during his tenure as vice president, he also angered fellow Democrats by cutting deals with Mitch McConnell that created sequestration and locked in most of the Bush-era tax cuts. Senate Majority Leader Harry Reid, in particular, felt that Biden had undercut the Democratic position by going around him to deal with McConnell directly.

Many Democrats, including some close to Obama, assume that, at some point, Obama will tell Biden not to run against Hillary. But the two have run against each other before—in 2008—finishing with both their friendship and the state of the Democratic Party intact. In the Obama administration, Biden often ended regularly scheduled phone calls to Hillary with the words "I love you, darling." And at the late senator Frank Lautenberg's funeral service in June 2013, Joe and Jill Biden bantered with seatmates Hillary and Huma. As Hillary got up to give the eulogy, Biden teased her about having to speak after Broadway star Brian Stokes Mitchell had just sung. "Good luck following that," Biden joked.

▲

Hillary, who had been largely quiet since CGI in June, returned to the political spotlight in the midst of the Weiner scandal, joining Obama for lunch at the White House on July 29 and Joe Biden for breakfast at the Naval Observatory the following day.

"It's largely friendship that's on the agenda," White House principal deputy press secretary Josh Earnest told reporters who pressed him to detail every aspect of the power lunch, including the fare. Earnest came prepared to tell them: grilled chicken, pasta jambalaya, and salad.

On an eighty-degree day, cool by Washington standards for the summer months, the two former rivals met on a patio outside the Oval Office. Obama had asked Alyssa Mastromonaco to set up the lunch after he ran into Hillary at the George W. Bush Library in Dallas several weeks earlier. As she had back in November 2008, Mastromonaco e-mailed her friend Huma to arrange the date. White House officials offered few details on the substance of the conversation, terming the meeting "chiefly social."

Obama, who had declined to bring the Clintons into the White House for social occasions early in his presidency, now just wanted to spend time with Hillary, according to White House aides. "The things that the president loves most are when he can have something without an agenda," said one Obama adviser, who noted that their meeting lasted for about two hours. "They were 'just visiting,' as my girlfriends would say."

In a different sense, many in the Clinton world view the Obamas' stint at the White House that way—they're just visiting.

Epilogue

Two harbingers for a Hillary campaign—one with mixed implications and one with a clear, if limited, upside—appeared within a week of each other in the fall of 2013.

On the morning of Halloween, the *Wall Street Journal* and NBC News released a poll that put a little bit of a scare into Hillary's most ardent supporters. Just like Ellen Tauscher had predicted two years earlier, Hillary's standing plummeted as voters increasingly viewed her not as an above-the-partisan-fray diplomat but as the Democratic front-runner for the presidency. The poll found that 46 percent of those surveyed had a "very positive" or "somewhat positive" view of Hillary, down from 56 percent in the same survey in April.

New York Times columnist Frank Bruni read the results as a long-overdue reality check. "Here we go," he wrote. "The beginning of the end of her inevitability.

"It's about time, because the truth, more apparent with each day, is that she has serious problems as a potential 2016 presidential contender. . . . Voters are souring on familiar political operators, especially those in, or associated with Washington. That's why Clinton has fallen." Bruni's was one of the first in a string of op-eds, magazine articles, and news stories that put a fine point on the steep challenges that Hillary still faced if she ran.

In late 2013, populism was in and the establishment was out in both parties. To liberals disillusioned with Obama because he had talked tough about bankers, insurers, and George W. Bush's national security policies only to embrace them all in the White House when it suited his goals, Hillary looked like a souped-up version of Obama's centrist half. They pined for freshman Massachusetts senator Elizabeth Warren to take Hillary on, hoping that Warren's feisty populist rhetoric, proven fund-raising ability, and gender would blend into the perfect antidote to Hillary in a primary. *The New Republic,* which already had delved deep into Band's financial dealings in a story about the wedge he had reportedly driven into Clintonworld, published a long piece about all of the reasons Warren could beat Hillary.

Bruni noted the distaste with which many observers watched Bill and Hillary setting up Chelsea Clinton for the inheritance of a political dynasty by making clear their belief that she could someday be president. But in Virginia a few days later, another Clinton spinoff, Terry McAuliffe, would capture the governor's mansion, suggesting that the Clinton mantle was hardly a weight too heavy to bear, even when conferred on a close associate with another last name.

If there was a silver lining in the *Wall Street Journal*–NBC poll, it was that of all the politicians and party groups tested, Hillary came in first: Obama was at 41 percent; the Democratic Party was at 37 percent; New Jersey governor Chris Christie was at 33 percent nationally, despite being on the verge of blowout reelection victory; and Ted Cruz was at 19 percent.

Christie's 22-point win set him up as the front-runner for the GOP establishment's support in the 2016 primary and to head the Republican Governors Association in 2014, a post from which he could strengthen ties to conservative candidates across the country by supplying the most powerful political adherent of all: money. Christie's primary problem, though, was just that: a primary problem. After he had embraced Obama in the aftermath of Hurricane Sandy—which helped Obama appear bipartisan in the last days of the 2012 campaign—many Republicans had soured on him.

By the tail end of 2013, there was no shortage of oft-named contenders for the Republican Party's 2016 nomination. Paul, the

Kentucky senator who had gone after Hillary on Benghazi, captured the hearts and minds of the GOP's increasingly vocal libertarian wing. Fellow Senate conservative Cruz had bolstered his standing with the base by encouraging Republicans to shut down the government in pursuit of an end to Obamacare. Rick Perry, the longtime Texas governor, and Governor Bobby Jindal of Louisiana, represented the western part of the Gulf Coast on the list of potent possibles. And, of course, there was Jeb Bush, who hailed from the only family deft enough to bring the moderates and conservatives together to deliver a Republican to the White House in the previous quarter century.

As votes were tabulated in New Jersey on November 5, Clinton-world was focused on Virginia, where McAuliffe, who had failed to get out of a Democratic primary four years earlier, edged out conservative favorite Ken Cuccinelli by about two-and-a-half percentage points. It was a closer-than-expected result, and Clintonites, who packed McAuliffe's election-night party, waited anxiously for a final call on the race.

Two hours after the polls closed, a veteran Clinton hand e-mailed from the party: "Everyone's a little nervous."

There was good reason to be. Bill and Hillary had ignored the risk of losing to put their full weight behind their old friend's candidacy. Loyalty, in its many forms, was perhaps the only trait they exhibited in greater abundance than political savvy. Early on in 2013, there had been efforts to minimize the degree to which the national press read McAuliffe's victory or defeat as a commentary on the Clintons. But by Election Day that was impossible. His campaign manager, Robby Mook, was in the small circle of operatives who were widely perceived to be in the running to head a 2016 Hillary outfit. Tom Steyer, the Hillary bundler and brother of Hillary's partner in the Too Small to Fail effort, Jim Steyer, spent millions of dollars on ads benefiting McAuliffe. As he had in 2009, Bill barnstormed Virginia, and Hillary made a special exception to her no-politics-in-2013 rule to raise money for McAuliffe and speak as a surrogate for him at a women's rally in Northern Virginia.

If Cuccinelli had pulled an upset over McAuliffe, especially after the national Republican Party had abandoned him for dead, the morning headlines would have been full of stories about how the Clintons couldn't get their pal across the finish line. The downside was far greater than the upside. McAuliffe's win was important, if less than pivotal: Some read it as a boon for Hillary and others wrote it off as meaningless for 2016—or, citing the smaller-than-expected margin, an indication of shifting Democratic fortunes.

The Clinton crew at McAuliffe's party let out a collective sigh of relief when the result was finally announced around ten p.m. and the race was called for McAuliffe. "Phew!" the Clinton hand said. "Nail biter!"

Hillary planned a more robust return to electoral politics in 2014, when she would start appearing on behalf of other candidates to build the party—and chits if she decided to campaign for herself again. All of the female Democratic senators had secretly signed a letter urging her to run early in 2013, and Warren said she wouldn't jump in. But speculation that Warren might run against her persisted. Biden was still building toward his own run, and several other candidates, including governors Andrew Cuomo of New York, Martin O'Malley of Maryland, and Jack Markell of Delaware, were considering their options. Cuomo, a scion of his father's liberalism and the Clinton's pragmatism, was a highly unlikely bet to run if Hillary did because her donor base fully eclipsed his. But, like in 2008, there was a hunger in parts of the Democratic base for a candidate who could fell her in the early states and sweep to the nomination.

There were also potentially damaging echoes of her 2008 campaign in the prenatal stages of the 2016 race. While she had off-loaded hired guns and brought in longtime aides when she went to the State Department, she still prized loyalty to a degree that sometimes overshadowed competence and sound judgment. Far less appreciated at the time, but nagging nonetheless, was that she might make the same fundamental mistake she had in 2008. Back then, she had run an old-school Democratic campaign, banking on victories in big states to win the nomination at the expense of the brilliant delegate-obsessive strategy Obama had pursued. More than anything, the sin was that she was such an excellent student of old campaigns that she had run one.

In 2013 she was gearing up to run a race that appealed to the Democratic desire to make history by electing a first—in this case the first Madam President—and functioned on the use of technology as a campaign weapon. It's what Obama had done in 2008. And, as Obama's popularity plummeted in late 2013, she ran the risk of running a campaign that positioned her as an encore to his election. Were the Clinton name, deep experience in the trenches of Washington, abiding loyalty, and the prospect of running a history-making campaign strengths or weaknesses? It would depend on how she used them. One mistake she seemed unlikely to repeat was planting her base of operations in the Washington suburbs. By November 2013, she had closed her Washington office and was transitioning her post-State staff to New York so that her entire operation could be closer to the Clinton Foundation nerve center.

But even without a physical presence in Washington, a three-legged support had been constructed to give her a stronger platform in 2016. In addition to Ready for Hillary, which was focused on building a grassroots network of supporters, across the country, Priorities USA, the pro-Obama SuperPAC that got its big fund-raising boost in 2012 when Bill and his inner circle blessed it, was gearing up to raise tens or hundreds of millions of dollars from major donors for a paid media campaign for the presidential election, and American Bridge, another Democratic SuperPAC, set up an offshoot called Correct the Record to get "earned media"—stories and television segments—to defend Democratic presidential candidates and go after Republicans. By mid-November, Priorities USA was in talks to bring in John Podesta, Bill's former chief of staff, and Jim Messina, the Obama campaign manager who had developed a strong rapport with Bill during the 2012 campaign, to run the operation.

David Brock, the pro-Hillary founder of Media Matters, headed up the Correct the Record organization and quickly hired 2008 Hillary campaign veterans Burns Strider and Adrienne Elrod to help run it. The flavor of Hillaryland was unmistakable, as Brock had to be reminded that he couldn't use the operation to slam Warren, since it was technically created to help the whole field of Democratic hopefuls. The trifecta—grassroots organizing, paid ads, and earned media efforts—positioned Hillary to benefit from the kind of full-scale outside operation that had become a crucial supplement to any modern campaign for the presidency long before she made an announcement.

Technically, the outside groups couldn't coordinate with Hillary, but they were so stocked with former Clinton hands—and so reliant on her high-dollar donors—that it was inconceivable that they would fail to take cues from her brain trust.

As she weighed whether to run—and she had said already that she was doing just that—one existential question facing Hillary was this: How could someone who believed she was the nation's best choice in 2008, who stood again on the verge of becoming America's first woman president, who felt called to public service by a higher power, as expressed in her devotion to the service-oriented Wesleyan faith, who had millions of supporters just waiting for the call, say no to one more full-tilt sprint for the ultimate prize?

"Because there are so many other ways to serve," she said. "I mean, that is truly the honest answer. It's not just putting you off because I'm not ready to answer the question.

"Look, I do have what I've called the responsibility gene. I do believe strongly in public service, and I do have, through my religious upbringing and my faith, a sense of obligation because I've been given so much," she said. "I mean, I am such a fortunate person. And I think I am called on to give back. And so I've been doing that all my life, and so it doesn't have to be one position or another."

But each time she had felt the call to serve, Hillary had answered it in the affirmative.

"I never thought I'd run for office, and then circumstances kind of conspired to suck me into the Senate race in New York. And it was almost like I was on the outside watching, saying, 'Oh, my gosh, look at this, it's coming around and happening to me,' " she said. "So

I did that and ran for reelection, then cared deeply about the direction of the country and ran for president. It was an incredibly intense campaign; didn't work out. I was ready to go back to the Senate, do my service there, because it had been a pretty tough time for New York—I mean, between 9/11 and the financial collapse, I mean, New York was in lots of trouble, and I care deeply about the people who entrusted me with being their senator. And then along comes the president and asks me to be the secretary of state."

In Hillary's telling, she's been drafted time and again—rather than volunteering herself. By the late fall of 2013, she had publicly acknowledged she was thinking about running, but she insisted she hadn't yet made up her mind.

"I never know what's going to happen next," she said. "And I really have never lived my life thinking I knew what was going to happen next. I really try to—I mean, it is very John Wesleyan, believe me. I really try to just do the best I can every day, because who knows what's going to happen next? I don't have any idea. So I'm one to just feel like every day I'm being true to my values and I'm contributing in some way, and maybe trying to do some good."

ACKNOWLEDGMENTS

This book began as a pitch from Bridget Wagner Matzie of Zach-ary Shuster Harmsworth, who had her sights set on Hillary Clinton even when the rest of the political world was focused on the 2012 presidential race. Pointed to us by a mutual friend, author Karin Tanabe, Bridget asked if we would be game to write a proposal for a book about Hillary's years at the State Department and her political future. It seemed like such a good idea, we marveled that no one else had thought of it. And thus, Bridget became our agent and friend. We can't thank her enough for the original idea, her advocacy, her guidance, and her edits. Nor could we be any more grateful to Karin for suggesting us to Bridget.

Our editor, Kevin Doughten, who had to pick up the book half-way through the process, brought his considerable talents to bear on weaving a set of stories into a narrative and pushing us for more inside-the-room details. We are forever indebted to him. We knew from the minute we met Kevin's boss, publisher Molly Stern, that she was an ass-kicker who would get the most out of not just us but her own team. We couldn't be more impressed with the work they have done.

In particular, we are grateful to Crown's Jacob Lewis, Maya Mavjee, Linnea Knollmueller, Barbara Sturman, Christine Tanigawa, Christopher Brand, Rachel Meier, Linda Kaplan, Christine Edwards, Candice Chaplin, Jay Sones, Annsley Rosner, Dyana Messina, and Carisa Hayes, each of whom owns a piece of this book. Claire Potter deserves special recognition for helping manage the project, from reading drafts to making herself available at all hours, on weekends and holidays, to ensure that each step moved the process forward.

Benjamin Kamisar was still an undergrad at Northwestern Uni-versity when we asked him if he would work as our lead research assistant. An excellent young journalist, he thoughtfully improved upon every project we gave him, transcribed countless hours of interviews, and maintained a give-me-more attitude throughout. We were blessed to have found the right man for the job. We are also grateful to Amelia Wedemeyer and Ellis Weintraub, who provided additional research assistance with professionalism and precision.

Chris Donovan, a producer for *Meet the Press,* freely gave advice and counsel, and Jonathan Capehart of the *Washington Post* provided moral support. We thank them for their friendship and insights.

Hugo Gurdon, Bob Cusack, and Ian Swanson of *The Hill* saw the value in letting Amie split her time between the White House and the book for much of 2013. John Harris, Jim VandeHei, Kim Kingsley, and Danielle Jones of *Politico* allowed Jon to pursue the book with the confidence that his job would be awaiting him when he returned. We are eternally grateful to all of you.

We would be remiss if we didn't mention the many businesses that unwittingly provided us with shelter and sustenance for our work: Starbucks in Georgetown, Shelly's Back Room, the lobby of the Ritz-Carlton, Ebenezers, and Stoney's.

Finally, we would like to thank most of our sources, some of whom sat with us multiple times, fetched physical documents from undisclosed locations, and were generally a fabulous bunch to work with. We are grateful, as well, to Hillary's post-State staff for their insights and assistance. To sources who pointed us in the wrong direction, we keep lists, too.

—J.A. and A.P.

My heart swells when I think about the sacrifices that my family made to allow me to take on this project. My wife, Stephanie Claire Allen, shares with me her love, her wisdom, her counsel, her laughter, and our two children. Asher Henry Allen couldn't yet walk when this book was first pitched and now he screams "home run" as he runs around the house, unwilling to drop his toy bat. Emma Pearson Allen wasn't even a thought in the summer of 2012, and now I can't remember what life was like before her. Though they cannot yet read this book, it is in so many ways for them—that they might assess a leader by her decisions, her character, and her judgment, and never pause at "her."

My contribution to this book begins where all human stories do, with a mother—in this case my mom, Marin Allen, who earned a Ph.D. while raising two small children, worked all day at the office and all night at home, taught me how to listen to what politicians say, and to this day demonstrates that strength and compassion are reinforcing traits. Similarly, neither I, nor this book, would be here without my father, Ira R. Allen, the most talented writer I know, who taught me his father's curve—or "drop"—and who talks baseball, politics, and journalism with me in the best running conversation of my life. It would be hard to imagine having published this book without my sister, Amanda Allen, whose love, support, and mockery have always spurred me to do better—and yes, Amanda, you are the good one.

The following people who inspired me personally and professionally have my deepest gratitude and affection: Joan Pearson, Kathy Rizzo, Martha Angle, Greg Giroux, Christopher Pearson, the Pearson family, the Bergman and Cohen families, Thom Rafferty, Jed Weiss, Dan McBride, Will Hessler, Robert Tomkin, Laura McGann, Martin Kady II, and Bill and Ronnie Weintraub.

And finally, to Amie, thank you for pouring your talent, your energy, and your soul into this project—and, of course, for putting up with me.

—J.A.

This book would not be possible without the love, friendship, and encouragement of my mom, Esther Parnes, who has always been the ultimate role model to me. I will never admire anyone more for their strength, wisdom, and moxie.

Sherry Parnes, you are everything: my sister, my best friend, my greatest fan, my biggest advocate, and my favorite comedian. No one gets my creative juices flowing more than you. To my dad, Henry Parnes—who almost lost his voice reading edits back to me when I was ill during this book-writing process—you instilled in me a love of reading and writing, and for that I am so grateful. Thanks also to Garri Hendell, the closest thing I have to a brother, for his continued love and guidance. And to my favorite little readers, J.W. and Cal, for being the cutest little guys ever and for providing an endless supply of hugs and kisses.

I will be forever indebted to Mickey Lipton, my sixth-grade English teacher who saw a glimpse of writing potential in a shy twelve-year-old girl and signed her up for her first journalism class. I would be absolutely nowhere without my mentor and friend Rick Bragg, the most elegant writer I've ever read, for opening the door to a world of journalism the aforementioned twelve-year-old would only dream about.

I'm also thankful for the help and friendship of journalists M. E. Sprengelmeyer, Niall Stanage, and my very first professional editor, Jon O'Neill, for inspiring me, offering words of wisdom, and cheering me on in the grandstands on this journey. And I owe thanks to Justin Sink for filling in on the White House beat when I went missing to work on this project. Thanks also to Steve Vasil and Peter Feldman for their advice and counsel.

I send enormous gratitude to my best friend in the world, Craig Bode, for listening to me ramble about this book and the characters in its pages for months and months and for reassuring me in the darkest hours that everything would be fine.

Thank you, as ever, to my dear friends for ensuring I didn't live a hermit's life while drowning in work on this project: Jamie Radice, (my perma-workwife) Karin Tanabe, Jennifer Martinez, Lesley Clark, Erika Bolstad, Julie Mason, Bethany Lesser, Michael Collins, Megan Chan, Vanessa Parra, Kendra Marr Chaikind, and Bridget Petruczok.

To my lifelong friends, Jarah Greenfield, Abby Tegnelia, and Dolly Hernandez, even though you're all spread out around the country and I rarely get to see you, I am so lucky to know you.

Finally, to Jon Allen, my partner-in-crime, we fought like hell at times, but you can't say it wasn't worth it.

—A.P.

NOTES

A NOTE ON SOURCING

This book was reported primarily through interviews with more than two hundred people, most of whom were granted anonymity to freely discuss their knowledge of Hillary Clinton, their insights into other players in Washington politics and policy, and sensitive conversations and actions that took place out of public view. Some sources were willing to speak "on the record," meaning that they are quoted directly and identified by name. They include, but are not limited to, former CIA director David Petraeus, former secretary of state Madeleine Albright, representatives Darrell Issa and Ileana Ros-Lehtinen, and deputy secretaries of state Jim Steinberg and Tom Nides. Many of the interviews were conducted "on background," meaning that sources' words appear in quotation marks but they are not identified by name. Those sources are identified by their office or some other characteristic that provides protection from being revealed—such as "Republican congressman" or "senior adviser." Still other sources simply provided information and guidance, leaving light fingerprints but not quotes in these pages. When dialogue appears in quotation marks, it was relayed to the authors by at least one of the participants in the exchange, a source who was present to hear it, or multiple sources who were apprised of the discussion and agreed on the content.

ONE: HILLARY'S HIT LIST

13 Bill Clinton had pleaded with Kennedy John Heilemann and Mark Halperin, *Game Change: Obama and the Clintons, McCain and Palin, and the Race of a Lifetime* (New York: HarperCollins, 2011), p. 219.

14 "entirely too nice" "Clinton Remembers Walter Capps," *AllPolitics,* CNN, November 12, 1997.

14 to give her their word, privately Ben Smith and Amie Parnes, "Clinton Asks Supers to Commit in Private," *Politico,* May 8, 2008.

15 because of Band Todd S. Purdum, "The Comeback Id," *Vanity Fair,* July 2008.

16 Florida State University football player Christina Wilkie, "Glory Days: Altmire Recalls His Season with FSU Football Coach Bobby Bowden," *The Hill,* December 16, 2009.

18 endorsed Barack Obama Josh Drobnyk, "Patrick Murphy Backs Obama," *Morning Call,* August 21, 2007, http://bit.ly/17Q696b.

23 packed with more than four hundred people Timothy McNulty, "Bill Clinton Appears at Fund Raiser for Ravenstahl," *Pittsburgh Post-Gazette,* November 26, 2008.

TWO: "BE GRACIOUS IN DEFEAT"

25 **$4 million–plus redbrick home** Zillow.com, accessed August 22, 2013.

26 **he did not intend to ask her** John Heilemann and Mark Halperin, *Game Change: Obama and the Clintons, McCain and Palin, and the Race of a Lifetime* (New York: HarperCollins, 2011), p. 251.

30 **memorial to "the built environment"** National Building Museum, www.nbm.org.

30 **nearly an hour late** Dana Milbank, "A Thank-you for 18 Million Cracks in the Glass Ceiling," *Washington Post,* June 8, 2008.

33 **"about time" for a woman** Shailagh Murray, "Pool Report from the Clinton-Obama Event at Mayflower," *Washington Post,* June 26, 2008.

33 **"I'm going to need Hillary"** Ibid.

36 **"root canal"** Heilemann and Halperin, *Game Change,* p. 263.

36 **more than $22 million** July 2008 monthly report of Hillary Clinton for President, Federal Election Commission, http://www.fec.gov/fecviewer /CandidateCommitteeDetail.do#2, accessed August 22, 2013.

THREE: CALCULATED RISK

50 **in late October** Jonathan Alter, *The Promise: President Obama, Year One* (New York: Simon & Schuster, 2010), p. 68.

50 **"who I had tea with"** Amy Chozick, "Obama, Clinton Tea Off," *Wall Street Journal,* December 28, 2007.

52 **$6.4 million debt** December 2008 monthly report of Hillary Clinton for President, Federal Election Commission, http://bit.ly/15O7mqD.

52 **Obama had offered her the job** Nico Pitney, "Officials: Obama Offered Clinton Secretary of State," *Huffington Post,* November 14, 2008.

53 **He came to see the political benefits** Bob Woodward, *Obama's Wars: The Inside Story* (New York: Simon & Schuster, 2010), p. 30.

54 **He had suggested Hillary** Alter, *The Promise,* p. 67.

58 **"I mean to make it hard"** Hillary Clinton, "townterview" by Suttichai Yoon and Veenarat Laohapakakul of *World Beat,* July 22, 2009, U.S. Department of State.

FOUR: US AND THEM

61 **mock-cupping the breast** Al Kamen, "One More Question . . . ," *Washington Post,* December 4, 2008.

62 **"Senator Clinton is pleased"** Ibid.

65 **"voice of reason"** Amie Parnes, "Gatekeeper: Cheryl Mills," *Politico,* April 24, 2009.

65 **"And she gets exactly that from Cheryl"** Ibid.

67 **Ellen DeGeneres** *Ellen,* October 14, 2005.

70 Bush's numbers were pathetic 2008 Pew Global Attitudes Project, December 18, 2013.

72 "the willing suspension of disbelief" John Bresnahan, "Clinton: Believing Petraeus and Crocker Requires 'Willing Suspension of Disbelief,'" *Politico,* September 11, 2007.

74 "Smart power is neither hard nor soft" Joseph S. Nye Jr., *Soft Power: The Means to Success in World Politics* (New York: Public Affairs, 2004), p. xiii.

81 limited the former president's international activities Memorandum of Understanding between the William J. Clinton Foundation and the Office of President-Elect Barack Obama, December 18, 2008, http://on-msn.com/16ia6Ao.

81 every living secretary of state Glenn Thrush and Amie Parnes, "Land Mines Ahead for Hillary," *Politico,* January 12, 2009.

82 issued an invitation Helene Cooper, "Clinton to Dine with Condoleezza Rice," *New York Times,* December 8, 2008.

83 "the vanguard of our foreign policy" Hillary Clinton, Statement before the Senate Foreign Relations Committee, "Nomination Hearing to Be Secretary of State," January 13, 2009, U.S. Department of State, http://1.usa.gov/18N3YP2; video at http://bit.ly/1890kWl.

84 "She can't show up the president" Thrush and Parnes, "Land Mines Ahead for Hillary."

84 the *Times* begged the committee "Bill Clinton's Donors," editorial, *New York Times,* January 10, 2009.

84 "multimillion-dollar minefield" "Vitter to Vote Against Clinton Nomination," Office of Senator David Vitter, January 15, 2009, http://1.usa.gov/19ENSrV.

85 "This is not goodbye" Amie Parnes, "Clinton Bids Colleagues Farewell," *Politico,* January 14, 2009.

FIVE: "BLOOM WHERE YOU'RE PLANTED"

92 Marshall's problem was less Alison Leigh Cowan, "Pick for Protocol Post Corrects Failure to File Taxes in 2 years," *New York Times,* June 18, 2009.

105 guaranteed a $1.3 million loan Adam Nagourney, "With Some Help, Clintons Purchase a White House," *New York Times,* September 3, 2009.

105 a tacit acknowledgment "McAuliffe Defeat Deals Latest Blow to Clinton Legacy," Associated Press, June 11, 2009.

SIX: FIRST AMONG EQUALS

111 Orszag had children by three different women "Peter Orszag, Just Engaged, Acknowledges New Baby with Ex-Girlfriend Claire Milonas," *Washington Post,* January 6, 2010.

117 Young Republicans "U.S. Secretary of Defense Robert M. Gates ('65) to Address William and Mary Graduates During Commencement Exercises, May 20, 2007," College of William and Mary, March 30, 2007, http://bit.ly/1anYn3P.

120 the unlikely pair Amie Parnes, "Cabinet Members Pile on the Love," *Politico,* October 6, 2009.

124 "the dilemma you face" Bob Woodward, *Obama's Wars: The Inside Story* (New York: Simon & Schuster, 2010), p. 222.

126 McDonough confronted Holbrooke James Mann, *The Obamians: The Struggle Inside the White House to Redefine American Power* (Viking: New York, 2012), accessed via excerpt on Slate.com.

126 McDonough shot Rothkopf a terse e-mail Helene Cooper, "The Adviser at the Heart of National Security," *New York Times,* July 9, 2010.

126 wrote a letter Rajiv Chandrasekaran, *Little America: The War Within the War for Afghanistan* (Random House: New York, 2012), pp. 1160–61 (e-book).

SEVEN: "WE DID IT, BUDDY"

130 a nearly comprehensive ban Larry Margasak, "Gore Employee May Have Misused Fund," Associated Press, October 2, 1999.

131 A former adviser to both Clintons Clinton Foundation Donor List, Fox News, December 18, 2008, http://fxn.ws/15hpyMU.

132 PepsiCo CEO Indra Nooyi Louisa Lim, "U.S. Exhibit at World Expo Opens to Mixed Reviews," National Public Radio, May 3, 2010.

132 Chevron, General Electric, Honeywell Frederik Balfour, "U.S. Pavilion in Shanghai Expo Confirmed," *Bloomberg Businessweek,* July 11, 2009.

132 Harman's company gave State Department report on Shanghai Expo, appendix XCVI.

133 Boeing, the host of her earlier session "Clinton Appeals for Sponsorship for US Pavilion," *China Daily,* November 16, 2009.

133 Two days before "President Hu Visits Shanghai World Expo Park," Chinese Government's Official Web Portal, http://bit.ly/1eAVuPI.

133 The reviews were fair John Pomfret, "Hillary Clinton Takes Break from International Issues, Visits World's Fair in China," *Washington Post,* May 23, 2010.

136 But Reines had sidestepped Ben Smith, "Reines Storm: Clinton Conflict Brews," *Politico,* March 24, 2009.

137 During a classic photo-op moment Jill Dougherty, "Clinton Reset Button Gift Gets Lost in Translation," *Political Ticker,* CNN, March 6, 2009.

138 One Russian newspaper "Button Gaffe Embarrasses Clinton," BBC News, March 7, 2009.

139 as she walked from an elevator Ken Bazinet, "Secretary of State Hillary Clinton Recuperating—Trying to Text—After Spill That Broke Her Elbow," *New York Daily News,* June 18, 2009.

141 a two-hour early morning surgery Mark Landler, "Clinton Will Undergo Surgery for Broken Elbow," *New York Times,* June 18, 2009.

141 She also missed out on Tina Brown, "Hillary, Take Off Your Burqa," *Daily Beast,* July 13, 2009.

141 **The week after her fall** Ben Smith, "Hillary Clinton Toils in the Shadows," *Politico,* June 23, 2009.

EIGHT: "USE ME LIKE AN APP"

156 **They had even invited him** Steven Lee Myers, "Twitter Meets Cuneiform," *New York Times,* April 22, 2009.
157 **On the very same day** Mark Landler and Brian Stelter, "Washington Taps into a Potent New Force in Diplomacy," *New York Times,* June 16, 2009.
166 **At a forum later that day** Jeffrey Gettleman, "Clinton Presents Plan to Fight Sexual Violence in Congo," *New York Times,* August 11, 2009.
169 **In January 2010** Josh Rogin, "Clinton Dines with Top Executives," *Foreign Policy: The Cable,* January 8, 2010.
170 **A few months after the dinner** John Poirier, "Tech Companies Seek Business in Syria," Reuters, June 24, 2010.
170 **But that was a smokescreen** Elise Labott, "Diplomats Blaze Uneasy Trail Along Digital Highway," CNN, July 1, 2010.

NINE: OBAMA GIRL

176 **"The clearance and vetting"** Jill Dougherty, "Clinton: Vetting Process for Administration Jobs a Nightmare," *Political Ticker,* CNN, July 13, 2009.
176 **"It's my secretary of state calling"** Sheryl Gay Stolberg and David M. Herszenhorn, "Bill Clinton Urges Fast Action by Senate Democrats," *New York Times,* November 10, 2009.
179 **"news watchers"** "Clarus Poll: Obama's Inner Circle," PR Newswire, December 16, 2009; Gallup Poll.
180 **"the whole eight"** Tavis Smiley, "One on One with Hillary Clinton," *Tavis Smiley Reports,* January 27, 2010.
183 **He cut radio ads** Eric Kleefeld, "Bill Clinton Records Radio Ad for Blanche Lincoln," *Talking Points Memo,* June 1, 2010.
183 **campaign for Mark Critz** Genaro C. Armas, "Dems Keep Murtha Seat During Special Pa. Election," Associated Press, May 19, 2010.
183 **and even auctioned off** Chris Gentilviso, "Hillary Raffles Bill to Ease Campaign Debt," *Time,* May 13, 2010.
183 **Obama's aides had tried and failed** Chris Cillizza, "Administration Officials Used Job to Try to Dissuade Senate Hopeful in Colorado," *Washington Post,* June 3, 2010.
184 **After he fired** Lloyd Grove, "Inside Obama's Tense Meeting," *Daily Beast,* June 23, 2010.
185 **"Don't take that picture"** "State Dinner Slip-up," CBS Video, http:// bit.ly/bBfnFU.
192 **like a sister to her** Maggie Haberman, "Anthony Weiner Explained Self to Bill Clinton," *Politico,* June 7, 2011.

192 Bill, embracing Chelsea Reliable Source, "Clintons Celebrate Wedding of Huma Abedin and Anthony Weiner," *Washington Post,* July 1, 2010.

193 Bill presided over Celeste Katz, Kevin Deutsch, and Rich Schapiro, "Queens Rep. Anthony Weiner Marries Huma Abedin with Former President Bill Clinton Presiding," *New York Daily News,* July 11, 2010.

195 The dossier contained Scott Wong, "DeMint Threatens to Filibuster START," *Politico,* December 2, 2010.

196 When the committee voted in September J. Taylor Rushing, "START Treaty Passes First Test," *The Hill,* September 16, 2010.

197 a powerful blow to Obama William Branigin, "Obama Reflects on Shellacking in Midterm Elections," *Washington Post,* November 2, 2010.

197 Clinton met with members *DipNote* Bloggers, "Secretary Clinton and Senators Kerry, Lugar Discuss the New START Treaty," U.S. Department of State Official Blog, November 17, 2010.

198 Biden, the former chairman Peter Baker, "Obama's Gamble on Arms Pact Pays Off," *New York Times,* December 22, 2010.

199 "I have to tell you" Peter Baker, "Clinton Battles Repeat of '94, with a Twist on '08," *New York Times,* October 25, 2010.

199 party dirty work for Obama Ben Smith, "Bill Clinton Pushed Kendrick Meek to Quit Florida Race," *Politico,* October 28, 2010.

200 a thirty-minute show from Clinton Perry Bacon, Jr., and Anne E. Kornblut, "Bill Clinton, Back in the White House Briefing Room," *Washington Post,* December 10, 2010.

202 Much was made in Washington "Inside Holbrooke's War with the White House," *Daily Beast,* January 14, 2011.

TEN: PROMISE AND PERIL

207 regime was "stable" Jeffrey Goldberg, "Hillary Clinton: Mubarak Regime Is 'Stable,'" *The Atlantic,* January 25, 2011.

207 "orderly, peaceful transition" Hillary Clinton, interview by David Gregory, *Meet the Press,* NBC, January 30, 2011.

209 "What is clear" Barack Obama, "Remarks by the President on the Situation in Egypt," White House, February 1, 2011.

210 "I really consider" Kirit Radia, "Secretary Clinton in 2009: 'I really consider President and Mrs. Mubarak to be friends of my family,'" ABC News, January 31, 2011.

210 "the promise and the peril" "Senate Confirmation Hearing: Hillary Clinton," *New York Times,* January 13, 2009.

212 "While some countries" Hillary Clinton, "Forum for the Future: Partnership Dialogue Panel Session" remarks, January 13, 2011, U.S. Department of State.

213 French president Nicolas Sarkozy Nicholas Watt and Patrick Wintour, "Libya No-Fly Zone Call by France Fails to Get David Cameron's Backing," *The Guardian,* February 23, 2011.

214 British prime minister David Cameron "Cameron: UK Working on 'No-Fly Zone' Plan for Libya," BBC News, February 28, 2011.

214 a set of mythological Valkyries Maureen Dowd, "Flight of the Valkyries," *New York Times,* March 22, 2011.

215 By March 12 "Arab League Backs No-Fly Zone in Libya," CNN, March 12, 2011.

218 "we urge our GCC partners" Jay Carney, press briefing, March 14, 2011, White House.

221 "leading from behind" Ryan Lizza, "The Consequentialist," *The New Yorker,* May 2, 2011.

222 Later Moussa would complain Ian Traynor, "Arab League Chief Admits Second Thoughts About Libya Air Strikes," *The Guardian,* June 21, 2011.

222 "I think most members" Susan Rice, remarks to press, March 16, 2011, U.S. Mission to the United Nations, http://1.usa.gov/eGAqa7.

223 "We definitely would like" Hillary Clinton, "townterview" by Nessma TV, Tunis, March 17, 2011, http://1.usa.gov/17WcjgT.

ELEVEN: BELOW THE WATERLINE

225 The president had been informed Mark Bowden, "The Hunt for 'Geronimo,'" *Vanity Fair,* November 2012.

227 "I find it hard to believe" Hillary Clinton, remarks at a roundtable with senior Pakistani editors, October 30, 2009, U.S. Department of State.

228 "It may well be" Lauren Appelbaum and Andrew Merten, "Obama vs. Clinton on Pakistan," NBC News, August 7, 2007.

229 At home, she concentrated Michael Novinson, "State Department Reaches Out to Pakistani-Americans," Scripps Howard Foundation Wire, June 12, 2009.

230 "In the United States, do you" Hillary Clinton, "townterview" by prominent Pakistani women journalists, Islamabad, Pakistan, October 30, 2009, U.S. Department of State.

231 Zardari countered by saying Peter L. Bergen, *Manhunt: The Ten-Year Search for Bin Laden—from 9/11 to Abbottabad* (New York: Crown, 2012), p. 562 (e-book).

231 the number of drone strikes "Pakistan Drone Strikes—Obama v. Bush," *New America Foundation,* updated July 28, 2013, http://bit.ly/14CVPPZ.

231 Raymond Davis, a CIA contractor Mark Mazzetti, "How a Single Spy Helped Turn Pakistan Against the United States," *New York Times,* April 9, 2013.

231 trying to prove ties Chris Arsenault, "Spy Game: The CIA, Pakistan and 'Blood Money,'" Al Jazeera, March 17, 2011.

232 Fortunately for Davis Mazzetti, "How a Single Spy."

232 Hillary, speaking in Egypt Hillary Clinton, interview by Steve Inskeep of National Public Radio, March 16, 2011, U.S. State Department.

232 "The understanding is" Josh Rogin, "Who Paid the Blood Money to Set Raymond Davis Free?" *Foreign Policy,* March 16, 2011.

232 a substantial shift in America's approach Elise Labott and Tim Lister, "Courier Who Led U.S. to Osama bin Laden's Hideout Identified," CNN, May 3, 2011.

236 two of the most powerful voices Bowden, "Hunt for 'Geronimo.'"

237 That Thursday NSC meeting Bowden, "Hunt for 'Geronimo.'"

237 skipped the gala Daniel Bates, "Obama Reveals Dramatic Moment When He Saw Photo of Bin Laden's Corpse," *Daily Mail Online,* May 2, 2013.

238 "Those were thirty-eight" Erik Hayden, "Hillary Clinton Says Photo May Just Have Been Her Allergies," *National Journal,* May 29, 2013.

Twelve: Hillary's Politics

240 "You can count on Kathy" David Catanese, "Bill Clinton Robocalls for Kathy Hochul," *Politico,* May 23, 2011.

240 Hochul defeated Republican "Statement of Canvass," May 24, 2011, New York State Board of Elections, http://bit.ly/R4Jqx9.

241 Her approval rating was at 66 Lydia Saad, "Hillary Clinton Favorable Near Her All-Time High," Gallup, March 30, 2011.

241 The Obama campaign even polled Mark Halperin and John Heilemann, *Double Down* (New York: Penguin, 2013), p. 78.

242 taking over as treasury secretary Ned Martel, "Geithner Once Proposed Hillary Rodham Clinton for Treasury Secretary," *Washington Post,* June 14, 2012.

243 a poll showing that 64 percent John McCormick, "Hillary Clinton Rise as Most Popular Politician Prompting Buyers' Remorse," *Bloomberg News,* September 16, 2011.

243 Bill endorsed Representative Brad Sherman Jonah Lowenfeld, "Bill Clinton, State and Local Officials Endorse Sherman in Contested West Valley District," *Jewish Journal,* August 5, 2011.

247 two ideas about Romney Ryan Lizza, "Let's Be Friends," *The New Yorker,* September 10, 2013.

248 "so close to paying" Ben Smith, "Clinton Still Working on Debt," *Politico,* December 10, 2010.

248 the two presidents came together Darren Samuelsohn, "Bill Clinton Upstages Obama Again at Green Buildings Event," Politico Pro, December 2, 2011.

249 "I never got to open" Bill Clinton, "We Can't Wait," remarks at Better Buildings Initiative, December 2, 2010, White House.

249 to play a round of golf Lizza, "Let's Be Friends."

249 "in doses" Halperin and Heilemann, *Double Down,* p. 61.

249 continued to offer his opinions Jodi Kantor, "With a Book, the Last Democrat in the White House Tries to Help the Current One," *New York Times,* November 4, 2011.

249 "When Bill Clinton was president" Barack Obama, "We Can't Wait," remarks at Better Buildings Initiative, December 2, 2010, White House.

250 "about the economy?" Darren Samuelsohn, "Bill Clinton Upstages Obama Again at Green Buildings Event," *Politico,* December 2, 2011.

250 "I just want to, I'll say again" Bill Clinton, "We Can't Wait," remarks at Better Buildings Initiative.

THIRTEEN: THE HRC BRAND

252 Hillary was just sitting down "We Came, We Saw, He Died," *Daily Mail Online,* October 21, 2011.

252 declined to say she regretted Hillary Clinton interview, *Fox News Sunday,* October 23, 2011.

252 "captured or killed soon" Elise Labott, "Clinton Makes Unannounced Visit to Libya," CNN, October 18, 2011.

253 On the trip to Libya Richard Stengel, "Q&A: Hillary Clinton on Libya, China, the Middle East and Barack Obama," *Time,* October 27, 2011.

253 the most enduring image of Hillary in command Diana Walker, photo in "Hillary Clinton and the Rise of Smart Power," *Time,* November 7, 2011.

260 an "apology tour" "Mitt Romney 'Apology Tour' Ad Targets Obama After Final Presidential Debate," *Huffington Post,* October 23, 2012.

260 promote democratic movements Josh Rogin, "Romney Campaign: Obama Failing on Democracy and Human Rights," *Foreign Policy,* July 27, 2013.

260 Chen Guangcheng John B. Thompson, "Chen Guangcheng: Rebel of the Year 2012," *GQ,* December 2012.

262 rendezvous point Jane Perlez and Andrew Jacobs, "A Car Chase, Secret Talks and Second Thoughts," *New York Times,* May 2, 2012.

263 "I want to kiss you" Susan Glasser, "Out of the Embassy and into the Fire," *Foreign Policy,* May 2, 2012.

263 Hillary put out a statement Hillary Clinton, "Chen Guangcheng," press statement, May 2, 2012, U.S. Department of State.

263 harshly critical statement "Liu Weimin's Remarks on Chen Guangcheng," bit.ly/1iuhiqv, accessed November 9, 2013.

264 Chen used his connections Seung Min Kim, "Chen Guangcheng Calls Into Congressional Hearing," *Politico,* May 3, 2012.

264 "apparent, according to these reports" Emily Friedman, "Romney: Will Be 'Day of Shame' for Obama If Chen Was Urged to Leave American Embassy," ABC News, May 3, 2012.

266 Chinese and American officials "Joint Statement on the U.S.–China Strategic and Economic Dialogue Outcomes of the Strategic Track," media note, May 4, 2012, U.S. Department of State.

268 November 2011 NATO air strike John H. Cushman Jr., "Obama Offers 'Condolences' in Deaths of Pakistanis," *New York Times,* December 4, 2011.

269 "We are sorry for the losses" Hillary Clinton, "Statement by Secretary Clinton on Her Call with Pakistani Foreign Minister Khar," July 3, 2012, U.S. Department of State.

Fourteen: The Bill Comes Due

271 more than five hundred donors Bobbi Bowman, "President Obama, Former President Clinton Wow McLean Fundraiser," *McLean Patch,* April 30, 2012.

272 Obama "deserves to be reelected" Bill Clinton, "Remarks by President Obama and Former President Clinton at a Campaign Event," April 29, 2012, White House.

272 Shortly before Bill delivered Nicholas Confessore, "Obama Donors Entreated to Retire Clinton's Debt," *New York Times,* April 28, 2012.

273 to help Kathleen Kane, a Hillary supporter Borys Krawczeniuk, "Clinton Backs Kane, but AFL-CIO Goes for Murphy," *Scranton Times-Tribune,* March 27, 2012.

274 "I am proud to endorse Mark Critz" Chris Good, "Bill Clinton Endorses Critz in Pennsylvania Democratic House Primary," ABCNews.com, April 12, 2012.

274 edged Altmire by 1,489 "2012 General Primary: Official Returns," Pennsylvania Department of State, April 24, 2012, http://bit.ly/189Bzq8.

274 Kane beat Murphy Ibid.

275 "invited me to the Oval Office" John C. Ensslin and Herb Jackson, "Rothman Visits Obama as Clinton Endorses Pascrell for 9th Congressional District Seat," *North Jersey,* June 1, 2012, http://bit.ly/15hxRs7.

275 Pascrell coasted Alex Isenstadt, "Bill Pascrell Trounces Steve Rothman in Primary," *Politico,* June 6, 2012.

276 by letting Berman ride Jonah Lowenfeld, "What's a Congressman to Do: Vote in D.C. or Ride with the President to George Clooney's House?" *Jewish Journal,* May 10, 2012.

277 wisdom of letting tax cuts Melissa Jeltsen, "Bill Clinton: Bush Tax Cuts Should Be Extended Temporarily," *Huffington Post,* June 5, 2012.

277 had come to the defense of Romney John Hudson, "Bill Clinton Joins the List of Bain Defenders," *Atlantic Wire,* June 1, 2012.

278 the economy rebounded Vicki Needham, "Experts Say Economy Should Grow Despite Who Wins White House in November," *The Hill,* September 2, 2012.

280 "a one-word answer: Arithmetic" Bill Clinton, speech to the Democratic National Convention, *New York Times,* September 5, 2012.

280 "It takes some brass" Ibid.

281 she settled into a chair "Photo: Hillary Clinton Watches Husband Deliver Convention Speech," CNN.com, September 6, 2012.

Fifteen: Benghazi

Note: In this and subsequent chapters, the abbreviation ARB refers to the State Department's Accountability Review Board report on Benghazi, which was prepared by a semi-independent panel picked by Hillary Clinton and released on December 19, 2012; it is online at http://1.usa.gov/TYkdAW. The abbreviation IPR refers to the Interim Progress Report for the Members of the House Republican Conference, a document containing the findings of GOP committees that was released on April 23, 2013; it is online at http://1.usa.gov/10xGqik.

283 delivered blunt assessments of Qaddafi's State Department cable, August 29, 2008, accessed from *New York Times* online database of WikiLeaks documents on November 7, 2013.
284 He arrived in Benghazi ARB, p. 13.
284 "go out and meet as many members" Greg Myre, "Slain U.S. Ambassador Chris Stevens Thrived on Tough Assignments," National Public Radio, September 12, 2012.
284 "as we expand U.S. expeditionary capacity" *Leading Through Civilian Power: The First Quadrennial Diplomacy and Development Review,* 2010, U.S. Department of State.
284 "famous for always maintaining" Hillary Clinton, "Secretary Clinton Remarks at Swearing-in Ceremony for Chris Stevens, Ambassador to Libya," May 14, 2012, U.S. Department of State.
284 "normalized security operations" IPR, p. 7.
285 in a March 28 cable State Department cable, March 28, 2012, "Request for DS TDY and FTE support," accessed from House Oversight and Government Reform Committee website on November 7, 2013.
285 Before Cretz could get a reply Eli Lake, "U.S. Consulate in Benghazi Bombed Twice in Run-up to 9/11 Anniversary," *Daily Beast,* October 2, 2012.
285 in a separate incident ARB, p. 15.
286 the original plan would remain IPR, p. 11.
286 When Stevens arrived to replace Cretz Ibid.
286 an IED had blown Lake, "U.S. Consulate in Benghazi Bombed."
286 "NO, I do not [repeat] not" IPR, p. 12.
286 expressing concern about a planned reduction State Department cable, July 9, 2012, "Tripoli—Request for extension of TDY security personnel," accessed from House Oversight and Government Reform Committee website on November 7, 2013.
287 In addition to attacking ARB, pp. 15–16.
287 Stevens traveled from Tripoli Eli Lake, "Who Outed the CIA Annex in Benghazi?" *Daily Beast,* May 24, 2013.
287 "At least one of the reasons" "The Latest on the Benghazi Hearing," *Political Ticker,* CNN, May 8, 2013, http://bit.ly/18PSV7O.
288 Hillary personally conveyed Ibid.
288 someone was spotted taking pictures Nancy A. Youssef, "In Talking Points Controversy, an Unanswered Question: Why Did CIA Say a Protest Preceded Benghazi Attack?" *McClatchy,* May 13, 2013.
288 That morning Stevens sent a memo State Department cable, Septem-

ber 11, 2012, "Benghazi weekly report," accessed from House Oversight and
Government Reform Committee on November 8, 2013.

289 asking whether Stevens had heard "Transcript: Whistle-blower's
Account of September 11 Libya Terror Attack," Fox News, May 8, 2013, http://
fxn.ws/12VVSPQ.

289 "the continuing efforts" "What They Said, Before and After the Attack in
Libya," *New York Times,* September 12, 2012.

289 failed to quell the outrage "Protesters Attack U.S. Diplomatic Com-
pounds in Egypt, Libya," CNN, September 12, 2012.

289 State Department was consumed Chris McGreal and Tom McCarthy,
"Benghazi Hearings: Hillary Clinton Issues Forceful Defence," *The Guardian,*
January 24, 2013.

289 met with a Turkish official "Benghazi Timeline: How the Attack Unfolded,"
CBS News, November 2, 2012.

289 a local police car left its post Julian E. Barnes, "Timeline: Military
Response to Benghazi Attacks," *Wall Street Journal,* May 8, 2013.

289 a low of 20 State Department Operations Center, e-mail during Benghazi
attack, September 11, 2012, ABC News, http://abcn.ws/TzmGGE.

289 as many as 125 Nancy A. Youssef and Suliman Ali Zway, "No Protest
Before Benghazi Attack, Wounded Libyan Guard Says," *McClatchy,* September 13,
2012.

289 "FUCK," Smith wrote Sarah Tory, "We Were Friends in Real Life and in
Internet Spaceships," *Slate,* September 12, 2012.

289 heard around Benghazi ARB, p. 23.

289 The attackers set fires Greg Hicks, former deputy chief of mission in
Libya, testimony, May 8, 2013, House Committee on Oversight and Government
Reform, http://1.usa.gov/103sFBL.

289 Within minutes ARB, p. 23.

290 Stevens began dialing Hicks testimony.

290 In the safe area ARB, p. 22.

290 Billowing smoke Ibid.

290 the other three Ibid.

291 set out for the compound Eric Schmitt, "C.I.A. Played Major Role in
Fighting Militants in Libya Attack," *New York Times,* November 1, 2012.

291 4:05 p.m. in Washington State Department Operations Center, e-mail
during Benghazi attack, September 11, 2012, at ABCNews.com, http://abcn.ws
/TzmGGE.

292 The security officers ARB, p. 24.

292 The five diplomatic security officers Ibid.

293 Leon Panetta "Pentagon Releases Official Timeline of Benghazi Attack,"
CNN, January 23, 2013, http://bit.ly/V4uOya.

293 Panetta would later Donna Cassata and Richard Lardner, "Panetta
Defends Military Response in Libya," Associated Press, February 7, 2013.

293 instruct special forces teams "Pentagon Releases Official Timeline."

293 By eleven-thirty p.m. in Benghazi ARB, p. 25.

295 Around two a.m. in Libya "Transcript: Whistle-blower's Account of September 11 Libya Terror Attack," Fox News, May 8, 2013, http://fxn.ws/12VVSPQ.

295 Hicks received a call Hicks testimony.

296 Meanwhile the CIA team ARB, p. 27.

296 After the mortar attacks Ibid.

297 "This is the first time" Hicks testimony.

297 Around seven-thirty a.m. local ARB, p. 27.

300 America's Ramstein Air Base "Hillary Clinton Senate Hearing on Benghazi," *Transcripts,* CNN, January 23, 2013, http://bit.ly/1fWxX9Z.

301 "We will wipe away our tears" Hillary Clinton, "Remarks at the Transfer of Remains Ceremony to Honor Those Lost in Attacks in Benghazi, Libya," September 14, 2012, U.S. Department of State.

302 "'Greater love hath no man than this'" Barack Obama, "Remarks by the President at Transfer of Remains Ceremony for Benghazi Victims," September 14, 2012, White House.

302 "The people of Egypt" Ibid.

303 The original draft John Dickerson, "Susan Rice and Her Attacks," CBS News, June 6, 2013.

303 militants with ties Josh Rogin, "Benghazi Talking Points Could Scuttle Top Diplomat Nominee," *Daily Beast,* June 5, 2013.

303 the easy availability of weapons "The White House's Benghazi E-mails," *New York Times,* May 15, 2013, http://nyti.ms/1eekOgI.

303 unhappy with the draft Ibid.

304 Toria Nuland Ibid.

304 "The penultimate point" Ibid.

305 Republicans would later use Dylan Byers, "ABC's Jon Karl: 'No Evidence Hillary Clinton Was Aware' of Benghazi Revisions," *Politico,* May 10, 2013.

305 But Sullivan "White House's Benghazi E-mails."

306 The language that had Ibid.

306 "No mention of Cairo cable" Ibid.

306 "Putting together the best" Louis Jacobson, "Jay Carney Says Susan Rice Didn't Play Down Terrorist Involvement in Benghazi," *PolitiFact,* May 13, 2013.

306 no demonstration in Benghazi Oren Dorell, "White House Releases Benghazi Emails," *USA Today,* May 16, 2013.

306 slightly varying versions Jacobson, "Jay Carney Says."

SIXTEEN: "ROAD WARRIOR"

315 He had cut a video Stephanie Condon, "Bill Clinton: Romney Thinks We're Dumb," CBS News, October 18, 2012.

315 "a heck of a secretary of state" Mark Leibovich, "Bill Clinton Presses On in Campaign for Barack Obama," *New York Times,* November 4, 2012.

316 she had more cash on hand October 2012 quarterly report of Hillary Clinton for President, Federal Election Commission, http://bit.ly/14D3Y74.

316 helped a handful of House candidates Michelle Breidenbach, "Former President Bill Clinton Campaigns for Slaughter, Hochul in Rochester," *Post-Standard,* October 19, 2012, http://bit.ly/QE1zfL.

317 jammed in a series of robocalls Alexandra Jaffe, "Clinton Cuts Robocalls for 45 Dem House Candidates," *The Hill,* November 5, 2012.

317 his own set of side trips and political tasks Caitlin Huey-Burns, "In Senate Races, Bill Clinton Takes on a Supporting Role," *Real Clear Politics,* October 31, 2012.

318 Bill would offer his support Glen Johnson, "Bill Clinton Cites Senate Balance in Email Appeal to Warren Supporters," *Boston Globe,* October 3, 2012.

319 "I take responsibility" Elise Labott, "Clinton: I'm Responsible for Diplomats' Security," CNN, October 16, 2012.

319 a forty-two-second video Ian Schwartz, "Unaired RNC Ad from 2012 Rips Obama for Benghazi: 3AM Call Was Ignored," *Real Clear Politics,* May 10, 2013.

320 even with unemployment at 7.9 Julie-Hirschfeld Davis, "Obama First Since FDR Re-Elected with 7.9 Percent Joblessness," *Bloomberg,* November 7, 2012.

320 Then he called Bill Clinton Ed Henry, "After Winning Re-Election, Obama Thanked Romney, Then Called Bill Clinton," Fox News, November 7, 2012.

Seventeen: Please Don't Go

321 reminisced like longtime friends Kristen A. Lee, "Obama, Clinton Reminisce on Their Long History During Final Trip," *New York Daily News,* November 20, 2012.

324 "No, Hillary," Panetta fired back Mark Mazzetti, "How a Single Spy Helped Turn Pakistan Against the United States," *New York Times Magazine,* April 9, 2013.

326 "the path we've taken" Tim Johnson, "Governments Seek New Burma Strategy," *Financial Times,* April 21, 2009.

327 Hillary visited both Suu Kyi Jason Burke and Sara Olsen, "Clinton Encouraged by Burma Reforms as She Meets Aung San Suu Kyi," *The Guardian,* December 1, 2011.

327 Suu Kyi traveled Ashley Fantz, "Aung San Suu Kyi Begins U.S. Tour," CNN, September 18, 2012.

329 "I could not be more grateful" Peter Baker, "For Obama and Clinton, a Partnership's Final Roadshow," *New York Times,* November 19, 2012.

Eighteen: Four Dead Americans

336 the president might have known Rep. Mike Rogers (R-Mich.), interview by David Gregory, *Meet the Press,* NBC, November 18, 2012.

337 the formation of a "special committee" Seung Min Kim, "Wolf Calls for Special Benghazi Committee," *Politico,* November 13, 2012.

338 spent 401 days on the road Megan Garber, "Hillary Clinton Traveled

956,733 Miles During Her Time as Secretary of State," *The Atlantic,* January 29, 2013.

338 an inn for visiting dignitaries Blair House: The President's Guest House, www.blairhouse.org.

339 both sides of the Thanksgiving break "Secretary Clinton: Travel to Australia, Singapore, Thailand, Burma and Cambodia," November 11–20, 2012; and "Secretary Clinton: Travel to the Czech Republic, Belgium, Ireland and Northern Ireland," December 3–7, 2012, U.S. State Department.

339 pushed back a planned trip Matthew Lee, "Illness Forces Clinton to Delay Trip to Morocco," Associated Press, December 9, 2012.

340 Friends of the Syrian People Robert Ourlian, "Timeline: Hillary Clinton's Health Woes," *Wall Street Journal,* December 31, 2012.

340 arming the Syrian rebels Michael R. Gordon and Mark Landler, "Backstage Glances of Clinton as Dogged Diplomat, Win or Lose," *New York Times,* February 2, 2013.

340 sustained the concussion Matthew Lee, "Hillary Clinton Hospitalized with Blood Clot," Associated Press, December 31, 2012.

341 a "head fake" "Hillary Clinton's Head Fake," editorial, *New York Post,* December 18, 2012.

341 a "diplomatic illness" Nick Wing, "John Bolton: Hillary Clinton Came Up with 'Diplomatic Illness' to Avoid Benghazi Testimony," *Huffington Post,* December 18, 2012.

341 "Benghazi flu" Katie Glueck, "Allen West: Hillary Clinton Caught 'Benghazi Flu,'" *Politico,* December 20, 2012.

341 had accused Huma Abedin Representatives Michele Bachmann et al. to Ambassador Harold W. Geisel, State Department deputy inspector general, June 13, 2012, http://bit.ly/NildkP.

342 State had released the ARB report William Burns, "Briefing on the Accountability Review Board Report, December 19, 2012, U.S. State Department, http://1.usa.gov/WpyFEl.

342 "Systemic failures" ARB, p. 29.

343 put on leave in response to the ARB Michael R. Gordon and Eric Schmitt, "4 Are Out at State Dept. After Scathing Report on Benghazi Attack," *New York Times,* December 19, 2012.

343 "no involvement to any degree" Josh Rogin, "Exclusive: Hillary's Benghazi 'Scapegoat' Speaks Out," *Daily Beast,* May 20, 2013.

343 "through the assistant secretary level" "Under Rubio Questioning, State Dept. Admits Senior Leadership Failed to Resolve Benghazi Security Concerns," Office of Senator Marco Rubio, December 20, 2012, http://1.usa.gov/R7e4po.

344 a blood clot in her head Jay Solomon and Ron Winslow, "Hillary Clinton in Hospital After Blood Clot Found," *Wall Street Journal,* December 30, 2012.

354 The QDDR had articulated *Leading Through Civilian Power: The First Quadrennial Diplomacy and Development Review,* U.S. Department of State, 2010.

356 "She was unhappy" Greg Hicks, former deputy chief of mission in Libya, testimony, May 8, 2013, House Committee on Oversight and Government Reform, http://1.usa.gov/103sFBL.

359 "got away with murder" Lindsey Graham, interview by Greta Van Susteren, *On the Record with Greta Van Susteren,* Fox News, January 28, 2013.

NINETEEN: "OUT OF POLITICS"—FOR NOW

360 "non-stop flying around" Hillary Clinton, *Living History* (New York: Simon & Schuster, 2003).

361 "in the pink" Victoria Nuland, State Department spokeswoman, daily press briefing, January 7, 2013, U.S. Department of State.

362 "Washington is a contact sport" Tom Nides, quoted by Ashley Southall, "A Gag Gift for Clinton as She Returns to State Dept.," *New York Times,* January 7, 2013.

364 "few big problems were solved" Michael O'Hanlon, quoted by Paul Richter, "Hillary Clinton's Legacy at State: Splendid but Not Spectacular," *Los Angeles Times,* January 28, 2013.

364 "Clinton looks awful" Michael Kinsley, "Hillary Clinton's Ego Trips," *Bloomberg View,* January 8, 2013.

366 "one of the most important advisers" Hillary Clinton and Barack Obama, interview by Steve Croft, *60 Minutes,* CBS, January 27, 2013.

366 "I was literally inaugurated" Ibid.

366 "I'm out of politics" Ibid.

367 "I won't lie" Hillary Clinton, interview by Kim Ghattas of BBC, June 14, 2011, U.S. Department of State.

367 "I'm proud of the work" Hillary Clinton, farewell remarks to State Department employees, February 1, 2013, U.S. Department of State.

367 63 percent of Americans approved Andrew Dugan, "Hillary Clinton Is Still Popular, More So Than Obama, Biden," Gallup, April 23, 2013.

TWENTY: READY FOR HILLARY

370 donor list was packed Parkhomenko for Delegate, campaign finance records, Virginia Public Access Project, http://bit.ly/18bYNvM.

370 "American politics may be headed back" Jonathan Martin and Maggie Haberman, "2016: Hillary Clinton vs. Jeb Bush?" *Politico,* November 8, 2012.

371 "I hope she goes" Nancy Pelosi, interview by Andrea Mitchell, *First Read,* NBC, December 18, 2012.

372 "gay rights are human rights" Hillary Clinton, remarks in recognition of World Human Rights Day, December 6, 2011, U.S. Department of State.

374 "late-to-the-party caution" Charles Babington, "Hillary Clinton Joins Other Dems in Backing Gay Marriage," Associated Press, March 18, 2013.

374 "Don't tell me the Democrats" Katie Glueck, "McConnell: Dems 2016 Lineup 'Rerun of the Golden Girls,'" *Politico,* March 15, 2013.

375 **Chelsea also recommended** Nicholas Confessore and Amy Chozick, "Unease at Clinton Foundation over Finances and Ambitions," *New York Times,* August 13, 2013.

375 **Chelsea grew concerned** Ibid.

376 **Teneo expanded rapidly** "About Teneo," *Teneo: Integrated Counsel for a Borderless World,* http://bit.ly/19HzMpy, accessed September 6, 2013.

376 **"exclusively with the CEOs"** Ibid.

376 **Bill had severed his financial ties** Maggie Haberman, "Bill Clinton Changes Relationship with Teneo," *Politico,* February 19, 2012.

376 **"You can do CGI or Teneo"** Josh Margolin, "There'll Be Hill to Pay!" *New York Post,* March 1, 2012.

376 **nearly twice as long** Bill Clinton, statement on the death of Mother Teresa, September 5, 1997, http://1.usa.gov/15jTl7z.

376 **"I couldn't have accomplished"** Bill Clinton, statement, March 1, 2012, Clinton Foundation, http://bit.ly/19HAdQC.

377 **on June 4, 2012** Huma Abedin to Thomas M. Gibbons, State Department bureau of legislative affairs, and Richard C. Visek, State Department bureau of the legal adviser, July 5, 2013, to satisfy request from Senator Chuck Grassley, http://1.usa.gov/17HVTLw, accessed September 6, 2013.

377 **Abedin's dual relationship** Maggie Haberman, Glenn Thrush, and John Bresnahan, "Huma Abedin Allowed to Represent Clients While at State," *Politico,* May 16, 2013.

377 **provided "strategic advice"** Abedin to Gibbons and Visek.

378 **"So far the State Department and Ms. Abedin"** Chuck Grassley, "State Department on 'Special Government Employees,'" July 25, 2013, Office of Senator Chuck Grassley, http://1.usa.gov/15jU7BG.

Twenty-one: The Last Glass Ceiling

379 **"work my heart out"** Robert Koenig and Jo Mannies, "Game Change? McCaskill Endorses a Hillary Clinton Run for President in 2016," *St. Louis Beacon,* February 1, 2013.

384 **by making six changes to the bio** Hunter Schwarz, "6 Changes Hillary Clinton Made to Her Twitter Bio," *BuzzFeed,* June 10, 2013.

388 **from 64 percent in April to 58 percent** Andrew Dugan, "Hillary Clinton Is Still Popular, More So Than Obama, Biden," Gallup, April 23, 2013.

388 **"Once Clinton left"** Paul Steinhauser and Ashley Killough, "What's Behind the Drop in Hillary Clinton's Numbers," *Political Ticker,* CNN, June 10, 2013.

390 **thought they could better position** Olivia Nuzzi, "Anthony Weiner Intern Reveals Why She, Others Joined New York Mayoral Campaign," *New York Daily News,* July 30, 2013.

390 **"another stress test"** Maggie Haberman, "Concern Grows for Huma Abedin Within Clinton World," *Politico,* July 30, 2013.

391 **Reines even gave an on-the-record interview** Amy Chozick and

Michael M. Grynbaum, "Coming to an Old Friend's Aid, with an Eye on the Clinton Image," *New York Times,* August 1, 2013.

393 *The New Republic* **published** Alec MacGillis, "Scandal Inc.: How Doug Band Drove a Wedge Through a Political Dynasty," *New Republic,* September 22, 2013.

396 **"I love you, darling"** Amy Chozick, "Biden and Clinton—Friends with Awkward Twist," *New York Times,* September 14, 2013.

Epilogue

399 **Hillary's standing plummeted** Peter Nicholas, "Hillary Clinton's Ratings Slip in New WSJ/NBC poll," *Wall Street Journal,* October 31, 2013.

399 **a long-overdue reality check** Frank Bruni, "Hillary in 2016? Not So Fast," *New York Times,* November 4, 2013.

400 **the reasons Warren could beat Hillary** Noam Scheiber, "Hillary's Nightmare?" *The New Republic,* November 10, 2013.

400 **Christie's 22-point win** New Jersey gubernatorial election results, *New York Times* online, November 6, 2013.

400 **to head the Republican Governors Association** Alexander Burns, "Bobby Jindal, Chris Christie to Lead RGA," *Politico,* October 8, 2012.

401 **two-and-a-half percentage points** Virginia Board of Elections, election-night results, November 5, 2013.

402 **secretly signed a letter** Conor Skelding, "At an Emily's List Event, No Doubt About Hillary 2016," *Capital New York,* October 29, 2013.

403 **Priorities USA was in talks** Ruby Cramer, "Obama Campaign Manager in Talks to Head Hillary Clinton Project," *BuzzFeed,* November 13, 2013.

Selected Bibliography

The following works provided insight into domestic politics, the relationship between Hillary Clinton and Barack Obama, and foreign policy, both in theory and in practice.

Alter, Jonathan. *The Promise: President Obama, Year One.* New York: Simon & Schuster, 2010.

Bergen, Peter. *Manhunt: The Ten-Year Search for Bin Laden from 9/11 to Abbottabad.* New York: Crown, 2012.

Chandrasekaran, Rajiv. *Little America: The War Within the War for Afghanistan.* New York: Knopf, 2012.

The Department of State. The First Quadrennial Diplomacy and Development Review (QDDR): Leading Through Civilian Power. Washington, D.C., 2010.

The Department of State. *Final Commissioner General's Report on the USA Pavilion at Shanghai Expo 2010.* Washington, D.C., 2010.

Heilemann, John, and Mark Halperin. *Game Change: Obama and the Clintons, McCain and Palin, and the Race of a Lifetime.* New York: HarperCollins, 2010.

Mann, James. *The Obamians: The Struggle Inside the White House to Redefine American Power.* New York: Viking, 2012.

Nasr, Vali. *The Dispensable Nation: American Foreign Policy in Retreat.* New York: Doubleday, 2013.

Nye, Joseph S., Jr. *The Future of Power.* New York: PublicAffairs, 2011.

Thrush, Glenn. *Obama's Last Stand.* New York: Random House, 2012.

Woodward, Bob. *Obama's Wars.* New York: Simon & Schuster, 2010.

INDEX